Body Talk

Psychology has traditionally examined human experience from a realist perspective, focusing on observable 'facts'. This is especially so in areas of psychology which focus on the body, such as sexuality, madness or reproduction. In contrast, many sociologists, anthropologists, feminists and post-structuralist, semiotic and psychoanalytic theorists have focused exclusively on the cultural and communicative aspects of 'the body', treating it purely as an object constructed within socio-cultural discourse.

This new collection of sophisticated discursive analyses explores this divide from a variety of theoretical standpoints, including psychoanalyses, social representations theory, feminist theory, critical realism, post-structuralism and social constructionism. The unifying theme of the contributions is that we need to move away from the binary divide between material and discursive analyses of the body, towards a position which allows us to recognize the interaction and inter-relationship between the two.

Body Talk reconciles the divide by putting forward a new 'material-discursive' approach, providing a qualitative, discourse analytic insight into sexuality, madness and reproduction, yet acknowledging the material reality of the body and of factors such as social class, ageing and material power. It also provides an introduction to social constructionist and discursive approaches which is accessible to those with limited previous knowledge of socio-linguistic theory, and showcases the distinctive contribution that psychologists can make to the field.

Jane M. Ussher is a senior lecturer in Psychology, and research director of the Women's Health Research Unit at University College London. She also works part time as a clinical psychologist. Her previous publications include *The Psychology of the Female Body* (1989), *Women's Madness: Misogyny or mental illness?* (1991) and *Fantasies of Femininity: Reframing the Boundaries of Sex* (1997). She is also editor of the Routledge *Women and Psychology* series.

Body Talk

The material and discursive regulation of sexuality, madness and reproduction

Edited by Jane M. Ussher

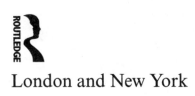

London and New York

First published 1997
by Routledge
11 New Fetter Lane

Simultaneously published in the USA and Canada
by Routledge
29 West 35th Street, New York, NY 10001

Typeset in Times by Routledge
Printed and bound in Great Britain by Creative Print and Design
(Wales), Ebbw Vale

British Library Cataloguing in Publication Data
A catalogue record for this book is available from the British Library

Library of Congress Cataloguing in Publication Data
Body Talk: the material and discursive regulation of sexuality,
madness, and reproduction/edited by Jane M. Ussher
Includes bibliographical references and index.
1. Body, Human–social aspects. 2. Body, Human–Psychological
aspects. 3. Women–Psychology. 4. Women–Physiology. 5. Sex
(Psychology). 6. Mental illness–social aspects. 7. Human
reproduction–social aspects.
8. Materialism. 9. Discursive psychology. I. Ussher, Jane, M.
[DNLM: 1. Feminist theory.]
HM110. B68   1997   97–15836
306.4–dc21   CIP

ISBN 0–415–15363–8 (hbk)
ISBN 0–415–15364–6 (pbk)

For Alison Madgwick

Contents

Contributors

Stephen Frosh is reader in Psychoanalytical Psychology at Birkbeck College, University of London, and Consultant Clinical Psychologist and Vice Dean in the Child and Family Department at the Tavistock Clinic, London. His most recent book is *For and Against Psychoanalysis*, to be published by Routledge in 1997.

Myra S. Hunter is clinical director of the Women's Health Research Unit at University College London and head of clinical psychology Services to women's health at University College London Hospitals. She has worked and published in the area of women's health for many years and has recently completed a six year study of menopause and midlife.

Hélène Joffe is a lecturer in psychology at University College London. Her publications include 'The Shock of the New: A Psycho-dynamic Extension of Social Representational Theory' in *Journal for the Theory of Social Behaviour* (June 1996) and 'Aids Research and Prevention: A Social Representational Approach' in *British Journal of Medical Psychology* (September, 1996). Her primary areas of interest are social representations theory, with specific emphasis on epidemics, and individualism.

Helen Malson is a lecturer in social psychology at the University of East London. She has spent several years researching the area of eating disorders and has published a number of journal articles on the subject. She is also the author of *The Thin Women: Feminism, post-structuralism and the social psychology of anorexia nervosa*, to be published by Routledge in 1997.

Irene O'Dea is a health psychologist, specialising in women's health. Since 1990 she has carried out research on osteoporosis, menopause and midlife with Myra Hunter at Guy's Hospital Medical School. She is currently living in Ireland.

David Pilgrim is visiting research fellow at the University of Liverpool and also works for Communicare NHS Trust as a clinical psychologist.

Anne Rogers is reader in sociology at the National Primary Care Research and Development Centre based at the University of Manchester. Her publications include *A Sociology of Mental Illness* (Open University Press, 1993), *Experiencing Psychiatry* (Macmillan, 1993) and *Mental Health Policy in Britain* (1996).

Janet Sayers teaches psychoanalysis at the University of Kent, and works part-time (both privately and for the NHS) as a Freudian therapist. Her books include *Biological Politics* and *Mothering Psychoanalysis*. She is currently working on a book provisionally titled *Boy Crazy: Analysing Men's and Women's Adolescent Memories and Dreams*.

Corinne Squire is at the University of East London. She is the author of (1989) *Significant Differences: Feminism and Psychology*, London: Routledge, and, with Ellen Friedman (1998) *Morality USA: Representations of Morality in Contemporary Culture*, Minnesota University Press, and the editor of (1993) *Women and AIDS: Psychology and Perspectives*, London: Sage.

Janet M. Stoppard is a faculty member in the Psychology Department at the University of New Brunswick in Canada. Her research interests include women and mental health, particularly depression in women, and feminist perspectives in clinical psychology.

Catherine Swann did her Ph.D on women's experience of PMS at the psychology department, University College London. She is currently a research manager at the Health Education Authority, and also lectures in Health Psychology.

Gary W. Taylor is a clinical psychologist working in the field of sexuality and health in the NHS in Brighton.

Jane M. Ussher is research director of the Women's Health Research Unit, and senior lecturer in psychology at University College London. She also works part-time in the NHS as a clinical psychologist. Her research interests are in gender and mental health, sexuality, and reproduction. Her most recent book is *Fantasies of Femininity: Reframing the Boundaries of Sex*, published by Penguin in 1997.

Acknowledgements

The idea for this book arose from a series of seminars that were organised at the Women's Health ResearchUnit (WHRU), in the Psychology Department, University College London. A central theme running through the research and theory being explored by each member of the group was the divide between the material and discursive aspects of experience. The issues which we wrestled with were ones I myself had been attempting to address for over a decade, without always having the language or the requisite background to do so. These included: In acknowledging the discursive aspects of menstruation and premenstrual syndrome, what do we do with the knowledge that women bleed, or that hormones vary across the cycle? In looking towards social constructionist theories of sex, what do we do with the material manifestations of arousal and desire? In arguing that anorexia is a product of discourses which circulate about femininity and the female body, how do we deal with the fact that many anorexic women die?

The material-discursive debate has been addressed in disciplines other than psychology for decades. Indeed, it was through turning away from psychology towards a range of disciplines including anthropology, semiotics, psychoanalysis, literary criticism and sociology that we found the greatest amount of insight into these issues. Yet psychologists do still have something to offer in this sphere, as is illustrated by the various contributions to this volume.

Lucy Yardley and myself initially proposed a jointly edited book on the subject of the material-discursive analysis of sexuality, health and illness. However, as the contributions we had both commissioned began to arrive, we realised that our interests and potential audiences were somewhat different, and the notion of two separate books was proposed. This volume is aimed at an audience with some prior knowledge of the material-discursive debate, and with a particular interest in the subject areas of sexuality, madness and reproduction. Lucy's volume, entitled *Material Discursive Approaches to Health and Illness*, is aimed at a more general health psychology audience, and also covers much of the background to these debates. I am grateful to Lucy for early discussions on this subject, and to Viv Ward at Routledge for her willingness to countenance these changes.

Thanks are extended to members of the WHRU who are not amongst contributors to this book, but who have taken part in the many discussions of this subject: Jo Bower, Jane Weaver, Christine Rutter, Julie Mooney-Somers, Alison Dixon and Mette Knudsen. I am also grateful to Jan Burns for discussions on sex, madness and reproduction over the last few years, as well as for providing inspiration, friendship and support.

An earlier version of parts of Chapters 1 and 8 appeared in Ussher, J.M. (1997) *Fantasies of Femininity: Reframing the Boundaries of Sex*, London: Penguin.

1 Introduction

Towards a material–discursive analysis of madness, sexuality and reproduction

Jane M. Ussher

'BODY TALK': WHAT DOES THIS MEAN?

> To talk of the body is to talk of corporeality, action and flesh. Or so it is said in science, psychology and the law.

Or:

> To talk of the body is to talk of discourse, of signs and signifiers, of represent-ations of fantasy and desire. So say poststructuralist, semiotic and psychoanalytic theorists.
>
> Which is the truth? Which way should we turn?

This is the perennial material-discursive divide. Those who stand on the 'material' side focus on the physical aspects of experience – on the corporeal body, the literal implementation of institutional control, the impact of the social environment, or on factors such as social class or economic status. Those who focus on the 'discursive' look to the social and linguistic domains – to talk, to visual representation, to ideology, culture and power. Theorists and critics from each side of the divide have seen the body as their rightful domain. To one camp it is a matter of physical flesh, to the other it is a matter of symbols and signs. So, again, which is the truth, which way should we turn?

This book explores a range of answers to these questions, from a variety of theoretical positions and epistemological standpoints, including psychoanalysis, social representations theory, feminist standpoint theory, critical realism, poststructuralism and social constructionism. Those who are looking for a battle of wills (or of words), or a rerun of either the nature–nurture or the realist–relativist debate should stop at this point. You will not find it here. For at one level the solutions to the material-discursive dilemma which are offered in this book are all the same. The view that we need to move away from the binary divide between material and discursive analyses of the body, towards a position which allows us to recognise the interaction and interrelationship between the two, is what unifies the individual contributions. What distinguishes them from each other is the way in which the material-discursive question is addressed, and the suggestions for future developments in research or theory which arise from the arguments that are outlined. A number of the contributors focus on theory and critique, outlining the problems in adopting either a solely material or discursive critique, then outlining the solutions that they have adopted in their own work. Others focus on empirical work, illustrating the way in which the material body is constructed and interpreted through discourse, and outlining the implications of this for understanding the supposed truths of sex, madness or reproduction. Some of the contributors do both.

   Those who argue for an entirely materialist analysis or, in contrast, take up the view that 'there is nothing beyond the text', are not amongst the contributors to this book. Their views may be implicitly evident – indeed it is the acknowledgement of the presence and power of these divided positions which underpins all of the analyses and arguments that are being put forth here – but the detailed exposition of each of these conflicting standpoints has already been conducted elsewhere. For those who require a brief introduction, I will outline the basic tenets of each position below.

THE MATERIAL-DISCURSIVE DIVIDE

Focusing on the material

Science, psychology and the law have traditionally examined all human experience from a realist perspective, within a positivistic framework which focuses on observable 'facts'. The aim of the expert has been to uncover objective 'truth', and to narrowly delineate the boundaries of the scientific or legal gaze. This is never more clear than in areas of expertise which focus on sexuality, madness or reproduction, where the material body stands at the centre of the scene. So sexuality is being reduced to instinctual drives, physiological arousal, penile pulse amplitude or vaginal swelling; reproduction to evolutionary concepts of mating, hormones or to the physical machinations of the womb; and madness to observable symptoms, inherited disorders or to the action of the brain. The classificatory systems, such as the Diagnostic and Statistical Manual of the American Psychiatric Association (DSM) which provide the boundaries for both research and clinical intervention in these areas, act to reify a positivist approach. The categorisation of sexual, reproductive or mental health disorders is based entirely on what can be measured or observed, thus reinforcing the focus on material phenomena in these different spheres. Equally, aetiological theories which have been developed to explain anything which falls outside of the norm have tended to remain within a reductionist domain. So, for example, phenomena as far-ranging as depression or schizophrenia, premenstrual or menopausal symptoms, deviant desires or sexual dysfunctions, homosexuality or male sexual mastery, have been attributed to internal hormonal or biochemical factors. These aetiological theories focus on the physical body as if that is all there is. As a consequence, any person who turns in this direction for help will find that attention to the body is all that they will get.

Take the case of sexuality. Within mainstream sex research male sexuality is reduced to testosterone and androgens, to the functioning of the penis, to erection and ejaculation; female sexuality to 'vaginal pulse amplitude', orgasmic responses, and the female arousal cycle. 'Sex' is unproblematically defined as heterosexual performance or response; attention focused on the actions of the penis in heterosexual intercourse. These easily observed and measured bodily 'realities' are dissected, explored, in the quest to finally uncover the mysteries of sex. Biological theories are offered as explanations for sexual violence, sexual problems and sexual deviation – as well as for the vagaries of 'normal' sex. All are deemed traceable to instincts, drives or to hormonal (im)balances; to the influence of a particular gene.

For example, one sexual scientist, Simon Le Vay, demonstrates this simple reductionist analysis of sex in his description of heterosexual intercourse, which he describes as such a simple behaviour that 'one hardly needs a brain to do it' (Le Vay, 1993: 47). Here is his description of the 'basic components' of 'coitus', step by step:

> (1) erection of the penis; (2) engorgement of the walls of the vagina and the labia majora, lubrication of the vagina by glandular secretions and transudation, and erection of the clitoris; (3) insertion of the penis into the vagina; (4) pelvic thrusting by one or both partners; (5) elevation of the uterus, with a consequent forward and upward rotation of the mouth of the cervix; (6) ejaculation of semen into the vagina; and (7) orgasm, the intensely pleasurable sense of climax and release, often accompanied by increases in heart rate, flushing of the skin, muscle spasms, and involuntary vocalizations.
>
> (Le Vay, 1993: 47)

Le Vay unquestioningly puts forward the notion of 'sex' as heterosexual intercourse. As in traditional sociobiological theories of sex, the woman's response follows that of the man – it is assumed that male arousal (and orgasm) comes first. Equally, female arousal is only considered here as vaginal response. Le Vay implicitly negates the symbolic domain, unconscious factors, or indeed any other form of sexual stimulation, or desire, as well as the social and discursive construction of 'sex'. This gives the material body pre-eminent status, and reinforces the power of the sexual scientist, whose theories and therapies are positioned as 'truth'. The fact that these theories reinforce phallocentric notions of 'sex' and of gendered power is ignored (Ussher, 1997).

In a similar vein, sexual problems are signified by a dysfunctional body. Take the case of male sexual dysfunction as it is classified in the DSM. With the exception of 'disorders of desire', where the problem is manifested by absence of interest or aversion to sex, it is the functioning of the material body, in this case the penis, which is at issue here. So the DSM-IIIR classifies male sexual problems as falling into the categories of male erectile disorder; inhibited male orgasm, and premature ejaculation. This perhaps explains why treatment for male sexual problems often focuses entirely on the material body, and why physical interventions, such as penile implants, are such a popular treatment for erectile problems in both Britain and the United States (see Teifer, 1986). These diagnostic categories and treatments also position sexual problems within an individualising framework, denying the fact that 'sex' is for the most part a dyadic activity, and that the responses and subjective experience of the man's partner are as relevant and significant as his own. They ignore the social meaning of sex (and of sexual 'failure'), as well as the importance of the discursive construction of the body and of desire.

Similar criticisms have been made about materialist analyses of madness and reproduction: The physical body is at the centre of theorising and of 'cure'; realist thinking leads to a negation of the meaning of symptomatology, or of aetiological factors based in the social domain; the power of the expert is pre-eminent (see Foucault, 1976; Ingelby, 1982; Ussher, 1991). In order to address some of these critiques, in recent years those working within a 'bio-psycho-social' framework, or those interested in social and psychological aspects of experience, have 'added on' a psychosocial-dimension to the traditional material interpretations of sex, madness or reproduction. However, the majority of scientists and clinicians working within this field still rely on realist assumptions, failing to question the social or discursive construction of bodily experience, the influence of their own subjectivity or ideological standpoint on the theories or therapies they develop, and the role of scientific or legal discourse associated with the body in social regulation and control (for an elaboration of these arguments applied to PMS, see Ussher, in press).

The turn to language

In contrast, many social theorists – including sociologists, anthropologists, social psychologists and feminists – have turned their attention exclusively to the cultural and communicative aspects of 'the body', often treating it as a phenomenon virtually unrelated to the biological processes traditionally studied in science and psychology. Here, the physical body appears as an object constructed within sociocultural discourses and practices; it stands as a symbol or a sign.

For example, in recent years, largely due to the influence of poststructuralist theorising, critical feminist attention has shifted to the power of symbolic representations of the sexuality of 'woman' and their role in the social regulation of women. This has led to critical analyses of how 'woman' is portrayed in a range of discursive contexts – from art (Pollock, 1988), film (Kaplan, 1983), popular culture (Douglas, 1994), literature (Gilbert and Gubar, 1979), pornography (Segal and McIntosh, 1993), to science and the law (for an analysis of the relationship between these different genres, see Ussher, 1997). The focus here has been on the regulatory power of discourse – control through that which Foucault termed the 'intelligible body'. Many of these critiques focus on that which semiotic theorists would term 'woman as sign',[1] the analysis of what 'woman' signifies or symbolises at a mythical level[2] – the representation of woman as object, or as fetish, and the splitting of 'woman' into Madonna or whore. These representations have been seen to maintain the position of woman as object or 'Other', in contrast to man who is subject or 'One', as representation plays a central role in the formation of subjectivity. As one critic commented, 'one becomes a woman in the very practice of signs by which we write, speak, see . . . This is neither an illusion nor a paradox. It is a real contradiction – women continue to become woman' (Blumm, 1984). Rather than sexuality being pre-given or innate, here it is seen as something which is performed or acquired. In the process of becoming 'woman', women follow the various scripts of femininity which circulate in the symbolic sphere, negotiating the contradictory representations and repertoires which are hegemonic at any point in time, in order to find a fit between what they wish to be and what is currently allowed (Ussher, 1997). The fact that women invariably take up (a few reject) the position of sexualised 'woman', who is always seen in relation to 'man', is attributed to the dominance of phallocentric discourse and the fact that gender is constructed within a heterosexual matrix (Butler, 1990).

These critical discursive or representational analyses have also had an impact on the way in which theorists and researchers conceptualise and research madness (Foucault, 1967; Gilman, 1988), reproduction (Ussher, 1989; Martin, 1989) and male sexuality (Segal, 1993; Frosh, 1994), with a number of significant consequences in terms of theory and clinical practice. For example, taxonomic categories of deviance or illness, which have been unconditionally accepted within science and psychology, have been deconstructed: the notion of the 'homosexual' or 'heterosexual; of 'paraphilias'; of sexual crimes; of vaginal penetration as 'sex' (and failure in this sphere as 'dysfunction'); of disinterest in sex or premenstrual distress as a 'problem'. These arguments fit neatly into a liberal or libertarian framework, and are in many ways parallel to the arguments made in the 1970s about the need to deconstruct categories of mental illness – the danger in labelling someone as 'schizophrenic' or 'depressed', and assuming that these are 'real' illnesses which are just waiting to be found, rather than being social categorisations placed on sets of symptoms or behaviours which deviate from the 'healthy norm'; a pathologising of those that threaten the status quo, and the peace or power of dominant social groups (Ingelby, 1982; Ussher, 1991).

Yet there is a down side to this deconstruction. Where we question the validity of social categories and the ideological intent behind them, we can be left with a scenario where nothing is 'real', everything is just a social label; an invention of those in power. So there is no such thing as a sexual problem, a sexual crime, or perversion. There is no such thing as a 'homo-sexual' or a 'heterosexual'. There is no such thing as a 'woman' or a 'man'. This can be seen to dismiss the experiences of many women and men. Women who suffer anxiety and stress associated with sexuality, who experience changes in mood across the menstrual cycle, are not delighted to be told that these are mere 'social constructions', not valid problems. Men who cannot obtain an erection, or who can only do so when dressed in particular clothes, may feel similarly. Equally, telling a gay man or lesbian that 'homosexuality' as an identity was an invention of the sexologists will invariably be met with derision. The positive adoption of a gay or lesbian identity has been one of the ways in which many men and women have cele-brated and made positive their position as sexual outsiders. The difference between heterosexuals and homosexuals is often emphasised rather than ignored.

One of the more worrying consequences of this line of argument is the recent move to take social constructionist arguments concerning the age of consent – the idea that there is no absolute age when it is *natural* to first have sex with a child, so the definition of such sex as 'abuse' is arbitrary – to support the sexual activities of paedophiles. At a recent conference on sexuality, the veteran sex researcher John Money deconstructed the notion of paedophilia by ironically drawing attention to the number of men suffering from 'twentyphilia' or 'thirtyphilia' – attraction to women in their twenties or thirties. Implying that there was no distinction to be made between those who are specifically attracted to women of a certain age (or women of a certain body type), and those who were specifically attracted to children, he went on to argue that many men who became sexually engaged with children were positive and loving in their relationships with them. In a social context where sex with children was normal, and where children had a free choice in whether to engage in it or not, his arguments may have some validity – although whether there can ever be a free 'choice' when there is so great a power imbalance is always questionable, and is one of the reasons for laws on age of consent. However, when adult–child sexual activity is against the law, and where the majority of adults who engage in such acts use threats or coercion, often leaving the child in a state of shame and self-blame, such libertarian deconstructions simply do not wash. The motivations of those apologists for paedophilia have to be seriously questioned (see Ussher, 1997).

Therefore, whilst we might criticise traditional realist theorising, the implications of adopting an extreme social constructionist or sociolinguistic approach must be carefully examined. In studying bodily experience, can we legitimately claim that 'there is nothing beyond the text'? For those who work in the fields of cultural theory, art history, film or literary criticism, the need to look beyond representation may not seem to be an issue of great importance. But those of us who work in the social sciences, in psychology or in medicine have to look to the material domain. We are continually faced with the day-to-day impact of the discursive construction of experience on material life. This is why this book is focusing on sexuality, madness and reproduction. These are arenas where a great deal of critical thinking has taken place, yet also where regulatory controls are exacted in the material world. These are arenas where the deconstruction of symptoms and syndromes has greatly challenged the legitimacy of expert intervention, but where individual women and men still come forward (or are referred) to clinicians for treatment or cure. Attempting to reconcile a critical analysis with a recognition of the materiality of people's lives is what this book is all about.

It is arguable that one of the factors which acts to hinder the development of coherent and pluralistic theories of sexuality, reproduction or madness, is the disciplinary split between those who focus on the corporeal body and those who focus on representation – the split between analyses of the material and discursive body. Yet this is a false divide, an inappropriate separation. To understand phenomena such as sexuality, madness or reproduction, we need to examine both bodily processes and practices, and the ways in which these processes and practices are constructed in the realm of the symbolic. We cannot separate the two. Thus the purpose of this book is to explore, illustrate and develop theoretical and methodological approaches which attempt to reconcile or address this divide, by combining critical sociolinguistic analyses with an appreciation of the reciprocal relationship between discourse and its material context.

One of the more constructive consequences of the 'turn to language' has been the development of qualitative studies of the discursive context and meaning of the body and bodily experience. This is research which focuses on the construction of meaning within language rather than on attempting to uncover the underlying 'truth' about the material body. Some of this work focuses on analyses of existing visual or textual representations, as has been outlined above. In the social sciences, much of it is empirical – interviewing individuals about their experiences, and examining the discursive constructions of that experience, which are evident in the resulting text. Discursive approaches are now commonplace in critical psychology, social psychology and many other social science disciplines. Yet to date there has been little discussion of how far a discursive approach can be applied to areas of experience where physical or material issues are at the fore. *Body Talk* directly addresses this issue.

Rather than summarise each of the contributions here, I will let each be read for itself, on its own terms. The order in which they are presented is relatively arbitrary. Each individual contribution can be taken and read on its own, but together they make something else, an integrated whole, which illustrates the need for a move beyond bipolar or dichotomous thinking, towards a material–discursive approach.

This book does not pretend to stand as the final statement on the subject. We are not attempting to provide the definitive solution to the problem of conceptualising the body beyond the material–discursive divide, or saying that reading this collection will answer all of the questions which arise in this debate. What we *are* doing is demonstrating that theorists, researchers and clinicians who work with the body – and particularly with sexuality, madness and reproduction – can no longer ignore the material–discursive debate. Yet, through critical analysis and creative research practice, we can move beyond a position of fragmented and divided thought, towards a more integrated analysis of the body, and of reproduction, madness and sex.

NOTES

1   Based on semiotic theorising, visual imagery – and in particular film – is seen as a system of communication, akin to language, wherein particular meanings are created through the use of 'signs'. This notion is based on the work of Saussure, who argued that the meaning of language is not based in the words or intentions of a speaker, but in the relationships between the elements of the sign system itself (see Hollway, 1989). Saussure argued that within language exists both the *signified* and the *signifier*. The signified is the object in the world, in our case 'woman', the biologically female person. The signifier is the collection of phonemes w-o-m-a-n, making up the word 'woman', which is the sign for a person who is born with breasts, a vagina, etc. The fact that the signifier 'woman' refers to the biological (or social) person that has breasts, etc. is arbitrary – is a construction within language. The fact that the word 'woman' connotes so many different and often contradictory things (beauty, desires, sexuality, emotion, fickleness, weakness, lability . . .) in the twentieth-century developed world is as a result of the sign system which operates in this cultural sphere.
2   Barthes has claimed that these signs operate as myth – not as a direct reference to the real world. Thus the signifier 'woman', either as image or as word, does not merely connote female sexuality or gender, but can have a whole new connotative meaning associated with it, which is provided by the particular culture and ideology in which the language or image is situated/produced. Thus 'woman' can become the sign for weakness, or danger, or sexuality (each a signified), making it a new sign, at a secondary level, that is often called a secondary level of signification.

REFERENCES

Barthes, R. (1975) *Mythologies*, New York: Hill & Wang.
Blumm, M. (1984) In T. de Lauretis, *Alice Doesn't Live Here Any More: Feminism, Semiotics, Cinema*, London: Macmillian, pp. 335.
Butler, J. (1990) *Gender Trouble: Feminism and the Subversion of Identity*, London: Routledge.
Douglas, S. (1994) *Growing up Female: Growing up Female with the Mass Media*, London: Penguin.
Foucault, M. (1967). *Madness and Civilisation: A History of Insanity in the Age of Reason*, Tavistock: London.
—— (1976) *The History of Sexuality*, vol. 1, London: Penguin.
Frosh, S. (1994) *Sexual Difference: Masculinity and Psychoanalysis*, London: Routledge.
Gilbert, S. and Gubar, S. (1979) *The Madwoman in the Attic: The Woman Writer and the Nineteenth Century Imagination*, Newhaven: Yale University Press.

Gilman, S.L. (1988) *Disease and Representation: Images of Illness from Madness to AIDS*, Ithaca, NY: Cornell University Press.

Hollway, W. (1989) *Subjectivity and Method in Psychology*, London: Sage.

Ingelby, D. (ed.) (1982) *Critical Psychiatry: The Politics of Mental Health*, London: Penguin.

Kaplan, A. (1983) *Women and Film. Both Sides of the Camera*, London: Methuen.

Le Vay, Simon (1993) *The Sexual Brain*, Massachusetts: MIT Press.

Martin, E. (1989) *The Woman in the Body: A Cultural Analysis of Reproduction*, Milton Keynes: Open University Press.

Pollock, G. (1988) *Vision and Difference: Femininity, Feminism and Histories of Art*, London: Routledge.

Segal, L. (1993) *Slow Motion: Changing Masculinity, Changing Men*, London: Virago.

Segal, L. and McIntosh, M. (eds) (1993) *Sex Exposed: Sexuality and the Pornography Debate*, London: Virago.

Teifer, L. (1986) In Pursuit of the Perfect Penis, *American Behavioural Scientist*, 29(5), 579–599.

Ussher, J.M. (1989) *The Psychology of the Female Body*, London: Routledge.

—— (1991) *Women's Madness: Misogyny or Mental Illness*, Hemel Hempstead: Harvester Wheatsheaf.

—— (1997) *Fantasies of Femininity: Reframing the Boundaries of Sex*, London: Penguin.

—— (in press) Premenstrual Syndrome: Reconciling Disciplinary Divides Through the Adoption of a Material–Discursive Epistemological Standpoint, *Annual Review of Sex Research*.

2 Women's bodies, women's lives and depression
Towards a reconciliation of material and discursive accounts

Janet M. Stoppard

INTRODUCTION

In both mainstream and feminist writing on women's mental health, depression has been identified as a problem that is particularly prevalent among women (McGrath *et al.*, 1990; Ussher, 1991; Weissman and Olfson, 1995). In the past, depression was likely to be viewed as a problem encountered during mid-life (e.g. involutional melancholia), coinciding with the end of a woman's reproductive life. Contrasting with this now outmoded view, epidemiological studies conducted in recent years in Western, industrialised countries have yielded evidence indicating that heightened vulnerability to depression among women is a feature of the full range of the female lifespan, beginning in adolescence (Nolen-Hoeksema and Girgus, 1994) and continuing through adulthood (Weissman *et al.*, 1993).

In concert with identification of depression as a problem that particularly afflicts women, theoretical formulations have been developed that incorporate gender-related influences (e.g. Belle, 1982; McGrath *et al.*, 1990; Jack, 1991). The observation that rates of depression are markedly higher among women than men also has prompted attempts to explain this gender-related difference (Nolen-Hoeksema, 1990; Cutler and Nolen-Hoeksema, 1991; Stoppard, 1993). Although gender-related differences in depression rates, and how they may best be accounted for, are not the focus of the present chapter, such findings have served to underline the importance of considering gender in attempts to explain and understand depression (Coyne, 1994).

The aim of this chapter is to explore the theoretical and epistemological (and methodological) implications of two main contemporary approaches to explaining depression in women.[1] These two approaches are encapsulated in the terms 'women's bodies' and 'women's lives'. The women's bodies approach focuses on the biological body, with particular emphasis on the reproductive female body. The women's lives approach addresses the social circumstances of women's everyday lives, including gendered sources of stress and their impact on women. The women's bodies approach is closely associated with medical-psychiatric perspectives on depression and can be considered as a variant of the dominant biochemical explanatory models governing practice in these fields (Weissman and Olfson, 1995). The women's lives approach derives in part from sociological investigations of the links between women's everyday life experiences and their reports of psychological distress (e.g. Brown and Harris, 1978, 1989), and from analyses, informed by feminist perspectives, of the systemic sources of inequality that shape and constrain women's everyday lives (e.g. McGrath *et al.*, 1990; Stoppard, 1993).

The women's bodies and women's lives approaches to explaining depression also have their counterparts in modes of intervention for treatment of depression in individual women. Thus, prescription of psychotropic (antidepressant) drugs represents the dominant treatment from the standpoint of the women's bodies approach, whereas various forms of psychotherapy, including cognitive-behavioural therapy (Beck *et al.*, 1979) and feminist-informed therapeutic approaches (Hurst and Genest, 1995) are more characteristic of the women's lives approach. Within mainstream clinical psychology, psychosocial (or diathesis-stress) models of depression currently abound (e.g. Gotlib and Hammen, 1992; Coyne and Whiffen, 1995). Whilst these psychosocial models, in some respects, are more compatible with the women's lives than the women's bodies perspective on depression, as will be elaborated later they also incorporate assumptions that are equally consistent with a women's bodies approach.

In much contemporary mainstream and feminist literature on women's mental health, the women's bodies and women's lives approaches to depression are presented as distinct theoretical orientations, with the implication that they are competing and antagonistic and, therefore, incompatible. One source of this apparent incompatibility is that the two approaches typically are taken up by researchers and practitioners with differing disciplinary affiliations. The women's bodies approach is dominant in biomedical research and practice; the women's lives approach predominates among those working within the social and behavioural sciences (psychology, sociology) and within the ranks of non-medical practitioners (clinical psychology, counselling, social work). Another source of perceived antagonism between the two approaches derives from their positioning with respect to recognition of women's disadvantaged social status, on the one hand, and the scientific status of knowledge on which theories of depression are based, on the other. From a feminist perspective, the women's lives approach is viewed as more progressive and potentially more emancipatory than the women's bodies approach and, therefore, as more in keeping with gender equality goals. From the perspective of mainstream depression researchers, however, the women's lives approach is characterised as politically motivated and consequently 'unscientific'. The women's bodies approach, presumably because of its grounding in biomedical knowledge, is viewed as having scientific legitimacy. Another way in which the women's bodies and women's lives approaches appear antagonistic is in their respective locations on opposing sides of the body–mind and nature–society divides. Thus, as currently operationalised and practised, these two approaches to depression in women appear to reinforce and promote the form of fragmented, dualistic thinking that has characterised modern attempts to understand and explain phenomena such as depression, defined as 'psychopathology'.

In the remainder of this chapter, I explore the strengths and limitations of, and contradictions posed by, these two approaches to depression in women. The position I wish to develop is that neither approach on its own can lead to an adequate understanding of depression in women. At the same time, by pointing to a need to consider both women's bodies and women's lives in theorising about depression, I am not advocating a move to the type of diathesis-stress model in which depression is seen to arise in the interaction of life stress and individual diatheses (personality and/or biologically based predispositions). Instead, the argument I want to develop is that, as currently formulated, neither the women's bodies approach, the women's lives approach, nor a combination of these two approaches, offers much promise as a route to explaining and understanding depression in women. The possibilities offered by these approaches are limited, in part, because of unexamined assumptions about the research methodologies that are appropriate for generating knowledge about depression in women. Specifically, each approach presupposes a realist epistemology coupled with a positivist research methodology. Presumptions about how 'depression' and 'gender' should be conceptualised also set limits on the women's bodies and women's lives approaches to explaining and understanding depression. Thus, the aim of this chapter can be restated as that of exploring how 'depression' arises in the intersection between women's bodies and their lives. This exploration involves sketching the outlines of a more dynamic, interdisciplinary, approach; one that has the potential to accommodate the biological, the psychological and the social when these concepts are reframed in terms of material-embodied and subjective-discursive aspects of women's lived experience.

CONTEMPORARY THEORETICAL PERSPECTIVES ON DEPRESSION IN WOMEN

Women's bodies as a source of depression

As documented by Ussher (1991), both historically and in the present women's bodies have served as a fertile source of explanations for women's health and mental health problems. With respect to depression, empirical (e.g. epidemiological) findings indicating a greater preponderance of women than men among the depressed predictably have led to a focus on those aspects of biology that differentiate female bodies from male bodies. That some women experience depression associated with embodied processes which involve hormonal change – e.g. premenstrually, post-partum, during menopause – has given some credence to a presumed link between depression in women and female reproductive biological processes. This link is underlined and at the same time symbolically represented in the naming of disorders. Women now can legitimately seek help from health professionals for premenstrual syndrome (PMS), post-partum depression and menopausal mood problems, and health professionals can legitimately claim expertise in treatment of these 'disorders'. Thus, the naming of disorders not only legitimises women's complaints but offers the promise of some form of treatment to alleviate their distress.

The women's bodies approach also fits comfortably with the prevailing biomedical framework within which depression is understood as a mental disorder caused by an underlying biochemical disturbance involving neurotransmitters in the brain. Biochemical models of depression are dominant within mainstream psychiatry (at least in Western countries and increasingly in the rest of the world) and provide justification for biochemical treatments (antidepressant drugs).[2] In a recent article, in which they overview research on depression in women, Weissman and Olfson (1995) identify investigations of the effects (and effectiveness) of antidepressant drugs with pregnant or breastfeeding women as an important topic for future research. Virtually no research on antidepressant drugs has been conducted with women of child-bearing age, because of the potential for harm to the foetus or to the breastfed infant, yet women (most of whom are of child-bearing age) are the major recipients of these psychoactive drugs.[3]

Critiques of the women's bodies approach

Critical analyses of the women's bodies approach have addressed the conceptual foundations of this perspective, as well as pointing to inconsistencies and contradictions in the empirical evidence marshalled in its support. Key conceptual concerns include the medicalisation and pathologisation of female reproductive biological processes that, while normal in women, are perceived as abnormal and dysfunctional when compared to the implicit standard of biological normality signified by the male body (e.g. Oakley, 1986; Nicolson, 1995c; Ussher, 1991). Moreover, research findings are largely inconsistent with hypotheses derived from the women's bodies approach to explaining depression in terms of changes in hormonal levels, whether associated with phases of the menstrual cycle (McFarlane and Williams, 1994; Walker, 1995), in conjunction with pregnancy and childbirth (Nicolson, 1992) or accompanying menopause (McKinlay *et al.*, 1987; Kaufert *et al.*, 1992).

Despite the many published critiques of the women's bodies approach, research and practice grounded in this perspective continue unabated.[4] And, among those whose work is governed by the framework of biological psychiatry, there is little acknowledgement or acceptance of the alternative women's lives approach to explaining depression in women.

Women's lives as a source of depression

The women's lives approach to explaining depression builds on critiques of biological models by pointing to potential sources of depression inherent in women's everyday lives. According to this approach, depression is readily explainable as a response to the stressful conditions of women's lives. Women bear the brunt of social-structural arrangements whereby, as wives and mothers, they are expected and required to take on primary, and often sole, responsibility for child- and family-care. In the 'private' confines of the family, girls and women are also more likely to suffer (often in silence) sexual and physical victimisation, forms of abuse that have been linked to women's vulnerability to depression (Cutler and Nolen-Hoeksema, 1991; Koss *et al.*, 1994). At the same time, gender-based inequalities in employment (including pay inequities, often justified in terms of women's primary commitment to the roles of wife and mother) ensure that relatively few women are in a position to support themselves and their children, thereby fostering economic dependence on men (or the state). Although, in recent decades, women have entered the paid labour force in increasing numbers, they tend to be clustered in low-paying jobs while continuing to bear the full burden of childcare and domestic work in the home (the so-called double day) (Lorber, 1994).

Women's economic dependency is supported by an ideology in which a woman's value is judged against a standard defined by the 'good' wife and mother, whilst, simultaneously, the work that women do in the home caring for others is devalued. Consistent with this analysis, Brown and Harris (1978), in their ground-breaking exploration of the social origins of depression, found that events occurring in the context of women's everyday lives served to 'provoke' depression if they undermined a woman's sense of herself as a 'good' wife and mother or threatened her continued ability to perform adequately in these roles. Additional findings by Brown and Harris have shown that risk of depression following occurrence of a 'provoking' event is exacerbated when the circumstances of a woman's life already are, or become (e.g. through marriage breakdown), characterised by economic disadvantage. Given these findings, it is hardly surprising that rates of depression are highest among women, such as single-parent mothers, who have limited economic resources (Belle, 1990).

Critiques of the women's lives approach

The women's lives approach to explaining depression informs therapeutic practice among many non-medical health professionals, and is the hallmark of practitioners whose interventions are guided by feminist analyses of women's oppression and exploitation within patriarchal social arrangements. Nevertheless, it is possible to mount a critique of the women's lives approach along the following lines.

First, much research based in a women's lives approach reflects an uncritical acceptance of the concept of depression as currently defined by the diagnostic criteria developed within mainstream psychiatry. The issue of how it is determined that a woman is depressed is rarely addressed and research findings showing higher rates of depression in women than men are interpreted as providing evidence in support of the women's lives explanatory approach. Findings of research that fail to yield evidence of higher rates of depression in women are problematic for this approach. Do such findings mean that women are no longer oppressed? Would equal rates of depression in men and women imply that the problem of women's oppression has been overcome?

Second, rejecting a role for women's bodies in understanding depression means that biologically based manifestations of 'depression' (as defined by diagnostic criteria) – such as sleep, appetite and digestive disturbances, and lack of energy to perform even ordinary everyday activities – cannot readily be explained.[5] Because the implications of these so-called 'vegetative' signs are often ambiguous with respect to a woman's physical health, when they occur women are likely to seek medical help for them.

Third, empirical findings do not fully cohere with an approach to explaining depression based on women's lives. By no means all women who are full-time housewives are depressed; the majority of women who combine the roles of housewife and mother with that of paid worker are not depressed; not all women who have been sexually abused become depressed; and not all single-parent women are depressed. Furthermore, not all depressed women have stressful lives. Of course it could be argued that merely being a woman in a patriarchal society is stressful in itself, but then why aren't all women depressed? If followed to its logical conclusion, this line of argument stretches the notion of depression to the point where it loses all meaning and also comes perilously close to the essentialist position of the women's bodies approach to explaining depression.

Another weakness of the women's lives approach is that the implications for action are less than clear, at least with respect to the individual woman who is depressed. Of course, it is possible to organise collectively around the goals of social, economic and political equality for women; this is unlikely, however, to do much to alleviate the distress of women who are depressed now. In the absence of alternatives, the options for most depressed women continue to be limited to drugs or individual psychotherapy, albeit modified by feminist influences.

Rather than continuing to debate the merits and shortcomings of theoretical positions proposed by 'experts', some feminist researchers have noted that a critical gap in research on women's mental health is the paucity of information on the views of women themselves about their health concerns (Walters, 1991; Pugliesi, 1992). This observation is in sharp contrast to the emphasis placed on exploration of women's accounts of their experiences within feminist perspectives on research methodology (cf.

Henwood and Pidgeon, 1995). Instead, much theorising about depression within the women's lives approach has drawn support primarily from epidemiological studies using survey methods to investigate the social determinants of health.

WOMEN'S ACCOUNTS OF THEIR DEPRESSIVE EXPERIENCES

Several recent studies have been reported in which women's accounts of their experiences in relation to 'depression' have been the focus of investigation. These studies have revealed that a link is drawn by women between their depressive experiences and their everyday lives. For instance, among women (in an urban area of central Canada) interviewed by Walters (1993), some did explain their feelings of depression as arising in relation to the stressful conditions of their everyday lives. These women attributed their experiences with depression to their heavy workloads, time pressures and caring responsibilities. At the same time, Walters found that some women also drew on explanations couched in terms of female biological processes (e.g. PMS, menopause) in accounting for their depressive experiences. Others also have explicated a 'women's bodies' discourse in the accounts of women who have experienced depression in conjunction with life events marked by bodily and biological changes, such as menstruation (Swann and Ussher, 1995), childbirth (Nicolson, 1992) and menopause (Lock, 1993).

Women diagnosed as 'depressed' by a medical professional have also been the focus of studies. For instance, based on participant observation of self-help groups for individuals who had been diagnosed as depressed, Karp (1992) described how group members (many of whom were women) drew on both biological and psychosocial explanations in their efforts to understand their depressive experiences. In this case, in keeping with the position promulgated in the self-help groups, explanations in terms of biological influences usually emphasised the role of biochemical disturbances. Although, according to Karp, group participants reported that they had gained some relief from being told by a medical professional that their problem was diagnosed as depression, one that had a biochemical cause, at the same time they continued to consider non-biological, personal-situational explanations for their depressive experiences. That is, neither a biochemical explanation nor an explanation in terms of psychosocial factors alone seemed entirely satisfactory to the participants in Karp's study.

In an interview study with individuals who had been diagnosed as depressed, Lewis (1995) also found that women's explanations for their depressive experiences reflected both biological (biochemical or hormonal) influences and social circumstances. Neither of these explanatory approaches, however, was judged by the women interviewed to be entirely satisfactory. Lewis noted a recursive quality in women's attempts to account for their depressive experiences; one in which biological and social explanations were taken up in succession, but without being integrated.

When research has addressed women's accounts, rather than experts' theories of the causes of depression, findings reveal the presence of both the women's bodies and women's lives approaches in the types of explanations drawn on as women seek to understand their depressive experiences. That women's accounts appear to mirror the same approaches that currently characterise experts' theories is hardly surprising. Both the women's bodies and women's lives approaches to understanding depression are widely disseminated in the popular media (e.g. women's magazines and 'women's' pages of newspapers) and in publications targeting health and social service professionals (e.g. newsletters and journals). At the same time, while these approaches are presented as alternative explanatory possibilities, for individual women such information provides little assistance in making sense of the feelings of confusion and ambiguity inherent in depressive experiences (Karp, 1992; Lewis, 1995).

Apart from their inability to offer women a sense of 'closure' in explaining their depressive experiences, the women's bodies and women's lives approaches do not operate in a social/cultural vacuum. When these explanatory approaches enter the realm of everyday understandings, they bring with them certain implications when taken up by individual women in accounting for their depressive experiences. Although experts' explanations of depression typically are presented as value-neutral, buttressed by the gloss derived from their legitimation as the products of 'scientific' research, they become less value-neutral when taken up by individual women. For a woman trying to understand bodily and subjective experiences that are often ambiguous as to whether they should be interpreted as signifying a physical problem ('Do I need to see a doctor?') or something else ('nerves', 'stress'?), whether she draws on an explanation in terms of women's lives or women's bodies will have somewhat different implications for how she sees herself and her situation.

If a woman seeks an explanation for her depressive experiences (low mood, lack of energy, etc.) in terms of bodily processes (e.g. hormonal changes associated with menstruation or menopause), she invariably attributes them to something outside her control and also removes the possibility that her own actions and subjective experiences are somehow implicated. It is not her fault; she is not to blame. Sustaining this interpretation, however, raises the possibility that her body, in some unclear and essentially mysterious way, is dysfunctional. Frequent media pronouncements on such topics as PMS and its deleterious psychological and behavioural consequences, and the myriad health problems said to result from reduced oestrogen production during menopause, add their weight to the social construction of the female body as inherently weak and disordered. In removing blame from the individual and transferring it to women's bodies, this approach also brings with it the implication that women could (should?) guard against future problems by taking the preventative action of ingesting medically prescribed substances (antidepressant drugs, hormonal replacements) to compensate for their inherent bodily weaknesses.[6]

Alternatively, if a woman attributes her depressive experiences to her social circumstances, this may exacerbate, rather than alleviate, feelings of distress, given the relative powerlessness of most women to change their situations. The conditions of many women's lives are governed by the requirements of caring for others, whether children, husbands or elderly parents. Yet the lack of access to, and control of, material resources characterising many women's lives limits options to pursue different ways of organising everyday domestic responsibilities (e.g. childcare). At the same time, in women's accounts of their everyday experiences, unpaid domestic and caring responsibilities tend to be 'normalised' as unexceptional, takenfor-granted features of their lives (e.g. Popay, 1992; Blaxter, 1993). Thus, women tend to downplay mental health problems, such as depressive experiences, interpreting them as predictable, and therefore understandable, consequences of the lives they lead (Walters, 1993). In this way, the 'antidepressant' (and emancipatory) potential of the women's lives approach is undermined. For example, among women who participated in Walters' study, more identified depression, rather than their weight, as a personal health concern; yet more expressed *worry* about their weight than about being depressed. Thus, the impact of the women's lives approach to explaining depression is dissipated by women's tendency to interpret their experiences as the normal consequences of everyday living. Whether this explanatory strategy leads to more or less depression is unclear, but to the extent that the sources of women's distress remain unarticulated and amorphous, their feelings of empowerment are unlikely to be enhanced.

Although women's accounts in relation to their depressive experiences may not explicitly be framed within the 'women's lives' explanatory approach, nevertheless they do draw on a 'stress' discourse in explaining their health problems (Walters, 1993). The notion of 'stress' has become part of the everyday understanding of health and ill health, reflecting the contemporary influence of experts' conceptualisations of stressful life experiences and the role of stress in the aetiology of various somatic and psychological problems (Pollock, 1988; Stroebe and Stroebe, 1995). Women's attribution of their depressive experiences to the stressful nature of their everyday lives can be seen as an aspect of this more general stress discourse. A drawback of this explanatory strategy, however, as Pollock (1988) has pointed out, is that the stress discourse potentially creates its own selffulfilling consequences, whereby people's awareness of 'stress' may itself engender distress. In drawing on the stress discourse in accounting for their depressive experiences, women can present their everyday lives as being relatively unproblematic; by identifying 'stress' as the problem, the source of depressive experiences is located outside the confines of everyday activities. Thus, use of the stress discourse serves to obscure, rather than reveal, how women's depressive experiences arise in the context of their lives. The meaning of 'stress' is further obscured by use of the term to denote both an external cause of distress and subjective distress (i.e. as a 'symptom').

In sum, neither the women's bodies nor the women's lives approach to explaining depression seems to have a great deal to offer individual women. Although women do draw on both approaches in their attempts to make sense of their depressive experiences, neither alone seems entirely satisfactory, and their explanatory efforts oscillate between the two (Karp, 1992; Walters, 1993; Lewis, 1995). Moreover, at the level of individual women, the consequences of taking up one or the other approach are, on the one hand, to implicate women's bodies further as deficient and inherently disordered or, on the other, to normalise and obscure how depressive experiences arise in the context of their everyday lives. If women's accounts merely reflect experts' formulations of causes of depression, albeit drawing on popularised versions, what is the status of women's accounts of their depressive experiences? What role do they have in theorising about depression?

Beginning research from women's accounts not only provides an important source of knowledge about the experiences of individual women that they (and/or health professionals?) call depression (Nicolson, 1995b). Such qualitative inquiries also facilitate exploration of the meaning of depressive experiences for women and how this meaning is constructed in the context of their everyday lives (Lewis, 1995). This lived experience includes the explanatory approaches available to women and on which they draw in their attempts to make sense of their depressive experiences. Explorations of women's accounts of their depressive experiences reveal that the process of arriving at an explanation for these experiences is one requiring negotiation of positions that appear resistant to a satisfactory resolution (Karp, 1992; Lewis, 1995). Thus, while women ask the question 'Why am I depressed?', they seem unable to derive a clear answer to this question from the possibilities available to them. From the perspective of depression experts, one response might be to dismiss women's accounts as merely reflecting lay (and therefore uninformed?) understanding of clinical phenomena more knowledgeably addressed by mental health professionals. An alternative response might be to interpret women's accounts as revealing limitations in contemporary conceptualisations of depression.

PROBLEMS WITH MAINSTREAM CONCEPTUALISATIONS OF DEPRESSION

The elements of vacillation and uncertainty present in women's accounts as they attempt to negotiate contradictory explanations for their depressive experiences have their counterparts in experts' theoretical formulations. The seemingly irreconcilable nature of theoretical positions that, on the one hand, give priority to biological processes and, on the other, emphasise social circumstances, appears to preclude the possibility of an adequate address to a phenomenon that is both embodied and subjectively experienced. In addition to the lack of rapprochement between explanatory perspectives, the issue of how depression should be defined for research purposes continues to be debated (Coyne, 1994). For the time being, this debate has been resolved by deferring to the diagnostic criteria enshrined in the Diagnostic and Statistical Manual of the American Psychiatric Association (1994). These criteria designate a variety of subjective (low mood, negative thoughts, lack of concentration) and physical (vegetative signs, inability to engage in everyday activities) experiences as symptoms of 'depression'.

One source of the lack of resolution apparent in attempts to explain depression, for depression researchers and depressed women alike, may lie in the tension between the subjective and physical embodiment, between the social and the biological. The women's lives and women's bodies approaches can be seen as representing different sides of the mind–body and society–nature dualisms. They address different parts of the puzzle, but provide no clear directions for integrating the pieces. This dualistic thinking not only is actualised in the division of labour in research on depression between those who follow a biomedical approach and those who pursue more psychosocial explanations, but is reflected in women's accounts of their depressive experiences. This dualistic discourse presents women with a choice between their bodies *or* their lives as the cause of their depression. At the same time, adding to the confusion, women experience their depressions both physically and subjectively, while lacking any socially shared discourse that could validate their experiences.

Psychosocial models of depression

Within mainstream psychology, psychosocial explanatory models of depression currently hold sway. Superseding earlier attempts to locate etiological processes primarily at the level of individual psychological functioning and content, proponents of psychosocial models acknowledge the role of the social environment by postulating that depression is caused by an interaction between individual psychological diatheses (e.g. cognitive vulnerabilities) and events arising in a person's everyday life that are experienced as stressful (Gotlib and Hammen, 1992; Coyne and Whiffen, 1995). Thus, specific events in a person's life that signify loss of a valued relationship or failure to achieve a desired goal are hypothesised to increase risk of depression when the individual has a congruent or 'matching' form of psychological diathesis.

Psychosocial theories of depression generally have been formulated and investigated within the positivist/realist epistemological framework dominant within mainstream psychology. When applied to the problem of explaining 'depression', such approaches bring with them limitations inherent in positivist methodologies. Little attention is paid to the subjective experiences of individuals diagnosed as depressed, except as these relate to investigator-defined psychological diatheses, such as cognitive 'vulnerabilities', typically assessed by 'standardised' questionnaires, which are 'objectively' scored. Incorporation of the 'social' into such theories is achieved in a way that serves to reinscribe dualistic assumptions, by first conceptualising the social as separate from the psychological, and then postulating their interaction. Thus, within mainstream approaches the social is treated as an object, capable of exerting causal influences, in interaction with psychological diatheses, in the aetiology of depression.

As conceptualised within psychosocial theories of depression, the social environment is defined in terms of stressful life events. Initial efforts to measure stressful life events relied on listings of events formulated by investigators. Recognition of the inflexibility of the events list approach, its inability to respond to idiosyncratic contextual aspects of individuals' lives, has led more recently to endorsement of the structured interview as the method of choice for assessment of the stressful features of depressed persons' social environments (Coyne, 1994; Wethington *et al.*, 1995). A prototypical example of this approach is the Life Events and Difficulties Schedule (LEDS), first developed by Brown and Harris (1978) to investigate the role of social factors in depression in women. This semi-structured interview is used to assess the presence of discrete events or ongoing circumstances in individuals' lives that they experience as distressing or upsetting (Brown, 1989).

What the LEDS methodology also does is to erase the background context in which everyday activities are socially organised. As employed in investigations of depression in women, the LEDS approach results in the nature of women's everyday lives being taken for granted; only unusual events and exceptional circumstances are recorded. The 'social', defined as the social environment, is operationalised in a restricted way as the current life circumstances of a particular woman. Thus, contemporary psychosocial theories are silent on the issue of how women's lives are regulated and influenced by wider social, political and economic conditions (e.g. lack of adequate childcare services, pay inequities and sexual harassment in the workplace), and how these conditions arise in social-historical context. Paradoxically, the way in which the 'social' is conceptualised in contemporary psychosocial theories of depression serves to 'decontextualise', rather than contextualise, women's experiences. Moreover, the overwhelming reliance on quantitative methods in research on psychosocial models of depression does not allow the meaning of the events and circumstances of women's everyday lives to be explored beyond 'common-sense' understandings, usually represented in highly condensed forms reflecting the standpoint of researchers. Mainstream methodological strategies, therefore, produce a conceptualisation of the 'social' that is impoverished in regard to both its material and discursive aspects.

A further limitation of psychosocial theories is that, while seeming to offer an alternative to reductionistic biological models of depression, the role of the body remains untheorised. Relying, as they do, on a definition of 'depression' adopted unmodified from a psychiatric conception of 'depressive disorder' (Coyne, 1994), itself derived from a medical model of 'mental illness', psychosocial theories are founded in assumptions that set the aetiology of depression squarely within the physically embodied individual. At the same time, psychosocial theories do not address embodied aspects of 'depression', manifested at the individual level as so-called 'vegetative signs' (e.g. sleep and appetite disturbances, debilitating lack of energy). Thus, in their neglect of embodied aspects of 'depression', mainstream approaches not only reinforce the body–mind form of dualistic thinking but also leave the 'women's bodies' approach to explaining depression unchallenged.

Social constructionist critiques of mainstream approaches

Social constructionist analyses of mainstream approaches to defining depression have drawn attention to the way 'depression' is socially constructed in language within interactions between medical practitioners and clients (Parker *et al.*, 1995). For instance, the DSM criteria for diagnosing 'depressive disorder' are stated in a manner that creates a sense of precision and objectivity which closer examination reveals to be spurious (Lewis, 1995). Aided by realist epistemological assumptions, the diagnostic process starts by labelling designated experiences as 'symptoms' of an underlying 'disorder' (in this case 'depression'), which is presumed to exist. This reification of the disorder is supported by a process of circular reasoning which begins by considering individuals' experiences in isolation from other aspects of their lives. These detached experiences are then reconceptualised as 'symptoms' of an underlying (and unobservable) disorder, one that can be detected only by means of the very experiences on which the initial diagnosis was based. From a social constructionist perspective, this diagnostic process can instead be reframed as operating to create 'depression' as a discursive object (Nicolson, 1992; Lewis, 1995). Saying that 'depression' is socially constructed is to point to the need to explore the way this term – its current meaning and use by professionals and lay people – has evolved in social-historical context. It also opens up for analytic consideration the role of language and social interaction in constructing experiences that researchers as well as ordinary people understand as 'depression'.

In considering depression from a social constructionist perspective, it is important to avoid the (mistaken) impression that the experiences currently labelled 'depression' are somehow being discounted as not 'real' or less valid because of their subjective character. Psychiatric diagnosis itself is not entirely inconsistent with a social constructionist perspective, given that its origins lie in clients' accounts of experiences shared with clinicians (Polkinghorne, 1992). In practice, nevertheless, the diagnostic process serves to foster reification of 'disorders' presumed to underlie clients' experiences. At issue here, however, are the implications for explaining and understanding the experiences now subsumed under the pathologising label of 'depression', if such experiences, as well as the accounts from which they are inferred, were themselves to be viewed as socially constructed.

Qualitative research methods, such as those focusing on people's accounts (e.g. interviews), provide one avenue for exploring individuals' subjective experiences and the meanings attached to these experiences. Use of qualitative approaches also is advocated by feminist researchers as a method for revealing the character of women's experiences in the context of their everyday lives (Henwood and Pidgeon, 1995; Nicolson, 1995a). Such approaches also hold promise for addressing the oft-reported observation and widely held belief that women as a group are particularly susceptible to 'depression'. Because of their affinity with a social constructionist epistemological position (Parker, 1994; Henwood and Pidgeon, 1995), qualitative methodologies also are more suited for elaborating the meanings of 'gender' in directions that extend beyond the individualised conceptions underpinning mainstream empiricist approaches to research. In mainstream psychological research, conceptualisations of 'gender' have focused almost exclusively on attributes of individual males and females, thereby precluding consideration of symbolic or social-structural aspects of gender (Harding, 1986; Kimball, 1994).

CONCEPTIONS OF GENDER AND EXPLORATIONS OF DEPRESSION IN WOMEN

In mainstream research on depression, gender typically is addressed in terms of assignment of 'subjects' to groups on the basis of 'sex', i.e. as signified by biological gender assignment as female or male. Investigation is likely to be directed towards determination of whether 'differences' (as tested statistically) between males and females are present on the dependent variables of interest. As Kimball (1994) has argued, this positivist research strategy has been deployed effectively by feminist psychologists to undermine and challenge cultural assumptions about gender-related differences, particularly in the domain of cognitive abilities and attainments. At the same time, this empiricist strategy undercuts feminist claims centred on ideas of female specificity with regard to positively valued 'human' qualities, such as caring and concern for others, manifested in a personal orientation in which maintenance of interpersonal relationships is paramount (e.g. Gilligan, 1982; Miller, 1986; Jack, 1991).

Kimball (1994) suggests that some resolution of the apparent conflict between the 'similarities' and 'differences' perspectives can be achieved by recognition of the multifaceted meaning of 'gender'. Thus, gender can be conceptualised not only as residing within the individual (e.g. as gender identity) but also as operating symbolically, within cultural meaning systems (Harding, 1986). Feminist researchers whose work is informed by the 'similarities' perspective tend to eschew exploration of symbolic gender, relegating such aspects of human experience to stereotypes, beliefs not grounded in an empirical reality. Symbolic aspects of gender, however, are central to, and embraced by, researchers who highlight the importance of knowledge of female specificity for understanding the 'psychology of women'. The divergence between these two approaches is further exacerbated by the different methodological commitments of their adherents (Kimball, 1994). Feminist empiricists typically employ positivist methodological approaches characterised by quantitative methods, whereas qualitative methods are more likely to be used by those exploring female specificity in a search for women-centred knowledge.

Gender can be understood in yet another way – as involving gendered aspects of the division of labour in society (Harding, 1986) interlinked with social-structural arrangements that serve to shape and constrain the contours of women's everyday lives (Lorber, 1994). The gendered division of labour permeates all aspects of productive and reproductive labour in society, encompassing both the 'public' and 'private' spheres of daily life. While conceptually distinct, these three aspects of the 'gender system' – the individual, symbolic and division of labour – are interrelated and mutually supportive, although on occasion may be in conflict with each other (Harding, 1986). Moreover, the gender system is an asymmetric one, in which characteristics, behaviours and endeavours associated with males generally are more highly and positively valued in a given social-cultural-historical context than those associated with females (Harding, 1986). For present purposes, conceptualising gender as a multifaceted 'gender system' raises the theoretical issue of which aspects of gender have relevance for understanding and explaining depression in women, and this issue leads in turn to the methodological question of how the role of gender in depression might best be explored.

Parallels can be drawn between the 'women's bodies' and 'women's lives' approaches to explaining depression in women on the one hand, and the 'similarities' and 'differences' perspectives in the psychological study of women (Kimball, 1994) on the other. The 'women's bodies' approach, because of its emphasis on individual biology and, in particular, reproductive biology, seems to have more in common with the 'differences' perspective. Women's vulnerability to depression is claimed to reside in the specific nature of the biology of the female body. The 'women's lives' approach, in contrast, is based on an assumption of gender similarity. Women's vulnerability to depression arises in the social circumstances of women's everyday lives rather than in underlying gender differences. Another distinction between the two approaches is that they appear to draw on different aspects of the gender system in conceptualising gender. In the women's bodies approach, gender is conceptualised primarily at the individual level, whereas in the women's lives approach gender is addressed at the level of the division of social labour. In other respects the two approaches have features in common. Research within both approaches has relied predominantly on positivist-quantitative methodologies informed by a realist epistemology. Moreover, neither approach has addressed gender symbolism at the discursive level.[7]

Thus, the 'women's bodies' and 'women's lives' perspectives appear to present 'partial', rather than competing, approaches to explaining depression in women. They are limited both in the way gender has been conceptualised and in the choice of research methodology. Research informing psychosocial theories of depression is characterised by similar limitations. While it may be tempting to suggest that research employing qualitative methods to explore women's subjective experiences would offer more promising directions for understanding depression in women, it is less clear how such approaches would provide an address to symbolic aspects of gender. When women's accounts of their experiences of depression have been explored, their explanations tend to be constructed in terms similar to those promulgated in professional circles (cf. Karp, 1992; Walters, 1993; Lewis, 1995). Another drawback of a turn to qualitative methods to explore women's accounts of their depressive experiences is the apparent inability of such methods to address the material body, and specifically those aspects of 'depression' that are physically manifested. This is especially the case when qualitative inquiry addresses 'depression' at the discursive level, because attention is focused on language, not the body.

TOWARDS A MATERIAL-DISCURSIVE APPROACH TO DEPRESSION IN WOMEN

At the level of theory and methodology, the kind of approach required is one that can accommodate both the subjective-experiential and the material-embodied in a way that escapes the dualistic modes of thinking underpinning mainstream research. At the same time, an appropriate approach would be one that can acknowledge ('validate') the debilitating and distressful character of the experiences, currently called 'depression', that are suffered by individual women. An important feature of such an approach will be the potential to provide accounts of depression in women that are more emancipatory and empowering than those currently available. Thus, accounts produced should serve to counteract the pathologising and victim-blaming inherent in prevailing models of depression.

A candidate for such an approach for understanding depression in women, one with the potential to produce less distorting and damaging knowledge, is standpoint theory (Harding, 1986; Smith, 1987).[8] Standpoint theory encompasses both an epistemology and a method for doing research (Harding, 1995). As an epistemology, it draws on a notion of 'strong objectivity' in which procedures for achieving 'objectivity' are uncoupled from the requirement of value-neutrality, a goal that in any case is not only unattainable but untenable (Parker, 1994; Harding, 1995). Thus, knowledge generated by research is acknowledged to be always socially constructed – the claim to produce 'objective facts' is revealed as a myth.

As a method, inquiry conducted from the position of standpoint theory involves beginning research from the perspective of those whose lives are shaped and constrained (or marginalised) by the dominant social order or 'ruling relations' (Smith, 1987). Thus, in seeking to understand depression, research is needed that begins from the perspective of women. Research from the 'standpoint' of women is required, not only because women as a group are marginalised in society, but also because women whose mental health is compromised are further marginalised through their involvement with professional systems having the mission of diagnosing and treating 'psychopathology'. One aim here would be to explore women's accounts of their experiences in relation to 'depression' as an important source of knowledge in its own right; knowledge that is often demeaned as 'subjective' (and consequently rejected) by mainstream researchers. While such accounts provide a source of knowledge about the lived 'realities' of women's everyday lives (knowledge that is not itself irrelevant to understanding depression), they also provide a starting point for an understanding of how both gender and depression are socially constructed.

From the social constructionist epistemology of standpoint theory, 'women's lives' are understood as social constructions – lived experiences that are at the same time socially constituted and discursively regulated. This understanding opens up explorations of women's accounts to inquiries into the social organisation of the gendered division of productive and reproductive labour as well as analyses of gender symbolism and cultural discourses that serve to maintain and buttress patriarchal social relations. Research of this kind, based in discursive analyses of women's accounts, has revealed how cultural discourses of 'femininity' (Swann and Ussher, 1995), the 'good woman' (Jack, 1991) and the good 'mother' and 'housewife' (Blaxter, 1993; Lewis *et al.*, 1994) regulate not only women's everyday practices as 'women' and as 'housewives', 'mothers' and 'wives', but also are implicated in the way they justify to themselves and explain to others the somatic and subjective experiences called 'depression'.

Standpoint theory can also accommodate a reframing of 'women's bodies' as socially constructed, if conventional notions of embodiment are updated. In mainstream research, the body tends to be taken for granted as a timeless biological organism. Instead, recent work in medical and cultural anthropology (Martin, 1987; Lock, 1993) and on the sociology of the body (Fox, 1993; Radley, 1994) presents a different view of the body as being socially produced and enmeshed in a web of socially constructed meanings. For instance, women's bodies can be understood as the product of social/cultural practices that not only regulate diet, but also the culturally idealised shape and size of the female body. At the same time, a woman's body is the instrument of everyday social practices that define the 'good woman' (Jack, 1991). Women's bodies are the vehicle for expressing what it means to be a good wife and mother (e.g. having a clean house, preparing nutritious home-cooked meals, ensuring that children are well-behaved and neatly dressed). Such everyday practices, while enacted physically, are discursively regulated. These culturally shared beliefs also shape and regulate the experiences of women whose social-material conditions do not conform to those of the conventional wife and mother, while simultaneously obscuring the source and impact of a particular woman's material circumstances.

In addition, while rethinking the role of women's bodies in depression, consideration needs to be given to alternatives to the reductionistic form of medical model that mainstream psychology has accepted unquestioningly from biological psychiatry (cf. Foss, 1994; Ross and Pam, 1995). Such revision is required to avoid the pitfalls of the socially constructed body–mind dichotomy, to illuminate instead the reciprocal links between a woman's lived reality and her subjective and embodied experiences (Yardley, 1996). One recent illustration of a non-reductionistic approach to female embodiment is Lock's (1993) work on differences in the experience of menopause in women in Japan and North America. For instance, Japanese women rarely report 'hot flushes', a symptom emblematic of menopause among North American women, and do not recount feelings of depression as a feature of menopausal experience. In accounting for these culturally based differences, Lock draws on the concept of 'local biology'. As developed by Lock, this notion derives from a perspective on human embodiment grounded in the 'lived body,' a body that is 'simultaneously a physical and symbolic artifact' (Lock, 1993: 373), both naturally and culturally produced. The position taken by Lock also acknowledges the plasticity of human biology, particularly at the level of physiology and chemistry, and its interdependence with culture. Thus, understanding of menopause requires exploration of how biology and culture intertwine to produce local experiences and situated knowledge (Lock, 1993: 374). Whether depression is a problem experienced by menopausal women is likely to depend as much on cultural beliefs and practices as on local biologies.

This more situated and culturally coded understanding of the female body also provides a framework within which to position findings in the emerging field of psychoneuroimmunology (Maier *et al.*, 1994). For example, in one recently reported study, a link was found between women's caring activities and their immune-system functioning. Specifically, among women caring for a relative with Alzheimer's disease, a voluntarily inflicted wound (to the forearm) took longer to heal than did a similar wound sustained by a group of matched women who were not caring for a terminally ill relative (Kiecolt-Glaser *et al.*, 1987). An understanding of the pathways involved in a process in which caring activities can influence immune-system functioning requires a less reductionistic and more complex model of human biology than that informing the 'women's bodies' approach to explaining depression.

Bringing a social constructionist perspective to bear on understanding embodied activity also provides an alternative way of conceptualising behaviours currently considered 'signs' of depression. For instance, Wiener and Marcus (1994) have analysed the interpersonal behaviours of 'depressed' individuals from a sociocultural perspective. Their research suggests that, rather than interpreting depressive interpersonal behaviours as outward manifestations of an underlying 'disorder', such behaviours can be understood as guided by shared social 'scripts'. This social knowledge is reflected in the systematic, reciprocated nature of exchanges between 'depressed' individuals and 'non-depressed' others. Thus, the analysis presented by Wiener and Marcus implies that people already have an implicit understanding of how to 'do' depression, and that so-called depressive behaviours are themselves socially constructed.

The socially constructed character of 'depression', as a contemporary mental health problem, is further suggested by historical studies of emotion in Western cultures. These studies point to a gradual shifting that has occurred over the last century from more expressive to less expressive forms of emotionality (Stearns, 1994). Depression is identified by Stearns as a paramount exemplar of contemporary modes of emotionality, reflecting a cultural emphasis on individualised, self-focused, inward-turning forms of emotional expression. The modern variant of individualism, in which individuals are expected to solve their own problems without help from others, fits well with emotional experiences, such as sadness and depression, characterised by withdrawal from others as a problem-solving strategy (Stearns, 1993).

CONCLUSION

Efforts to explain 'depression' in women need to draw on and integrate knowledge that is multifaceted and interdisciplinary, to address both the material–embodied and subjective–discursive aspects of experiences labelled as depression. Only then will it be possible to understand how depression arises in the intersection between women's bodies and women's lives. As long as depression continues to be conceptualised as an individual problem, best investigated within a positivist methodological frame, women will continue to blame experiences currently classified as 'depressive symptoms' on their bodies or their lives, and will continue to be a major source of clients for the mental health professions.

Research informed by a standpoint epistemology opens up avenues for exploring how 'depression' is constructed in discursive processes. Availability of alternative discourses for understanding the meaning of depression, whilst having the potential to offer individual women more affirming, empowering and less stigmatising, self-blaming ways of interpreting their experiences, also could have material consequences. Currently, women form a large majority of those 'treated' for depression, and consequently are the major recipients of mood-altering prescription drugs. Alternative discourses on 'depression' could serve to undermine the increasing domination of biochemical modes of intervention (encouraged by the marketing strategies of transnational pharmaceutical companies) within medical-psychiatric practice.

In pursuing material-discursive approaches to understanding depression in women, an important goal will be to situate knowledge about what is now called 'depression' within social-cultural-historical context. Such contextualised understandings will include knowledge illuminating how women negotiate the tensions and contradictions that arise between their socially constructed lives and their material-embodied lives (cf. Yardley, 1996). A perspective that can encompass both material and discursive aspects of lived experience, that can keep both aspects in view, at this juncture appears to have the most to offer in the search for more emancipatory understandings and explanations of the 'problem' of depression in women.

NOTES

1 Exploration of the ideas on which this chapter is based was greatly facilitated by a sabbatical leave (1994–95) spent as a visiting academic in the Psychology Department, University College London, and as a visiting research fellow with the Women's Health Research Unit, Psychology Department, UCL. I am indebted to Dr Jane Ussher (Psychology Department, UCL, and Director of the Women's Health Research Unit) for enabling this opportunity and for many stimulating discussions on topics central to the present work.

    My thinking in the area of depression in women, and on the need for material-discursive approaches for explaining and understanding what is called 'depression', also has benefited in significant ways from discussions with Dr Sian Lewis, currently with the National Primary Care Research and Development Centre, University of Manchester, and with Dr Lucy Yardley, Psychology Department, UCL.

2 In Canada and the United States, drug treatment of depression is being promoted through a toll-free telephone service offering consumers information on 'symptoms' of depression for self-diagnostic purposes and on modes of treatment available. A parallel telephone service is offered to medical practitioners providing advice on prescribing of antidepressant drugs. Three-quarters of the cost of initiating these services has been donated by five major pharmaceutical companies (as reported in the Canadian national newspaper, the *Globe & Mail*, 'Phone Line to Aid Depression Sufferers', 4 May 1996, pp. A7).

3 One wonders if such research is also needed to justify and support an even larger worldwide market for antidepressant drugs.

4 The biological models informing much contemporary theory and research within psychiatry, and which provide a warrant for biochemical approaches to treatment, have recently been critiqued as 'pseudoscience' (Ross and Pam, 1995).

5 Whilst it might be argued that somatic 'symptoms' of 'depression' can be understood as 'normal' or 'natural' responses to events in women's lives, it still needs to be explained why particular events elicit these specific 'symptoms' rather than others and why so-called 'vegetative' signs tend to co-occur with depressed mood, feelings of hopelessness and low self-esteem.

6 Lock (1993: 378) takes this line of thinking further to sketch a possible future in

which older women could be denied treatment for health problems, such as heart disease and hip fractures, if they have not 'imbibed' hormonal replacement therapy (HRT).
7   Of course, as Harding (1986) has pointed out, gender symbolism pervades all aspects of research, from problem formulation to justification procedures.
8   In her earlier work (e.g. Harding, 1986), the term 'feminist standpoint theory' is used by Harding; in more recent statements (e.g. Harding, 1995) the qualifier 'feminist' is omitted.

REFERENCES

American Psychiatric Association (1994) *Diagnostic and Statistical Manual of Mental Disorders: DSM-IV*, Washington, DC: American Psychiatric Association.
Beck, A.T., Rush, A.J., Shaw, B.F. and Emery, G. (1979) *Cognitive Therapy of Depression*, New York: Guildford.
Belle, D. (1982) *Lives in Stress: Women and Depression*, San Diego, CA: Sage.
——(1990) Poverty and Women's Mental Health, *American Psychologist*, 45, 385–389.
Blaxter, M. (1993) Why do Victims Blame Themselves? In A. Radley (ed.) *Worlds of Illness: Biographical and Cultural Perspectives on Health and Illness*, London: Routledge, pp. 124–142.
Brown, G.W. (1989) Life Events and Measurement. In G.W. Brown and T.O. Harris (eds), *Life Events and Illness*, London: Unwin Hyman, pp. 3–45.
Brown, G.W. and Harris, T.O. (1978) *Social Origins of Depression: A Study of Psychiatric Disorder in Women*, London: Tavistock.
——(1989) Depression. In G.W. Brown and T.O. Harris (eds), *Life Events and Illness*, London: Unwin Hyman, pp. 49–93.
Coyne, J.C. (1994) Self-Reported Distress: Analog or Ersatz Depression?, *Psychological Bulletin*, 116, 29–45.
Coyne, J.C. and Whiffen, V. (1995) Issues in Personality as Diathesis for Depression: The Case of Sociotropy-Dependency and Autonomy-Self-Criticism, *Psychological Bulletin*, 118, 358–378.
Cutler, S. and Nolen-Hoeksema, S. (1991) Accounting for Sex Differences in Depression Through Female Victimization: Childhood Sexual Abuse, *Sex Roles*, 24, 425–438.
Foss, L. (1994) Putting the Mind Back into the Body: A Successor Scientific Medical Model, *Theoretical Medicine*, 15, 291–313.
Fox, N.J. (1993) *Postmodernism, Sociology and Health*, Buckingham: Open University Press.
Gilligan, C. (1982) *In a Different Voice: Psychological Theory and Women's Development*, Cambridge, MA: Harvard University Press.
Gotlib, I.H. and Hammen, C.L. (1992) *Psychological Aspects of Depression: Toward a Cognitive-Interpersonal Integration*, New York: Wiley.
Harding, S. (1986) *The Science Question in Feminism*, Ithaca, NY: Cornell University Press.
——(1995) 'Strong Objectivity': A Response to the New Objectivity Question, *Synthese*, 104, 331–349.
Henwood, K. and Pidgeon. N. (1995) Remaking the Link: Qualitative Research and Feminist Standpoint Theory, *Feminism and Psychology*, 5, 7–30.
Hurst, S.A. and Genest, M. (1995) Cognitive-Behavioural Therapy with a Feminist Orientation: A Perspective for Therapy with Depressed Women, *Canadian Psychology*, 36, 236–257.

Jack, D.C. (1991) *Silencing the Self: Women and Depression*, Cambridge, MA: Harvard University Press.

Karp, D.A. (1992) Illness Ambiguity and the Search for Meaning: A Case Study of a Self Help Group for Affective Disorders, *Journal of Contemporary Ethnography*, 21, 139–170.

Kaufert, P., Gilbert, P. and Tate, R. (1992) The Manitoba Project: A Reexamination of the Link between Menopause and Depression, *Maturitas*, 14, 143–155.

Kiecolt-Glaser, J.K., Glaser, R., Shuttleworth, E.C., Dyer, C.S., Ogrocki, P. and Speicher, C.E. (1987) Chronic Stress and Immunity in Family Caregivers of Alzheimer's Disease Victims, *Psychosomatic Medicine*, 49, 523–533.

Kimball, M.M. (1994) The Worlds We Live in: Gender Similarities and Differences, *Canadian Psychology*, 35, 388–404.

Koss, M.P., Goodman, L.A., Browne, A., Fitzgerald, L., Keita, G.P. and Russo, N.F. (1994) *No Safe Haven: Male Violence Against Women at Home, at Work, and in the Community*, Washington, DC: American Psychological Association.

Lewis, S.E. (1995) A Search for Meaning: Making Sense of Depression, *Journal of Mental Health*, 4, 369–382.

Lewis, S.E., Nicolson, P. and Spencer, C. (1994) 'Lost selves': Accounts of Depression and Motherhood, paper presented at the London Conference of the British Psychological Society, December 1994.

Lock, M. (1993) *Encounters with Aging: Mythologies of Menopause in Japan and North America*, Berkeley, CA: University of California Press.

Lorber, J. (1994) *Paradoxes of Gender*, New Haven: Yale University Press.

Maier, S.F., Watkins, L.R. and Fleshner, M. (1994) Psychoneuroimmunology: The Interface Between Behavior, Brain, and Immunity, *American Psychologist*, 49, 1004–1017.

Martin, E. (1987) *The Woman in the Body: A Cultural Analysis of Reproduction*, Boston, MA: Beacon Press.

McFarlane, J.M. and Williams, T.M. (1994) Placing Premenstrual Syndrome in Perspective, *Psychology of Women Quarterly*, 18, 339–373.

McGrath, E., Keita, G.P., Strickland, B.R. and Russo, N.F. (1990) *Women and Depression: Risk Factors and Treatment Issues*, Washington, DC: American Psychological Association.

McKinlay, J.B., McKinlay, S.M. and Brambilla, D.J. (1987) The Relative Contributions of Endocrine Changes and Social Circumstances to Depression in Middle-Aged Women, *Journal of Health and Social Behavior*, 28, 345–363.

Miller, J. B. (1986) *Toward a New Psychology of Women*, Boston: Beacon Press.

Nicolson, P. (1992) Explanations of Post-Natal Depression: Structuring Knowledge of Female Psychology, *Research on Language and Social Interaction*, 25, 75–96.

——(1995a) Feminism and Psychology. In J.A. Smith, R. Harre and L. Van Langenhove (eds), *Rethinking Psychology*, London: Sage, pp. 122–142.

——(1995b) Qualitative Research, Psychology and Mental Health: Analysing Subjectivity, *Journal of Mental Health*, 4, 337–345.

——(1995c) The Menstrual Cycle, Science and Femininity: Assumptions Underlying Menstrual Cycle Research, *Social Science and Medicine*, 41, 779–784.

Nolen-Hoeksema, S. (1990) *Sex Differences in Depression*, Stanford, CA: Stanford University Press.

Nolen-Hoeksema, S. and Girgus, J. (1994) The Emergence of Gender Differences in Depression During Adolescence, *Psychological Bulletin*, 115, 424–443.

Oakley, A. (1986) Beyond the Yellow Wallpaper. In A. Oakley *Telling the Truth About Jerusalem*, Oxford: Blackwell, pp. 131–148.

Parker, I. (1994) Qualitative Research. In P. Banister, E. Burman, I. Parker, M. Taylor and C. Tindall, *Qualitative Methods in Psychology: A Research Guide*, Buckingham: Open University Press, pp. 1–16.

Parker, I., Georgaca, E., Harper, D., McLaughlin, T. and Stowell-Smith, M. (1995) *Deconstructing Psychopathology*, London: Sage.

Polkinghorne, D.E. (1992) Postmodern Epistemology in Practice. In S. Kvale (ed.), *Psychology and Postmodernism*, London: Sage, pp. 146–165.

Pollock, K. (1988) On the Nature of Social Stress: Production of a Modern Mythology, *Social Science and Medicine*, 26, 381–392.

Popay, J. (1992) 'My Health is all Right, but I'm Just Tired all the Time': Women's Experience of Ill Health. In H. Roberts (ed.), *Women's Health Matters*, London: Routledge, pp. 99–120.

Pugliesi, K. (1992) Women and Mental Health: Two Traditions of Feminist Research, *Women and Health*, 19(2/3), 43–68.

Radley, A. (1994) *Making Sense of Illness: The Social Psychology of Health and Disease*, London: Sage.

Ross, C.A. and Pam, A. (1995) *Pseudoscience in Biological Psychiatry: Blaming the Body*, New York: Wiley.

Smith, D.E. (1987) *The Everyday World as Problematic: A Feminist Sociology*, Toronto: University of Toronto Press.

Stearns, C.Z. (1993) Sadness. In M. Lewis and J.M. Haviland (eds), *Handbook of Emotions*, New York: Guildford, pp. 547–561.

Stearns, P.N. (1994) *American Cool: Constructing a Twentieth-Century Emotional Style*, New York: New York University Press.

Stoppard, J.M. (1993) Gender, Psychosocial Factors and Depression. In P. Cappeliez and R.J. Flynn (eds), *Depression and the Social Environment: Research and Intervention with Neglected Populations*, Montreal and Kingston: McGill-Queen's University Press, pp. 121–149.

Stroebe, W. and Stroebe, M.S. (1995) *Social Psychology and Health*, Pacific Grove, CA: Brooks/Cole.

Swann, C.J. and Ussher, J.M. (1995) A Discourse Analytic Approach to Women's Experience of Premenstrual Syndrome, *Journal of Mental Health*, 4, 359–367.

Ussher, J.M. (1991) *Women's Madness: Misogyny or Mental Illness*, Hemel Hempstead: Harvester Wheatsheaf.

Walker, A. (1995) Theory and Methodology in Premenstrual Syndrome Research, *Social Science and Medicine*, 41, 793–800.

Walters, V. (1991) Beyond Medical Agendas: Lay Perspectives and Priorities, *Atlantis: A Women's Studies Journal*, 17(1), 28–35.

——(1993) Stress, Anxiety and Depression: Women's Accounts of Their Health Problems, *Social Science and Medicine*, 36, 393–402.

Weissman, M.M., Bland, R., Joyce, P.R., Newman, S., Wells J.E. and Wittchen, H. (1993) Sex Differences in Rates of Depression: Cross-National Perspectives, *Journal of Affective Disorders*, 29, 77–84.

Weissman, M.M. and Olfson, M. (1995) Depression in Women: Implications for Health Care Research, *Science*, 269, 799–801.

Wethington, E., Brown, G.W. and Kessler, R.C. (1995) Interview Measurement of Stressful Life Events. In S. Cohen, R.C. Kessler and L.U. Gordon (eds), *Measuring Stress: A Guide for Medical and Social Sciences*, New York: Oxford University Press, pp. 59–79.

Wiener, M. and Marcus, D. (1994) A Sociocultural Construction of 'Depression'. In T.R. Sarbin and J.I. Kitsuse (eds), *Constructing the Social*, London: Sage, pp. 213–231.

Yardley, L. (1996) Reconciling Discursive and Materialist Perspectives on Health and Illness: A Re-Construction of the Biopsychosocial Approach, *Theory and Psychology*, 6, 485–508.

3   Mental health, critical realism and lay knowledge

David Pilgrim and Anne Rogers

INTRODUCTION

Our basic argument in this chapter is as follows. A persuasive case can be made about the *causes* of mental health problems within traditional realist frameworks. Also, the experienced *meanings* expressed by people with these problems can be usefully explored within a variety of hermeneutic frameworks. However, more satisfactory integrative accounts to these often counterposed positions could be guided by critical or sceptical realism. In order to flesh out this general claim, we will draw upon and summarise four interlinked aspects of some of our recent work on mental health. First, we will summarise some main features of competing theoretical approaches to mental health problems within the social sciences (Pilgrim and Rogers, 1994). Second, views from within the mental health service users' movement will be noted (Rogers and Pilgrim, 1991). Third, we will draw upon some data from a study of psychiatric patients' views (Rogers *et al.*, 1993). Fourth, we will summarise some findings from a recent study on views of non-psychiatric patients about mental health (Rogers *et al.*, 1995).

SOCIAL SCIENCE AND PSYCHIATRIC PROBLEMS

It is possible to identify four social scientific orientations which have had peak periods of popularity and now coexist as sedimented layers of work about mental health problems. These are social causationism; interpretive microsociology; political economy and poststructuralism. We will dwell more on the last of these because it has been the basis for a strong constructivist position, which we consider has been an unwarranted overreaction to realism. For ease of reading, discussions of these four approaches will be listed separately.

Social causationism

This is the oldest tradition and it accepts the legitimacy of psychiatric nosology. Diagnostic categories like 'depression' or 'schizophrenia' are mainly accepted as being non-problematic and interest focuses on the social causes of mental illnesses. (At times, though, there are disputes about criteria for 'caseness' in community studies). Epidemiology has established a class gradient of mental illness but has still not resolved the direction of causality in this regard. One of the earliest studies in psychiatric epidemiology, which sought to establish a link between schizophrenia and social class (Faris and Dunham, 1939), took place in the context of the development of 'human ecology' as a theoretical trend within the Chicago School of sociology (Park, 1936).

Some social psychiatrists as well as sociologists can also be situated within this tradition (e.g. Barton, 1957; Murphy, 1982). The bulk of the work has entailed epidemiological surveys of community populations or hospital admissions, although one of the earliest critiques of the disabling or iatrogenic impact of psychiatric institutions on their residents is also evident (Brown and Wing, 1962). The social causation thesis probably peaked in popularity in the 1950s, although one of its most-quoted exemplars appeared in the late 1970s (Brown and Harris, 1978). Thus there is no neat set of boundaries to periodise this and subsequent trends discussed below. They are sedimented layers of knowledge which overlap unevenly in time.

Interpretive microsociology

During the 1960s, versions of microsociology appeared which challenged the methodological dominance of epidemiology. The theoretical roots of this were to be found mainly in symbolic interactionism and social phenomenology (Goffman, 1961; Scheff, 1966; Lemert, 1967), and the methodological emphasis was on ethnographic studies of institutional life and everyday rule enforcement, using participant observation and personal accounts. Symbolic interactionism allowed a perspective to emerge from the 'underdog'. In particular, a voice could be given to the 'unofficial' side of the hospital, a voice which countered the uncritical accounts of medical life by structural-functionalists. This interpretive approach also subsumed the emergence of ethnomethodology and at times shaded into philosophical inquiry (Coulter, 1973). Despite the challenge of poststructuralist work to reorientate the sociology of thought and talk, examples of traditional interpretive work were evident in the 1970s (e.g. Emerson and Pollner, 1975; Goldie, 1977; Horwitz, 1977) and beyond (e.g. McKeganey, 1984; Gabe and Thorogood, 1986; Rogers, 1993). What interpretive microsociology introduced, *contra* the social causationists, was the relativisation of mental health and illness and the notion that both of these are socially negotiated. This prefigured a theme in poststructuralist work.

Political economy

During the 1970s, doubts began to emerge about social science settling into an interpretive scheme. In particular, Marxian critiques became evident which tried to set the organisation of psychiatry into a macroeconomic context. Scull (1977, 1979) analysed the emerging social control role of psychiatry in the nineteenth century and its functional value for the capitalist State. This was extended to a political economy approach to explain the emergence of deinstitutionalisation in response to fiscal pressure after the Second World War. Within this scheme, Scull rejects a phenomenological or ethnographic approach to his topic and is guided in the main by economistic notions, backed up by documentary evidence. Accordingly, Busfield (1986) describes Scull as a 'Marxist-functionalist', but Weberian resonances are apparent in his work on professional dominance and social closure in relation to asylum doctors (Scull, 1979).

Sedgwick (1972, 1980) also reacted against anti-psychiatry and its sociological associates by emphasising the question of the fiscal crisis of the State and its impact on the fate of the mentally ill. At the same time, in anticipation of poststructuralist notions, unlike Szasz he argues that all illness descriptions (not just those of mental illness) reflect value judgements and are the precondition of medicine controlling such disvalued states (see Sedgwick, 1980: 34–38). However, Sedgwick's concern was not merely to deconstruct illness but to challenge political passivity when faced with the real distress of individuals. A political economy approach to evaluating schizophrenia and its treatment can also be found in the work of some social psychiatrists (e.g. Warner, 1985).

Poststructuralism

Over the past decade the influence of Foucault has been apparent throughout the social sciences, and his impact on work on psychiatry has been particularly profound. At the outset, in the 1960s, his own work was on the emergence of the asylum (Foucault, 1961, 1965). This has led some commentators to link Foucault to the humanistic protest of the 'anti-psychiatrists'. However, his work is an epistemological break in the field. It stands separately from both microsociology and structuralism in relation to psychiatry.

The methodological implications of Foucauldian scholarship are novel – empirical knowledge claims are of interest not to produce (only) knowledge in itself but also to read and reread or deconstruct that knowledge. This task is near to interpretive sociology, so both could be placed in a hermeneutic framework, but focuses on discourses not individual social actors. Moreover, it does not accept the presuppositions of humanism, such as a coherent or stable subjectivity, nor does it privilege individual agents in its inquiry. Instead it opposes or seeks to transcend the 'personalistic' or 'homocentric' features of the older interpretive tradition. On a second front, the over-determining role of the state or political economy is rejected. Whilst their influence or role is conceded, stable or predictable causal patterns are not. Thus a priori essentialism is challenged.

In the 1980s, sociology in this poststructuralist framework issued a set of discourses on discourses. It opened up the inevitability of plural social realities and the precarious nature of knowledge claims. The 1980s began with overtures to a motif of the decade, with announcements of the 'twilight of man [*sic*]' (Lemert, 1979). Earlier, in 1977, signs of British departures into a Foucauldian critique of structuralism appeared, exemplified by the establishment of the journal *Ideology and Consciousness*.

Foucault's own work on institutional psychiatry was categorised by his followers as scene setting – documenting the prehistory of the discipline or the conditions which made it possible (Miller, 1986; Gordon, 1990). New formations of psychiatric work were subsequently the focus of deconstructionists. Twentieth-century psychiatry was described as eclectic, and its ambit now extended beyond the boundaries of both the asylum and madness. In particular, psychological as well as biodeterministic features of psychiatry were highlighted.

The Great War was identified as a crucial phase of transition from biological to psychological theory, from madness to neurosis and from inpatient to outpatient work. The deconstruction by Stone (1985) of the emergent 'shell-shock' problem of the time shows that the eugenic discourse of Victorian psychiatry was incommensurable with a discourse about 'England's finest blood' – officers and gentleman and working-class volunteers were breaking down under the strain of a war of unprecedented attrition and stalemate. Military neurosis changed irrevocably the face of psychology and psychiatry.

Because of the expansion of the ambit of psychiatry to include outpatient voluntary relationships with non-psychotic patients, poststructuralists tend to reject the anti-psychiatric emphasis on the destructive and oppressive features of modern psychiatry. Miller and Rose (1988) put this succinctly: 'We argue that it is more fruitful to consider the ways that regulatory systems have sought to promote subjectivity than to document ways in which they have crushed it.' Not surprisingly, their focus has been more about newer psychological discourses in contemporary society than the legacy of Victorian biological psychiatry (Rose, 1985, 1990; Miller and Rose, 1988).

Miller (1986) points out that Foucault did not reject the role of repressive power when introducing the importance of productive power. None the less, as the work cited above and below indicates, Foucauldian analyses about the twentieth century (i.e. a period later than Foucault's own focus) downplay the role of coercion in the psychiatric system. Such a focus on productive power also necessitates Miller and Rose sustaining a series of dismissals of Marxian accounts of psychiatry. Scull's social control thesis is rejected as a 'crude reductionist explanation' (Miller, 1986: 31). His critical history of nineteenth-century British psychiatry is described as 'valuable, but the narrative labours under the weight of the sociological baggage it has to support' (Miller, 1986: 30). And Rose goes further in his condemnation of the limited value of a coercive social control analysis, followed on by Scull's economistic explanation for decarceration policies in the twentieth century:

> Rather than seeking to explain a process of de-institutionalisation, we need to account for the proliferation of sites for the practice of psychiatry. There has not been an extension of social control but rather the psychiatrisation of new problems and the differentiation of the psychiatric population . . . The modern dispensation of psychiatry, far from being merely repressive or negative has constituted a new discipline of mental health.
>
> (Rose, 1986: 83–84)

It is a moot point whether or not all Western societies are now 'psychiatric societies' to the same degree as the United States of America (cf. Castel *et al.*, 1979). However, the diffuse and ubiquitous presence of psychological problems and their proposed resolution cannot be denied, not only throughout the 'psy complex' but also in management styles, selling, women's (and now men's) magazines and Sunday supplement columns. Technologies of the self derived from both humanistic and psychodynamic psychology are indeed now deeply implicated in many aspects of contemporary societies.

If we step back from these four positions, it is our view that the most recent challenge from poststructuralism is quite persuasive when highlighting the shortcomings of both naive causal reasoning (*erklären*) within social causationism and political economy, and the individualism intrinsic to interpretive humanism (*verstehen*). However, it is also clear that poststructuralism itself has thrown out the baby with the bath water about some aspects of both material reality and individual human agency. It remains trapped with all of the strengths and weaknesses of (philosophical) idealism. Consequently, its suspicion and cynicism about material reality leads to a form of epistemological nihilism, whereby nothing can ever be decided about the world. We are left instead with a vertiginous quicksand of unending deconstruction, plural realities and the undecidability of propositions. Thus, although poststructuralism has been a refreshing corrective to approaches to mental health which were positivistic, economistic or personalistic, it contains its own problems of idealism and nihilism. Consequently, our view is that, while all of the four positions noted above have made legitimate contributions to knowledge claims about mental health and society, none of them can enjoy a sense of sustainable pre-eminence.

Faced with this mixed picture, we would argue that a critical realist framework potentially integrates the strengths of the four positions, while avoiding their major weaknesses. Critical realism (Bhaskar, 1989) affirms physical reality, both biological and environmental, as a legitimate field of inquiry but recognises that its representations are characterised and mediated by language, culture and political interests rooted in, for instance, race, class, gender and social status. Thus, while critical realism retains empirical inquiry as legitimate, it rejects a naive positivist view of the world – that reality is discoverable by scientific methodologies which are disinterested or value-free. Equally it rejects the idealism of poststructuralism. So, while the map is not the territory, coexisting maps and territories warrant legitimate investigation from a *variety of sceptical* perspectives, which imply multiple methodologies. For Bhaskar, the latter would implicate a range from experimentalism to ethnography because he does not deny the different research questions which the physical and the social sciences attempt to answer.

As well as this epistemological feature of critical realism, another is its implication for social science. For the purpose of this chapter, in particular, which advocates the legitimacy of lay knowledge about mental health, Bhaskar's work cautions against the possibility of expert knowledge about human beings in society being predictive. This is in keeping with other critical theorists, such as Wilden (1972) following Bateson, who demonstrates the futility of social science's predictive pretensions because it deals with open not closed systems. While the latter occur, or are contrived by natural science, to permit systematic investigations to describe, explain and predict the world, in open systems only the first two of these are possible. The complexity and inventiveness of human agency and praxis in varying social contexts simply defy expert predictions. This is particularly important for psychology, which still keeps alive aspirations towards accurate prediction and a disciplinary incremental movement towards the status of a natural science.

A third epistemological advantage of critical realism is that it gives due weight to material reality. In the case of explaining mental health problems, for example, this would mean conceding the causal influence of both poverty and physiological processes. Thus mental health problems are not *merely* constructions – say the outcome of the dominant cognitive interests of psychiatrists, patriarchy or the ruling class, even if and when these interests are in operation. Just because biodeterminism in psychiatry has been associated with vested élite interests, and biological theories tend to become hegemonic under right-wing government social policies, does not mean that biodeterministic notions are always reactionary inventions. If this is doubted, it is instructive to examine the conduct of a person with Alzheimer's disease or temporal lobe epilepsy or, for that matter, a fevered patient with florid hallucinations.

Critical realism offers these epistemological advantages but it also provides an important *democratic* potential by cautioning against scientism, i.e. a naive overreliance on the scientific production of knowledge by, and on behalf of, elite groups in society. Like the critical theory of the late Frankfurt School (Habermas, 1971, 1987) it implies that the knowledge produced by ordinary people could be the focus of an emancipatory approach to social scientific research. (Note that Bhaskar's sympathy with Habermas is partial – see Bhaskar, 1989: 189). Within an emancipatory approach to social science, lay knowledge is viewed as having equal, though not superior, status to expert knowledge about mental health. The term lay *knowledge* is preferred here because of its attendant connotations of validity, rather than *belief*, which is the preferred term of most current health psychologists and is also present in the earlier work of sociologists of health and illness.

A good example of the implicit (but only thinly veiled) positivism of psychological investigation is that of seeking lay 'beliefs' from preconstructed questionnaires rather than via open-ended dialogues. The former approach is exemplified in the work of Furnham and his colleagues (e.g. Furnham and Pendred, 1983; Furnham and Lowick, 1984; MacCarthy and Furnham, 1986). Apart from dialogues with respondents being pre-empted, these studies emphasise that lay views are, or must be, checked against a version of reality which is defined by current expert knowledge. This is put succinctly at the end on a paper on lay theories of the causes of alcoholism, viz.:

> Finally, it must be noted that, although research into lay beliefs produces interesting and potentially useful information, it can never replace research into the *actual* causes of various phenomena. Empirically tested academic theories represent the most accurate, valid and useful form of knowledge we can produce.
>
> (Furnham and Lowick, 1984: 331, emphasis in original)

It is our view that the certainty of the latter statement is not warranted. This is not to say that lay knowledge necessarily should be privileged over expert knowledge. But it is to acknowledge that sometimes lay people develop forms of knowledge which are legitimate and occasionally even superior to the current state of professional knowledge. In the field of mental health, with the dubious conceptual validity of professional notions like 'schizophrenia' and the poor track record of clinicians at either helping patients or making predictions about their conduct, lay people have every right to claim a mandate about a topic which has thrown experts into confusion and provoked incredulity, distrust and hostility in their patients. This is not to argue, though, that the conceptual and therapeutic weaknesses of the mental health industry provide a unique opportunity for lay knowledge to shine. Other examples are when professional epidemiology has *followed* the lead given by lay campaigners about industrial diseases such as asbestosis and pneumoconiosis.

Lay knowledge is in part constructed and reconstructed with reference to scientific and medical knowledge, as has been noted by DeSwaan (1990). This is apparent in the work by Cornwell (1986), who found that working-class women in the East End of London constructed notions of health and illness with reference to both their own experience *and* to biomedical notions. Similarly, sometimes professional views are also subjected to 'layification'. For example, there is some evidence to suggest that GPs' assumptions and causal frameworks are as close to lay notions of depression and neuroticism as they are to traditional psychiatric knowledge and that

GPs' own lay views coalesce with knowledge gained through secondary socialisation as medical practitioners (Pilgrim and Rogers, 1994).

Having reviewed some epistemological points which have culminated in our advocacy of studying lay knowledge about mental health, we will not move to reporting some examples of this approach within our own recent research. These refer to: The growth of a new social movement of psychiatric patients; the views the latter have about the roots of their difficulties; and the views which non-patients have about mental health problems.

THE BRITISH MENTAL HEALTH SERVICE USERS' MOVEMENT

A testimony to the link between lay knowledge and collective social action is the strong presence of a new social movement – the mental health service users' movement – with its own variegated ideology (Rogers and Pilgrim, 1991). Though some themes of earlier anti-psychiatric humanism resonate within this movement, the emphasis is on direct action and a reformulation of mental health problems using lay knowledge and experience. The political opposition to psychiatry from users' groups (and black groups) has tended to focus on a concern about the nature of service delivery and professional theory and practice, with a particular rejection of expert biological approaches to etiology and treatment. As well as demanding free counselling for all, there are demands to regulate drug use strictly and to phase out ECT and psychosurgery (Survivors Speak Out, 1987). Though this has been the main focus, the ideology of the users' movement contains both a critique of medical knowledge and a reconstruction of biophysical reality. The notion of a person as a passive patient or consumer is displaced by a new identity of user or 'survivor'. This reconstruction is most evident in the rejection of social identities constructed around psychiatric nosology and diagnoses, e.g. being a 'schizophrenic' or a 'psychotic patient'. Consumerism is also eschewed. The latter discourse is associated with a new managerial philosophy and is rejected by the mental health users' movement because of, as one respondent noted to us, 'its connotation with Tory consumerism, but also because consumer implies you are getting something of value . . . ' (Rogers and Pilgrim, 1991).

The notion of user or 'survivor' as a new social identity necessarily implicates a re-construction of mental health need; one which contains a link between felt or expressed need and material resources within a wider social context identified by patients. This is evident from the quote from this key respondent in the users' movement in the 1980s, which associates need with an underlying philosophy about the values and ethos of community responsibility and resources, and the utility of mutual aid.

If we are going to be useful to people who present as distressed we've got to change the way we operate. We've got to have neighbourhood drop-in centres, we've got to have people who've been through the system available to those who are about to go through it and we've got to have an enormous sharing of responsibility as to what happens when one of us freaks out.

(Rogers and Pilgrim, 1991)

The rejection of a psychiatric identity and its attendant negative constructions of people as burdensome, ill and out of control, brings with it a re-construction of need and demand which is not easily met within the existing configuration of service delivery. To an extent aspects of recent reforms with, for example, increased recognition of the importance of 'local voices', and health needs assessment undertaken at a population level which extends beyond traditional psychiatric criteria, are more commensurate with this new social movement's identity and demands. The voluntary sector, which allows the fluidity of roles and responsibilities between provider and provided for, also finds favour with many users (Rogers *et al.*, 1993). This is consistent with the notion that ordinary people produce health as well as 'consume' health services. The voluntary sector, however, remains marginal and financially and organisationally precarious compared to services provided by the statutory sector. At the same time, there has been a fragmentation of the cultural legitimacy of collective social action together with blocked avenues previously available to 'consumers', such as the Community Health Councils.

PATIENTS' VIEWS OF PSYCHOLOGICAL DISTRESS

Individuals' reconstruction of biomedical concepts in the light of their own illness experience is more explicit in accounts from mental health service users about mental illness. In a national survey we conducted, 516 respondents who had had at least one episode as a psychiatric inpatient were asked what they viewed were the reasons for their first contact with mental health services (Rogers *et al.*, 1993). Remarkably few described this early contact as being because of 'mental illness'. Of those answering the question, fewer than 11 per cent considered this to be the reason for contact with services. Given that most of these people would have been labelled by psychiatrists as having suffered from some form of mental illness, this indicates at the outset that a substantial discrepancy exists in the basic way in which professionals and users of services construe the fundamental problem. It may be that to a large extent the discourses of psychiatry and psychiatric patients are incommensurable.

It is interesting to note that the subgroup of patient which did prefer the illness label showed a greater tendency to view services more positively than those fellow patients who eschewed an illness description. The open-ended questions about initial contact with services, and views on what led to problems, resulted in types of description which demonstrate the complexity of the understandings patients had about themselves. It is notable that this complexity contrasts with the narrower constructions imposed by psychiatric diagnosis ('mentally ill', 'schizophrenia', 'reactive depression' and so on). Moreover, given that these descriptions are so diverse, it would seem highly implausible that any single acceptable solution to emotional distress (be it medical or otherwise) is actually tenable. The mixed list of responses obtained sometimes entailed firm views about causality, whilst at other times descriptions were merely given and perplexity remained about any pertinent antecedent events. Patients often alluded to a variety of life circumstances surrounding their initial problem. For example:

> Lost job and I became a recluse. Mother informed the doctor when I refused to sign on one morning.

> I was engaged to a girl and two weeks before the wedding she broke it off. I cut my throat in her parents' house. Prior to this my mother threatened to cut me off if I married the girl. Tensions caused by this caused rows between me and my fiancé, which left me feeling confused and very hurt.

> I had been sexually abused by my father since I was seven. I coped until the death of my grandfather when I was aged nineteen. Then I began to talk about it and get depressed. When I told my husband he began to abuse me. I just couldn't handle this after being abused for so long before.

> Stress due to promotion and second marriage – fear of failure of both at the same time.

> Me not caring about myself and society not caring about me.

> The direct issue was the loss of my baby. The indirect one was problems with my neighbours and my job.

> Family stress due to my mother's illness led to me having hallucinations.

> Long periods of unemployment. Society in general saying that there was plenty of work to be had, so those out of work were seen as being lazy. Employers told you that you were no good by not employing you.

> I was depressed and upset following the death of my mother. We had a difficult relationship and I never felt wanted by her. While she was alive I felt that she never loved me. After her death there was no chance to put that right. Also earlier abuse by a family member affected me and the relationship I had with my husband as a result.

It is clear from the above accounts and others from this research project that lay understandings about the cause of distress were elaborate and take a multiplicity of factors into consideration. People in this study were likely to view their problems emerging as a result of a battle between 'endogenous' or individual predisposition – such as nature, temperament, family characteristics – and 'exogenous' factors related to a person's way of life – such as employment and domestic arrangements. While, in principle, these lay views are compatible with an eclectic view of mental disorder which takes into consideration social and psychological factors as well as biodeterminism (Goldberg and Huxley, 1980), this did not translate into the professional understandings encountered by these same respondents *in practice*. If a biopsychosocial model is present in the socialisation of psychiatrists and other mental health workers, this was not obvious to the respondents.

The typical psychiatric formulation of personal problems tended to be in biomedical terms – as indicated by patient reports of the type of diagnosis and treatment given. In contrast, it was evident that contact with health services in the eyes of patients resulted from a complex of cumulative personal and domestic events. Particular, precipitating or 'triggering' factors were often difficult to identify as a unitary cause of a 'breakdown'. People seem to experience mental distress as a continuum of everyday life, without an easily identifiable genesis. There is also a rational and logical link between the content of lay knowledge and the experience of services. The further services were from 'medicalised' (and particularly hospital) settings and the nearer they were to people's everyday existence, the greater the acceptability these had in the eyes of patients. In terms of therapeutic interventions, the nearer the intervention was to modes of lay relating (i.e. 'talking' treatments), the greater the lay vote of confidence. Equally, GPs were preferred for their engagement with a lay view and conceptualisation of need, as well as their ability to respond to material needs of patients, which also featured in their constructs of distress.

ORDINARY ACCOUNTS OF MENTAL HEALTH

The lay knowledge described above is an example of how individuals reconstruct biomedical concepts in the light of their own illness experience, contact with services and professionals, and their psychiatric 'career'. Because the majority of these respondents had had extensive contact with services, it meant that their construction of knowledge was constantly reinforced both by their experience of illness and their contact with professionalised services. In other words, they were experts in mental health through their experience of distress and service utilisation. The question that then arises is this: What is the nature of lay knowledge in the absence of an officially identified period of mental illness or contact with psychiatric services?

A recently completed research project undertaken for the Health Education Authority (Rogers *et al.*, 1996) explored different types of families' constructs about positive mental health. Respondents made links between psychological processes, meaning and action in the absence of an identifiable period of mental illness. This study revealed a complex relationship between lay epidemiology and the mental health practices undertaken by individuals – in terms of maintaining mental health and emotional support.

The accounts given by family members differed in nature from those who had been psychiatric patients (discussed above). The research we conducted on users' views of psychiatric services was seemingly devoid of safe 'public' accounts – there appeared to be no necessity to hide criticisms of professionals or treatment or to evade emotional issues. Clearly undergoing the vagaries of becoming a psychiatric patient removes shyness or reticence about these issues. With the 'non-clinical' set of respondents, there was a clear demarcation between private and public accounts. Personal disclosure for its own sake and the expression of distress was often viewed as exhibitionistic and unwarranted, and the motives of people who do this were subjected to questioning.

While respondents often found difficulties in finding the appropriate terminology or in expressing what they considered to be inexpressible, they did consider that, in principle, what caused mental healthiness or ill health was their legitimate province, a province which is more usually deemed worthy of expert, but not lay, opinion. Relative to physical health, mental healthiness is less tangible to construe. Physicality gives a direct empirical sense of knowing about our physical well-being, both by outward signs and subjective symptoms. By contrast, reflectiveness about people's own behaviour and inner mental states is less well-developed. Indeed, some theories (like the depth psychologies) have it that we have to remain ignorant of most our psychological states most of the time in order to survive, function and preserve a positive sense of self. Perhaps one of the reasons for this better articulation around physical illness relates to the extent to which people perceive that they have control over physical health-maintaining activities as opposed to mental health ones. As one respondent noted in relation to child-rearing:

> I don't think of it [mental health] the same as physical health really. You can't control things as you can with getting cancer . . . like getting food and getting their sleep and keeping them safe. Whereas mental health is more difficult.

For some respondents, situating mental health in the body is the only reference point of understanding. In response to the question 'What does the term mental health mean to you?,' responses included: 'Something to do with the brain or something' and 'That's what's in your head, isn't it really?'. This biological construction is not merely a feature of lay ignorance, given that a part of the professional discourse about mental health and illness focuses singularly on assumed bodily determinants of behaviour (examples of this include biological psychology, organic psychiatry and sociobiology). Unlike physical health, which is often the focus of people's everyday lives, mental health remains in the background, unacknowledged and, as this respondent notes, only makes its presence felt when things go wrong.

> It's a very difficult thing to explain [mental health], because you don't go around thinking about it, most of the time . . . things are just chugging along really. Then it can strike you out of the blue. Suddenly you realise

you are not coping, and it's different from being ill physically because somehow you are aware you are not feeling too good. I mean with both [physical and mental health] you've got ill and not ill but most of the time with physical health you're somewhere in between. But with mental health you're just not aware what's going on until it's too late.   .

'Balanced', 'emotionally controlled', 'stable' or 'coping' were other phrases used to describe mental well-being, and were much more common than phrases such as 'the way one feels' or 'being happy'. Although both men and women used expressions which implied the ability to cope or control things in everyday life, women were more likely to make reference to feelings, e.g. 'what you are feeling like inside', and men to identify themes of stability, control and rationality. At other times, the preconditions of maintaining stability and coping were seen to extend beyond the individual. This was most notable in relation to the female respondents, who emphasised other people's support and communication with the outside world. These and other gendered notions may shed light on the interpretation by some social scientists that men do not readily use their emotions as a resource in the public and private sphere (Hothschild, 1983). What our data does imply is that to do so overtly may, for men, imply weakness and loss of control.

The various ideas put forward by respondents about the causation of mental healthiness and unhealthiness mirrored the discourses of mental health professions and academic disciplines. These ranged from the biological, to the psychological through to the sociological. However, the emphasis was clearly on social causes. There were also a variety of ways in which respondents *expressed* these theories, which involved a combination of medical and psychological terms and understanding, combined with a lay view. Not all potential causes were given the same weight. A preference for life events, family problems and economic hardship was mentioned frequently, but genetic causes were noted much less often – and usually as an addendum to these other cited causes. Major life events were cited as the predominant cause of poor mental health. Events recurrently mentioned were divorce, bereavement, unemployment and financial difficulties. Financial difficulties, employment stress and unemployment were the most frequently cited factors considered to affect mental well-being.

Financial hardship was mentioned by respondents from families from all backgrounds. In the middle-class families, this tended to be in recognition of the pressures people faced from different class backgrounds to themselves. In terms of the frequency with which certain life events or long-term difficulties were mentioned, financial difficulties featured more in accounts of the working-class respondents. Adequate financial arrangements and job security were the basis of both good physical and mental health according to most of our respondents.

It's all down to money. All your problems are money problems. All the problems on them pages [interviewer's schedule] are to do with money.

Money, your job and your health. That's the main three ingredients. If you've got a job and it's secure you've cracked it.

While the dominant view about the causes of mental health problems was essentially one of social causationism, the struggle to preserve mental health emphasised individual ingenuity. In other words, agency not structure was privileged. Individuals generally considered that they had little control over external constraints and stressors, so they focused in their own lives on what they believed they could control – their own conscious actions. Methods of maintaining mental health emphasised self-reliance and the striving of autonomy. This had both inner or subjective features and outward relational characteristics. The former entailed drawing consciously on reserves for coping. The latter involved using the support or positive feedback of others to boost one's own morale or finding time alone. Cognitive strategies which emphasised moral obligation and personal responsibility allow people to cope with threatening change as indicated by this respondent:

I think they have to come to terms with them, then decide how they are going to fit into the new world around them or how they are going to make their little world fit them. They can change the external factors or fit into the new environment. I don't think there's a lot of other choice really.

Sport was viewed as a means of maintaining mental healthiness. However, this strategy was linked to more than the good physical feelings that were attributed to regular exercise. While the latter were reported, it was also the case that the collective familial and community identity associated with football was also a source of emotional support, especially for men. Collective activities such as football symbolise more than the culture of narcissism advocated by commentators such as Lasch (1979). The identification the respondents had with the sport referred to the companionship of fellow supporters and the vicarious achievements and struggles shown by their favoured team.

DISCUSSION

Our overview of the strengths and weaknesses of differing perspectives within social science towards mental health problems led to us pointing towards critical or sceptical realism as a guiding framework to retain the strengths of both realism and constructivism. We then went on to explore the democratic potential of this approach, which legitimises an examination of all forms of knowledge including that produced by lay people. The latter is particularly pertinent in the field of mental health, which is characterised by a highly divided and contested range of competing professional discourses. It is clear from people who have had contact with psychiatric services, and those who are asked to reflect on mental health, that ordinary people have complex views. The latter subsume: an emphasis on social causationism in relation to the causes of mental health problems; a commitment to individual agency and cognitive ingenuity when coping with or solving problems; and an ambivalence about sustaining or challenging a mind–body dualism. Biodeterministic views, favoured by many experts, are not always rejected but they are rarely emphasised.

Three particular implications will be noted in conclusion. First, lay people recognise material reality (structure) as being central to the creation of mental health problems, while at the same time conceding that in the absence of direct control over those determinants they are obliged to make the best of their capacity to take responsibility for problems arising in their lives (agency). Compared to the fruitless dichotomy sustained for decades by advocates of each position in social science, lay people offer an immediate integration (on 'structuration', cf. Giddens, 1979). Second, such an integration would suggest that modes of professional inquiry, which themselves respect and affirm this co-presence of attributions about social causes and of personal constructions, would offer a more democratic approach to knowledge than either the naive realism of biodeterminism or the esoteric idealism of poststructuralism. Third, the accounts of ordinary people are not merely a curious adjunct to expert constructions – they also constitute testimonies to the real material conditions in which individual perspectives and human relationships are situated.

REFERENCES

Armstrong, D., Bird, J., Fry, J.S. and Armstrong, P. (1991) Perceptions of Psychological Problems in General Practice: A Comparison of General Practitioners and Psychiatrists, *Family Practice*, 9, 173–176.
Barton, R. (1957) *Institutional Neurosis*, Bristol: Wright & Sons.
Bhaskar, R. (1989) *Reclaiming Reality: A Critical Introduction to Contemporary Philosophy*, London: Verso.
Brown, G. and Harris, T. (1978) *Social Origins of Depression*, London: Tavistock.
Brown, G. and Wing, J. (1962) A Comparative Clinical and Social Survey of Three Mental Hospitals, *Sociological Review*, monograph no. 5, 145–173.
Busfield J. (1986) *Managing Madness: Changing Ideas and Practice*, London: Hutchinson.
Castel, F., Castel, R. and Lovell, A. (1979) *The Psychiatric Society*, New York: Columbia Free Press.
Cornwell, J. (1986) *Hard Earned Lives*, London: Tavistock.
Coulter, J. (1973) *Approaches to Insanity*, Oxford: Martin Robertson.
DeSwaan, A. (1990) *The Management of Normality: Critical Essay in Health and Welfare*, London: Routledge.
Emerson, R.M. and Pollner, M. (1975) Dirty Work Designations: Their Features and Consequences in a Psychiatric Setting, *Social Problems*, 3, 243–254.
Faris, R. and Dunham, H.W. (1939) *Mental Disorders in Urban Areas*, Chicago: University of Chicago Press.
Foucault, M. (1961) *Folie et deraison: histoire de la folie à l'âge classique*, Paris: Plon.
——(1965) *Madness and Civilisation*, New York: Pantheon.

Furnham, A. and Lowick, V. (1984) Lay Theories of the Causes of Alcoholism, *British Journal of Medical Psychology*, 57(4), 319–332.

Furnham, A. and Pendred, J. (1983) Attitudes Towards the Mentally and Physically Disabled, *British Journal of Medical Psychology*, 56(2), 179–188.

Gabe, J. and Bury, M. (1988) Tranquillisers as a Social Problem, *Sociological Review*, 36, 320–352.

Gabe, J. and Thorogood, N. (1986) Prescribed Drug Use and the Management of Everyday Life: The Experience of Black and White Working Class Women, *Sociological Review*, 34, 737–772.

Giddens, A. (1979) *Central Problems in Social Theory*, London: Macmillan.

Goffman, E. (1961) *Asylums*, Harmondsworth: Penguin.

Goldberg, D. and Huxley, P. (1980) *Mental Illness in the Community*, London: Tavistock.

Goldie, N. (1977) The Division of Labour Among Mental Health Professionals – A Negotiated or an Imposed Order? In M. Stacey and M. Reid (eds), *Health and the Division of Labour*, London: Croom Helm.

Gordon, C. (1990) *Histoire de la folie*: an unknown book by Michel Foucault, *History of the Human Sciences*, 3, 13–26.

Habermas, J. (1971) *Toward a Rational Society*, London: Heinemann.

——(1987) *The Theory of Communicative Action*, Boston, MA: Beacon Press.

Hochschild, A. (1983) *The Managed Heart: The Commercialisation of Human Feeling*, University of California Press: San Francisco.

Horwitz, A. (1977) The Pathways into Psychiatric Treatment: Some Differences Between Men and Women, *Journal of Health and Social Behaviour*, 18, 169–178.

Lasch, C. (1979) *The Culture of Narcissim*, New York: Norton.

Lemert, C.C. (1979) *Sociology and the Twilight of Man: Homocentrism and Discourse in Sociological Theory*, Carbondale: Southern Illinois University Press.

Lemert, E. (1967) *Human Deviance, Human Problems and Social Control*, Englewood Cliffs: Prentice Hall.

MacCarthy, B. and Furnham, A. (1986) Patients' Conceptions of Psychological Adjustment in the Normal Population, *British Journal of Clinical Psychology*, 25(1), 43–50.

McKeganey, N. (1984) 'No Doubt She's Really a Little Princess': A Case Study of Trouble in the Therapeutic Community, *Sociological Review*, 321, 328–348.

Miller, P. (1986) Critiques of Psychiatry and Critical Sociologies of Madness. In P. Miller and N. Rose (eds), *The Power of Psychiatry*, Cambridge: Polity Press.

Miller, P. and Rose, N. (eds) (1986), *The Power of Psychiatry*, Cambridge: Polity Press.

——(1988) The Tavistock Programme: The Government of Subjectivity and Social Life, *Sociology*, 22(2), 171–192.

Murphy, E. (1982) Social Origins of Depression in Old Age, *British Journal of Psychiatry*, 141, 135–142.

Park, R. (1936) Human Ecology, *American Journal of Sociology*, 43, 1–15.

Pilgrim, D. and Rogers, A. (1994) Something Old, Something New . . . : Sociology and the Organisation of Psychiatry, *Sociology*, 28(2), 35–46..

Rogers, A. (1993) Police and Psychiatrists: A Case of Professional Dominance?, *Social Policy and Administration*, 27(1), 259–267.

Rogers, A. and Pilgrim, D. (1991) 'Pulling down Churches': Accounting for the British Mental Health Service Users Movement, *Sociology of Health and Illness*, 13(2), 129–148.

Rogers, A., Pilgrim, D. and Lacey, R. (1993) *Experiencing Psychiatry: Users' Views of Services*, London: Macmillan.

Rogers, A., Pilgrim, D. and Latham, M. (1996) Understanding and Promoting Mental Health in Families. Family Health Research Programme London.

Rose, N. (1985) *The Psychological Complex*, London: Routledge.

——(1986) The Discipline of Mental Health. In P. Miller and N. Rose (eds), *The Power of Psychiatry*, Cambridge: Polity Press.

——(1990) *Governing the Soul: The Shaping of the Private Self*, London: Routledge.

Scheff, T. (1966) *Being Mentally Ill: A Sociological Theory*, Chicago: Aldine.

Scull, A. (1977) *Decarceration: Community Treatment and the Deviant – A Radical View*, Englewood Cliffs: Prentice Hall.

Scull, A. (1979) *Museums of Madness: The Social Organisation of Insanity in Nineteenth Century England*, Harmondsworth: Penguin.

Sedgwick, P. (1972) Mental Illness is Illness, paper presented at the National Symposium on Deviance, York, England.

——(1980) *PsychoPolitics*, London: Pluto.

Stone, M. (1985) Shellshock and the Psychologists. In W.F. Bynum, R. Porter and M. Shepherd (eds), *The Anatomy of Madness*, London: Tavistock.

Survivors Speak Out (1987) *Charter of Needs*, London: Survivors Speak Out.

Szasz, T. (1961) *The Myth of Mental Illness: Foundations of a Theory of Personal Conduct*, London: Secker.

Warner, R. (1985) *Recovery from Schizophrenia: Psychiatry and Political Economy*, London: Routledge & Kegan Paul.

Wilden, A. (1972) *System and Structure: Essays in Communication and Exchange*, London: Tavistock.

4 AIDS panic

Corinne Squire

PROLOGUE

The materiality of the body, its physical and psychic reality, seems inescapable, and beguiling. Science, which aims to discover the laws of the material world, finds strenuous tests in the body's complexity.[1] The body's accessibility both makes these tests possible, and helps persuade the popular imagination of biological science's legitimacy: surely something we know so intimately and well must be an important focus of scientific study (Doane, 1990). In politics, the body's materiality guarantees the interests of particular social identities, through the 'experience' that grounds much feminist, black and gay politics, for instance (Brodbeck, 1992). Lived bodily experience also seems to ground individual unity and identity, telling us, in a deep and incontrovertible way, who we really are.

However, the body's materiality is never as certain as it appears. The science of the body is perpetually under challenge, from science's own failures and its inherent scepticism, from external critiques of science's ulterior motives, and from descriptions of science as narrative, not truth (Harding, 1986; Jacobus *et al.*, 1990). In addition, other stories of the body compete with the scientific one – that of religion, and that of social improvement, which has progress rather than truth as its goal. [2] The politics of a materially fixed body-identity also holds itself together with great difficulty against the divergent meanings the similar bodies of, for instance, 'black people', 'gay men' or 'women' have to their occupants (Riley, 1988; Dent, 1992). Even the notion of an embodied self is in some accounts a fictional unification of bodies and subjectivities that are multiple and fragmented (Marcus, 1987).

It is not sufficient, though, to treat all efforts to understand the body as stories, simply constructing their own, narrative, realities. Such a description makes it impossible to determine why some stories are told more, and have more effects, than others; or how a person can act and feel as if their identity is firmly and unproblematically vested in their body. Through a combination of narrative persuasion and institutional powers, some regimes of knowledge are more far-reaching than others. To understand this combination, a double reading of the body's materiality and discursivity is required.

In this piece I shall assume not that discourse is all-determining, but that the division between the discursive and the material is difficult, even impossible, to sustain. The material is discursive; equally, the discursive is material. Such a doubled understanding has long-standing precedents within Enlightenment thought, where the body has always functioned not simply as the guarantee of material science, but also as the intersection between matter and spirit where rationality emerges, and makes science possible. In this tradition, the body is both the guarantee of science and the symptom of science's limits. What lies beyond these limits, outside material truth, is conceptualised variously, as divine truth; secular, individual truth and discursive, social truth.

Following Michel de Certeau, I shall argue that the division between discourse and the material is less relevant today than the division between 'method' – the regulations and formulations emblematised in science – and practices and stories of the 'everyday' (de Certeau, 1984: 65, 78). Like de Certeau I shall be interested in what appears 'outside', in this case 'outside' the science, specifically the psychology of HIV, both in popular culture and in people's stories.

EXTERIORISING AIDS PANIC

Psychology's focus on disciplinarily defined behaviours, cognitions, attitudes and emotions, that are not directly or reliably measurable, can look like an abdication of science. Its interest in the effects of social factors on subjective experience also seems to distance it from science. Nevertheless, most psychology continues to define itself strongly as science. However vague or recalcitrant its objects, it subscribes to scientific principles, aiming for valid and reliable tests of hypotheses that are explanatorily general but non-trivial. The possibility of a chain of causation linking psychic with biochemical or biophysical events, and thus connecting psychology with other sciences, is a powerful disciplinary subtext. Psychological investigations are understood as responsible and necessary first steps in uncovering these connections. Most significantly, psychology assumes that subjectivity and the social have their own level of material reality, and that they are susceptible to a scientific, or pre-scientific, description, explanation and management.

Within psychology, as within biology and medicine, AIDS ups the scientific stakes. AIDS research operates as the touchstone of scientific advances on the body.[3] Since behaviours and attitudes are widely seen as key to understanding the condition, psychology has an accepted academic and policy role here. But AIDS is so fraught with cultural metaphors and intrinsic uncertainties that this scientifically materialist approach is always challenged by another: a response that I shall call AIDS panic. This panic revolves around notions of bodily vulnerability, debilitation and death; sexuality, and homosexuality especially; racial Otherness and foreign contamination; pleasure;

and scientific and other epistemological uncertainties. AIDS panic can be paralysing or hostile, even murderous. But it is an unavoidable response to a condition that is fatal, whose transmission has proved difficult to regulate, and that is associated with taboo activities and socially feared groups. AIDS science, though, including psychology, tends to ignore or externalise AIDS panic.

Science is always conducted in part against cultural panic. AIDS science declares itself the regulator of AIDS panic. It tries to isolate, visualise and name the virus, its components and effects, and to develop strategies to curtail its spread and symptoms. AIDS panic operates as a kind of exterior to AIDS science, an 'outside' in de Certeau's words: the repository of left-over, unexplained or undendurable bits of reality or languages, that cannot be codified. Often this panic-inducing unknown appears in scientific discourse as an 'epidemic of signification' (Paula Treichler's description of AIDS discourses in Western cultures generally), spewing out fearsome images and hateful words. It is particularly clear in the case of such AIDS science that discourse is material, and the material discursive (Treichler, 1989: 31). Scientific vocabularies around the condition have shaped diagnostic, treatment and prevention practices. At the same time, AIDS science is itself heavily inflected by the patriarchal, heterosexist, racist assumptions of the language that writes it, assumptions that lead to partialities or omissions, apocalyptic warnings, melodramatic over- or under-statements. AIDS science is committed not to understanding but to rooting out its own panic. As a result, this panic remains unacknowledged, yet integral: A property of the external objects science struggles to subdue.

Within the psychology of HIV the exteriorisation of AIDS panic is perhaps even more noticeable. Psychologists working on HIV/AIDS are generally, perhaps, more self-conscious about social stereotyping than are biological writers, and so HIV-related psychology displays fewer of the homophobic and misogynist generalisations that characterised early medical writing on the epidemic (Treichler, 1989: 46, 49). However, psychologists are also concerned not to jeopardise their field's shaky scientific status. One result is that they are committed to a 'scientific' generality that can neglect the specificity of AIDS. Dominant prevention models of health belief, reasoned action and social learning (Amaro, 1995), concepts of the interaction between HIV and personality (Kobasa, 1991), and assumptions about the importance of self-esteem in promoting competent behaviour (Tashakkion and Thompson, 1992), for instance, are often translated wholesale from other domains where they have gained legitimacy. HIV counsellors rely predominantly on models of, for example, cognitive coping strategies or emotional bereavement stages that have been developed around other health issues and then generalised. The scientific assumption of generality thus allows analogies to be drawn between risky sex and smoking; death of a gay partner and death of a heterosexual spouse; global self-esteem, well-being and competence, and the same features in an HIV risk context; a positive HIV antibody test and a cancer diagnosis. HIV psychology's concern to be scientific also leads it to treat cultural discourses of HIV as epiphenomena, or at most as extra stressors, not shapers of the epidemic – factors that the bright light of scientific knowledge will disperse. Treichler's panicky signification 'epidemic' thus disappears from the scene.

The social particularity of the epidemic also remains underconceptualised in much HIV psychology, which persists in using a predominantly individual frame of understanding (Amaro, 1995). Some psychologists with an interest in social action have suggested that HIV and AIDS be recognised as largely social constructions, demanding social understanding and action (Institute of Medicine, 1995: parts 2 and 4). Even in these accounts, the 'social' is treated scientifically, as an entity that can be described and evaluated, factor by factor. Such work aims to transform the cultural discourse around AIDS from a nebulous, poisonous miasma into a rational expression of knowledge. Again, the assumption here is that AIDS panic can be erased by a science that comprehends and conquers it – by, for instance, thoroughly researched campaigns of HIV information and education (Flora *et al.*, 1995).

A few psychologists have addressed HIV as a discursive phenomenon, exploring the complex articulations of the condition without reducing them to descriptions of what happens. Within psychology, though, this work has tended to be ruled by a kind of secondary determinism; derived from science, though not strictly scientific. While such research does not treat language as transparent, as telling us about the reality of people's lives, it is a quest for the hidden subtext, for what is 'really' being said. It does not say that the multiple, contradictory messages within, for instance, a drug user's account of AIDS are wrong, nor does it reduce them to a single meaning. However it sorts out definitively what they are, and tells us which is most important. Connors, following such an analysis, argues that though all the meanings 'make sense to [the drug user] on some level', personal experience 'often wins out in the final discernment of the meaning of AIDS' (1995: 78). This drive towards definite, often single meanings passes over the panic-stricken ambiguities that permeate AIDS discourse. In addition, this form of research often presents HIV discourses in people's talk as reified speech elements that have little connection, beyond some shared content, with other significations of HIV, for instance on television or in pamphlets. This reifying analysis again facilitates scientific explanation, but it rules out messier, more wide-ranging accounts of AIDS discourse.

Psychologists working around HIV are, of course, doing the right thing when they try to help people deal with the condition or avoid infection; when they expand the 'reality' of HIV by addressing it through social relations, social policy and mass media; and when they attempt to give a comprehensive account of what people say about their HIV experience. I am suggesting, though, that some substantive aspects of HIV, aspects I have identified with AIDS panic, get forgotten in these endeavours. They appear in HIV-related psychology by implication only, in glossed-over contradictions or confusions; and in psychology's references to bigotry, resistance to education, 'slipping' in safer sexual practices, 'resignation' and 'denial'.

AIDS panic is dealt with much more directly and extensively in cultural studies (see, for instance, Carter and Watney, 1989; Crimp, 1989; Sontag, 1988; Boffin and Gupta, 1990; Murphy and Poirier, 1993).[4] Cultural theorists seem more likely to recognise an epidemic of signification when they see one, and to think it 'matters': that it is material, and that it is of consequence. Moreover, cultural studies is less concerned than psychology to impose a scientific order on the chaotic meanings and realities of the epidemic, and so it is more able to see 'outside' this order.

I want to investigate two forms of AIDS signification in this chapter: popular images of viral epidemic and stories about HIV told by some seropositive people. I shall treat these significations not as 'discourse' separate from 'reality', but as manifestations of, and responses to, AIDS panic. In so doing, I want to clarify the place of AIDS panic for a psychology of HIV. I do not want to capitulate to this panic, but to recognise it is valuable in itself, and also helps us to put into perspective the more authoritative, scientific account of HIV that suppresses AIDS panic.

Since considerable theoretical and practical gains have emerged from cultural studies of AIDS panic, this chapter's method borrows from that field. The chapter does not use formalised psychological methods that tend (even if focused on 'discourse') to be searching for one defining meaning and exploring its convergence with 'reality'. It is, rather, a textual analysis, concerned with multiplicities and contradictions of meaning.

VIRAL PANIC

I have suggested that psychologists underestimate AIDS panic. They treat it as an irrational cultural response which it is the business of psychology to fight, helping to develop other, more rational and optimistic understandings instead. This section of the chapter discusses the extent and complexity of AIDS panic. I shall look first at significations that are self-consciously 'about' AIDS, and then at the recent 'epidemic of signification' around bacterial and viral pathology. Taken together, these phenomena constitute a broader 'viral' panic, generated by AIDS, yet touching other points in the nexus of cultural anxiety.

When Treichler (1989) suggested that a signification 'epidemic' had arisen around HIV, she noted the plurality and conflicts of AIDS meanings, and their fatal, panicky intensity. Not only illness and death, but pleasure, non-reproductive sexuality (anal intercourse, sex for money), femininity, and racial and national 'others' are implicated. This is an epidemic of transgressive meanings, endlessly exchanged and transmitted. In it, HIV metaphorically represents other signs with panic-inducing meanings, while conversely those signs can themselves be metaphors for AIDS. The encouragement of HIV testing among pregnant women in poor urban communities of colour in the US, for example, is in part a sign of racist panic about the colour of the national 'family' (Amaro, 1993). At the same time, policy attempts to control the same women's reproduction, by welfare penalties for example, have as one subtext the fearful cost, and pathos, of 'AIDS babies'.

In the overdeveloped world, the homosexual body acts on AIDS meanings as a unifying object of fascination, around which panic coalesces (Treichler, 1989: 50; see also Bersani, 1989). Instances of this concentration in HIV discourse include the implication of lesbians far more often than their epidemiological profile would justify; analised First World imaginings of Third World sexual practices; the casting of female prostitutes as reservoirs in a quasi-homosexual exchange of body fluids between men; the suggestion that women infected by bisexual men are collusive in gay male sexuality; the homosexualisation of injecting drug users by viewing them as sexually indiscriminate; and the 'queering' by association of haemophiliacs (Treichler, 1989; Patton, 1993). Leo Bersani speculates that when the townspeople of Arcadia, Florida, set fire to the house of a family whose three children were said to be HIV positive, they were envisaging a man being fucked: 'In looking at three hemophiliac children, they may have seen – that is, unconsciously represented – the infinitely more intolerable image of a grown man, legs high in the air, unable to resist the suicidal ecstasy of being a woman' (1989: 212).

AIDS panic does not circulate freely in popular discourses: they regulate it, much as science does. As AIDS science has diffused into the popular media, and as advocacy groups have forced their own discourses into the mainstream, conventional manifestations of AIDS panic have become muted.[5] Popular media have their own structures of panic control, too. Television, for example, the most widespread source of AIDS information in the overdeveloped world, has to balance marginality – the result of, for instance, explicit representations of sexuality and drug use, and of non-realist representations – against the mass audiences achieved by a bland focus on 'family' (Treichler, 1993).[6] Television AIDS narratives are also caught up in some specifically televisual preoccupations with how to present sexuality, the balance between education and entertainment, and being 'real'. Treichler quotes the Movies and Ministeries Vice President of NBC saying, 'We tried to make an honest depiction, something where people would say, "Hey, that's real. That's not phony, that's not TV" ' (1993:168). AIDS panic tends to get cancelled out in such media debates. Moreover, as television genres, especially the 'disease-of-the-week' movie format, mutate to encompass this new disease, AIDS panic becomes domesticated, confined within safe limits. AIDS panic in the popular media can, too, be read in various ways, and often, as many cultural analysts have pointed out, the readings are socially and personally dangerous, especially to people infected by HIV. Moreover, because these significations are unreflexive, they tend to repeat and reify themselves, and in doing so remove AIDS panic from the possibility of serious consideration. Nevertheless, the sense of something ineffably horrible remains strong in media significations. They are, after all, allowed – even supposed – to picture (as science is not) the entirety of the material world, not just that part of it susceptible to controlled investigation. And so cultural discourse remains an arena where AIDS panic finds an intermittent but important voice, especially in local media, where care about (and monitoring of) AIDS reporting remains lower.

In August 1993, the front pages of US tabloids screamed the story of a woman '[s]hocked by a false AIDS test'. When Rebecca Clark of New Jersey offered to give blood to the Red Cross, screening showed she could be HIV positive. Her doctor re-administered the test, and discovered at the same time Clark's pregnancy – a state that often produces false positive results. This and subsequent tests were negative, but the Red Cross refused to take her off what a local paper (the *Trentonian*) called its 'black list' of deferred donors. But Clark wanted to give blood in case her son, who shared her rare blood type, needed it. The story resurrected a significatory tension that has often accompanied the AIDS epidemic, between stigmatising and helping the deathly, sexualised, pathetic figure of the person infected or affected by HIV – in this case, a person who, though negative, once falsely tested positive. The Red Cross marked Rebecca Clark for life, the *Trentonian* wrote, with 'the scarlet letter "D" for deferred'. This criticism, referring to the sin-signifying 'A' that adulterous Hester Prynn wears in Hawthorne's novel *The Scarlet Letter*, assumed a welcome distance between past judgements on the female body, and present judgements on the AIDS body. Ironically then, the report emphasised that Clark was an ideal and blameless woman. It dwelled on her normal, happy family life, and pictured her small son with her on the front page. At the same time, a suspicion of syphilitic contamination clung to her as it almost always does to women in popular media accounts of AIDS (Gilman, 1988; Patton, 1993). The conjunction of Clark and the scarlet 'D', turning HIV and adultery into parallel stigmata, cast a subtextual doubt on her. The report also invoked other panic-inducing questions about the power of apparently benevolent institutions like the Red Cross, and about science's knowledge; one paragraph explaining how HIV tests always pose a small risk of false positive and false negative results had the rhetorical effect of suggesting medicine was impotent before the virus. Even here, then, at its most explicit, AIDS panic is associated with other fears that it reinforces, and from which it in turn draws strength.

A signification of AIDS with a very different focus was the movie *Kids* (1995), in whose somewhat wooden narrative a virginal good girl, manipulated into sex once by a confused young Don Juan, tests HIV positive and tries to find him. The film's explicitness about sex and drugs, and general teenage hedonism, led to heated denunciations of it, parents agonising over what was happening to today's children, and teenagers applauding its 'realness'. The panicky tone of the film's plot and its ambience of excess, does not, though, erase their rhetorical effectiveness. Panic was put to work here as an inducement to moral and behavioural clarity. It is likely, however, that panic on its own has little effect on the HIV risk of a teen population. The film is also suffused with a continual visual pleasure, often in the young people's bodies, that racks up AIDS panic by its complete dissociation from the AIDS narrative. Moreover, this is not really much of an 'AIDS' movie. AIDS stands in here for a slew of other issues: drugs, relationships, contraception and young women's exploitation.

The tracing of diverse meanings in presentations of AIDS has as its corollary the possibility of reading AIDS in images with other overt concerns. Such readings have indeed been made, particularly around film, in a history that passes from *Fatal Attraction* (1987), sometimes called the first AIDS movie; through *Basic Instinct* (1992), to *Interview with the Vampire* (1994) – almost unavoidably an 'AIDS movie' given its thematic concerns with blood, death and ambiguous sexualities (Hanson, 1991; Ricapito, 1995). Such readings-in of AIDS, while often valuable, often coexist with equally plausible other readings; readings of the *Aliens* series around not just AIDS but femininity and maternity (Creed, 1987), for example. In order to examine AIDS panic's particular metaphorical contribution to other significations, I am going to look at a set of productions more directly connected with AIDS, which I shall call the Hot Zone constellation.

A 1992 *New Yorker* article, 'Crisis in the Hot Zone' (Preston, 1992) described the 1976 outbreaks of *Ebola* viruses, haemorrhagic fever viruses with 60–90 per cent fatality rates, in Sudan and Yambuku, northern Zaire. It also told of a similar infection appearing in 1989 in the US, among Philippine monkeys in a primate quarantine unit. A best-selling book on the subject (Preston, 1994) followed, as did two Hollywood film projects with closely related themes – one dropped during development, the other, *Outbreak* (1995), starring Dustin Hoffman and drawing large audiences. Two books covering haemorrhagic fever viruses, AIDS and a range of other infectious diseases appeared around the same time, as did *The Forgotten Plague* (Ryan, 1994), a study of tuberculosis from its nineteenth-century dominance to its present-day return, often in combination with HIV (see also Rothman, 1994). Other events renewed the Hot Zone concern: Flesh-eating bacteria scares, predominantly in Europe; anxiety over new strains of *E. Coli*, BSE, legionnaires' disease, and Lyme disease and similar conditions in the US (Revkin, 1995); a 1992 epidemic of a new cholera bacterium in Madras; and another episode of *Ebola* in Zaire (Altman, 1995), just as *Outbreak* was released. It was AIDS, though, that had catalysed a resurgence of scientific interest in infectious diseases, and that primed public interest in these other conditions, with their similar dangers. The rhetoric of the Hot Zone texts also echo and intensify AIDS significations; without AIDS panic, they could hardly have been written.

Hot Zone narratives are explicit about the panic-inducing effects of the organisms they describe. The visualisation of these effects is important, even in written examples of the genre, where what you would see happening to the body is detailed at length, even gloatingly (Horton, 1995: 24). If you are infected with *Ebola Zaire*, the *New Yorker* article reveals, 'your eyeballs bleed. You vomit a black fluid . . . In the pre-agonal stage . . . the patient leaks blood . . . from the nose, mouth, anus, eyes, and from rips in the skin . . . ' (Preston, 1992: 59). Film versions of the story choose particular visual signs. *Outbreak* goes for initial sweat and convulsive jerking, and later pallor with distinct reddening at the eyes and nose. Among other horrors, these pictures of disintegration inevitably recall, media images of AIDS bodies disappearing, wasting, sweating, pale, and marked by red sarcomas.[7] Visual horror is an understandable Hot Zone focus, given the threat to a visually constituted bodily narcissism that illness poses. But we might also argue, following Lee Edelman (1993), that the homophobia which foregrounds fear of narcissism in AIDS discourse makes the visual an especially strong concern, whose intensity now spills over into related significations of disease.

Science brings horror under control, and its visual regulations (through, for instance, microscope images or chromatography) have particular power (Foucault, 1979; Juhasz, 1993). In many Hot Zone narratives the discovery and visualisation of the pathogenic agent marks an interim resolution. We see or read of the scientist staring at the sparse, immobilised organisms, tiny and deadly; or in the case of the tuberculosis bacillus, first stained and displayed by Robert Koch in 1884, a 'beautiful blue' (quoted in Ryan, 1994: 12). In the cultural narrative of AIDS the discovery of HIV occupies a similar place, as Shilts' account of the scientific race to isolate the virus demonstrates. The turning point came when a scientist 'peered at the cultures' from an AIDS patient and saw cells dying off, the sign of a previously unknown retrovirus (Shilts, 1987: 227). Yet, since transmission but not the virus itself can be controlled, the visualisation of HIV has less significance than the picturing of its pathways and sources. Mappings of risky contacts made by individuals – such as Gaitan Dugas, Patient Zero, allegedly the source of many early US cases (Shilts, 1987: 147), or Magic Johnson, whose announcement of seropositivity was followed by numerous tabloid images of ex-girlfriends; and speculative HIV lineages stretching back to Haiti, Africa, monkeys or the CIA – had wide media currency. These discursive tracings prefigure the efforts to see and know transmission and origin in the Hot Zone narratives, which usually have as another important structural element the exposure of source or mode of transmission. In *Outbreak* the exposure takes the form of a photo-image, found by the virologist-heroes, of the monkey that is the viral 'host'. In Garrett's (1995) account of one Bolivian virus, mode of transmission – mouse urine, in this case – is exposed narratively, when the denouément of the chapter traces for the reader the line of contamination.

In cultural texts, unlike scientific ones, science's failures to repress viral panic are written into the script, often into the images. Viruses cannot be seen directly and are highly unstable, changing shape, properties and effects. Although these failures have multiplied in the Hot Zone constellation, HIV's variability and flexibility, and the persistently raised possibility of unknown co-factors, still emblematises such uncertainty about the adequacy of the scientific picture (Garrett, 1995). A shadowy cultural image persists of HIV itself passing from hand to hand, breath to breath. Concretising this indeterminacy, the electron microscope picture of *Ebola* is widely reported to look like a question mark (Horton, 1995: 24). In *Outbreak* the camera follows unseen particles as they travel across crowded places and through air ducts, carried on saliva droplets or menacingly invisible. Then we see the microscope image of a mutated, airborne form of the virus. At the end of all the Hot Zone narratives, science has gained control, but the stories still leave us with a dystopian 'what if . . . '. As the recent *Ebola* epidemic began to be contained, the *New York Times* headlined, 'No-one can say why virus striking Zaire is so deadly' (Altman, 1995). In longer documentary accounts like *The Hot Zone* (Preston, 1994), the containment of deadly viruses remains inexplicable and decimation continues to lie in wait. It is as if the now-buried fears of HIV claiming the whole white, middle-class, heterosexual US population return again in these more distant possibilities.

The Hot Zone constellation also displays a set of social biases that repeat, in an overt way, the concealed stereotypes driving AIDS panic. 'Crisis in the Hot Zone' suggests that cutting down the rainforests is causing viruses to spread out of the dark and steamy reservoirs of infection that once contained them. Exploding populations and increased contact between previously separate groups are also indicted. Here viral panic turns disease into ecological vengeance and the ecosystem into Frankenstein, and sets up the rainforest, the African and the prostitute in uneasy equation. These speculations recapitulate early AIDS mythologies about sexual excesses, cross-species and cross-race contact, and dark Africa. One virologist interviewed for 'Crisis in the Hot Zone' cites AIDS: 'as a biologist, from a deeply philosophical viewpoint, I don't think there's any difference' (Preston, 1992).

Hot Zone texts construe not just the body but the US as under attack from within. This attack depends either on the possibility that viruses such as those in the haemorrhagic fever group will arrive with international travellers; or, in the case of the rabies bacterium, over the Mexican border; or on the notion of 'Urban Thirdworldisation' (Garrett, 1995) – for instance when drug-resistant strains of TB live among poor people of colour whose lack of use of, or access to, health care are said to help such diseases spread and become more stubborn. Even without the TB–AIDS connection, this free-wheeling paranoia has a specific resonance with the discourse of 'the dragon within' (Joseph, 1992) that presents HIV as a kind of traitor identified variously with the inner city, the minority population, gay men, the medical profession, and the political establishment supposed to represent 'us' all (see also Shilts, 1987).

Towards the end, the *Outbreak* narrative turns towards the possibility of a 'Nam-style fire-bombing of the US town infected by the 'Motava' virus. The image that marks this turn is that of a US map, on which is projected the likely spread of the virus in 48 hours. Quickly, fatal orange dots cover the space, spreading like the dense web of Gaitan Dugas's travels mapped out in scientific journals and popular accounts (Shilts, 1987: 438). The most dramatic scenes in both film and written Hot Zone texts involve a visual metaphorisation of the danger from unseen invaders: 'Americans', their vulnerable bodies clad in isolating spacesuits, feeling like they are 'going into outer space' (Preston, 1992: 73), venture into a contaminated space, a 'hot zone' – a lab at Biosafety Level 4, the Ugandan cave where the *Marburg* virus was thought to originate (Preston, 1994: 402). AIDS itself is used here as an index of the dangers; it, too, is a Level 4 agent. More specifically, the spacesuit image recalls those that appeared in early television treatments of the AIDS epidemic that invariably showed a person hospitalised with AIDS being cared for by medical staff in protective suits, gloves and masks.

The Hot Zone productions exhibit a particularly intense fascination with the militarism of virology. This charm leads the books to picture scientists with swooning romanticism as frontier cowboys, and prompts the movies to rely on biological warfare subplots and protagonists who are colonels as well as doctors. In 'Crisis in the Hot Zone' the infatuation also leads to a full-blown onslaught of war terms. The viruses are capable of 'explosive' transmission. They 'penetrate' and 'take over' cells and 'crush' the immune system; the body goes through 'crash and bleed out', a military term for shock and haemorrhage (Preston, 1992: 58–60, 63; 1994: 46). This militarism is paralleled in AIDS discourse in floods of references to the 'war' we must wage, the 'holocaust' being wreaked, the 'Beirut' of the AIDS body, Manhattan as 'ground zero', etc. As Michael Sherry (1993) points out, the use of such powerful metaphors is hardly surprising. It does, though, indicate the limited supply of effective rhetorical resources available. It also provides some examples of how these resources can be used against governments and health professionals either subsumed in AIDS panic or devoted to its suppression, as in the rhetorical guerilla warfare conducted by ACT UP (AIDS Coalition To Unleash Power). I would also suggest that a certain magic seems to attend militarist descriptions of viruses, as if by taking on a language of peril dangers can be contained, the success of regulation assured, while viral panic continues to gain expression. Moreover, coming after AIDS the militarism of the Hot Zone constellation also seems to operate like a kind of unleashed expression of an AIDS-related desire to regulate panic more forcibly and completely than can science.

All the Hot Zone accounts say that in the absence of a scientific solution, the answer to viral panic is increased disease surveillance worldwide, under the control not of the UN but of the US Centers for Disease Control (CDC), which they identify as the only agency able to deal with viral panic. In the case of TB in the US the suggestions involve 'monitoring' (Ryan, 1995: 417) or, more precisely, 'directly observed' chemotherapy, drugs taken under the eye of a health professional (Horton, 1995: 26) These suggestions recall earlier US proposals for internal HIV quarantine and contact tracing, and the compulsory HIV antibody testing of applicants for permanent residency, and selected visitors.[8] Such efforts to regain panoptical control over the rights of black citizens and residents, and women's and gay men's sexuality, extend in the regulation of Hot Zone panic to encompass the entire US 'sphere of influence', as if in imaginary compensation for the general failure of the earlier efforts.

In their more democratic incarnations, Hot Zone texts describe the world as a giant out-of-balance immune system, imagine a 'rational global village' (Garrett, 1995: 620), and call for collaborative CDC, UN, and host-country disease monitoring, and the empowerment of Third World women to reject unsafe sex; or more simplistically for the 'adoption' (Ryan, 1994: 417) of underdeveloped by overdeveloped nations; or even for the US to act as the 'World's Doctor' (*New York Times*, editorial, 11 May 1995). At such moments, questions like 'Collaboration, monitoring and empowerment for whom?' – and doubts about paternalism – inevitably arise (*New York Times*, letters, 20 May 1995). Here the parallels with questions raised about US policy on AIDS in the Third World are very close.

Despite these parallels, in one way the Hot Zone texts achieve meanings and effects that AIDS discourses rarely do. Even before the recent *Ebola* outbreak, these texts were supporting strong public arguments about the cost-effectiveness in terms of US lives of setting up UN or CDC stations worldwide to monitor infectious diseases. Similar utilitarian arguments about HIV never achieved much support: the US lives thought to be at stake were low-valued, and the benefits of educating everyone in the US about their risk seemed outweighed in most calculations by the costs of such taboo speech. If *Ebola* was marginal to the overdeveloped world by virtue of its Africanness, it was also brought 'home' to the US by the transmission possibilities of international air travel, and by the implicit parallel with HIV, which was 'over there' and is now 'over here', and which was a disease of 'them' but now may infect 'us'. In addition, *Ebola* was far enough away to contemplate its dangers calmly, especially as its transmission is associated with no more reprehensible behaviour than encountering infected body fluids through caring for the sick.[9]

Despite this difference, a general viral panic seems to characterise popular discourses of infectious agents. Many features of these discourses have been drawn from AIDS significations: their visual horror; their attempts, never quite successful, at regulating this horror; their inculcation with social biases, neocolonial paranoia, and militarism. Without AIDS, viral panic would not be so alluring. Conversely, with this new haemorrhagic-fever articulation, AIDS panic – which had been attenuating as homosexual men died, crack and IV drugs became less popular and adult heterosexuals did not get sick – gained a new metaphorical force.

Viral panic discourse is an important indication, for those working on

HIV issues, that irrational and troubling aspects of the epidemic, still outside scientific articulation, continue to occupy an important cultural place. As the next section of the chapter demonstrates, specific features of AIDS panic – its focus on toxicity, invasion and insulation; its preoccupations with the visible; its resort to medicine – continue to play themselves out, though in new ways, in the discourse of some seropositive people.

LIVING WITH AIDS PANIC

This section looks at stories produced by people infected by HIV, in order to see how these stories are affected by AIDS panic; how they regulate such panic; and how they also coexist with narratives of a well and happy life, an accommodation that constitutes a kind of living with AIDS panic.

The stories were told during interviews with twenty-two seropositive people about their experiences of support groups and other forms of support (Squire, 1995). In discussing these issues, interviewees almost inevitably described their relationship to HIV itself. I shall treat these interviews as texts, not truths, and as indicators of discourses and practices in operation, not as these discourses' or practices' proofs or foundations. This section, perhaps more clearly than the previous one, assumes the materiality of discourse. All interviewees themselves assumed that HIV's materiality was structured by signification at the cultural level, in individual states of mind and sometimes in its actions on the immune system.[10] For many interviewees, even the discourse of the interviews assumed a minor constitutive place in living with HIV, giving them a chance to articulate their successes, confusions and, occasionally, their fears.

Interviewees all described a time after diagnosis – days for some, a year for others – when they were taken over by an AIDS panic that resembled in many respects that in the Hot Zone constellation or in the 'epidemic of signification' described by Treichler (1989). They were filled with stigma, shame, fear and despair. They shut themselves up in their houses, they avoided contact with others, and they thought of nothing but the virus. 'When I first found I'm positive I thought I will die in a few weeks . . . I told myself I don't need to buy any clothes because I will die soon . . . I never went anywhere, I don't talk with no-one', Helana said (interviewees' names have all been changed). They were the virus, dirty and dangerous; 'a vial of poison', as one man put it. Often this panic was visualised. Interviewees' image of HIV was of television's person-with-AIDS, so skeletal as to be hardly human. They figured themselves as visual objects of panic, the focus of a quasi-scientific, knowing, controlling public gaze. They were sure others would be able to see their contamination. Laura told how she believed, 'oh those people are gonna look at me and say "she's positive" '. Mina, a visual arts student, described her first presentation at college:

they switch on the lights you know . . . everybody behind can look at you ... and I thought, ... 'My HIV's being mirrored out now', and thought they're going to be able to see through me or something ... I almost fainted just thinking about all those things standing in front of the wall, everybody looking out at me.

For psychologists AIDS panic is a stage, often noted in the literature, that people affected by HIV must work through. However, interviewees described it continuing, alongside more conventionally adaptive responses, long after diagnosis.

Interviewees also described a contemporary ability to deal with AIDS panic, something that they had achieved by constructing a way to live with HIV and to talk of it rationally and hopefully. This discourse refused fatalism without denying illness, and opposed depression though still allowing it. Meeting, initially just seeing other seropositive people who looked very different from the spectral TV image, was an important step. Helana found a support group 'very helpful' in overcoming her feeling of imminent death: 'It's always, like, woman there ten years who is positive ... it makes you feel like probably you can live.' Mina described shutting her eyes before she walked into her first support group meeting and just listening to the voices, a less dangerous form of knowledge than vision, to determine if she knew anyone there. Then in a moment of personal and narrative revelation she opened her eyes and stepped in. Now, she said, she feels she belongs in such groups more fully than anywhere else: 'I used to think I was the only one, and that's the major thing I go for, to ... be together and share our feelings and just basically comfort one another.' Up against the wall at her college presentation, yet supported invisibly by all the other seropositive women she knew, she 'took a deep breath', turning herself from a transparent image into a three-dimensional, living body, overcame her panic, and finished the seminar. Laura, a recent migrant from Africa, told of emerging quickly from the depression and abjection of diagnosis into a relatively calm state of living with HIV. Her AIDS panic had different culturally accepted signs, visceral rather than visual: 'heaviness' was a sign of tiredness, a 'noisy' stomach indicated diarrhoea, bones were 'cracking'. But this difference seemed less responsible for her rapid adjustment to living with HIV than was her almost immediate induction after diagnosis into a welcoming group of seropositive women who countered the fatality of AIDS panic. 'Community', though, was never a perfect solution in these stories. Aside from the demographic and medical divisions that occasionally divided groups, interviewees all included accounts of moments when they were inevitably on their own with panic – with nihilism, depression and death.

Another strategy was for interviewees, even those whose existence was most determined by HIV, to keep parts of their lives separate from the condition. Often this strategy was one of discursive control: interviewees did not tell even those friends who would be sympathetic, or tried not to talk about HIV except with other infected friends. At other times, though, the strategy structured lives rather than talk. Interviewees ignored their HIV status in planning their actions, and avoided others with HIV, for instance. As John, ill himself and with a positive partner, said, 'I'm a bit sick of, this is going to sound awful, being surrounded by ill people.' Well interviewees like Helana carried their deliberate forgetting far enough to be amazed at times to remember their seropositivity. These forms of resistance, by distancing interviewees temporarily from HIV, checked but did not suppress AIDS panic. The resistances produced an implicit and sometimes explicit ambiguity in the interviews: Were the speakers still trailed by fear and self-loathing, or had they really vanquished them? Such ambiguity tends, in most psychological work on HIV, to be resolved. The seropositive person is judged either to be in denial, a state of variable and debatable benefit, or to have accepted their condition. The answer the interviews themselves gave was that both were true. AIDS panic and a more rational, 'scientific' state were in continual coexistence.

Medical discourse appeared to offer control of AIDS panic to some inter-viewees, particularly men with experience of illness, who often presented full discussions of particular infections or treatments and talked about wanting to know everything there was to be known. '[The] doctor says, "oh god, you know far more than I do because you have time to read the relevant journal"', John said. However, interviewees like John were not simply appropriating existing medical knowledge, but supplementing it with a knowledge developed by activists. John did not read journals so much as treatment newsletters produced by grass-roots organisations, a genre often highly critical of orthodox medicine and driven by an intimate sense of AIDS panic. Interviewees tended finally to endorse medical expertise; despite noting the irrelevance of T cell counts, they would also say what they were, for instance. It is important to remember, however, that the qualifications were ubiquitous, and that interviewees also articulated medicine's failures to regulate AIDS, failures that transmuted, in their discourse, into what they usually called a 'realistic' conviction of HIV's terminality. Interviewees' use of medical knowledge to control AIDS panic was thus highly nuanced. Medicine's insufficiency limited science's regulatory power and left panic a place in their stories – the place of the real. In a conventional psychological study of, for instance, attitudes or decision-making, the interviewees' vacillations about medical expertise might have looked confused or maladaptive. In these inter-views they appeared as sensitive adjustments to the epidemic's scientific uncertainties and cultural power.

Another mode of panic control lay with the alternative therapies described by all the interviewees. This form of knowledge seemed at first to suppress or, in its own terms, to 'transcend' AIDS panic. Interviewees described a journey towards 'owning the virus', or towards a spiritual enlightenment that rendered HIV irrelevant. This was not, as in the Hot Zone texts, a military struggle: Andy, the interviewee most committed to it, explicitly distanced himself from how 'some people visualise their cancer or whatever as a rock and . . . the thing they're going to beat it with as a bloody great big mallet . . . '. Instead Andy described visualisation in this way: 'I sort of see . . . dark colours representing, you know the HIV and . . . it's just washed clean away with golden, with wonderful golden [light]'. We might ask, as does Martin (1994), whether the complex-systems account of the body and its processes articulated in such everyday accounts promotes individualism and fatalism. This interpretation would be difficult in view of the narratives' own qualifications of the complex-systems model. All interviewees expressed questions or doubts about alternative therapies' efficacy or their assignment of personal blame for illness. Andy himself commented on the catch-22 hermeticism of a story that turned even depression and failures in his health into useful indicators of his spiritual progress. Thus the therapies were always slightly problematic in the narratives. They offered only momentary transcendence, a Utopian instant outside of AIDS panic, a transitory resistance to stigma, victimhood, passivity and fear. They seemed to provide more a way to live with AIDS panic than to erase it. Andy's visualisations, for example, though temporarily effective, had to be endlessly repeated, perpetually driving out dark with light.

Looking at the overall narrative structure of the interviews, it became clear that here, too, AIDS panic is always present but never either fully controlled or controlling. Andy, for instance, charted a conversion narrative: a life of distractions, devoid of deep significance; then the devastation of the diagnosis; then the gradual construction of a meaningful existence around spirituality – holistic cancer therapies, reflexology, shamanism. The entire recorded narrative placed itself outside HIV, as if to disavow it. Nevertheless, when the tape was switched off, another story got told. This was the tale of Andy's habitual marijuana use, how it damaged his immune system, and how it might compromise his otherwise sure hold on life. At this point, HIV's panic-inducing unpredictability and power regained a place in the interview.

A second narrative, very different, was that of Rachel. Her story since becoming ill was of a string of disappointments: Her work bored, stressed and finally exhausted her, friends neglected her, her mother misunderstood her, doctors failed her and AIDS service organisations depressed her. Each subplot's close was followed by another enraged mini-narrative of desperate search, almost as if they were all the same story. This story of utter negativity seemed at first to be spinning endlessly in AIDS panic. But even here there were moments when the panic was mitigated. In an aside, Rachel mentioned a man she had met at a drop-in, who had recovered from the condition now debilitating her. Later she noted how her mother's incomprehension actually helped her, giving her a partial escape from HIV. At the end, she described (ironic but hopeful) writing to a faith-healer. Even the repetitions in her narrative, driven by an anger so strong as to seem independent of particular events, maintained a sense that something else, beyond the horror of AIDS, was possible.

It is not helpful, I think, to try to resolve these narratives' contradictions. We are not trying to find out which strand had most to do with the speaker's life (as we would if we took the interviews as reflections of a separate lived reality), or which strand is textually the stronger (as we might if we were hunting down the interviews' 'real meaning'). Instead a psychologist approaching HIV through narrative would want simply to explore how these double meanings worked together to maintain AIDS panic at the same time as enabling a hopeful, healthy life often largely dissociated from AIDS.

CONCLUSION

Within the psychology of HIV, it is the suppression rather than the indulgence of AIDS panic that seems dominant. I have tried, following Deleuze and Guattari's (1987)[11] notion of wrong but productive readings, to 'misread' AIDS panic, usually something that we want to dispel or overcome, as an entity that psychologists working around HIV should remember, not forget. The discourse of an enlarging viral panic encourages such remembering. So too does the perpetual, though contained, presence of AIDS panic in interviews with seropositive people.

Paula Treichler (1989: 70) calls us to live with HIV in a dual way, recognising but not paralysed by its dangers, listening to AIDS science but not privileging it, and resisting discursive certainties of existing discourses: seduced neither by the excesses of AIDS panic itself, nor by the possibility of repressing that panic. The interviews I have described demonstrate that doubled life. A psychology that itself took on this duality might be able to address more productively the subjective effects of HIV.

NOTES

1 The most notable instance is consciousness, which has recently become a topic of increased speculation in biology, psychology and physics (see Edelman, 1987; Dennett, 1991; Penrose, 1994: 348ff; Changeux and Connes, 1995.).
2 These narratives often coexist within discourses of the body. Those of improvement and science are frequently interwoven, as in medicine. Despite the fact that science largely supersedes religion, the two narratives continue to conflict – as around abortion – or act in parallel, each feeding the authority of the other – around abortion, again, and in debates about medical advances in promoting reproduction and staving off death (see Friedman and Squire, 1998).
3 In medicine, this research is conducted at the forefront of virology and immunology, themselves cutting-edge fields (Patton, 1989; Treichler, 1989).
4 Even this field at times seems to divert or simplify panic, in injunctions towards wholly positive thinking or images, or in efforts to convert mourning into political organisation, as Bersani (1989) and Marshall (1991) suggest.
5 This chapter considers activist and educational discourses around HIV/AIDS only tangentially. For important considerations, see Crimp (1989), Marshall (1991), Patton (1995) and Sherry (1993).
6 At the same time television AIDS narratives display some other general cultural patterns, replaying homosexuality as effeminacy, oscillating between belief in

(and scepticism about) science, interested in the law as a story that makes sense of intractable issues. Treichler's (1993) discussion of *An Early Frost* notes the legitimising power of the protagonist being a lawyer. A more thoroughgoing example is *Philadelphia*'s use both of this trope and of a narratively structuring 'trial film' form.

7 At a greater remove, they also resonate with nineteenth-century accounts of tuberculosis (Sontag, 1988).

8 Again, the stringent policing of disease has earlier precedents in TB (Rothman, 1994) and syphilis.

9 Viruses have taken over from germs in cultural fears of illness. Panic narratives of bacterial illness follow a similar pattern, as Garrett's (1995) book indicates. Bacteria, treatable and more easily visualised, both scientifically and popularly, can perhaps more safely support a lurid myth of pathology, as with the flesh-eating scares of the early 1990s. With viruses, 'invisible invaders' as one book title (Radetsky, 1991) has it, the horror seems to lie more with what is unknown and unseen – source, transmission and the virus itself (rather than its effects). However the categories overlap; some bacterial phenomena offer the same uncertainties of nature, origin and spread to the cultural imaginary, and the horror of viral effects, particularly when these are fatal, remains a subtext always ready to surface.

10 However, interviewees worked with different notions of signification. Some used language to present the material scientific truth of their bodies; some described other, psychic realities; some were concerned most with how the story sounded or how it hung together.

11 Deleuze and Guattari's metaphor for such misreading – apt in this context, where AIDS panic is largely homosexualised and universally laden with horror – is the text's impregnation with a monster child, performed by an approach 'from behind' (1987).

REFERENCES

Altman, L. (1995) No-one Can Say Why Virus Striking Zaire is so Deadly, *New York Times*, 13 May, pp. 1, 5.

Amaro, H. (1993) Women's Reproductive Choices in the Age of AIDS. In C. Squire (ed.), *Women and AIDS: Psychological Perspectives*, London: Sage.

——(1995) Love, Sex and Power: Considering Women's Realities in HIV Prevention, *American Psychologist*, 50, 437–447.

Bersani, L. (1989) Is the Rectum a Grave? In D. Crimp (ed.), *AIDS: Cultural Analysis/Cultural Activism*, Boston, MA: MIT Press.

Boffin, T. and Gupta, S. (eds) (1990) *Ecstatic Antibodies*, London: River's Oram Press.

Brodbeck, G (1992) Body Odor: Gay Male Semiotics and *L'écriture féminine*. In David Porter (ed.), *Between Men and Feminism*, London: Routledge.

Carter, E. and Watney, S. (1989) *Taking Liberties: AIDS and Cultural Politics*, London: Serpent's Tail.

Changeux, J.-P. and Connes, A. (1995) *Conversations on Mind, Matter and Mathematics*, Princeton, NJ: Princeton University Press.

Connors, M. (1995) Response to 'Social Science Intervention Models for Reducing HIV Transmission'. In Institute of Medicine, *Assessing the Social and Behavioral Science Base for HIV/AIDS Prevention and Intervention*, workshop summary, background papers, Washington, DC.

Creed, B. (1987) From Here to Modernity: Feminism and Postmodernism, *Screen*, 28(2), 47–67.

Crimp, D. (ed.) (1989) *AIDS: Cultural Analysis/Cultural Activism*, Boston, MA: MIT Press.

de Certeau, M. (1984) The Practice of Everyday Life. Berkeley, CA: California University Press.

Deleuze, G. and Guattari, F. (1987) *A Thousand Plateaux: Capitalism and Schizophrenia*, Minneapolis, MN: Minnesota University Press.

Dennett, D. (1991) *Consciousness Explained*, New York: Little, Brown.

Dent, G. (1992) Black Pleasure, Black Joy. In G. Dent (ed.), *Black Popular Culture*, Seattle, WA: Dia Center for the Arts/Bay Press.

Doane, M.A. (1990) Technophilia: Technology, Reproduction and the Feminine. In M. Jacobus, E. Fox Keller and S. Shuttleworth (eds), *Body/Politics*, London: Routledge.

Edelman, G. (1987) *Neural Darwinism*, New York: Basic Books.

——(1993) The Mirror and the Tank. In T. Murphy and S. Poirier (eds), *Writing AIDS*, New York: Columbia University Press.

Flora, J., Maibach, E. and Holtgrave, D. (1995) Communication Campaigns for HIV Prevention: Using Mass Media in the Next Decade. In Institute of Medicine, *Assessing the Social and Behavioral Science Base for HIV/AIDS Prevention and Intervention*, workshop summary, background papers, Washington, DC.

Foucault, M. (1979) *History of Sexuality*, vol. 1. London: Allen Lane.

Friedman, E. and Squire, C. (1998) *Morality USA: Representations of Morality in Contemporary US Culture*, Minneapolis, MN: Minnesota University Press.

Garrett, L. (1995) *The Coming Plague*, New York: Farrar, Straus and Giroux.

Gilman, S.L. (1988) *Disease and Representation: Images of Illness from Madness to AIDS*, Ithaca, NY: Cornell University Press.

Hanson, E. (1991) The Undead. In D. Fuss (ed.), *Inside/Out*, New York: Routledge.

Harding, S. (1986) *The Science Question in Feminism*, Ithaca, NY: Cornell University Press.

Horton, R. (1995) Infection: The Global Threat, *New York Review of Books*, 6 April, pp. 24–27.

Institute of Medicine (1995) *Assessing the Social and Behavioral Science Base for HIV/AIDS Prevention and Intervention*, workshop summary, background papers, Washington, DC.

Jacobus, M., Fox Keller, E. and Shuttleworth, S. (eds) (1990) Introduction. In *Body/Politics*, London: Routledge.

Joseph, S. (1992) *The Dragon Within*, New York: Carroll and Graf.

Juhasz, A. (1993) Knowing AIDS Through the Televised Science Documentary. In C. Squire (ed.), *Women and AIDS: Psychological Perspectives*, London: Sage.

Kobasa, S. (1991) Aids Volunteering. In D. Nelkin, D. Willis and S. Parris (eds), *AIDS: A Disease of Society*, Cambridge: Cambridge University Press.

Marcus, L. (1987) Enough About You, Let's Talk About Me: Recent Autobiographical Writing, *New Formations*, 1, 77–94.

Marshall, S. (1991) The Contemporary Political Use of Gay History: The Third Reich. In Bad Object-Choices (ed.), *How do I Look? Queer Film and Video*, Seattle, WA: Bay Press.

Martin, E. (1994) *Fragile Bodies*, Boston: Beacon Press.

Murphy, T. and Poirier, S. (1993) *Writing AIDS: Gay Literature, Language and Analysis*, New York: Columbia University Press.

Patton, C. (1989) *Inventing AIDS*, New York: Routledge.

——(1993) 'With Champagne and Roses': Women at Risk from/in AIDS Discourse. In C. Squire (ed.), *Women and AIDS: Psychological Perspectives*, London: Sage.

——(1995) *Fatal Error*, New York: Routledge.

Penrose, R. (1994) *Shadows of the Mind*, Oxford: Oxford University Press.

Preston, R. (1992) Crisis in the Hot Zone, *New Yorker*, 26 October, pp. 58–81.

——(1994) *The Hot Zone*, New York: Random House.

Radetsky, P. (1991) *Invisible Invaders*, New York: Little, Brown.

Revkin, A. (1995) New Lethal Illness Carried by Ticks is Identified, *New York Times*, 12 July, pp. 1, B2.

Ricapito, M. (1995) Creeping Back into Vogue, *New York Times Art and Leisure*, 13 August, pp. 11, 18.

Riley, D. (1988) *Am I That Name? Feminism and the Category of 'Women' in History*, Minneapolis, MN: Minnesota University Press.

Rothman, S. (1994) *Living in the Shadow of Death*, New York: Basic Books.

Ryan, F. (1994) The Forgotten Plague: How the Battle Against Tuberculosis Was Won – and Lost, New York: Little, Brown.

Sherry, M. (1993) The Language of War in AIDS Discourse. In T. Murphy and S. Poirier (eds), *Writing AIDS: Gay Literature, Language and Analysis*, New York: Columbia University Press.

Shilts, R. (1987) *And the Band Played on*, New York: St Martin's Press.

Sontag, S. (1988) *AIDS and its Metaphors*, London: Farrar, Straus and Giroux.

Squire, C. (1995) *Group Portraits: HIV Support Groups*, report, Nuffield Foundation.

Tashakkion, A. and Thompson, V. (1992). Predictors of Intention to Take Precautions Against AIDS Among College Students, *Journal of Applied Social Psychology*, 22, 736–753.

Treichler, P. (1989) AIDS, Homophobia and Biomedical Discourse: An Epidemic of Signification. In D. Crimp (ed.), *AIDS: Cultural Analysis/Cultural Activism*, Boston, MA: MIT Press.

——(1993) AIDS Narratives on Television: Whose Story? In T. Murphy and S. Poirier (eds), *Writing AIDS: Gay Literature, Language and Analysis*, New York: Columbia University Press.

5 Screaming under the bridge

Masculinity, rationality and psychotherapy

Stephen Frosh

INTRODUCTION

In recent years, the influence of feminist thinking on psychology, psychoanalysis and systems theory has come to be felt in analyses of masculinity as well as femininity (e.g. Seidler, 1989, 1991; Mason and Mason, 1990; Segal, 1990; Frosh, 1994). These analyses, for all their differences, have converged on a vision of masculinity as something surprisingly fragile. It is as if this entity of which we might once have been so confident, this dominant force in the world, has no substance to hold it together, no definite and permanent reality. Rather than men being sure-footed and imperious in our identity, constructivist perspectives in social, psychoanalytic and systemic thinking have revealed us as slippery, furtive creatures, unsure about the grounds for our continuing domination of social structures, unclear about our role in work, parenting or loving, uncertain about what it means to 'be a man'.

In this chapter, I will explore the relationship between the destabilising impact of the feminist critique and the possibility of alternative discursive constructions of 'masculinity'. In particular, I will argue that a useful contrast can be made between a narrow rendering of masculine 'rationality' and a notion of 'the body' as a site for the eruption of irrational, apparently unwilled impulses. This idea is well expressed by Julia Kristeva's concept of the 'semiotic' as the disruptive underside of (linguistic) experience. I will also suggest that the body, being repressed in conventional masculinity, has ways of making itself felt. Sometimes this can be seen happening in the context of therapy, and I shall provide two examples of therapeutic interchanges in which some such thing seems to occur.

UPSETTING THE RATIONAL MAN

In large part, the contemporary deconstruction of masculinity has gone hand in hand with the growth of a postmodern sensibility that challenges the taken-for-granted superiority of *rationality*, with which masculinity has historically been closely connected (Seidler, 1994). The 'discovery' that an obsessive concern for rationality operates at the cost of an integrated response to experience is one which has come as difficult news to many men, because it opens us out to all the confusions of feeling and uncertainties of being that are supposed to characterise the 'feminine'. Nevertheless, this is a genuine contemporary (re)discovery: however powerful an instrument for making sense of the world rationality may be, there is only so far one can go with it before it starts to fall apart. In particular, the intrusions of what might, tendentiously, be called 'the unconscious' into everyday life serve as a constant reminder of the fragility of the rational carapace under which men strive to shelter.

This querying of the status of rationality is linked to the upheavals of modernity and the confusions of the postmodern sensibility. Each of us, as a human subject, is faced with the need to find a series of identities that can map on to the fluctuations of the contemporary cultural environment. At the extreme, as personal and cultural identities are called into question by globalisation, technological change and the breakdown of traditional mechanisms of order, a resurgent irrationality comes to the surface. This can be seen in the ravages of the new nationalism spawned by the passing of recent political monoliths, in the growth of fundamentalism as a force on the world stage, and in the multiplication of 'alternative' religions, lifestyle groups, and psychotherapies. It can also be observed in some celebrations of postmodernism, in which fragmentation and excess seem triumphant (see Frosh, 1991).

What is clear from the dangerous way in which this new irrationalism often operates is that it is necessary to develop ways to deal with the breakdown of rationality and the revelation of the importance of the irrational – particularly the importance of emotion – without abandoning completely the struggle to maintain an ethical order grounded in experience and available for inspection and symbolisation. What is doomed to explode under the pressure of its own contradictions is not reason *per se*, but a form of rationalism that attempts to write off huge chunks of experience as meaningless. Rationality itself, defined loosely as the attempt to make meaning out of experience, should therefore not be abandoned, but rather *extended* to encompass the sphere of the irrational – emotion, anxiety, creativity, love and fear of the other. In some ways, this parallels the traditional goal of psychoanalysis, that of bringing unconscious material to light so that it can be worked on, integrated into the system of the psyche, and placed under the general command of reason. Not that this is ever completely possible: as Žižek (1991) has compellingly demonstrated, the anxiety produced by the Real – by those aspects of experience which are unavailable to symbolisation and which find their final destination in death – is always with us, arising out of the suspicion that something unknowable lurks around the corner. Nevertheless, to adapt Freud's famous formula concerning the transformation of 'hysterical misery into common unhappiness' (Breuer and Freud, 1895: 393), much is to be gained from the process of trying to symbolise the unsymbolisable, in order to make it part of the arena of human intercourse.

The deconstruction of masculinity is a particularly apposite arena for the attempt to reclaim the irrational and put it into words. Rationality and control of self and others go together as aspects of masculine mastery, treating experience as controllable and homogeneous, amenable to domination and to the power of the will. Masculinist ideology idealises this logic of rational order, in which all things are subject to the imposition of an organising power, and contrasts it with the apparent chaos and unpredictability of emotionally driven disorder. This logic in turn is part of a wider series of contrasts that include science versus nature, instrumentality versus expressiveness, and masculine versus feminine – all contrasts in which the second term presents a threat to the first, and therefore has to be dominated. Consequently, the dawning realisation that science and instrumentality cannot be relied upon, and that those subjugated entities (such as women) which have been dominated and silenced might be finding their voice, puts masculinity into turmoil as well.

As traditional masculine sureties dissolve, what men are often faced with is the sense that we have no arguments left. It is as if the premise upon which Western masculine identity has been based, a premise concerned with separateness, self-sufficiency and self- (as well as other-) control, is no longer sustainable. Putting things in order, using language instrumentally, repressing emotion and avoiding intimacy – these characteristics of masculine self-identification now do not look like good bets for survival. This is particularly true of survival in relationships, where demands for obedience are more likely than ever to meet resistance, and where reciprocity implies emotional sharing and nurturing and a capacity to tolerate emotion in oneself and others.

There are various ways of conceptualising this new situation, reflected for example in debates about the 'phallus' (Frosh, 1994), romantic love (Chodorow, 1995) or fathering (Samuels, 1993). The idea being worked with here, however, is that what is required of men now is a means of symbolising the body. This idea takes 'the body' as emblematic of that aspect of human experience which is not willed, yet is intrinsic to our being. A central attribute of masculinist ideology is to oppose the body in this sense, and the emotion associated with it, in order to maintain the fantasy that everything can be controlled. When the body is recognised, it tends to be in another discourse, one in which it is the instrument of the will, to be honed and worked upon so that it will be able to achieve what is expected of it, for example in war or sport. Its illnesses and its emotions, its uncontrollable aspects, are kept out of sight, straightforwardly denied or opposed. Thinking psychoanalytically here, what is going on in repudiating the body may be a continuing refutation of the power of the mother, of whom the boy was once part, towards whom he was dependent, and from whom he needs to distance himself in order to construct his ever-fragile masculine identity. The fantasy at work here is that in relieving himself of the body, pretending that it has no value as an element in a speaking subjectivity, the male can also be free of the messy dependency associated with femininity – can, once again, be in control of emotion, irrationality and the anxiety which they produce. This is an important aspect of the seeming impossibility of creating a truly reflexive theory of masculinity: men's own experience is left unconstruable because masculinity is based on its repression.

In the contemporary psychoanalytic literature on gender development, a substantial critique of the notion that boys must repudiate the mother in order to grow into their masculine identity has been put forward by numerous writers. Benjamin (1995) is representative of a notable tendency to argue that the lack to be found in the boy is not so much because of his loss of his mother, but because of his failure to find a father who is present in any form other than as a symbolic prohibition – who is really there for the boy, who is in the positive sense 'embodied'. The splitting entailed in this leaves everyone impoverished.

> And so it was no accident that Freud's theory gave the woman a son to love, in his view the only unambivalent love. To the mother was granted the fulfilment of the wish for identificatory love not just in relation to her father but in ideal love of her son; to the son was given the grandiosity that was mirrored by the mother who renounced it. But Freud's story also gave the son an ideal love, a forever unrequited love of the father who cast him out as a murderous rival.
>
> (Benjamin, 1995: 114)

What is needed for non-polarised gender development, Benjamin argues, is the possibility of an 'overinclusive' identification with both the same-sex and the other-sex parent. For the boy, this is too often inhibited by the failure of the father to allow an identificatory love to form. In the terms of the argument here, one could say that the lack of an embodied, loving father leads to the reduction of masculine identity to an abstract, disembodied ideal; the body, split off into the mother, is rejected as a consequence.

The 'body' in all this is something that, through its materiality and specificity, demands that the abstractions of 'pure thought' are abandoned and that something muddled, messy and uncontrollable is allowed into the symbolisation of experience. One necessary component of a reformulated theory of the body and a reconstructed masculinity is a language in which this symbolisation can take place. In contemporary theory, the fullest conceptualisation of this kind, of the way the body can be a potentially subversive force, can be found in Kristeva's (1980) notion of the 'semiotic'. In terms of language, the semiotic refers to the rhythms and sounds that flesh out the purely linguistic elements of speech and writing. More generally, the semiotic can be thought of as that dimension of experience linked with and underpinning the symbolic order of language and culture, but also constantly threatening to disrupt it.

> The semiotic is a set of pre-signifying impulses and drives that chaotically circulate in and through the infant's body . . . In the broadest terms, the

semiotic is the input of the undirected body, while the Symbolic is the regulated use and organised operations of that body in social production.

(Grosz, 1992: 195)

It will be apparent from this that the semiotic is easily regarded as a register for traditional images of femininity – bodily, chaotic, made marginal by the operations of the symbolic order, unable to speak its own name. Nevertheless, while acknowledging the shared marginality of the semiotic with the feminine, Kristeva insists on its pre-gendered nature, making it a possible site of resistance and subversion in all subjective experience – male as well as female. *All* subjects are infiltrated both by the symbolic and the semiotic, subjected to the law but also 'ruptured by the boundless play of semiotic drives' (Elliott, 1992: 222). The continuing existence of the semiotic offers a prospect for heterogeneity and disruption within every human subject, male or female, and this prospect can always be glimpsed somewhere, whether in art, in language, in madness or in dreams.

THERAPY, NARRATIVE, GENDER

One powerful component of therapeutic encounters is their capacity to disrupt the expectations and preset, rationalised stories with which the participants in therapy – therapists and clients – face one another. This presumably has something to do with the way the therapeutic arena functions as a space which is both alienating and deeply personal. The client or clients talk about themselves, and this talk then becomes an object to be revolved and examined in the process of therapy – that is, the clients' selves and relationships become constructed in discourse as more or less material entities. This means they can be worked on, a process which is highly charged emotionally rather than being purely cognitive, because our investments in ourselves-in-discourse are very deep and intense. When therapy has an impact, it allows a person to take back a transformed version of the material originally offered up for examination; fully achieved, this creates a new internal structure available for the next round of the cycle. This whole procedure might be thought of as alienating because the *subjects* of therapy are taken as *objects* of inspection or reflection, by themselves as well as by the therapist, and a division appears between the 'I' who does the inspecting and the 'I' who is inspected. But as the two re-fuse, there is also the potential for a deeply personal, hence non-alienated, crisis to occur. In Lacanian terms, the movement of the subject's discourse from the Imaginary in which it is originally couched, to the Symbolic dimension in which it returns, mediated by language, may face her or him with an experience of 'interruption' in which what was taken to be true of the self can no longer be sustained.

In different ways, this notion of how therapy operates is common to many forms of psychotherapy, including both psychoanalytic and systemic work. Typically, the person in therapy produces a series of often partially suppressed representations of self and others which can become manifest in discourse in forms that are, to varying degrees, fluid or fixed. When they are fluid, they are sometimes subversively open to question and to change; when they are fixed, they may block the possibility of transformation across a wide range of different discursive problems, including those of gender. But what might be hoped, particularly in the light of the discussion above concerning the linked rigidity and fragility of masculine identity, is that therapy could offer a place for expression of the subjugated voice of the semiotic – that is, an arena where the rational organisation of masculine character armour can be wrong-footed, flipped over judo-style, allowing something else to break through. This 'something else' would be expected to be a crisis-ridden recognition of the inadequacy of the rational posturing of masculine identity, particularly in relation to its inability to articulate emotional states. Language should break down, something should appear in the crack; a little bit of the 'real' or a little murmur of bodily impulse or confusion – something non-literal, non-representational; something problematic. If masculinity deconstructs, it should implode, revealing an underside which is not merely 'feminine', but non-rational and possibly gender-transgressive.

Among many contemporary psychoanalytic and systemic therapists, the general conditions for this kind of analysis and for the practice flowing from it have been set by an encounter with postmodernism that has led to an assertion of the primacy of narrative approaches to therapeutic work (for example, White and Epston, 1990; Parry, 1991; Hoffman, 1993; Wax, 1995). The particular version of deconstructive narrative practice adopted by such therapists has focused on the production of alternative narratives to those with which people enter therapy; alternatives that may make possible new ways of perceiving and feeling about experience. This approach contests the traditional 'expert rationalist' model of therapy, in which the therapist knows something about the 'truth' underlying the patient's or family's conflicts and can decode this truth to reveal the right path for further development. Instead, postmodernist therapists argue that there is no one particular truth concerning an experience – no right path – and no particular expert discoverer or interpreter for any other person. Instead, there is only the possibility of a more free discursive activity, a more vibrant recognition of the complexity of people's accounts and of the very powerful sense in which these accounts can be said to constitute experience.

There is an important debate to be had about the extent to which this emphasis on linguistic productivity makes contemporary therapy genuinely postmodern – especially if postmodernism is understood as a revelation of the insufficiency of language and the impossibility of rationality (Frosh, 1995). In particular, some of what passes for postmodern *family* therapy seems to miss the point that many of the conflicts producing psychological distress act at the edge of language – that is, they cannot be articulated and so continue to work as a source of irrational alienness within individuals or family groups. The task of the therapist here is usually not one of remaining silent in acknowledgement of the meaninglessness of linguistic display, which is the implication of at least some postmodernist analyses, but rather it is to struggle to resymbolise, to put into words that which has not been, or cannot be, spoken. This is an old-fashioned and pre-postmodernist insight within psychotherapy: the point of therapy is to make meaning known.

Despite this critique of its postmodernist credentials, however, the narrative or discursive approach in therapy offers a way into the articulation of alternative renderings or readings of masculinity, precisely because it opens up a space for the inspection and contained questioning of received assumptions. As masculinity comes into focus in this form of therapy, the notion that it is somehow fixed and has its form determined by pre-given forces is subverted by the suggestion that another story might be there to be told – that something else might be operating to make men behave the way we do. Sometimes, it takes only a small and tentative suggestion, a tiny push, for the walls to come tumbling down.

THE MOMENT THE BODY BREAKS THROUGH: SOME ILLUSTRATIVE MATERIAL[1]

The argument above is that the deconstruction of masculinity apparent in contemporary Western culture might also be seen in a powerful way in therapy, and that the likely form this will take is as moments of breakdown in rationality, followed by the gradual articulation of an apparently non-rational position. The particular nature of this position will be as an expression of the 'semiotic': a breakthrough of the body into consciousness, an experience of being governed by something outside oneself which is nevertheless representative of the 'truth' of one's emotional experience. In therapy which is attuned to these gender dynamics, it may be possible to pick up on these semiotic breakthroughs and find ways of resymbolising them, to produce a new positioning in masculinity which is also emotionally more complete.

What follows are two illustrations of points early on in therapy in which some such non-linguistic voice can perhaps be heard – moments of breakdown or breakthrough in which something unexpected happens and the preset discourse of the men involved is uncannily subverted. The examples are taken from transcripts of first sessions in family therapy, with two different families and two different therapists. The first example is from a session with a male therapist. The parents (Mr and Mrs X) have presented themselves very conventionally in gender terms. Mrs X is worried about her younger son, Paul, who is a bright boy in trouble at school, particularly for fighting and wildness. She thinks he might be unhappy and it might be her fault, because she does not offer him enough and also because the family is too isolated socially for the children's good. Mr X presents himself as brusque and to-the-point; he thinks the school is the main problem. He acknowledges that Paul is a 'handful', but believes the school should be able to manage him and that their complaint about Paul signals the school's inadequacy. He has only agreed to come to therapy to appease the school, expecting the therapist to say there is nothing wrong with Paul. He cuts across his wife's talk a good deal to emphasise this external location of the problem.

As the session goes on, however, it becomes apparent that Paul is lonely and unhappy; that he feels he is a monster who cannot do anything right and is always knocking people over, figuratively and in actuality. Towards the end of the session, the therapist asks him who he thinks he takes after, eliciting no response. There is then the following sequence.

THERAPIST	If you could think of somebody who was really sympathetic, really on your side, how would they describe you, what would they say about you?
PAUL	You'd have to ask *her* that. I don't know what to say . . .
THERAPIST	Well, no, I was just thinking about what *you* would imagine: somebody who likes you, is on your side, what would they say about you?
PAUL	(*Heavy sigh*)
THERAPIST	Somebody who doesn't want to just be critical of you, who wants really to think about you seriously.
PAUL	(*Long pause*) Ummm . . .
THERAPIST	It's a difficult question . . .
PAUL	If they were in a good mood . . . little terror (*laughs*).
THERAPIST	Sorry? You have good moods . . . ? Oh, if they're in a good mood . . .
PAUL	Little terror.
THERAPIST	They'd say you were a little terror. Right.
PAUL	(*To father*) You say that, don't you? Admit it, you do, don't you?
FATHER	A holy terror, yes.
PAUL	A holy terror.
THERAPIST	A holy terror. And that would be somebody who was sympathetic to you, who liked you, would say that about you?
PAUL	Yes.
THERAPIST	OK. (*To parents*) Would you agree with that, is that a . . . fair statement, if somebody were sympathetic to him, they would say that?
MOTHER	Yes.
FATHER	I wouldn't, no. There are times when . . . There's outbursts . . . Did you ever see the film *Cabaret*? Do you remember Liza Minnelli under the railway bridge?
THERAPIST	No . . . (?)

FATHER   It didn't impinge on your memory? It stuck with me because he said this to me when he was at infant school . . .

MOTHER   Oh, that's right.

FATHER   Liza Minnelli went under the bridge when the train went over and she screamed at the top of her voice to release the tension, and he often said to me that at infant school he felt like standing up and screaming. [That] seems to have stopped? . . . Do you still do that?

PAUL   Still do it now.

FATHER   . . . It has to be some release, of some description.

PAUL   If we're all in one room, sometimes I say, 'Can I just go out now?' and I go out, I go to my bedroom, I close the door and I have a great big shout.

THERAPIST   Where does that tension come from?

PAUL   And all the windows . . .

FATHER   I don't know . . .

PAUL   I just can't hold it back . . .

FATHER   . . . In some ways he's a *doppelgänger*. In fact I say to [my wife] at a certain age I'm going to disappear and you'll have to take over completely. I can understand that frustration with . . . in some ways the boredom of life, at times. Things crowd in on you and you have to break the pattern of whatever you're doing, do something different. And I suspect it's . . . a fraction of this . . . and it may occupy half an hour, it may occupy a day, but once that pressure is released, then you can follow a normal path. And I suspect that's what's happening to him.

There are obviously numerous frames within which this episode can be placed, affecting the interpretation of its meaning. Clearly, gender is not the topic of conversation. Nevertheless, there is a gendered element in the passage that bears on the breakdown of rationality and language in the terms developed earlier. The first thing to note is the explosion of emotional energy, linked to the father saying something about himself and his own feelings, in identification with his son. This explosion, like most such occurrences, comes with no preliminary gradient, as if Mr X suddenly finds his feelings breaking through and, either deliberately or involuntarily, does not hold them back. Is this a conventional masculine event? If there is meat in the general argument that the core characteristic of 'masculinity' is a rational representation of self and reality, then this moment of breakthrough can be interpreted as an eruption of the feminine into the masculine language of control. The semiotic dimension of experience – the rhythmic, bodily, maternally invoked underside of language – overwhelms, momentarily at least, the symbolic. Indeed, Mr X employs precisely the sexualised language of breakthrough and volcanic eruption, of pressure and explosion, that is embodied in the emotional tone of the interaction. Straightforwardly, if crassly, the rhythmic associations of the feminine semiotic transgress the boundedness of masculine linguistic control.

Of course, this account re-enacts the stereotypes of gender expressed in 'masculine' and 'feminine' divisions and is itself open to deconstruction. In the therapy itself, what is going on is not an adoption of a feminine mode of being, whatever that might mean, but a complex identificatory process that undermines the rigidity of Mr X's starting point. Having not taken up the question of who is like whom in the family, Mr X responds to an invitation to think sympathetically about his son first with irony ('holy terror'), but then with an affiliation with his trouble which is actually mediated by an identification with a female figure – Liza Minnelli, observed screaming as a train bangs on past, in a film (*Cabaret*) that itself trades on sexual ambiguity. This image has stayed with Mr X over a period of decades, and is clearly one that acts as a nodal point for reflection and self-scrutiny. The pressure of his life, its boredom and its depression, become condensed into the scream. This is a familiar and conventional phenomenological image, but it is a powerful one nevertheless; and it is an evocative moment in which self-boundaries give way to a howl of rage.

Is this a gendered phenomenon, or is the Liza Minnelli association an accidental one? In terms of the masculinity–rationality homology outlined above, it has to be counted as gendered, with particular emphasis on a special form of linguistic breakdown. Mr X's language, restricted and staccato for most of the session, is energised here by a sensation which most of the time is denied. To some extent it can be said that his language becomes embodied, that he speaks out of a richer symbolic than is usual for him. The scream, however, is altogether an antagonist of this symbolic; it is pure semiotic, it is the breakthrough of the undercurrent when words can no longer keep experience at bay. Mr X's association is to the outer limit of his self-knowledge, containing within it all that is lacking in his apparent mastery, all that is made missing by his attempts at control. The figure of the screaming woman is thus no accident in gender terms; it is a response to domination and also a hint at the lack of emotional contact which domination obscures. It is, therefore, a potential moment of breakdown in the carefully structured order of sexual difference.

The second illustration comes from an interview with a female therapist. Mr Y is a mental health professional who has come with his family (Mrs Y and two teenage sons) because of the physical fights he is getting into with the boys. He begins the session by saying that he is the 'problem', but then he develops a rhetoric of loyalty and privacy which positions his wife as unsupportive and possibly treacherous, because she confides in a female friend outside of the family. Under the guise of accepting responsibility for his violence, he develops an alternative and preconceived narrative in which he is insufficiently supported by his wife, who thus is not fulfilling her role. This idea is silently accentuated by the fact that Mr Y is black and an immigrant, thus potentially more isolated and deserving of an alliance from his white wife. Out of the initially disarming rhetorical strategy of accepting his status as an abuser, Mr Y thus alters the frame so that he can be seen as a victim, and this is placed in gendered terms in relation to appropriate husband and wife roles.

Having followed this trajectory, the therapist asks for a detailed account of an episode of violence. This produces a new reading of events. One son, Ray, has been describing how violence often begins over small issues, particularly disputes over television programmes. He then talks in graphic and disturbing terms about the most recent episode, which culminated in him smashing a favourite piece of his father's furniture and fighting with his father.

THERAPIST	And did you get injured by the fight?
RAY	Well he hit me in the head when we were doing that, and then when he came up and realised what had happened he pushed into my room and hit me in the face, and I had to go to casualty the next day because my jaw was hurting.
THERAPIST	Did that mean having X-rays and things . . . was there any breakage?
RAY	No.
THERAPIST	And were there big bruises?
RAY	No there was just bruising along here (*indicating chin line*). They didn't swell up.
THERAPIST	Right, and was your father injured too?
RAY	I don't know.
THERAPIST	Were you injured (*to Mr Y*)?
FATHER	No. (*Inaudible*) . . . He's . . . I kept on . . . I tried to restrain him before that . . . that was the first time I have felt that . . . we have always had, the children and I, have had a very physical, we are quite physical . . . we have cuddles and kisses and so on, but when it comes for me to chastise them I've chastised them but never . . . the first time I have lost complete control, that was the first time . . .
THERAPIST	That's very frightening, isn't it?
FATHER	Yes. Um, I have chastised, always I have control, this time I chastised I suddenly lost control and what was more frightening was . . .
THERAPIST	And was there just you and Ray in the house, or was there anybody else around?
FATHER	Everybody else . . . Mrs Y has . . . for the past few months she has . . . consciously not . . . intervened. So when I went upstairs – oh, no that's not true, she does intervene sort of . . . probably I'll later explain . . . in an odd sort of way . . .

THERAPIST   So, there were just the two of you having this fight?

FATHER   Not a fight. I was trying to restrain Ray, but when I heard upstairs, the bang was . . . something got damaged . . . and I went along and saw . . . and . . . I suddenly lost control of myself and I slapped him, and I realised . . .

THERAPIST   If I asked Ray, would he think it was a slap or a punch, which do you think . . . ?

RAY   No, it was a slap.

THERAPIST   Slap.

FATHER   But what was more frightening was I had . . . it was not out of chastising, it was more, it was literally loss of control.

Again, there are a number of interpretive frames which could in principle be employed, but the focus in this interchange is on what happens to the discourse of the father. As in the previous example, there is nothing in the extract that overtly deals with gender; rather it is concerned more generally with violence and loss of control. This of course is a characteristically problematic issue for men, and one would have little difficulty in exploring the way breakdown of control and bursting through of rage is an indication of the masculine problematic of dealing with emotion, intimacy and frustration. All this is present in the extract, as it is too in the session as a whole.

But one additional element arises out of this rage/control dynamic in the extract to suggest that, in addition to control breaking down, something else is breaking through, something transgressive in gender terms, yet also uncomfortably uncertain. Mr Y comments that

we have always had, the children and I, have had a very physical, we are quite physical . . . we have cuddles and kisses and so on, but when it comes for me to chastise them I've chastised them but never . . . the first time I have lost complete control, that was the first time.

As in the previous example, there is a failure of language here, but its form is different. Rather than articulating an image of the intrusion of the unspeakable into the realm of the symbolic (the scream), Mr Y *enacts* the breakdown through the incoherence and fragmentation of his own speech. He is attempting to articulate an economy of the physical that places him as warm and embracing – conventionally feminine in the context of teenage sons. But this economy has spiralled out of control; his repertoire of physical contact is not sufficiently subtly calibrated to allow him the full range of expression, and precisely because he has no emotional language he cannot convert his feelings into symbolisable form. What seems to happen is that his closeness with the boys also enables a passionate crossing-over into a violence which is experienced as uncontainable, because it cannot be put properly into words. All this is communicated, however, not so much in the content of his language as in its failure: he has no words, nor any body with which to fill the space created by their absence.

Mr Y himself comments at the beginning of the session that he is not trying to be 'macho' in taking responsibility for everything. He struggles throughout, however, not to think of himself as a failure, and deals with this threat by gender-stereotypic projections on to his wife and criticism of her role failure in not protecting him from a persecutory outside. In the extract given above, the new component is that the specificity and drama of the son's account faces Mr Y with the loss of his positive link with others, and with a sense of his own violence as an isolating force in his life. It is not his wife turning towards outsiders, but her turning away from him, that comes into focus; even more poignantly at this moment, it is the destruction of the intimate positive contact with his sons that faces him with a gaping loss. Masculinity is at issue here – all the material on control and violence is relevant. But what might be felt most intensely by Mr Y is the way the limitations of his masculine positioning are constraining him to drive his family away, when it is – at least consciously – intimacy with them to which he aspires. All his intentions, all his rationality, dissolve in the face of a rhythm, a background noise, that is inarticulable, perpetual and full of despair.

It is this background noise, this rhythmic pulsation, which comes to the fore as one starts to reconstruct masculinity. In the face of dissolving certainties concerning the nature of, and values appropriate to, masculinity, men have to seek alternative ways of being that are less likely to close off the possibilities of engagement with the actualities of the contemporary social environment. Tackling masculine violence is one central element in this process, as the two vignettes given above suggest. Clearly, this process involves a long and complex challenge to men to take responsibility for all the effects of our actions on others – to be less dependent in an infantile sense, more capable of recognising the hurt we cause. A central part of this challenge is to consider the ways in which the masculine denial of emotion and affiliation towards control – passed off as an alliance with rationality – produce disfigured and rage-filled encounters with others. In therapy, particularly where the therapeutic procedure is to focus on the generation of alternative narratives, there is a prospect that emotion and the irrational can be allowed to break through to disrupt the bleakness of the masculine denial.

Much of this hinges on the extent to which the body is allowed to speak as a site of resistance to the narrow rationalism that denies meaning to anything which is not instrumental and under control. 'Embodiment' has numerous connotations here, ranging from allowing space for dependence and intimacy to enjoyment of sensuality and unpredictability. It means integrating the abstract with the concrete; developmentally, for the boy, it means constructing masculine identities which do not have to be made secure by renunciation of the mother and all that she symbolises. It means finding words adequate to the articulation of something which is not easily codable; finding a rich language in which the semiotic can be felt, a poetic discourse of everyday life.

IN PLACE OF A CONCLUSION

This chapter began with an assertion of the problematic status of 'masculinity' under contemporary conditions, and a claim that this is linked with the need to find a new way of voicing the irrational without losing all semblance of reason. Through an invocation of the 'body' as a site of resistance to any narrow version of rationality, it was argued that the semiotic register of experience might at times break through to disrupt the discourse of rational masculinity. Sometimes, it was suggested, a highly charged emotional encounter of the kind observable in psychotherapy might become an arena in which this kind of disruptive/reconstructive work can take place. If the so-called crisis of masculinity is not to become a destructive howl of rage, work of this sort is necessary. Therapy does not always have this effect any more than writing does, but we all struggle on in our own ways, uneven, inconsistent and inconsequential as they may be.

NOTE

1 The work reported in this section has been carried out as part of a research project run in collaboration with Charlotte Burck at the Tavistock Clinic, London. Funds supporting the research were provided by the College Research Fund of Birkbeck College, University of London.

REFERENCES

Benjamin, J. (1995) Sameness and Difference: Toward an 'Over-Inclusive' Theory of Gender Development. In A. Elliott and S. Frosh (eds), *Psychoanalysis in Contexts*, London: Routledge.

Breuer, J. and Freud, S. (1895) *Studies on Hysteria*, Harmondsworth: Penguin (1974).

Chodorow, N. (1995) Individuality and Difference in How Women and Men Love. In A. Elliott and S. Frosh (eds), *Psychoanalysis in Contexts*, London: Routledge.

Elliott, A. (1992) *Social Theory and Psychoanalysis in Transition* Oxford: Blackwell.

Frosh, S. (1991) *Identity Crisis: Modernity, Psychoanalysis and the Self*, London: Macmillan.

——(1994) *Sexual Difference: Masculinity and Psychoanalysis*, London: Routledge.

——(1995) Postmodernism Versus Psychotherapy, *Journal of Family Therapy*, 17, 175–190.

Grosz, E. (1992) Kristeva, Julia. In E. Wright (ed.), *Feminism and Psychoanalysis: A Critical Dictionary*, Oxford: Blackwell.

Hoffman, L. (1993), *Exchanging Voices: A Collaborative Approach to Family Therapy*, London: Karnac.

Kristeva, J. (1980) *Powers of Horror*, New York: Columbia University Press (1982).

Mason, B. and Mason, E. (1990) Masculinity and Family Work. In R. Perelberg and A. Miller (eds), *Gender and Power in Families*, London: Routledge.

Parry, A. (1991), A Universe of Stories, *Family Process*, 30, 37–54.

Samuels, A. (1993) *The Political Psyche*, London: Routledge.

Segal, L. (1990) *Slow Motion: Changing Masculinities, Changing Men*, London: Virago.

Seidler, V. (1989) *Rediscovering Masculinity*, London: Routledge.

——(1991) *Recreating Sexual Politics*, London: Routledge.

——(1994) *Unreasonable Men*, London: Routledge.
Wax, M. (1995) How Secure are Grünbaum's *Foundations?*, *International Journal of Psychoanalysis*, 76, 547–556.
White, M. and Epston, D. (1990) *Narrative Means to Therapeutic Ends*, New York: Norton.
Žižek, S. (1991), *Looking Awry*, Cambridge, MA: MIT Press.

6 Adolescent bodies
Boy crazy memories and dreams

Janet Sayers

Adolescence marks a watershed in our embodiment as sexual beings. Yet this is often overlooked by psychologists – not least by psychoanalysts, despite Freud being one of the first to draw attention to the psychological impact of becoming embodied, in adolescence, as sexually mature. He arrived at his discoveries through analysing his own and others' memories, dreams and fictions about adolescence (e.g. Freud, 1896, 1899, 1907, 1919).

In this chapter I will draw on similar material. I will draw particularly on a three-part study involving interviews with women and men I have met through my work as a university lecturer and therapist, asking students in lectures anonymously to write down their adolescent memories, and arranging for students in two parallel single-sex state secondary schools to write down (again anonymously) their best-remembered recurring childhood and recent dreams.

I will quote examples from this study (in which I have, of course, changed all identifying details), together with examples from other autobiographical and fictional accounts of adolescence, to highlight three distinct but interrelated discourses in terms of which women and men, including psychoanalysts and feminists, write and talk about the experience of becoming sexually embodied in adolescence. I will focus specifically on what I will call discourses of disconnection, connection, and 'boy crazy' romance and grandiosity.

DISCONNECTIONS

Losing sight of his early discoveries regarding the formative impact of becoming sexually embodied in adolescence, Freud (e.g. 1923a) stressed in his later work the disconnection of the boy as a toddler from his mother on construing the absence of a penis in girls as signifying that, were he to realise his desire for sexual connection with his mother, he too might lose his penis as girls seem to have lost theirs. Freud's followers in the United States – the so-called 'US ego psychologists' – in turn argue that boys should disconnect and 'dis-identify' from the mother so as to forge a distinct male identity (e.g. Greenson, 1968).

Whether or not this is indeed necessary to their gender development, boys often arrive at adolescence depicting themselves as disconnected from their mothers. Several students from the boys' school in my study, for instance, but none from the girls' school, recounted recurring nightmares of being physically disconnected and separated from their mothers in early child-hood. A 17-year-old, for example, wrote:

> I used to have a dream about being separated from my mother as she was taking me to school. There was always a very strong sense of loss in this dream – it was particularly vivid, and at the same time quite frightening. It was a dream that reoccurred very frequently for some time.

Many men similarly recount their adolescent experience of the bodily changes involved in becoming sexually mature in terms of disconnection from their mothers and others. It was in these terms – in terms of being disconnected from talk with his parents about sex – that Jonathan, a Canadian lawyer whom I interviewed for this study, recounted his first wet dream, also disconnected and uncontained as regards his age and the season when it occurred. He said:

> I remember when I was 11 . . . it may have been later than 11 . . . probably in the spring . . . it might have been the winter. It could have been in the fall. I don't remember . . . I went to a party . . . We danced. I danced close to a very attractive girl. And, I was a kid, nobody had ever told me about wet dreams. I didn't know anything about anything. And that night I had my first wet dream, which was very disconcerting, because I didn't know anything about it. My father always told me about sex, but he was always a few years too late, so I thought something terrible had happened to me . . . I think I put two and two together. But it is very disconcerting not to know quite what's happening. I was clearly very sexually stimulated, but I think it was the first time that I'd ever kissed a girl, so it was kissing, sexual stimula-tion, and then just falling apart . . . [because] I didn't know what was happening. So it's embarassing, because it's just all over the place. It's upsetting because I wasn't sure if something was wrong with me, and it was rather pleasant. So it was a mixture of all these things together, and I think it was probably a bit shocking that this could happen.

Jonathan stressed that the experience was 'shocking', 'upsetting' and 'disconcerting' because he felt disconnected from talking with his parents about such things. He went on to tell me of his recurring high school night-mare of not being able to talk, of 'being in front of everyone, in a play, and not knowing what the words were'. He told me of his loneliness as a child and teenager, that he never had 'close friends, very close, just one person who was a friend'.

Others similarly recall their loneliness, disconnection and isolation from others in remembering their adolescent erections. Far from being able to talk about and share this experience with others at the time, they dwell on how they concealed it from them. For example, Alex, an accountant, told me how, sitting upstairs at the front of the bus coming home from school, and discovering he had an enormous erection, he immediately thought how he could best hide the fact from his fellow-passengers. Fearful of getting up lest they see what was happening to his body through his trousers, he preserved his distance. He stayed sitting even though this meant not getting off the bus when it arrived at his stop, and even though this meant being discovered by the bus conductor not to have the money necessary to pay the extra fare.

It is also in terms of disconnection with others that men recount memories of their more wayward adolescent sexual thoughts and fantasies. Gordon, a retired trade unionist, emphasised that he still could not connect or talk with others, including me, about them. He told me that, as a teenager, he suffered:

> complete lack of understanding of sexuality, its problems, masturbation, etc. These were terrific problems. I had no brothers and sisters . . . feelings of guilt. Um. Er. The physical needs which aren't answered. Fantasies which have to substitute for relations with the other sex.

When I asked whether he remembered these fantasies, he replied:

> Well, yes I do. But I don't think I would like to draw them in detail. They're pornography, aren't they? They're mental pornography really. I wouldn't like to elaborate. It would take being on the psychiatrist's couch with a compensatory £1000 cheque, and even then . . .

There was no way, he indicated, he would share his teenage sexual thoughts with me, just as there was no way he shared them with anyone else at the time.

Tom, a librarian in his mid-twenties, likewise told me of being cut off from talking with others about his sexual dreams and daydreams as a teenager. He told me how, in his early teens, he became obsessed with erotic images of women trussed up and killed, and of himself as masochistic victim of men's anal penetration and attack. Disconnecting and divorcing himself from talking with others about these images of his and others' embodiment as sexual beings – images that became all the more alarming and uncontained, perhaps, for not being talked about and shared – Tom resorted to writing down his fantasies in compendious notes and never-to-be-published novels.

Like Tom as a teenager, and protected by anonymity, several students from the boys' school in my study wrote down their sexual fantasies. Just as grown men often recall first having sex with partners they scarcely knew, and with whom they had no other connection (see e.g. Faulkenberry *et al.*, 1987), students in my study recounted dreams involving impersonal, empty surroundings, and sex with anonymous women, ending, as in the following account from a 15-year-old, in split-off, involuntary-seeming masturbation. He wrote that in his best-remembered recent dream:

I was in some kind of public transport, either a bus or a tube, when this really attractive girl came up to me and asked if I wanted to come round her house to meet her friends. This place was massive, but there wasn't any people there. Then I forget what happens for a while, but I can remember performing oral sex with this woman in a '69' position. I woke up in the middle of the night and found myself masturbating.

More often students from the boys' school cut themselves off from even the minimal connection – with their unknown reader – involved in writing down their fantasies. A sizeable minority (eleven out of eighty-eight of the 14- and 15-year olds) elected not to write down their recent dreams. One 14-year-old wrote, 'The only ones I can remember are embarassing.'

Just as this boy admitted that embarrassment stopped him writing down his dreams, teenage boys in other studies speak of being disconnected from talking honestly with their peers about their sexual thoughts and feelings. Boys between the ages of 14–16 attending a working-class school in Glasgow recently told a researcher:

If you ask any boy if he's a virgin every one will say 'No', 'I done it on holiday', and all that. That's the pure one: 'I done it on holiday at Ayr' . . . You would not go and have a big conversation amongst all your mates . . . You may come out with a joke and that. You never have a pure conversation at all . . . You don't go and pour your heart out and all that. You keep your feelings to yourself.

(Wight, 1994: 721, 722)

Men and boys not only describe being disconnected from talking honestly with others in adolescence about their sexual feelings and experiences. They also describe being disconnected from themselves, particularly from their bodies. They describe themselves, in adolescence, in terms analogous to the mind–body dualism of Cartesian individualism.

The psychoanalyst Anna Freud adopted similar terms in writing about adolescence. She argued that young people, experiencing what she termed the increased 'libido' of puberty as out of control, often disconnect and distance themselves mentally from their sexual drives. They divorce thought and action. Their impressive reasoning ability, she added, is often impelled by longing to 'master' their instincts 'on a different psychic level' (Freud, 1936: 162). She also observed that many adults in analysis remember adolescence in similarly disconnected terms. They remember the facts, including presumably the bodily facts, shorn from their accompanying passions (Freud, 1958).

Two young men in my study graphically depicted this adolescent divide of bodily fact and psychological feeling. A 17-year-old wrote:

I dreamt that I was asleep and standing by my self watching me sleep. Speech bubbles appeared. They said 'IS THIS ME?' At this stage the person who said the above woke up and was standing by another 'me' asleep. Again the 'This is me' reappeared and this kept on happening until I (real me) woke up!

A 29-year-old postgraduate student similarly represented the bodily and psychological changes he remembered from early puberty as disconnected. He tabulated them under two separate headings:

Physical	*Mental*
Developing hairy legs	Always falling in love
Permanent erection!	Becoming very political
Aching legs	Feeling isolated
Sweating feet	Sleeping a lot – always tired
Voice breaking	Always thinking about sex/women

In theorising adolescence, Anna Freud (e.g. 1936, 1958) described not only the adolescent's disconnection of his mind and body, she also described adolescents' disconnection of their past and present selves. She recounted how, faced with the bodily desire, mobilised by puberty, to have sex with those they have known from infancy – namely members of their immediate family – adolescents defend against this desire by severing themselves psychologically from their childhood attachments. They cling to others instead. They often identify with them in the process. In recounting this development, Anna Freud drew on the account by her colleague Hélène Deutsch (1934) of women and men who become increasingly divided in their teens between a hollow inner self and an 'as if' external self based on imitating others.

Many years later, the psychoanalyst R.D. Laing (1960) recounted cases of young people experiencing themselves as disconnected from their 'being-for-themselves' by their bodily and social 'being-for-others'. Madness, in his view, often involves the young person walling up and dividing off his unembodied-seeming inner childhood 'true self' from invasion by what he experiences as, or wants to experience as, an entirely different, separate and disconnected embodied 'false self' façade.

Novelists write in similar vein. They write of adolescents disconnecting from their seemingly immaculate former self on first experiencing and consummating their sexual desire. This is particularly eloquently observed by Alain Fournier in his classic novel, *The Lost Domain*. More recently, the New York journalist, Eva Hoffman, represents this division in her autobiography *Lost in Translation*. She symbolises adolescent disconnection of past and present in her own case in terms of her 'exile', as she puts it, on leaving Poland for Canada when she was 13.

Psychoanalysts working with disturbed young people describe yet another division occurring in adolescence – between love and hate. They recount cases of young people driven to distraction by dread lest the impulse to act out sexually their fantasies of hate disconnected from, and uncontained by, love destroy them or others (see e.g. Laufer and Laufer, 1989). More often researchers find that young men complacently describe themselves dividing and disconnecting not so much their love from their hate, but love from sex. A recent study, for instance, found that, unlike women, most men said affection was not the motive impelling their first sexual intercourse (Michael *et al.*, 1994).

Often adolescents deal with the biological realities of puberty not only by disconnecting affection and sex, love and hate, past and present, body and mind. They disconnect from their sexual desire by locating it in others – often in the girls or women with whom they first had sex. Several of the men I interviewed for this study talked in these terms. They spoke of being initiated into sex not by their own desire but by that of girls or women they happened to meet. Perhaps this was, in part, a transference phenomenon – an effect of myself, a relatively unknown woman, prompting them to recall their teens.

Whether or not this was a factor, Brian, a graphic artist in his mid-forties, was not untypical in describing the bodily drive impelling him into first having sex as coming not from him but from a girl from another school whom he chanced to encounter at a club:

> She was much more experienced than I was . . . she was the one who took the lead role. I suppose, as boys of that age, you think about it. But, when it comes to doing it, you don't do anything. It was down to her the first time, and after a few drinks . . . just to give you courage to do it. It was after a disco, and we went to a park, and she started er, um, taking the initiative, so we ended up doing it there in the park. And I remember because I had white jeans on, and when I got home I had terrible grass stains all over these jeans, and I tried to scrub them off before my parents came home.

Just as Brian disconnected and arguably hid the evidence of his desire as much from himself as from his parents by dwelling on his partner's sexual experience and seduction of him, so too several students from the boys' school in my study recounted dreams in which they disconnected from their desire for sex by attributing it to others. A 15-year-old described this process particularly candidly in recounting a dream about his sister galvanising him into having the sex he admitted he wanted to have with her. He wrote:

> My most recent dream was last night – I dreamt I was with my sister . . . She said she wanted to lose her vaginity [*sic*] but not to be a bastard. She asked me to have sex with her . . . So I agreed, but I actually wanted to have sex with her! . . . She pointed to my trousers, and she took them off and pulled me down on top of her . . . I then got my penis and put it into her vagina and we started having sex . . . she reached her orgasm as I ejaculated. Then she got dressed and went to her bedroom. I am still a virgin!

But he seemed to feel guilty, not a virgin at all. Perhaps it was his still remaining conscious of his sexual desire for his sister, having not sufficiently disconnected from it in shifting his desire on to her, that drove him to confess this dream. Whatever his motive, he was the only boy to recount a manifestly incestuous dream.

More often students from the boys' school kept intact their image of themselves as virginal and sexually innocent by disconnecting from their contrary guilty sexual impulses by describing the latter as coming from girls or women with whom they had no other connection apart from sex. Examples include the masturbation dream recounted earlier in this section (see p. 88). The frequency with which boys and men in my study thus disconnected from wanting sex tallies with the surprising finding that men often – indeed slightly more often than women – describe themselves as being subjected to, and victims of, others' sexual overtures. One study, for instance, found that 97.5 per cent of men students (compared to 93.5 per cent of women students) reported being coerced by others into unwanted sexual activity, including kissing, petting and intercourse (Muehlenhard and Cook, 1988).

In sum: many recount their experience of sex and of their changing bodies in adolescence in terms of disconnection both from themselves and others. Others, by contrast, recount their experience of their bodies and of sexual changes in their bodies in adolescence in terms of their connection with others.

CONNECTIONS

Unlike Freud (e.g. 1905), who described the development of the sexual instinct in infancy in terms disconnecting its manifestation (oral, anal or genital) from others, the psychoanalyst Melanie Klein (e.g. 1959) emphasised that we are all emotionally and psychologically connected with others from the moment of birth. She insisted that, from earliest infancy, our internal world is peopled by loving and hating relations with others, in the first place with the mother.

Similarly, Klein's student and colleague, Donald Winnicott, put much emphasis on our initial connection, as babies, with others. Reiterating the point, he wrote: 'I once said: "There is no such thing as an infant," meaning, of course, that whenever one finds an infant one finds maternal care, and without maternal care there would be no infant' (Winnicott, 1960: 586, n.4).

Quoting Winnicott approvingly, the feminist sociologist (now psychoanalyst), Nancy Chodorow (1978), argues that the connection of mother and baby, insisted on by Winnicott, persists in girls from infancy into adulthood. This is because, being female like the mother, there is no need for the girl to disconnect and dis-identify from her in forging a female-based identity.

Certainly girls often remain intensely aware, from early childhood, of being emotionally connected with their mothers, and also with other women and girls. From nursery school onwards, they play, more often than boys, in emotionally close and intimate groups of two or three with other girls (see e.g. Rutter and Rutter, 1992). By middle childhood they are often very perceptive, sensitive and attuned to emotional connections between themselves and others, as Lyn Brown and Carol Gilligan (1992) found in their study of pupils attending a private girls' school in Cleveland, Ohio. Eight-year-old Jessie, for instance, said that if she got into an argument with one of her friends, rather than go silent, sulk and stalk off (as boys and men often do), she would make sure to quickly get together again with her friend to make good their otherwise threatened continuing closeness with each other. After a fight, Jessie said:

> always the next day at school we hug and say we are ready and say hi, because we both forget about it. I think I would lose her because she's very easy to lose, you know. If I say no and I walked out the door, she would come and drag me in again and . . . start crying and I don't want that to happen.
>
> (Brown and Gilligan, 1992: 57)

Girls accordingly often arrive at adolescence very much aware of their emotional connection with each other. They are also very conscious of continuing connection and involvement with their mothers, both for good and ill.

Whereas several secondary school boys in my study recounted nightmares of physical disconnection from their mothers (see p. 86 above), girls more often recounted nightmares of imprisoning physical connection and closeness, of being bodily ensnared by maternal or other adult female figures. A particularly vivid example comes from a 12-year-old who wrote the following recurring childhood dream:

> I am on a giant web and there is a giant spider coming towards me. She is smiling but as she gets nearer she lets out a horrible scream, so high it hurts my ears. She becomes scary and ugly. She gets really close to me and I am stuck on the web unable to move. She looks like she is going to kill me and then she scuttles back to the beginning, puts on a smile, and it begins again. It goes on for ages.

Women and girls likewise often recount puberty in terms of nightmares of the bodily changes involved harmfully connecting them with their mothers in making them women like them. Ellen, for instance, a scientist in her late fifties, told me:

> I insisted on wearing boys' clothes from about 8 till about 13. I wore boys' shorts with proper button-up flies . . . and I was really angry when it turned out I was a girl after all, and that there was no getting round the fact that I was a girl . . . My mother one day said, 'I think you'd better start wearing a top.' She didn't say very much, she just said, 'I think you've got to start wearing a top,' and I realised it was because my breasts were developing. And I was really angry about that, and upset.

Ellen remembered hating her mother for using the fact of her developing breasts to emphasise that she was becoming a woman like herself. She also remembered hating her mother for packing sanitary towels at the top of her trunk for all the other girls to see when she opened it in her dormitory at school.

Others recount memories of menstruation in more mixed terms. They describe both wanting to talk with their mothers about menstruation, and being baulked and disappointed by their mothers' evident hatred of, and contempt for, what makes them bodily the same. A 25-year-old student, for instance, recalled herself, aged 11:

> wondering how I was going to tell my Mum that we had been told about periods at school. This took me weeks and I was expecting some big adult discussion with her after my revelation. She simply replied, 'Ah you know it all now – boobs and bums!'

Other students also described themselves as rebuffed. One student, recalling early puberty, wrote, 'I can remember starting my periods and thinking I was dying . . . [and] running to my mother who laughed.'

Many equate menstruation with dying and death. They equate woman-hood generally with bodily mutilation and vulnerability. Unlike students from the boys' school in my study, several from the girls' school depicted their mothers and other maternal figures in their dreams as being eaten by others, as pushed over cliffs, as fat, poisoned, decapitated, killed and rotting. Their imagery is consistent with social attitudes portraying sexually mature, reproductive femininity as damaged and damaging, as disgusting and repulsive (see e.g. Bordo, 1991).

Kleinian psychoanalysts often interpret such imagery in the anecdotes, memories, and dreams patients recall in therapy – in so far as their associa-tions warrant it – as reflecting hatred of the mother and her body. They write that this in turn often results in fear lest the mother similarly hate and attack them and their bodies (see e.g. Klein, 1928).

Certainly several students in my study recounted dreams of damaged female figures attacking them, as in the following example from a 14-year-old:

> Me and my family [mother, brother and sister] were squashed in a Tupperware box. We managed to get the lid off and we got out and we were in a huge room . . . the only other thing in the room was a shop mannequin with no arms or legs. Suddenly my family disappeared and I was left alone . . . I remember her [the mannequin] taking the duffel coat I was wearing. Then she grabbed my arms.

Another girl, aged 13, recounted a dream linking an image of her mother as ill with an image of herself being attacked by a girl like herself. She wrote that in her dream:

> My Mum was very ill and my dad and sister were being kept in an old

Edwardian house . . . One night, I peered down the drive and saw a girl in a long white nightgown, big brown plaits, eyes, vampirish teeth, blood-red lips and a pale white face . . . as soon as I got to the back door she pressed against me from behind. I ran again but she followed me . . . I ended up along the glass corridor at school and she pressed me against the glass and columns. She pushed me through the glass . . . She came down and stabbed me over and over again . . . I woke up terrified. I had this dream thirteen times, and then a little while ago, my friend had the same dream.

Experiencing their mothers and other grown women as sick or damaged, and experiencing their connection with them as confining and imprisoning, many look for comfort from girls their own age. Just as the above-quoted 13-year-old described sharing and having identical dreams with her friend, women and girls often recount sharing with their friends their worries lest, in becoming women, their bodies are no good. They share with them their anxieties about being too big or too fat.

Psychoanalysts and feminists describe this preoccupation as it occurs in anorexia and bulimia in terms of the relationships of adolescent girls to their mothers. They characterise anorexic and bulimic abuse and starvation of the body as both an attempt by girls to fend off the mother, whom they equate with their maturing bodies, and as repeating their childhood connection with their mothers through food. (I detail these theories further, and provide case examples, in Sayers, 1988, 1995b respectively.)

Thankfully most adolescent girls do not become either anorexic or bulimic. But many feel dissatisfied with their bodies. Several research studies report that pre-teen and teenage girls, particularly early maturing girls, often have a poor body image and want to be thinner than they are (see e.g. Duncan *et al.*, 1985). They find that women students link being unhappy and depressed with not being physically attractive (see e.g. Boggiano and Barrett, 1991).

Similarly, many students in my study linked concern about their bodies to not getting on with others. One student, for instance, remembered herself, aged 13, 'feeling fat, ugly and unloved at home'. Often they linked concern about their bodies not with thoughts about their families, but with thoughts about their peers. A student in her early twenties described herself in her early teens as 'feeling insecure and very discontented with my body, feeling that being accepted by my friends was the most important thing in the world'. Another wrote that, when she was 13, 'I was picked on by Emma [my friend] for being overweight.'

In her novel, *Cat's Eye*, Margaret Atwood (1988) describes girls in early adolescence picking on and taunting each other about their appearance as reflected in a looking-glass. She writes:

Cordelia brings a mirror to school. It's a pocket-mirror, the small plain oblong kind without any rim. She takes it out of her pocket and holds the mirror up in front of me and says, 'Look at yourself! Just look!' Her voice is disgusted, fed up, as if my face, all by itself, has been up to something, has gone too far.

Girls in my study recounted similar dreams of being confronted with unflattering, distorting mirror images of themselves, making them look 'short and very fat', as one 14-year-old put it.

The psychoanalyst Jacques Lacan (1949) describes the toddler's fascination with his mirror image in terms of his consolidating himself in identifying and, in the process, mis-identifying himself with what is in fact disconnected from himself – his mirrored reflection. By contrast, as Atwood tells it, girls in adolescence are also concerned with their mirror image because it informs them what they look like to others.

Some describe their teenage preoccupation with how others see them in positive terms, linked to happy memories of themselves and their mothers. Hazel, for instance, a retired hospital matron, talking to me about her teens, said:

> I remember a specific incident, as I said we wore these dresses, white collar and cuffs, and one day my mother made me a dress which was so pretty, with a full skirt, in a light blue, and a big sash round the waist, and she allowed me to go and buy my own hat to go with it, and I felt so different in this dress. And I found I had a power – I had sexual power. That's when I discovered it. Because boys looked at me, and turned their heads. And I thought oh this is great, this is an area where I shine.

Others describe more negatively their experience of their family's response to their teenage good looks. One young girl put her response particularly vehemently. She said:

> I kind of put on a mental suit of armour. I clamp myself in it, and then walk into the room. Grandma opens her arms up and cries, 'You're beautiful! Isn't she a beauty? Look at my beauty!' and I want to scream. I feel like my nipples are sticking out for everyone to see, and I can feel my thighs sticking together, and I think of little things, like whether there are any of those gooey specks of dirt between my toes. That admiration is excruciating! It swoops down on you . . . All those eyes on you, thinking, 'Ooh, ah – hasn't the little girl gone and got all developed?'
>
> (Apter, 1995: 58)

Feeling alienated from their families, particularly from their mothers, by their sexual development and maturation, many talk about it instead with their friends. This is very movingly described by Anne Frank in the teenage diary she kept in the Amsterdam attic where she and her family hid from the Nazis during World War II. In it she confided in an imaginary friend, Kitty. She told her of increasing tensions between her mother and herself. In one entry, for 5 January 1944, after recounting how wounded she felt when her mother laughed at her, Anne writes comforting memories of sharing with another girl her experience of her sexually changing body. She writes:

> I remember that once [before I came here, when I was just14] when I slept with a girl friend I had a strong desire to kiss her, and that I did do so. I could not help being terribly inquisitive about her body, for she had always kept it hidden from me. I asked her whether, as a proof of our friendship, we should feel one another's breasts, but she refused. I go into ecstasies every time I see the naked figure of a woman, such as Venus, for example. It strikes me as so wonderful and exquisite that I have difficulty in stopping the tears rolling down my cheeks. If only I had a girlfriend!
>
> (Frank, 1953: 114–115)

Students in my study similarly recounted memories and dreams of sharing with other girls the experience of becoming sexually mature. They also recalled sharing with them their first sexual encounters with others. A housewife in her early forties told me how, when she was 13, 'All we talked about was had you had your period, and had you been kissed.' Another woman, also in her forties, shared with me, as she doubtless shared with her peers at the time, the experience of her first kiss. In retelling the experience, she situated it in terms of the impact of her being kissed on her connection with other girls she then knew. She told me:

> I could actually taste what he tasted like when he kissed me . . . I probably blocked out the sense that it was quite frightening by, probably what I did for quite a long time, was actually standing in its place the fact that this was a very high-status activity that I was engaging in here, being kissed in the double seats in the pictures, by a boy, which put me ahead of the game as far as other girls were concerned . . . And it was frightening, kind of strange, as in like this is very odd . . . I suppose it's very vivid because it's the first intimate encounter with another human body . . . a real feeling of being a grown-up, a strange grown-up experience. And I didn't dislike it because I was so transfixed by how meaningful it was.

A 13-year-old from my secondary school sample similarly dwelt on her mixed feelings about sexually connecting with someone else on kissing them. She recounted a recent dream in which, she wrote:

> I was at home sitting on the sofa in the kitchen with everything in the kitchen as it should be. My mum, dad and older brother were also in the kitchen and a boy called Shane was sitting next to me. Then we started kissing each other, and while he was kissing me my mouth had disgusting-flavoured herbs and spices in it and felt really dry. I didn't want to stop kissing Shane so I carried on.

When it comes to sexual intercourse, however, rather than dwelling on their experience of their own and their partner's desire, they more often dwell on the impact of their having sex on their friendships with others. A 12-year old, for instance, wrote that in her best remembered recent dream:

> I was in bed in my dormitory [at camp] and I heard a handful of gravel hit the window. I went over and opened it. Kevin and his friend climbed up a tree and got in. I slept with Kevin and I thought, 'I wonder what Anna will think. I am two years younger than her and I am sleeping with a boy and she hasn't kissed one yet.'

Two other girls reconciled having sex with togetherness with their family and friends by recounting dreams of group sex. One girl, aged 13, wrote:

> This is quite rude but we were all having sex. I was with Steve, Sue was with Ben and Anna was with Simon and Brian. And then Anna, Sue and I started running, hopping and jumping with orange and pink scarves around us and nothing else on.

The other girl, aged 17, recorded a dream of 'A sex session between my parents and me and my brother. I remember questioning the moral tasteless-ness in the dream, but everyone else was saying: "Go on, go ahead." Never reached full-blown sex (thank God!).'

Whatever the connection with family and friends depicted in these dreams, their authors' cautions regarding their dreams' 'rudeness' and 'tastelessness' indicate their anxiety lest writing or talking about sex invite others' disap-proval, and thereby threaten their connection with them. Perhaps a similar fear contributed to no girl (apart from the three quoted above) writing an explicitly sexual dream, and to no girl recounting a masturbation or lesbian dream. This is consistent with other findings that, fearing the impact on their connection with others of talking about their sexual desire, girls in adolescence are often silent about it (see e.g. Tolman, 1994).

Girls and women are much more ready to talk and write about their adolescent desire in terms of 'boy crazy' romance. Boys and men are by contrast more likely to talk and write in 'boy crazy' terms about themselves as the embodiment and incarnation of what they and others most desire of men as heroes and gods, as I will now illustrate and explain.

BOY CRAZINESS

First, though, a word about gender. In the above two sections of this chapter I have quoted men and boys talking and writing about their experience of adolescent sexuality in terms of disconnection, and women and girls talking and writing about this experience in terms of their connection with others. As I have also indicated, some theorise this difference between the sexes as an effect of men being pressurised from early childhood to disconnect from their mothers in the interests of forging a separate male gender identity, while girls remain connected with their mothers in being the same sex.

But connection and disconnection – and the associated discourses of community and individualism – are not in themselves gendered. By contrast 'boy-craziness' – by which, as indicated above, I mean grandiosely or romantically imagining oneself or others as idealised heroes or gods – is patently gendered. It is also often advanced by psychoanalytic theorists as means of disconnecting – in infancy or adolescence – from the woman who first mothered us.

In a pivotal essay, published towards the end of his life, Freud (1923b) argued that the sexual embodiment of children as boys or girls is constituted by their situating themselves, in late infancy, in terms of having or not having a penis. The French psychoanalyst Jacques Lacan (e.g. 1958) in turn argued that the centrality of the penis in this respect derives from the privilege accorded the phallus as symbol of sexuality in patriarchal society. He argued that, in the absence of the mother recognising 'the law of the father' structuring patriarchy, the child is at risk of psychosis. He is in danger of remaining or being drawn into the psychotic illusion of being all to his mother, of being everything – symbolised, according to Lacan (see e.g. Lacan, 1955–56), by the phallus – that she desires.

Similarly, the literary theorist and psychoanalyst Julia Kristeva (1977) argues that the mother's interest in something beyond herself and her child – symbolised, according to Kristeva (following Freud), by the 'father of individual pre-history' (Freud, 1923a: 31) – is the precondition of a gap being opened up between the two of them without which the child would remain prey to the horror of 'abjection', of disappearing back into the mother's body. In effect Kristeva, like Lacan, insists on the intervention between mother and child of a 'third term' symbolised by man as patriarch or phallus to enable the child to move forward from, and escape the abjection and psychosis threatened by imagining himself the same as his mother.

Whether or not this is true of infancy – and it is to infancy that Lacan and his feminist disciples restrict their account of the origins in child development of our society's patriarchal and phallic organisation of sexual desire – many non-Lacanians write about adolescence in terms of young people freeing themselves from the regressive pull of childhood and early mothering by identifying, in adolescence, with the forward movement signified by men as heroes or patriarchs.

Jung (1912), for instance, deplored the fate of the young man, the eternal child – the 'puer aeternus' as he called him – trapped in being nothing but the glorious but evanescent and fleeting playboy dream of his mother. He wrote of the importance of young men escaping the grip of the mother's unconscious, of their modelling themselves on the heroes of myth and legend in overcoming the dragon of death, representing the mother. The Jungian psychiatrist, Anthony Stevens, similarly insists that:

> The arrogance of youth is a necessary arrogance ... the bond to the mother has to be loosened ... The son is then free to go the way of the hero ... These myths express in symbolic form the experience of

Everyman . . . Failure to overcome the monster signifies failure to get free of the mother.

(Stevens, 1990: 125)

Similarly, the US ego psychologist Peter Blos (1967) argues that, in adolescence, boys must free and disconnect themselves from an 'archaic' or 'omnipotent' image of the mother, internalised in earlier childhood as means of becoming independent of her external control. Blos (1984) argues that liberating and disconnecting himself from the mother depends on the adolescent boy identifying with an idealised image, first of the father and then of other men in his place. Blos lauds in these terms the ego-boosting effect of teenage boys identifying with the male icons of film, music and sport.

Blos's followers write in similar vein. They argue that boys in adolescence should identify with men idealised on the model of the father if they are to acquire the masculinity they say is necessary to their having sexual intercourse. They commend heterosexual sex for yet further enhancing the young man's inflated image of himself – his 'phallic prowess', his male 'gender-role identity' (Tyson and Tyson, 1990: 291).

Certainly many students from the boys' school in my study recounted self-inflating dreams of themselves physically equalling or bettering currently idealised male sports idols. A 14-year-old, for instance, recounted a dream in which 'There was crowds and crowds of people. I was playing tennis against Andre Agassi and Pete Sampras at the same time. They didn't win a point. And I won. The grass tennis court was bright green and the crowd cheered me.' Many other students from the boys' school, but none from the girls' school, recounted similar dreams of themselves embodied as sports or rock heroes.

Others recounted dreams – that might well have been group productions informed by magazine, film or video pornography – of themselves as sexually magnetic, as phallic conquistadors. One student, again a 14-year-old, wrote:

My most recent memorable dream, which occurs over and over again, is where I start at a party, with lots of really nice girls, and they all really fancy me and aren't afraid to show it . . . Then two of them follow me home, and I shag them both, lick them out and they give me a blow job.

A 21-year-old student similarly bragged of his 13-year-old macho achievements. He listed them as follows:

- I started high school
- I had my first French kisses
- I was in love with my female teacher
- I destroyed my father's car
- I grew over 6'1"
- I lost my virginity
- I invented a couple of songs.

Older men similarly represent themselves (as teenagers) as magnificently inventive, big, violent, and as masters of sex. Chris, for instance, a salesman in his late thirties, told me how, fearful as a teenager of becoming forever immersed and embroiled in crippling identification with his mother (with her poverty and illness), got away through making much of himself as a Don Juan. From his teens onwards he made it his business to seduce women into crediting him with being the perfect male embodiment of their desire. (I recount his story further in Sayers, 1995a).

Judy, a teacher in her early sixties, like Chris, remembered her mother in her teens as an oppressive incubus weighing her down. She recalled trying to free herself as a teenager from becoming the same 'sexually repressed' creature as her by cultivating a contrary image of herself analogous to the housewife whore of Buñuel's film, *Belle de Jour*. She imagined herself with 'lots of strange men adoring me, wanting to have me'.

Most of all, however, Judy remembered a dream from when she was 15 of herself as a man whom women craved. In her dream she modelled herself on the naval hero of the novel *Hornblower* that a male relative had lent her, and on the rulers she assumed the boys she was with at prep school would become on leaving Eton and Oxford. She also modelled herself on her world-famous physicist father. She eroticised this grand male amalgam. In her dream, she said:

> I'm standing on a ship deck. I'm a man in uniform, a naval officer . . . I've asked a young girl, or two young girls, to swim out to the ship in the evening from the harbour where we're anchored. It feels like some South American place . . . I am a man, anything goes, the world is mine. The women/girls have not arrived. But . . . I know they'll come.

Whereas Judy described herself as disconnecting from oppressive identification with her mother by imagining herself as a superlative, sexually irresistible male lover, others recount disconnecting from their mothers in adolescence not through identifying with idealised men but through desiring them. In this they draw on another myth: the myth of the heroine rescued from imprisonment by a wicked maternal figure by the love of a great or wonderful man. It is, of course, the story of *Sleeping Beauty*, *Snow White* and *Cinderella* – of the heroine saved by an intrepid knight or handsome prince from remaining in a coma, from staying boxed up in a coffin or from being kept as a drudge by a cruel or envious witch or stepmother.

Kleinian psychoanalysts tell a similar tale of children who, feeling horribly constrained by intense love and hate of the woman who first mothered them, escape through idealising the father and other men in her place (see e.g. Klein, 1955; Chasseguet-Smirgel, 1964). Moreover, as the feminist psychologist Dorothy Dinnerstein (1976) points out, men's absence – their relative disconnection, both emotional and physical, from children's early care – makes them all the more ready repositories of idealising fantasy in not being there to disprove it.

These writers focus on infancy to the neglect of adolescence – not so the psychoanalyst Karen Horney. Drawing on her and her daughter's experience of adolescence (see Sayers, 1991), she observed that, experiencing themselves as outwitted and bettered by their mothers, teenage girls often begin what often becomes a lifelong subordination of all their other wishes and interests – including commitment to work – to pursuing and getting a man. She called this pursuit boy crazy, hero-worship (see e.g. Horney, 1935; Paris, 1994).

Women and girls in my study recounted memories and dreams of adolescence in similar terms. They recounted tales of escaping rivalrous, ambivalent and imprisoning connection and identification with their mothers by making men the centre of their lives. They remembered their sexuality in adolescence in terms of boy crazy romance.

Hating her mother, and hating the thought, in early adolescence, of becoming bodily the same as her, Ellen (see pp. 92–93 above), for instance, told me that she early learned to masturbate as a child to console and comfort herself for her mother's lack of love for her and preference for her older brother. As a teenager, however, Ellen traded physical for emotional comfort. She masturbated less frequently. Instead, she said, masturbation often gave way to her telling herself male-centred romances to which she added each night. She recalled that:

> One was about skiing, because my mother took us skiing when we were about 14. The culminating point in this fantasy – because my mother didn't take us out in sleighs, you saw other people going out in sleighs – and in this fur-lined sled this boy would declare his love. It took months from meeting this boy on the slopes, ending up with my being completely loved, and doted on by this boy.

Women often mock themselves, in retrospect, when they recall the girl-meets-boy pulp fiction that fuels stories like those Ellen told herself. One woman, for instance, writes:

> I was an addict from the age of 12 to 17. I sacrificed my O levels to Mr Boon's books, and even my piano Grade 6. While practising scales, I read Mills & Boons at the music stand. I even made a tape of arpeggios to foil my mother while I walked among men with V-shaped torsos and powerful thighs. I couldn't get enough of these tales of devastating attraction, terrible misunderstandings, heart-wrenching partings and, in the end, sweet reunion.
>
> (Stewart-Liberty, 1996: 10)

In adolescence itself, however, such fictions are often deadly serious. Despising her mother for her duplicity, weakness and fears of being poor, 12-year-old Victoria tells an interviewer:

> I'm hoping some day I will fall in love with a man and we will be happy and live happily ever after . . . He is going to be at least six foot and have

a beard and a mustache and he's going to be really nice and gentle and . . . the perfect prince.

(Brown and Gilligan, 1992: 151)

Similarly, a 13-year-old girl in my study, like the 12-year-old whose dream I quoted above (see p. 92), recounted a dream of being physically beset and crawled over by 'a massive spider' with horrible staring eyes in the kitchen of the house where she lived alone with her mother. After recounting this creepy-crawly image, associated with her mother, she took refuge in a dream of a schoolmaster honouring her with his prolonged regal regard. In her dream, she wrote:

I am sitting on the roadside and a car keeps driving past me. I look into the window and see Mr Jenkins, my history teacher. He sees me and grins and waves slowly, like the Queen. This continues for a long time.

More ominously, a student in her early twenties pictures herself, aged 14, saying:

Oh no, let me out. Which one am I? Why can't she leave me alone? Claws, hate, loathing, pills, bathroom, mirror . . . Look at your eyes. They're filled with tears and hurt. Look at your face. It's so unfair. Unfair. Unfair. Why does she have to do it to me? What's wrong with me? She's jealous, she hates me, she wants to be me. She wants my life. She wants to eat me. Get away. Leave me alone . . . Dream about love. Men love me. *He's* always there. And so is he. And also him. I must keep them close. I must always keep them. Who cares if she hates me? I've always got him. I'll take him and I'll get him . . . MINE.

Images of feeling clawed at, mirrored, eaten and taken over by women (above all by women as mothers), and of finding solace in the idea of having and possessing a man, are not the monopoly of women and girls. Men and boys recount similar images, but they often express them in less emotional, more crudely embodied phallic terms.

Benjamin, for example, aged 13, indicates to his New York psychoanalyst that he is frightened of being as weak as his mother subjected to his father's violence. He then goes on to indicate that he hopes to escape experiencing himself to be as weak as her through being strengthened by being fucked by a man with an enormous penis. He says:

he 'crotch gazed' at men all the time, especially on the bus and the subway when they were in one place long enough to be stared at. He would wonder how big their penises were, wonder if he could guess by the size of the bulge in their pants. And then he went on, 'Sometimes I imagine that the man notices me staring at him, and he takes me back to his apartment. We get undressed and he has a very big penis and he fucks me.'

(Berenstein, 1995: 53)

Benjamin's analyst anticipates how, acting on this idea, and seeking to find men to embody his inflated phallic image of them, Benjamin might become launched on an endless and hopeless quest, on 'a constant search for a bigger penis, a more powerful phallus, a more genuine man' (Berenstein, 1995: 58). Writing more generally, feminist exponents of Lacan's development of psychoanalysis recount the harm done women as well as men by acting on the illusion that they or others might embody such idealised images – more or less explicit, veiled or concealed – of man as phallus (see e.g. Minsky, 1996). What, then, is to be done?

CONCLUSION: BEYOND MEMORIES AND DREAMS

Failing to address the damage done by idealising men as phallic gods, heroes or patriarchs, some psychoanalysts, as we have seen, recommend women – but particularly men in adolescence – to adopt this tactic as means of disconnecting from the mothers of their infancy. Others, on the contrary, are committed to deconstructing the images patients bring to therapy, including the image of man as patriarchal superego. They seek to unpack these images by encouraging their patients to free-associate to the distinct, separate and often incoherent elements in the otherwise integrated and seemingly coherent narratives – fictions, memories and dreams – they bring to therapy.

The aim of such deconstruction is to enable patients to recover and reconnect with their otherwise disconnected and unconscious or projected fantasies and desires, so as to reintegrate the feelings dividing them from themselves and others on a surer basis than is afforded by, for instance, idealising men as gods.

Feminists go further. They seek to expose, challenge and overturn the harm done women by men's social dominance that does so much to feed our idealising illusions about them. And this includes exposing the discourse of boy-craziness, and the related discourses of disconnection and connection, in terms of which, as I have sought to illustrate and explain in this chapter, women and men often write and talk about their own and others' sexual embodiment in adolescence.

REFERENCES

Apter, T. (1995) *Secret Paths*, New York: Norton.
Atwood, M. (1988) *Cat's Eye*, London: Virago.
Berenstein, F.H. (1995) *Lost Boys*, New York: Norton.
Blos, P. (1967) The Second Individuation Process of Adolescence, *Psychoanalytic Study of the Child*, 22, 162–186.
——(1984) Son and Father, *Journal of the American Psychoanalytic Association*, 24(5), 301–324.
Boggiano, A.K. and Barrett, M. (1991) Gender differences in depression in college students, *Sex Roles*, 25(11/12), 595–605.
Bordo, S. (1991) *Unbearable Weight*, New York: New York University Press.

Brown, L. and Gilligan, C. (1992) *Meeting at the Crossroads*, Cambridge, MA: Harvard University Press.

Chasseguet-Smirgel, J. (1964) *Feminine Guilt and the Oedipus Complex, Female Sexuality*, London: Virago (1981).

Chodorow, N. (1978) *The Reproduction of Mothering*, Berkeley: University of California Press.

Deutsch, H. (1934) The Psychological Type: 'as if'. Reprinted as Some Forms of Emotional Disturbance and Their Relationship to Schizophrenia. In *Neuroses and Character Types*, New York: International Universities Press (1965).

Dinnerstein, D. (1976) *The Rocking of the Cradle*, London: Souvenir Press.

Duncan, P., Ritter, P., Dornbush, S., Gross, R. and Carlsmith, J. (1985) The Effects of Pubertal Timing on Body Image, School Behavior and Deviance, *Journal of Youth and Adolescence*, 14, 227–236.

Faulkenberry, J.R., Vincent, M., James, A. and Johnson, W. (1987) Coital Behaviors, Attitudes and Knowledge of Students who Experience Early Coitus, *Adolescence*, 22, 321–332.

Frank, A. (1953) *The Diary of Anne Frank*, London: Pan Books.

Freud, A. (1936) *The Ego and the Mechanisms of Defence*, London: Hogarth Press (1968).

——(1958) Adolescence, *Psychoanalytic Study of the Child*, 13, 255–278.

Freud, S. (1896) The Aetiology of Hysteria, *Standard Edition*, vol. 3, London: Hogarth Press.

——(1899) Screen Memories, *Standard Edition*, vol. 3, London: Hogarth Press.

——(1905) Three Essays on the Theory of Sexuality, *Standard Edition*, vol. 7, London: Hogarth Press.

——(1907) Delusions and Dreams in Jensen's 'Gradiva', *Standard Edition*, vol. 9, London: Hogarth Press.

——(1919) The Uncanny, *Standard Edition*, vol. 17, London: Hogarth Press.

——(1923a) The Ego and the Id, *Standard Edition*, vol. 19, London: Hogarth Press.

——(1923b) The Infantile Genital Organization, *Standard Edition*, vol. 19, London: Hogarth Press.

Greenson, R. (1968) Dis-Identifying from Mother, *International Journal of Psychoanalysis*, 49, 370–374.

Horney, K. (1935) The Overvaluation of Love, *Feminine Psychology*, New York: Norton (1967).

Jung, C.G. (1912) *Symbols of Transformation, Collected Works*, vol. 5, London: Routledge (1956).

Klein, M. (1928) Early Stages of the Oedipus Complex, *Love, Guilt and Reparation*, London: Hogarth Press (1975).

——(1955) Envy and Gratitude, *Envy and Gratitude and Other Essays*, London: Hogarth Press (1975).

——(1959) Our Adult World and its Roots in Infancy, *Envy and Gratitude and Other Essays*, London: Hogarth Press (1975).

Kristeva, J. (1977) Stabat Mater, *Tales of Love*, New York: Columbia University Press (1987).

Lacan, J. (1949) The Mirror Stage as Formative of the Function of the I as Revealed in Psychoanalytic Experience, *Écrits*, trans. A. Sheridan, London: Tavistock (1977).

——(1955–56) On a Question Preliminary to Any Possible Treatment of Psychosis, *Écrits*, London: Tavistock (1977).

——(1958) The Signification of the Phallus, *Écrits*, London: Tavistock (1977).

Laing, R.D. (1960) *The Divided Self*, London: Penguin (1965).

Michael, R.T., Gagnon, J.H., Laufmann, E.O. and Kolata, G. (1994) *Sex in America*, Boston: Little, Brown.

Minsky, R. (1996) *Psychoanalysis and Gender*, London: Routledge.

Muehlenhard, C.L. and Cook, S.W. (1988) Men's Self-Reports of Unwanted Sexual Activity, *Journal of Sex Research*, 24, 58–72.

Paris, B. (1994) *Karen Horney*, New Haven: Yale University Press.

Rutter, M. and Rutter, M. (1992) *Developing Minds*, London: Penguin.

Sayers, J. (1988) Anorexia, Psychoanalysis, and Feminism, *Journal of Adolescence*, 11, 361–367.

——(1991) *Mothering Psychoanalysis: Hélène Deutsch, Karen Horney, Anna Freud, Melanie Klein*, London: Penguin.

——(1995a) *The Man Who Never Was: Freudian Tales*, London: Chatto & Windus.

——(1995b) Consuming Male Fantasy. In A. Elliott and S. Frosh (eds), *Psychoanalysis in Contexts*, London: Routledge.

Stevens, A. (1990) *On Jung*, London: Penguin.

Stewart-Liberty, O. (1996) I Lost My Heart to Mills & Boon, *Independent on Sunday: Real Life*, 21 July.

Tolman, D.L. (1994) Doing Desire: Adolescent Girls' Struggles for/with Sexuality, *Gender and Society*, 8, 324–342.

Tyson, P. and Tyson, R.L. (1990) *Psychoanalytic Theories of Development*, New Haven: Yale University Press.

Wight, D. (1994) Boys' Thoughts and Talk About Sex in a Working Class Locality in Glasgow, *Sociological Review*, 42(4), 703–737.

Winnicott, D.W. (1960) The Theory of the Parent–Infant Relationship, *International Journal of Psycho-Analysis*, 41, 585–595.

7 The discursive construction and regulation of dissident sexualities

The case of SM

Gary Wilson Taylor

In 1987 police in Bolton seized a video showing adult men engaging in consensual sadomasochistic (SM) sex. A massive investigation ensued, codenamed 'Operation Spanner', which, over the next two years and at a cost of over half a million pounds, led to the arrest of forty-two men. Sixteen were committed to trial, initially at Lambeth Magistrates Court and then at the Old Bailey, charged under Sections 20 and 47 of the Offences Against The Persons Act of 1861. On 19 December 1990, eleven men were found guilty of assault and given sentences of up to four and a half years in prison. A further twenty-six were cautioned for the rather bizarre offence of aiding and abetting their own assault. Their convictions were upheld at appeal in February, 1992. As a result of the Spanner Investigation, a further prosecution was made in 1990 against Alan Oversby for his provision of a body-piercing service to fetishists and SM-devotees. In the trial, a differentiation was drawn between adornment which is purely decorative or aesthetic and that which is for the purposes of sexual or sadomasochistic gratification. On the grounds that Oversby's services were considered to be sexually arousing to his clients, he was given a fifteen-month suspended jail sentence.

These court cases exemplify quite alarmingly the way in which the state attempts to regulate sexual expression. As Kershaw (1992) has pointed out, they set a precedent whereby we no longer own our own bodies. Indeed, in his summing-up, Judge Rant made it clear that it was the responsibility of the judiciary to decide what constitutes acceptable sexual practices. The law has made a forceful entry into the realms of sexual pleasure in an attempt to dictate to us what we may do. Of course, this is not a precedent – we have never owned our own bodies. Since at least 1750 AD, the state has attempted to regulate the way in which we give and receive sexual pleasure (Bresler, 1988). Judicial legislation against that which has come to be known as SM dates from at least 1777, when de Sade was incarcerated, while in the United Kingdom consensual SM has been illegal since 1934 (*R.* v. *Donovan*, 1934). The law's long-standing intolerance, subjugation and punishment of homosexuality and other unacceptable sexual practices has been well documented (Bresler, 1988), as have its attempts to legislate against abortion, suicide, self-harm, drug use . . . Clearly our own bodies are, and perhaps always have been, the property of the state (see Weeks, 1990; Ussher, 1997, and Chapter 8).

The effective judicial regulation of our bodies and how we use them in the pursuit of sexual pleasure is dependent upon the more covert ideological construction of a hegemonic sexuality and the practices which contravene it. Historically, this has been achieved primarily through the apparatus of religion. Here, I wish to concern myself with the way psychology, psychotherapy and psychiatry are used, not only to legitimise legislation against SM and non hegemonic sexualities, but to define and regulate, both discursively and materially, the way in which we express our sexualities. In this chapter, I intend to offer a review and critique of the essentialist construction of SM within psychological discourses; that is, the notion that 'SM' resides *within* individuals as a discrete and objectively categorisable phenomenon or identity, and that it possesses meaning which is fixed and unvarying. I will provide a Foucauldian-Marxist analysis of these discourses and their purpose, addressing the way in which they are legitimised through the apparatus of science and the scientific method. I will then offer an account of the social constructionist position on sexuality and explore the way in which the aforementioned discourses impact on the way in which individuals construct and make sense of their SM identities and practices. Finally, I will attempt to conclude my review and analysis in the context of the constructionist and material–discursive debates which continue to rage around the theorisation of sexuality.

A BRIEF HISTORY OF THE ESSENTIALIST THEORISATION AND TREATMENT OF SM

Introduction

The terms 'sadism' and 'masochism', which are taken from the names of the authors de Sade (1740–1814) and Sacher-Masoch (1836–95), emerged within psychiatric and medical discourse towards the end of the nineteenth century (Krafft-Ebing, 1886). Since that time, the term 'sadomasochism', which was first used by Freud (1905), has become firmly rooted in the emergent clinical taxonomy of psychopathology and diffused throughout psychological and psychoanalytic theory and the language of everyday life. Indeed, it is perhaps noteworthy that the aforementioned legislation against SM has come at a time when popular culture increasingly embraces representations of such sexual dissent. In popular music, film, video, advertising, fashion, dance, in nightclub entertainment, SM and its accordant imagery have become ever more prevalent, albeit in a rather non-threatening, desexualised and glamorised form. This popularising and glamorising of SM and fetishistic imagery has also coincided with increased political awareness and militancy on the part of SM-ers. This is largely a result of the more general politicisation of sexuality and gender represented by the lesbian, gay, queer and feminist movements, as well as a response to the recent proclamations and directives of the British judiciary. Increasingly, demands are being made, similar to those in the past concerning homosexuality (Bayer, 1981), that SM be decriminalised and depathologised.

Currently, 'sexual sadism' and 'sexual masochism' remain psychiatric disorders within both the Diagnostical and Statistical Manual (DSM-IV) (American Psychiatric Association, 1994) and the International Classification of Diseases (ICD-10) (World Health Organization, 1992). Furthermore, SM continues to be described as pathological in current psychological and psychiatric textbooks (Davison and Neale, 1990) and continues to be discussed alongside non-consensual and explicitly criminal behaviours such as child sexual abuse and rape. It is, essentially, still regarded as a 'pathological way of loving' (Berliner, 1947), an ironic observation given that the dominant culturally sanctioned model of heterosexual sex necessitates an inequable distribution of power involving the psychological, physical and sexual subjugation of women (Ussher, 1991, 1997). Indeed, it is interesting to note that, in contrast to the Spanner trial, a recent case involving the prosecution of a man who, with her consent, branded his wife on her buttocks, ended in acquittal (Hamilton, 1996). This verdict was reached, presumably, on the grounds that the 'assault' took place within wedlock and involved the heterosexual domination of a woman by her husband and as such is reinforcing, rather than threatening to, the established order. It would appear that both the pathologisation and the criminalisation of SM are dependent upon the degree to which the behaviours are politically dissident and undermining of hegemonic notions of 'normal sex'.

SM: pre-medicalisation and prevalence

The use of pain to enhance sexual arousal would seem to have existed throughout human history (Moser and Levitt, 1987). It features in the *Kama Sutra* of about AD 450 (Vatsyayana, 1962), the *Koka Shastra* dating from 1150 (Kokkoka, 1965), *The Perfumed Garden* from about 1400 (Nefzawis, 1963) and the *Anganga Ranga* from 1500 (Malla, 1964). Unambiguous examples of 'SM' may also be found in European literature dating from the nineteenth century (Moser and Levitt, 1987) and has also been shown to have formed a quintessential part of religious and monastic life since at least the sixth century (Medway, 1994). There is ample evidence to demonstrate that SM-type practices have existed throughout history and across a diversity of cultures, including ancient Egypt, Arabia, India and the Orient (Ellis, 1903; Bloch, 1935; Moser and Levitt, 1987). Its prevalence and acceptability among contemporary Western populations has also been demonstrated. For example, Kinsey *et al.* (1953) found that, of their perhaps somewhat biased sample, 24 per cent of men and 12 per cent of women reported being aroused by SM stories. Further anecdotal evidence of the commonality of sadomasochistic fantasy is provided by Friday (1982; 1993), while a study by Hunt (1974) found that of a sample of 2026 questionnaire respondents, 4.8 per cent of men and 2.1 per cent of women had obtained sexual pleasure from receiving pain. Similar results were found from a survey of 3700 randomly selected college students commissioned by *Playboy* magazine (1976): 2 per cent had tried and liked inflicting or receiving pain, while 3 per cent had tried and liked bondage or master–slave role-playing (cited in Moser and Levitt, 1987).

Although attracting some medical curiosity in the eighteenth and nineteenth centuries, it was only in 1886 that such practices became diagnoses of sexual pathology. Indeed, 'Sadomasochism is a good example of the way a pathological condition is established by the medical community, for until it became a diagnosis it received little attention and was not even classified as sin' (Bullough and Bullough, 1977: 210).

Sexology and the genesis of sexual pathology

In *Psychopathia Sexualis*, Krafft-Ebing (1886) first established the official use of the terms 'sadism' and 'masochism' within medical discourse. However, his aetiological theory of SM, as due to a 'congenital hereditarily tainted constitution' involving a 'pathological intensification of the masculine sexual character [in sadism and a] degeneration of the psychical peculiarities of women [in masochism]' (Krafft-Ebing, 1886: 133), has been criticised as vague and speculative (Marcus, 1981; Thompson, 1994). Krafft-Ebing cites no empirical evidence to substantiate his claims. His model does not appear to be grounded in data and is biologically reductionist despite the lack of any actual empirical evidence for the role of biology or neurology in such sexual variance. His theoretical position has also been criticised as inherently moralistic, patriarchal and heterosexist, and as characterised by an insufficient awareness of sociocultural issues (Thompson, 1994). There is no clear operational definition. His theories are derived entirely from clinical single-case studies and from historical and anecdotal illustrations, while his position as a forensic psychiatrist meant that his sample tended to comprise persons guilty of violent criminal offences. For example, his analysis of the origins of sexual sadism makes reference to the eroticised nature of primitive rituals involving human and animal sacrifice and to the 'degenerate caesars' and their 'delight in having youths and maidens slaughtered before their eyes'. There is also reference to an infamous array of serial killers and child murderers; case studies include an epileptic who 'bit off pieces of his consort's nose and swallowed them', and a man (case 24) partial to eating cats and rats who gratified his sexual desires with dead 'putrid bodies'. Parallels are also drawn with those who have a penchant for 'sodomising [decapitated] geese' or 'wallowing in the warm steaming entrails of dead chickens'. Further to this (and perhaps not surprisingly), sadism is presented as incompatible with a 'normal sex life' and as a 'disease' giving rise to uncontrollable 'attacks' of depravity and violence. Such factors may explain his conflation of consensual SM with 'violence' and with 'pathology', and his inferred association between sexual sadism and murder, infanticide, genocide, rape, paedophilia, necrophilia and bestiality, and their association in much subsequent theorising on SM (Greene and Greene, 1974; Thompson, 1994).

Hirschfeld, the German sexologist, introduced the term 'metatropism' for SM and speculated, similarly to Krafft-Ebing, that it involved a reversal of gender roles, with the male (masochist) taking on and 'exaggerating the femininity and passivity of a woman' and the female (sadist) taking on the 'masculinity and aggressiveness of a man'. Thus, for Hirschfeld, masculine sadism and feminine masochism were simply excesses of the normal sexual impulse, while in the opposite sex they become complete metatropic deviations from normality (Ellis, 1935: 172). Again, such theorisation takes as its starting point a biologically reductionist understanding of gender and the inequality of power that exists between the sexes, then labels the contravention of these 'God given laws' and this 'pre-ordained' and 'natural' inequality as 'perversion'.

Freud and the instinctual theorists

Similarly to Krafft-Ebing and Hirschfeld, Freud also positioned sadomasochistic desire within an evolutionary Darwinian model of gender-determined sexual aggression. He argued that:

> The sexuality of most male human beings . . . contains an element of aggressiveness and a desire to subjugate; the biological significance of it seems to lie in the need for overcoming the resistance of the sexual object by means other than the process of wooing. Thus sadism would correspond to an aggressive component of the sexual instinct which has become independent and exaggerated and, by displacement, has usurped the leading position.
>
> (Freud, 1905: 71)

The process by which sadism was assumed to give rise to masochism, and the way in which they become 'independent and exaggerated', was to occupy much of Freud's subsequent theorising and was crucial in the genesis of his theory of instinctual drives. However, Freud's analysis of SM is somewhat confused by his vague and varying use of the term, which he applied to sexual practices, instinctual drives and, with the publication of *A Child is Being Beaten* (Freud, 1919), to a diversity of behaviours including characterological, non-sexual traits (Maleson, 1984). Evaluation of the theory is also complicated by its continual and often radical revision, not least because of the problem posed by masochism to the functioning of the pleasure principle. Freud appears to have made two attempts to negate this difficulty, first in suggesting, similarly to Ellis (1903), that any strong excitation in an infant, including that which might be punitive, could produce 'sexual' arousal, and second (and more fundamental), by postulating the existence of a second primary instinct capable of overriding that which seeks pleasure; the death instinct (Freud, 1920), an innate self-directed drive towards destruction of the self.

Freud eventually differentiated masochism into several types (Freud,

1924), most importantly primary erotogenic (sexual) and secondary moral masochism. Erotogenic masochism was (eventually) conceived as being the result of a fusion of the death instinct with libido (Freud, 1920). Freud argued that (primary) sadism involves the outward projection of this drive into objects while moral masochism arises from a transformation of this primary sadism which, fuelled by the death instinct and such factors as castration anxiety and Oedipal guilt, is turned inward upon the self. For Freud, primary sadism and masochism represent neurotic distortions of instinctual drives resulting from regression or fixation, due to unresolved Oedipal conflicts, to a pre-Oedipal anal-sadistic stage of sexuality: 'Masochistic sexual practices allow for partial gratification of genital aims by paying the price for pleasure, accepting pain as an appeasement for castration, stressing one's helplessness or denying Sadistic impulses' (Sack and Miller, 1975: 245).

Freud's (multiple) understandings of SM appear somewhat confusing, and often contradictory: indeed, one is left feeling that, like Freud, 'no satisfactory explanation has been put forward' (1905: 72). Since Freud, something of a dichotomy has emerged in psychoanalytic discourse, with most theorists advocating either drive theories relating SM, similarly to Freud, to the sublimation and conflict of the primary instincts (Reik, 1940; Brenner, 1959; Gero, 1962), or to an 'object-relations' approach whereby SM is seen as determined primarily by environmental antecedents during infancy (Sadger, 1926; Berliner, 1947, 1958; Loewenstein, 1957; Storr, 1964; Glasser, 1979; Mollinger, 1982; Atkins, 1987). However, what they all share is the notion that SM is a sexual practice resulting from psychic conflict residing within the individual.

Object-relation theories

Unlike Freud, object-relation theorists emphasise the way in which SM reflects the early internalisation of objects. Sadger (1926) was among the first to propose and explore such an approach, relating SM to the Freudian stages of psychosexual development. Sadger begins with a discussion of the genesis of love and hate during early infancy. He starts from the premise that 'the satisfaction of the ego-needs, the appeasing of hunger and the cleansing of the body cannot be attained without a simultaneous strong excitation of the (oral, anal and genital) erotogenic zones' (Sadger, 1926: 484). And:

> Just as the young infant learns to love all those who stimulate and satisfy its sexuality, so it learns to hate all those who in any way interfere with its sexual life. This is the deepest root of love and hate and the source of their indissoluble connection.
>
> (Sadger, 1926: 485, 486)

Both love and hate are regarded as unavoidable and must be directed at those who are close, usually the mother.

Sadger places considerable emphasis upon the importance of breast-feeding and its association with oral-eroticism. The infant, observed Sadger, will often suckle on the breasts with great passion and aggression, sometimes even causing them to bleed. There is a desire on the part of the infant to 'incorporate the breast into itself', to master it and be its dictate in order to satiate its own desires at will. This involves fantasies of 'biting off the nipples', of 'castrating them'. Thus sadism, as a primary instinctual drive, is intrinsically related to a need for mastery. However, more crucial is the withdrawal of the breasts which, he claims, incites anger and hatred, 'severely mortifying the child's primary impulse of mastery' (1926: 488) and, in becoming conflated with love and attachment, establishing a primary and primitive 'sexualised power dynamic'. A similar process applies to self-care and toileting behaviours as the child is made increasingly responsible and even punished for its failures. In this way, claims Sadger, and since all love relations after the age of five are a recapitulation or 'transference' of the first, 'the tiny child's encounter with love and hate becomes a proto-type' for all subsequent relationships (1926: 488). To paraphrase Berliner (1958), SM experiences represent, in the unconscious, the subject's original relationship with the love object. Sadger concluded that 'whoever hates more than he loves, that is, whoever originally felt more keenly the withdrawal of sexual stimuli than he had felt the positive pleasure these had afforded, will have a tendency to sadism' (1926: 489). A related process is espoused for sexual masochism in which, suggests Sadger, sexual arousal is 'linked with the feeling of being in the power of some stronger being' (1926: 490). There is a primary identification with, and a fusion of, sexual arousal, power and/or pain.

Some object-theorists have gone further in emphasising this primitive unification of love and hate. For example, Mollinger (1982) argues that in its omnipotence and its inability to distinguish self and object representations, the 'symbiotic infant' (Kernberg, 1976) experiences itself as both the victim and the instigator, both the sadist and the masochist (cf. Klein, 1988). Even as differentiation proceeds, and objects acquire their own internal represen-tation, the infant is unable to hold on to love and hate within the same object (or within the self) and so they are split off, isolated, intensified and directed outward (as sadism) or inward (as masochism). Such a conceptuali-sation of the genesis of SM relies upon an understanding of parents as 'narcissistic' and as incapable of meeting the needs of their children (Panken, 1983). At best, psychoanalytic theorists tend to regard such parents as intensely ambivalent with a tendency towards hostility (Berliner, 1958), as inconsistent and irrational (Nydes, 1963), as over-controlling and manipulative (Montgomery, 1989) and as lacking self-control (Pestrak, 1991). Glasser (1979), for example, claims that 'even a comparatively super-ficial observation of [the SM-devotee's] family relationships will reveal serious disturbance, the most common features being a mixture of excessive dependent involvement and violent pseudo-rejection' (1979: 230). However, no evidence is cited to substantiate such claims; indeed, it has been noted that SM-devotees frequently exonerate or deny any hostility or aggression on the part of parents (Pestrak, 1991). Nevertheless, Pestrak refers to this as a 'denial and distorted perception of the child–parent relationship sustained by the parent's use of projection and other defence mechanisms' (1991: 90). A high incidence of sexual and physical abuse in the histories of devotees is also alluded to in the literature (Grossman, 1991), but again without empirical corroboration.

Psychoanalytic theories of SM have primarily focused on intrapsychic conflicts ameliorated through the displacement of the sexual aim. However, some object-relationists have concentrated on the function of interpersonal mechanisms in the maintenance of SM practices (Sack and Miller, 1975). For example, Avery (1977) suggests that sadism serves the function of intimidating a potentially abandoning object into staying, while for Berliner (1947), Horney (1935) and others, masochism involves an identification of the victim as lovable, as good, and as needing protection and mastering. Using such frameworks, SM becomes crucially related to a fear of object loss, ultimately derived from 'a fear of annihilation and a loss of self' (Mollinger, 1982: 387), and perhaps not dissimilar to the significance attached to castration fear by Freud (1905) and to those ideas espoused by Glasser (1979) relating to 'the core complex'. For Glasser, SM is an immature and primitive form of loving involving the 'sexualisation' of aggression due to a fear of annihilation. He argues that by sexualising aggression and turning it into sadism, the object is maintained as a source of pleasure rather than destroyed. Other theorists have also emphasised the relationship between SM and difficulties pertaining to intimacy (Glasser, 1979; Schnarch, 1993) and to anxieties and conflicts around dependency, autonomy and control (Frosh, 1993), as well as to its role as a re-enactment of trauma (Stoller, 1975).

Perhaps because of their tendency to 'essentialise' the phenomenon, to try and isolate it and root it in the individual's psychological structure and establish a single aetiology, psychoanalytic discourses on SM appear conflictual and, it could be argued, overly confident in their speculation. Indeed, psychoanalysis has had to conclude, finally, 'that there is no single, well-defined entity, syndrome, disease or pathogenic agent that lies at the core of all the neurotic, characterologic, psychotic and perverse behaviour that we call "sadomasochistic"' (Grossman, 1991). SM remains insufficiently defined and poorly understood. This, as Maleson (1984) acknowledges, means that 'the decision to employ the term may often be based on the judgements and normative concepts of the analyst' (1984: 336). Furthermore, there are no accounts of psychoanalytic formulations of SM being based on, or corroborated by, empirical research. Consequently, psychoanalytic models of SM have been criticised for being derived from informed abstracted theorising, based exclusively on clinical single-case design (Gosselin and Wilson, 1980; Thompson, 1994). Perhaps because of this tendency for analytic theory to be based on SM-devotees who present for therapy, the 'psychological unhealthiness' of SM and therefore of its practitioners is often assumed as *a priori*. Moreover, assumptions concerning 'non-clinical participants', their experiences and psychological state, remain uncorroborated.

Behavioural and biological theories

The behavioural model of SM rests upon the basic premise that all sexual behaviour is the result of learning. Initially this was postulated to be a simple paired association, as exemplified by Sacher-Masoch's alleged beating from his aunt after being caught observing her during coitus. However, as Jaspers (1963) has commented, while 'perversion rises through the accidents of our first experience [and] gratification remains tied to the form and object, once experienced this does not happen simply through the force of simultaneous association' (Jaspers, 1963: 323). McGuire *et al.* (1965) argue that this initial experience is crucial only in that it provides a fantasy for masturbation which, through a process of conditioning, becomes a more permanent and encompassing 'sexual deviation': 'In accordance with conditioning theory any stimulus which regularly precedes ejaculation by the correct time interval should become more and more sexually exciting. The stimulus may be circumstantial or it may be deliberate' (McGuire *et al.*, 1965: 186). According to McGuire *et al.*, the value of a stimulus as a masturbatory fantasy is determined by whether it is the first real sexual experience. Subsequent masturbation ensures that its stimulus value is increased while other sexual stimuli are extinguished through lack of reinforcement or are experienced as aversive or unpleasant. More operantly based formulations of SM, derived from animal experimentation – in which a positive reinforcer is paired with an 'unpleasant' stimulus, thus creating a conditioned 'masochistic' response – are reviewed by Sack and Miller (1975).

That sexual arousal can be conditioned in humans has been demonstrated by Rachman and Hodgson (1968), who paired a fetish object, the conditioned stimulus, with an arousing, unconditioned stimulus, and produced a conditioned sexual response in 'normal male' participants. The efficacy of behavioural treatment strategies in 'unlearning' sadomasochistic behaviours has not been well demonstrated. For example, the use of aversion therapy in the 'treatment' of sadomasochism is described by Marks *et al.* (1965) with variable rates of 'improvement' at two-year follow-up (cited in Bancroft, 1974). However, the use of electric shock in the treatment of masochists has obvious drawbacks and at least one study has shown that such treatments can be sexually arousing to the patient (Bancroft, 1974). Similarly to psychodynamic formulations, behavioural conceptualisations of SM would appear to be largely uncorroborated by empirical research and are derived primarily from the treatment of small, self-selected clinical samples. They also appear somewhat oversimplistic and reductionist.

Another viewpoint, not considered in any depth here, suggests that SM, along with paedophilia, homosexuality and other 'sexual anomalies', is caused by 'differential brain pathology' (Goodman, 1987; Marshall *et al.*, 1990). It is argued that SM is determined, or influenced, by genetic, hormonal or chromosomal abnormalities operating within the central nervous system. Similar speculations may be found in Krafft-Ebing (1886); however, the validity of such a model remains unproven. The efficacy of treatment strategies derived from such speculation also appear to be unproven, while related ethical and political considerations are entirely ignored.

Neuropsychological and anthropological theories

Other psychological models of SM have concentrated on the psycho-physiological association of pleasure and pain (Sack and Miller, 1975). Ellis (1903) was among the first to argue that all states of arousal are physiologically indistinguishable and that pain may stimulate sexual arousal just as it may fear or anger. For Ellis, 'sadism-masochism' was a universal and normal feature of sexual relations rather than a congenital and pathological aberration. Ellis believed that 'pain', whether it be the discomfort of initial penetration or the consequence of intense and harsh flagellation, could be directly experienced as pleasure. Pain, he argued, could become a form of erotic symbolism, 'a psychic condition in which part of the sexual process tends to assume unusual importance', similarly to the way in which objects might become fetishised. Pain is paired with an intense emotional feeling in order to enhance sexual arousal. In this sense, pain may provide a general excitement, which can amplify sexual feelings (Tomkins, 1962) or be labelled as sexual by those experiencing the pain (Weinberg *et al.*, 1984). The similarity of the physiological responses to pain and orgasm is also noted by Kinsey *et al.* (1953). Further to this, Sack and Miller (1975) argue that pain can only be experienced 'phenomenologically'. In drawing upon the extensive literature on the psychology and management of pain, they point to examples such as the use of hypnotic suggestion as an anaesthetic for major surgery and, in citing the work of Zborowski (1969), to the operation of cultural and individual variations in pain responsivity (cf. Melzack, 1973). They also criticise 'dichotomous models' of pain and pleasure, arguing that the words actually refer to 'different qualities of experience which need not be mutually exclusive' (Sack and Miller, 1975: 254).

In concentrating on 'spanking', one of the core components of SM, Levitt (1971) argued that the bottom, apart from possessing obvious sexual characteristics, is also enervated by the same third and fourth sacral nerves as the genitals, which carry 'pleasurable sensations' to the central nervous system. Given that the bottom is able to tolerate considerable trauma without serious damage, Levitt found the use of 'bottom spanking' in fore-play to be a common and explicable phenomenon. Mains (1991) cites evidence which suggests that pain can trigger opiate-like chemicals within the brain which release endorphins, resulting in a form of 'adrenaline rush' comparable to that experienced by athletes or skydivers. He argues that 'pain is not enjoyable because it is a second rate substitute [for pleasure, but because] it is pleasure' (Mains, 1991: 38). Polhemus and Randall (1994) argue a similar point in their reference to SM practices as a form of consciousness-raising, likening it to medieval flagellation and to the painful spiritual rituals common among Native American and Hindu cultures. Polhemus, an anthropologist, continues:

> SM's capacity to open such doors of perception might derive from the simple operation of opiate-like brain chemicals. However, at least as important a part could be played by the ritualistic structuring of SM experience. The power of ritual has been largely forgotten in our modern world . . . Ritual structures action, focuses attention upon meaningful symbols, slows down time and sets an event apart from the everyday. Most of all, those who participate in a ritual event become more than the sum of the parts of a community.
>
> (Polhemus and Randall, 1994: 117)

Similar arguments may also be found in a number of the essays written by devotees contained in Thompson (1991).

Empirical and ethnological research on SM

The psychoanalytic and psychological models of SM reviewed have been developed with minimal reliance upon empirical research, and have been based almost exclusively on small samples of people presenting to clinical services. Most literature concerning SM therefore tends to be primarily theoretical and clinical in nature and tends to make *a priori* assumptions regarding the psychological well-being of its practitioners. As Breslow *et al.* point out, 'despite the attention given to Sadomasochism in the scientific literature, few attempts have been made to study Sadomasochists' (Breslow *et al.*, 1986: 84). Those few studies which have attempted to investigate SM among non-clinical participants include Spengler (1977), Lee (1979), Kamel (1980), Breslow *et al.* (1986), Moser and Levitt (1987), Gosselin and Wilson (1980), Weinberg and Falk (1980), Weinberg *et al.* (1984) and Taylor (1995). However, most of these, as postal questionnaire surveys of sexual behaviour, have tended to be superficially descriptive and provide little data with which to corroborate or develop psychological understandings of SM.

The studies generally suggest that SM-devotees develop their interests at various ages, that its expression is extremely varied and may take place within individual, group, anonymous, intimate or professional contexts. Furthermore, they suggest that devotees vary in terms of the importance and exclusivity of their SM interests and differ in terms of their preferred position along the dominance–submission continuum. Most participants in the studies tended to have a positive self-image while self-reported rates of depression were low, as were the reported frequencies of sexual and emotional abuse during childhood (Breslow *et al.*, 1986 – based on the return of 272 postal questionnaires). Of their sample of 178, Moser and Levitt (1987) found that 5 per cent were to some degree distressed by their involvement in SM, 16 per cent had consulted a mental health professional, and 5 per cent had a psychiatric admission. However, there is no comparison with a matched non-SM control group and no evidence of if (or how such) 'ill health' might be related to SM. The extent to which such samples are representative of persons who practise SM is also open to question. Spengler's (1977) study of 245 gay male SM-devotees suggests that it is adjustment, acceptance and openness of one's sexuality, rather than *being* sadomasochistic, which is crucially related to psychological well-being.

In one of the few published studies by psychologists using non-clinical SM participants, Gosselin and Wilson (1980) secured a sample of 133 male and 25 female SM-devotees (aged between 20 and 80) who advertised in British SM contact magazines. Participants were required to complete an Eysenck Personality Questionnaire (EPQ) and a Wilson Sex Fantasy Questionnaire, and to provide details of their sexual behaviour, fantasies, personality and pathologies. Gosselin and Wilson found few differences between non-'sexually deviant' controls and SM participants. They did not differ in their childhood experiences of corporal punishment, although devotees' upbringings were marginally stricter. Rates of orgasm and self-rated libido were also similar. SM sexual practices were found to be extremely varied, although the majority tended to be predominantly masochistic. Gosselin and Wilson (1980) and Gosselin (1987) also stress the contractual nature of SM practices and the centrality of behaviours not necessarily related to the administering or receiving of 'pain'. Gosselin and Wilson's psychometric measures suggested that, of their male SM participants, submissives tended to be more introvert and less stable than dominants who, in turn, were less 'stable' but as extrovert as 'normal' males. Dominant women were the most extrovert but also scored higher on neuroticism. However, no participant displayed clinically significant levels of neuroticism or psychoticism, and their scores were all within a normal range. Participants also failed to display particularly high levels of guilt or other general indicators of obsessional or neurotic characteristics. However, the study only provided a limited number of measures derived from the EPQ, a questionnaire not commonly used in clinical psychological assessment.

A similarly designed study by Taylor (1995), using the Clinical Assessment Questionnaire, revealed a diverse mean profile for a mixed SM cohort. Participants tended to score over and above the average range on intelligence, dominance, imagination and radicalism, and below average on conformity. On the clinical factors, agitation and psychopathic deviation were the only scales on which there was a significant, albeit small, mean deviation above the average range. These scales are also as much a measure of sensation-seeking and disinhibition, and so in isolation cannot be taken as indicative of pathology. However, since the sample for this study consisted of only nineteen, these results may only be taken as suggestive.

The empirical research cited here, and those studies presented earlier regarding prevalence, would appear to suggest that SM involves a complex interplay of various behaviours, beliefs and sensations which often extend into 'normal' sexual practices, which are contemporaneously and historically prevalent and which, it would seem, do not necessarily indicate the existence of any 'mental ill health'. Nevertheless, within most psychological discourse, as the aforementioned review testifies, SM has been constructed as an objectively observable and quantifiable practice, it is generally hypothesised as having a unitary and universal aetiology, as in some way residing within or belonging to the person who exhibits it, as consistent and explicit in its presentation and unvarying (or unimportant) in its meaning to those who practise it. Furthermore, and perhaps most significantly, SM has been constructed as a psychosexual disorder and remains a psychiatric illness reified within the DSM and the ICD. Why?

SEXUALITY, PATHOLOGY AND SOCIAL CONTROL

Foucault (1976) argued that since at least the seventeenth century language has been used to subjugate dissident sexualities, with desires transformed into discourse – religious and pseudo-scientific – in order that they be controlled:

> Through these various discourses, legal sanctions against minor perversions were multiplied, sexual irregularity was annexed to mental illness, from childhood to old age, a norm of sexual development was defined and all the possible deviations were carefully described . . . [medicine] created an entire organic, functional, or mental pathology arising out of 'incomplete' sexual practices; it incorporated them into the notions of 'development' and instinctual 'disturbances'; and it undertook to manage them.

> (Foucault, 1976: 36, 41)

Dissident sexualities, argued Foucault, have not been repressed – they have been multiplied and fractured, while discourses have been legitimised and empowered to define and to control. He cites the 'taxonomic' explosion of sexual pathologies toward the end of the last century; Westphals' 'creation' of the homosexual in 1870, Krafft-Ebing's creation of zoophilia, sadism and masochism, and Rohleder's classification of mixoscopophiles, gynecomasts, prestyophiles and sexoesthetic inverts, to name but a few (cited in Foucault, 1976: 43). The function of these discourses (i.e. the 'deviancing' of 'alternative sexualities') is, according to Foucault, to consolidate and proliferate sexual hegemony (i.e. procreative, patriarchal, heterosexual monogamy) in order that labour capacity be maximised and political conservatism and inequable and divisive social relations be perpetuated. Scientific discourse, according to Foucault, in its 'uncovering of truth', is subordinated to the imperatives of pseudo-morality which, in turn, are subordinate to economics and the distribution of power (Reiche, 1970; Foucault, 1976; Weeks, 1990). SM, then, may be seen as having been discursively and materially constructed as a perversion so as to reinforce, legitimise and perpetuate forms of sexuality which are subservient to the requirements of the state.

Such a conceptualisation, with regards to the 'mental health professions', necessitates a refutation of their position as independent, positivistic and scientifically objective and neutral disciplines, since they are the agents through which these scientific truths are constructed, validated and disseminated. It becomes necessary to question their role as being

> instrumental in maintaining the societal status quo by (a) Endorsing and reflecting dominant social values, (b) Disseminating those values in the persuasive form of so-called value free scientific statements, and (c) Providing an asocial image of the individual as essentially independent from socio-historical circumstances.
>
> (Prilleltensky, 1989: 800)

Indeed, 'not only do psychologists [etc.] rarely challenge existing social beliefs, they also actively endorse and facilitate [their] reproduction' (Prilleltensky, 1989: 795). This is because they, too, are the 'socialised products' of their cultural and political environments, and their chosen areas of research, their methods, their results and their interpretation are all intrinsically tied to their own subjective positions. If one accepts that the 'human sciences' are 'necessarily subjective' and informed by sociopolitical issues relating ultimately, at least from a Foucauldian-Marxist perspective, to social control, the distribution of power and the means of production, then the supposed objectivity of the positivistic method, when applied to psychological and psychiatric diagnosis and classification, is thrown into doubt. This has led some researchers to question the validity of a number of 'psychiatric disorders' reified within the DSM and the ICD, and to question the utility and function of diagnostic classification and the very existence of a whole range of syndromes including 'schizophrenia' (Boyle, 1990), 'sexual dysfunction' (Boyle, 1993) and female reproductive syndromes such as PMS, postnatal depression and the menopause (Ussher, 1989, 1991). Just as diagnoses of psychosis were used against opponents of the Soviet state, and slaves who insisted on escaping the plantations were diagnosed as 'drapetomaniacs', so contemporary psychopathologisation may be seen not as reliant upon objective truths and as serving the advancement of science and the betterment of humankind, but as social constructions subservient to political and economic imperatives.

In establishing disorders as illnesses or dysfunctions which reside as some kind of 'essence' within individuals, the psychological professions create the reason for their existence and their territories of influence. Through the rhetoric of science, they create, reinforce and perpetuate an image of science as a 'privileged way of knowing' (Kitzinger, 1987: 12), 'as a natural, apolitical domain of technical expertise, advancing inexorably and dispassionately towards objective and empirically verifiable truth about the nature of reality' (1987: 15) and as a legitimate, empirically validated and humane method of managing people's distress *and dissent*. With this relocation of dissidence as illness (Conrad and Schneider, 1980), and the expanding medicalisation of 'everyday life' (Illich, 1975), the psychological professions increasingly serve as agents of social control, immersed in a misrepresentative vocabulary and an 'aura of scientifically grounded neutrality' (Gerhardt, 1989: 268).

Social constructionism

Social constructionism provides an alternative to this essentialist and positivist paradigm. It is a perspective which eschews the concept of a singular, objective, empirically validatable truth, existing out there 'in-the-world', waiting to be uncovered through the application of 'the scientific method'. It involves a rejection of the notion that complex phenomena may be explained by referring to some supposed inner truth or essence. Equally, there is a rejection of the assumption that there *must be* a unitary, fundamental and rational underlying pattern of exposition ordained by nature. It is therefore a perspective which eschews reductionism and determinism in all its forms. In contrast to *essentialist positivism*, realities become constructions (Berger and Luckmann, 1967), while truth becomes multiple and subjective. 'Psychiatric disorders' may be seen as disparate behaviours and internal 'cognitive constructions', emanating from interchanges between persons and their environments which are defined as pathological by those with the power and purpose to do so. In this sense, SM becomes merely a label (Scheff, 1974), a manufactured illness (Szasz, 1970; Bullough and Bullough, 1977), a 'social construction' (Rian, 1982; Weinberg *et al.*, 1984; Eisenberg, 1988; Cochrane, 1989).

From a social constructionist perspective, biology may be seen as providing only the *preconditions* for our sexualities, a set of potentialities which take on meaning only in terms of their social, cultural activation. The constructionist paradigm assumes that there is no insistent or essential human drive or desire which pre-exists the entry into language and culture (Ortner and Whitehead, 1981): 'Desire is constituted in the very process of that induction, in which the component instincts and the polymorphous perversity of the young human are involuntarily conscripted into the demands of culture' (Weeks, 1982: 299). It is a perspective concerned with the way individuals are constituted by the social world, the way the world of language and symbols come to dwell within them; the way we discursively construct our sense of self and our sense of the world around us from the discourses that are available to us. In this regard, social constructionism draws upon ideas from Lacanian psychoanalysis as well as poststructuralist and symbolic interactionist perspectives (Plummer, 1982, 1995). It is also informed by phenomenological and existential ideas, especially Sartrian notions of 'existence as preceding essence' and of 'being-in-the-world' (Sartre, 1957). However, what all these perspectives share is an emphasis upon the individual's active role in structuring their reality within limiting sociohistorical contexts.

A DISCURSIVE ANALYSIS OF SM IDENTITIES AND PRACTICES

If we accept that SM, as an identity and as a set of practices, is socially constructed through the discourses that are available, then from a constructionist perspective it becomes possible, indeed purposeful, to investigate the way in which these discourses are used by people to define, shape and make sense of their sexualities and so explore the way in which SM sexualities are discursively and materially constructed. One method by which these 'symbols' may be accessed is through an analysis of their representation in language. Such a method is consistent with the social constructionist approach, since it assumes that our sense of self and of the world is constituted in and through discourse. The aim of its analysis is to unravel the process by which this discourse is constructed, by identifying varying discourses and positioning them in their sociocultural contexts. From a discursive analysis of audiotaped interviews with twenty-four SM devotees recruited through SM networks, the authors (see Taylor, 1995; Taylor and Ussher, in press) were therefore able to explore the ways in which participants defined and made sense of their sexualities using a number of interpretive repertoires or 'ways of understanding'. In terms of definition, all participants incorporated the notions of consensuality, an inequable balance of power, sexual arousal and compatibility of definition. However, what was especially interesting was the way participants constructed discursive aetiological frameworks within which they could make sense of their SM. An analysis of these discourses revealed eight common interpretive repertoires, eight ways in which participants made sense of their SM. These discursive themes often overlapped, were (occasionally) contradictory and were employed to varying degrees by different participants. They involved SM being understood and positioned as dissidence, as pleasure, as escapism, as transcendence, as learned behaviour, as intrapsychic, as pathology and, finally, as 'inexplicable'.

SM as dissidence

The mode of this discourse's expression differed in accordance with the political and personal orientation of the individual, but involved an understanding of SM as deliberately, consciously and militantly antithetical to a sexual hegemonic, to patriarchal heterosexuality. Its most common form, expressed primarily by female participants, was within a feminist discourse in which SM was regarded as parodying sexual relations considered as traditionally subjugating, oppressive and exploitative of women:

> In SM relationships you are playing in what I think is a very corrupting way with what, once upon a time, was a legal right for a husband to beat his wife with a stick. We're actually now playing, experimenting with things that were oppressive but we're doing it in a totally different way.

> I think SM is as much about politics as anything else.

There was a recognition of sexual relationships as inherently involving an inequable balance of power but with an understanding of this power dynamic as reflexive and as not necessarily weighted in favour of men. Instead, SM was positioned as a parody of abusive, divisive sexual relations; it turns it on its head, ridicules it, undermines it, exploits it, exposes it with the ultimate intention of destroying it.

Another related discourse positioned SM as oppositional not so much to patriarchy but to what many devotees referred to as 'vanilla sex', conventional non-SM sexual relations, which were positioned as conformative, uninteresting, unadventurous and unerotic. Within this discourse there was a celebration of perversity, of difference consistent with many of the ideas embraced within 'queer politics':

> It's in yer face perversion. I suppose I like outraging people, upsetting the balance, you know girls are supposed to be like this or sex is supposed to be like that.

SM as pleasure

Another discourse involved positioning SM and 'SM identity' as 'fun', as 'having a laugh', as 'mucking about', as play. Much of the language used by participants and devotees generally reflected this fairly obvious association between SM and 'having fun' – 'playmates', 'sex play', 'playroom', 'sex toys', 'SM games', 'sex games' were all commonly used phrases. This is not to say that the suspension of disbelief and the 'seriousness of sex play' was not crucial to many participants; only that the objective of the 'play' was, first and foremost, about giving and receiving pleasure.

SM as escapism

This discourse positioned SM as transcendence or escapism of the mundane, of the ordinariness or alienation of everyday life. There was an emphasis upon SM as in some way compensating for a perceived lack in their life, such as in countering feelings of aloneness, drudgery or boredom:

> I work in an office all week nine to five, Mr Straightsville. When the weekend comes and I can do SM it's like an antidote: it invigorates me, keeps me going.

> I love the ritual of SM, it's like another world, it's all contrived, fantastical, nothing's real, everything is constantly changing. It's pure escapism I guess.

The language of SM and phrases such as 'scene' and 'role-play' also indicate the role of SM as escapist fantasy, not necessarily as an avoidance of reality but as another (alternative) reality, with its own conventions and its own inherent benefits for the participant:

> It's play-acting. It's like going on to a stage, you can step out of yourself and pretend to be something you're not. I can be a man, a woman, someone's teacher, their father, their baby, their prisoner, anything.

Some of these discourses, in positioning SM as a possible avoidance, a denial or an escape from oneself, or at least certain aspects of oneself, imply that such a narrative might be related to a more intrapsychic discourse. However, it also raises another potential discursive theme: SM as therapy.

SM as transcendence

One transcendence discourse involved positioning SM within a spiritual or mystical framework. The 'high' participants described as resulting from SM (without, prior to or with orgasm) was also credited with near-mystical significance. It was spoken of as a heightened state of consciousness or as in some way making them more astute, more enlightened or more alive. Some participants credited SM as possessing ceremonial significance. For example, one referred to his SM induction as a 'rite of passage', another as 'an awakening'. SM was credited almost with the status of religion. Participants adhered to its rituals and conventions and devoted themselves to its practice. They made references to 'new age primitivism' and likened it to religious flagellation and to non-Western spiritual practices involving the endurance and infliction of pain and suffering.

A second (related but more secular) discourse, used to varying degrees by a dozen participants, involved an interpretation of SM as causing an adrenaline rush or an endorphin high. The process and content of this 'high' was similar to the previous discourse, but was attributed to a more physiological cause. However, one consequence of this 'physiological discourse' was an understanding of SM as potentially addictive, like any pleasurable drug:

> I know guys who have SM sessions two, three times a week and they're now into situations where they're into really heavy stuff, and they come out of sessions looking a real mess, and I think it's almost like some kind of addiction where you tolerate the effects and so need more and more to get the same buzz out of it.

> I think I'm actually quite addicted to SM. I'd probably find it difficult to go without the euphoria. It's very addictive and you can't get it from anything else.

SM as learned behaviour

A discourse closely related to this, and drawn upon by six participants, incorporated an understanding of SM as the result of a learned association usually originating in childhood. Such discourse usually involved some awareness of SM as having a neurophysiological component in which pain and arousal become inseparably paired:

> Pain and sexual arousal have become more and more indistinguishable to me. It's as if over the years my brain has kind of, er, combined them, like I can no longer tell them apart, so that now during sex I find any sensation of pain immediately excites me.

SM as intrapsychic

A more 'psychodynamic-systemic' discourse was also apparent. This spanned a variety of interrelated discourses but generally involved SM being in some way related to certain psychological aspects of their personalities, often understood as the result of experiences in childhood. Participants also referred to the detached nature of much SM contact, and its relationship to their difficulties or avoidance of intimacy, but the most dominant 'intrapsychic' discourse was on the importance of control and its role in SM as a continuation, re-enactment or reversed re-enactment of earlier power issues:

> I guess I'm quite a controlling person in everything. I find not being in control very difficult to handle perhaps because I'm afraid of being, er, out of control which is how I was a few years ago. That was a very difficult time for me. Perhaps being a top is about, um, overcompensating. At that time things got out of hand 'cause someone else had all the power and they let me down badly, really messed me up. I've discovered the best person to put my trust in is myself. (I: So to not be in control is to be vulnerable?) Yeah.

A further discourse was around SM as retribution, or as somehow related to guilt or unhappy or abusive childhoods. It was this discourse which seemed most clearly related to the next: that of SM as pathology, but it was also the one most passionately rejected by participants as an explanation of their SM.

SM as pathology

Although participants rarely applied this discourse to themselves, most knew of someone whose SM was (or was potentially) indicative of pathology. Many participants clearly had difficulty understanding the practices of other devotees and sometimes dismissed their behaviour as 'unhealthy' because they felt it was extreme:

> I think there have to be limits, like being on your own and cutting yourself I think is really weird and cigarette burns, that's going beyond SM. I think that's about mental health. Someone who gets a buzz from having cigarettes put out on them I think is in touch with something quite disturbed.

Behaviours were also seen as 'unhealthy' if they did not adequately incorporate an awareness of consent or, for some, if they went beyond the context of immediate sexual arousal:

> He thought that just because I was submissive in bed that I would be submissive in the relationship. He was a total power freak. I don't think he understood that the SM was about sexual pleasure. I mean, his whole life was based on having to dominate: he definitely had a problem.

> Of course a lot of S&M-ers are messed up. Just like everyone else; I mean why should we have a monopoly on mental health? For some, the SM thing's probably incidental for others, yeah, I'm sure it's tied up with, I don't know, a bad childhood or something, but that doesn't mean SM is practised by mad people any more than with vanilla. It's just more difficult to make sense of, that's all.

SM as inexplicable

A number of participants regarded their own behaviour as 'weird' but tended to attribute this to 'the inexplicable' rather than 'the pathological'. Indeed, one of the most common discourses, used to varying degrees by all participants, incorporated some ideas around SM as defying comprehension:

> I just accept it as a bit odd but that's OK. Why try and explain everything ? I don't need to make sense of it. Perhaps if it were understandable it would be less appealing. I mean, what's this problem that everyone has about having to make sense of everything the whole time?

THE ESSENTIALS OF CONSTRUCTIONISM: SM AND THE MATERIAL–DISCURSIVE DEBATE

Psychology, psychiatry and psychoanalysis have attempted to construct SM as an 'essentialist' sexual aberration generally indicative of psychopathology and ill health. They have also put forward a variety of hypotheses to account for its aetiology and presentation. More recently, social and postmodernist discourses consistent with feminist and queer politics have countered these constructions. Within the aforementioned analysis, it is possible to identify these and other discourses as 'introjected constructions' and to see how they jostle with one another within people's 'understandings of the self'. Such an approach provides important insights into the way people's internal worlds are constructed and how their identities and practices are formed, interpreted and, at times, exonerated. It clarifies the way in which SM can only be understood through a 'phenomenological analysis' of its (often multiple) subjective meanings and that these meanings can only be understood within their socio-cultural and historical context. The analysis also highlights the way in which psychology, rather than being neutral, detached and purely descriptive, is actively involved in constructing the phenomenon under its gaze.

However, this social contructionist–discursive analysis of SM sexualities does pose a number of related difficulties. The reduction of a given phenomenon to the level of discourse tends to deny its operation on a more material level, individually and collectively, biologically and politically. The social constructionist approach tends to carry with it a denial of the existence of anything real beyond the level of narrative. There is a negation of the material world, and of the body, which is lost in a kind of 'constructionist solipsism'. This can be discounting of many people's realities – their sense of themselves as an 'SM-er', as 'lesbian', as 'gay', is negated; it is dismissed as nothing more than a construction. Yet one is left feeling that there *is* something real, some *essence* beneath these layers of constructed meaning, but that its emergence in, and interaction with, the material world is left unexplored, for if it is acknowledged at all it is dismissed as unknowable. Perhaps what is needed is a more integrative theoretical and epistemological framework which acknowledges the discursive–material dualism of sexuality and within which this emergence and interaction might be more fully explored.

While the social constructionist approach may be keen to emphasise the cultural and social relatedness of people's stories, their impact can also easily be reduced to the level of narrative. The body, the societal structure – the materiality of power within which discourses are generated, enacted and received – can easily be ignored. For example, while SM may be understood as a discursive construction, like most sexualities it is generally acted out within the confines of the body. It is experienced (at least in part) materially; as pain, pleasure, arousal. Thus, while it may carry symbolic and subjective meaning it also has very real material consequences; for the body and for society. At its extreme we are, potentially, still faced with difficult questions concerning the rights of individuals to consensually endanger (or take) their own or another's life in the pursuit of sexual pleasure. There are also difficult ethical and political implications, debated by a number of feminist and queer theorists, as to the role of SM in reinforcing, perpetuating and exonerating real-life inequalities, oppression and violence (Linden *et al.*, 1982; Jeffreys, 1990; Califia, 1994; Edwards, 1994). Clearly SM, whatever it is, is not *just discursive*.

REFERENCES

American Psychiatric Association (1994) *Diagnostic and Statistical Manual of Mental Disorders* (DSM-IIIR), Washington DC: American Psychiatric Association.

Atkins, R.N. (1987) The Origins of Masochism, *Integrative Psychiatry*, 5(1), 49–52.

Avery, N.C. (1977) Sadomasochism: A Defence Against Object Loss, *Psychoanalytic Review*, 64, 101–109.

Bancroft, J. (1974) *Deviant Sexual Behaviour*, Oxford: Clarendon Press.

Bayer, R. (1981) *Homosexuality and American Psychiatry: The Politics of Diagnosis*, New York: Basic Books.

Berger, P. and Luckmann, T. (1967) *The Social Construction of Reality*, New York: Anchor.

Berliner, B. (1947) On Some Psychodynamics of Masochism, *Psychoanalytic Quarterly*, 16, 459–471.

——(1958) The Role of Object Relations in Moral Masochism, *Psychoanalytic Quarterly*, 27, 38–56.

Bloch, I. (1935) *Strangest Sex Acts*, New York: Falstaff Press.

Boyle, M. (1990) *Schizophrenia: A Scientific Delusion*, London: Routledge.

——(1993) Sexual Dysfunction or Heterosexual Dysfunction, *Feminism and Psychology*, 3.

Brenner, M. (1959) The Masochistic Character, *Psychoanalytic Quarterly*, 18, 197–226.

Bresler, F. (1988) *Sex and the Law*, London: Muller.

Breslow, N., Evans, C. and Langley, J. (1986) Comparisons Among Heterosexual, Bisexual and Homosexual Male Sadomasochists, *Journal of Homosexuality*, 13(1), 83–107.

Bullough, V. and Bullough, B. (1977) *Sin, Sickness and Sanity: A History of Sexual Attitudes*, New York: New American Library.

Califia, P. (1994) *Public Sex: The Culture of Radical Sex*, Pittsburgh, PA: Cleis Press.

Cochrane, R. (1989) *The Social Creation of Mental Illness*, London: Longman.

Conrad, P. and Schneider, J.W. (1980) *Deviance and Medicalization*, St Louis, MI: Mosby.

Davison, G.C. and Neale, J.M. (1990) *Abnormal Psychology*, John Wiley & Sons.

Edwards, T. (1994) *Erotics and Politics: Gay Male Sexuality, Masculinity and Feminism,* London: Routledge.

Eisenberg, L. (1988) The Social Construction of Mental Illness, *Psychological Medicine*, 18, 1–9.

Ellis, H. (1903) *Studies in the Psychology of Sex*, New York: Random House.

——(1935) *The Psychology of Sex*, London: Heinemann Medical.

Foucault, M. (1976) *The History of Sexuality*, vol. 1, Harmondsworth: Penguin (1984).

Freud, S. (1905) *Three Essays on the Theory of Sexuality*, The Pelican Freud Library, vol. 7, London: Penguin.

——(1919) *A Child is Being Beaten*, Standard Edition, vol. 17, London: Hogarth Press, pp. 175–204.

——(1920) *Beyond the Pleasure Principle*, Standard Edition, vol. 18, London: Hogarth Press, pp. 7–66.

——(1924) *The Economic Problem of Masochism*, Standard Edition, vol. 19, London: Hogarth Press, pp. 157–172.

Friday, N. (1982) *My Secret Garden*, London: Quartet.

——(1993) *Men in Love*, London: Hutchinson.

Frosh, S. (1993) The Seeds of Masculine Sexuality, in J.M. Ussher and C. Baker (eds), *Psychological Perspectives on Sexual Problems: New Directions in Theory and Practice*, London: Routledge.

Gerhardt, M. (1989) *Ideas About Illness. An Intellectual and Political History of Medical Sociology*, London: Macmillan.

Gero, G. (1962) Sadism, Masochism, and Aggression: Their Role in Symptom Formation, *Psychoanalytic Quarterly*, 31, 31–42.

Glasser, M. (1979) Some Aspects of the Role of Aggression in the Perversions, in I. Rosen (ed.), *Sexual Deviation*, Buckingham: Open University Press.

Goodman, R.E. (1987) Genetic and Hormonal Factors in Human Sexuality: Evolutionary and Developmental Perspectives, in G. Wilson (ed.), *Variant Sexuality, Research and Theory*, London: Faber and Faber.

Gosselin, C. (1987) The Sadomasochistic Contract, in G. Wilson (ed.), *Variant Sexuality, Research and Theory*, London: Faber and Faber.

Gosselin, C. and Wilson, G. (1980) *Sexual Variations: Fetishism, Sadomasochism and Transvestism*, London: Faber and Faber.

Greene, G. and Greene, C. (1974) *S-M: The Last Taboo*, New York: Grove Press.

Grossman, W.I. (1991) Pain, Aggression, Fantasy and Concepts of Sadomasochism, *Psychoanalytic Quarterly*, 60, 22–52.

Hamilton, A. (1996) SM in Marriage OK, *Gay Times*, April.

Horney, K. (1935) The Problem of Feminine Masochism, *Psychoanalytic Review*, 22, 241–257.

Hunt, M. (1974) *Sexual Behaviour in the 1970s*, Chicago: Playboy.

Illich, I. (1975) *Medical Nemesis*, New York: Pantheon.

Jaspers, K. (1963) *General Psychopathology*, Manchester: Manchester University Press.

Jeffreys, S. (1990) *Anticlimax. A Feminist Perspective on the Sexual Revolution*, London: The Women's Press.

Kamel, G.W.L. (1980) Leather Sex: Meaningful Aspects of Gay Sadomasochism, *Deviant Behaviour*, 1, 171–191.

Kernberg, O. (1976) *Object Relations Theory and Clinical Psychoanalysis*, New York: Aronson.

Kershaw, A. (1992) Love Hurts, *Guardian Weekend*, 28 November.

Kinsey, A.C., Pomeroy, W.B., Martin, C.E. and Gebhard, P.H. (1953) *Sexual Behaviour in the Human Female*, Philadelphia: Saunders.

Kitzinger, C. (1987) *The Social Construction of Lesbianism*, London: Sage.

Klein, M. (1988) Envy and Gratitude, *Envy and Gratitude and Other Works, 1946–1963*, London: Hogarth Press.

Kokkoka, R. Von (1965) *Thekoka Shastra*, trans. A. Comfort, New York: Stein & Day.

Krafft-Ebing, R. von (1886) *Psychopathia Sexualis*, trans. F.S. Klaf, New York: Bell.

Lee, J.A. (1979) The Social Organisation of Sexual Risk, *Alternative Lifestyles*, 2, 69–100.

Levitt, E.E. (1971) Sadomasochism, *Sexual Behaviour*, 1(6), 68–80.

Linden, R.R., Pagano, D.R., Russell, D.E.H. and Star, S.L. (1982) *Against Sadomasochism: A Radical Feminist Analysis*, East Palo Alto, CA: Frog in the Well.

Loewenstein, R.M. (1957) A Contribution to the Psychoanalytic Theory of Masochism, *Journal of the American Psychoanalytic Association*, 5, 197–234.

McGuire, R.J., Carlisle, J.M and Young, B.G. (1965) Sexual Deviations as Conditioned: A Hypothesis, *Behaviour Research & Therapy*, 2, 185–190.

Mains, J. (1991) The Molecular Anatomy of Leather. In M. Thompson (ed.), *Leatherfolk: Radical Sex, People, Politics and Practices*, Boston, MA: Alyson.

Maleson, F.G. (1984) The Multiple Meanings of Masochism in Psychoanalytic Discourse, *Journal of the American Psychoanalytic Association*, 32(2), 325–356.

Malla, K. (1964) *Theanganga Ranga*, trans. R. Burton, New York: Lancer Books.

Marcus, M. (1981) *A Taste for Pain*, London: Souvenir.

Marks, I.M., Rachman, S. and Gelder, M.G. (1965) Methods for Assessment of Aversion Treatment in Fetishism with Masochism, *Behavioural Research*, 3, 253–258.

Marshall, W., Laws, D. and Barbaree, H. (eds) (1990) *Handbook of Sexual Assault*, New York: Plenum.

Medway, G.J. (1994) Those Were the Days, *Fetish Times*, 5, 30–33.

Melzack, R. (1973) *The Puzzle of Pain*, New York. Basic Books.

Mollinger, R.N. (1982) Sadomasochism and Developmental Stages, *Psychoanalytic Review*, 69(3), 379–389.

Montgomery, J.D. (1989) Preface. In J.D. Montgomery and A.C. Grief (eds), *Masochism: The Treatment of Self Inflicted Suffering*, Madison, CT: International Universities Press.

Moser, C. and Levitt, E.E. (1987) An Exploratory–Descriptive Study of a Sadomasochistically Oriented Sample, *The Journal of Sex Research*, 23(3), 322–337.

Nefzawis, S. (1963) *The Perfumed Garden*, ed. A.H. Walton, trans. R. Burton, New York: Putnams & Sons.

Nydes, J. (1963): The Paranoid Masochistic Character, *Psychoanalytic Review*, 50, 55–91.

Ortner, S.B. and Whitehead, H. (1981) *Sexual Meanings: The Cultural Construction of Gender and Sexuality*, London: Cambridge University Press.

Panken, S. (1983) *The Joy of Suffering: Psychoanalytic Theory and Therapy of Masochism*, New York: Aronson.

Pestrak, V.A. (1991) The Masochistic Personality Organization: Dynamic, Etiological and Psychotherapeutic Factors, *Journal of Contemporary Psychotherapy*, 21(2), 83–100.

Playboy (1976) What's Really Happening on Campus, *Playboy*, October, 128–131, 160–164, 169.

Plummer, K. (1982) Symbolic Interactionism and Sexual Conduct: An Emergent Perspective. In M. Brake (ed.), *Human Sexual Relations: Towards a Redefinition of Sexual Politics*, New York: Pantheon.

——(1995) *Telling Sexual Stories. Power, Change and Social Worlds*, London: Routledge.

Polhemus, T. and Randall, H. (1994) *Rituals of Love, Sexual Experiments, Erotic Possibilities*, London: Picador.

Prilleltensky, I. (1989) Psychology and the Status Quo, *American Psychologist*, 44 (May), 795–802.

Rachman, S. and Hodgson, R.J. (1968) Experimentally Induced Sexual Fetishism: Replication and Development, *Psychological Record*, 18, 25–27.

Reiche, R. (1970) *Sexuality and Class Struggle*, London: New Left Books.

Reik, T. (1940) *Masochism in Modern Man*, New York: Aronson.

Rian, K. (1982) Sadomasochism and the Social Construction of Reality. In R. Linden *et al.*, *Against Sadomasochism: A Radical Feminist Analysis*, East Palo Alto, CA: Frog in the Well.

Sack, R.L. and Miller, W. (1975) Masochism: A Clinical & Theoretical Overview. *Psychiatry*, 38, 244–257.

Sadger, J. (1926) A Contribution to the Understanding of Sado-Masochism, *International Journal of Psychoanalysis*, 7, 484–491.

Sartre, J.-P. (1957) *Being and Nothingness: An Essay on Phenomenological Ontology*, trans. H.E. Barnes, London: Methuen.

Scheff, T.J. (1974) The Labelling Theory of Mental Illness, *American Sociological Review*, 39, 444–452.

Schnarch, D.N. (1993) Inside the Sexual Crucible, *Networker* March/April

Showalter, E. (1987) *The Female Malady: Women, Madness and English Culture 1830–1980*, London: Virago.

Spengler, A. (1977) Manifest Sadomasochism of Males: Results of an Empirical Study, *Archives of Sexual Behaviour*, 6, 441–456.

Stoller, R. (1975) *Perversion: The Erotic Form of Hatred*, New York: Dell.

Storr, A. (1964) *Sexual Deviation*, London: Penguin.

Szasz, T. (1970) *Manufacture of Madness*, New York: Harper & Row.

Taylor, G.W (1995) Making Sense of SM: A Social Constructionist Account, unpublished D.Clin. dissertation, South Thames Clinical Training Course and University of Wales, College of Cardiff.

Taylor G.W. and Ussher, J.M. (in press) *Sadomasochism: A Discourse Analytic Study.*

Thompson, B. (1994) *Sadomasochism*, London: Cassell.

Thompson, M. (ed.) (1991) *Leatherfolk: Radical Sex, People, Politics and Practices*, Boston, MA: Alyson.

Tomkins, S.S. (1962) *Affect, Imagery, Consciousness*, New York: Springer.

Ussher, J.M. (1989) *The Psychology of the Female Body*, London: Routledge.

——(1991) *Women's Madness: Misogyny or Mental Illness*, Hemel Hempstead: Harvester Wheatsheaf.

——(1997) *Fantasies of Femininity: Reframing the Boundaries of Sex*, London: Penguin.

Vatsyayana (1962) *Kama Sutra*, trans. R. Burton, New York: Lancer Books.

Weeks, J. (1982) The Development of Sexual Theory and Sexual Politics. In M. Brake (ed.), *Human Sexual Relations: Towards a Redefinition of Sexual Politics*, New York: Pantheon.

——(1990) *Sex, Politics and Society. The Regulation of Sexuality Since 1800*, London: Longman.

Weinberg, T.S. and Falk, G. (1980) The Social Organisation of Sadism and Masochism, *Deviant Behaviour*, 1, 379–393.

Weinberg, T.S., Williams, C. and Moser, C. (1984) The Social Constituents of Sadomasochism, *Social Problems*, 31, 379–389.

World Health Organisation (1992): *International Classification of Diseases* (ICD-10), WHO.

Zborowski, M (1969) *People in Pain*, London: Jossey-Bass.

Additional legal references

R. v. *Brown* [1993] 2 WLR 556; [1992] 2 All ER 75 (the Spanner case).

R. v. *Donovan* [1934] 2 KB 498; [1934] All ER Rep 209.

8 Framing the sexual 'Other'

The regulation of lesbian and gay sexuality

Jane M. Ussher

INTRODUCTION

What does it mean to be lesbian or gay? Is it simply a matter of sex – of the functioning of the flesh – or is it all about politics and identity? Is it defined by matters of love and desire, or is it an issue of how people describe themselves? Why is it that some people are lesbian or gay, and others are not? Is it a matter of essential difference, or is it merely a sexual choice? How can people change from heterosexual to 'lesbian' or 'gay' halfway through life; are they *really* gay? Indeed, what does *really* being gay mean, if such a statement makes any sense at all?

The question of 'homosexuality' has perplexed theologians, sexologists, social theorists and lawmakers for centuries. It continues to provide almost a lurid fascination for both lay people and experts alike, with many of the above questions being repeatedly (if naively) asked. In the burgeoning discipline of gay and lesbian studies – or queer theory – the complexity of sexuality, and the need for more complex theorising, has been exposed. The voices of the previously silenced sexual 'other' – lesbians and gay men – have irrevocably changed the nature of the debates in this sphere. Many of the concerns of earlier commentators, such as the issue of treatment or cure, are no longer deemed to be any part of the agenda at all. But other questions continue to be debated, such as the issue of what does it *mean* to be positioned as sexual 'other' in a heterosexual social sphere, and what factors precipitate the development of an individual person's sexuality as heterosexual, lesbian or gay.

Arguably, at the heart of these debates is the often unspoken question of whether homosexuality is a matter of the material body or a matter of discourse. Experts and lay people alike have oscillated between the two layers of analysis. Historically, homosexuality has been defined as a physical act; a form of sexual deviancy which was regulated through the literal control or confinement of the material body. In the late nineteenth century, the newly developed discipline of sexology precipitated a shift towards the consideration of homosexuality as something people *are*, rather than as an act that people *do*. Conceptualising homosexuality as identity led to the regulation and control of the 'homosexual person', regardless of whether or not they ever engaged in same sex sex. Throughout, both scientific and popular explanations for homosexuality have focused on the flesh – with reductionist biological theories dominating academic debate on this subject from the late nineteenth century through to the present day. However, post-structuralist and social constructionist theorists have vociferously challenged this essentialist position, arguing that both 'sex' and sexuality are discursively constructed. This has led to the concept of 'homosexuality' being deconstructed, which might appear to suggest that the material body plays little part in the equation. Yet more recent critics have brought us the notion of sexuality as performance. We seem to be back to homosexuality as something people *do* rather than something they *are*. The difference today is that this sexual performance is discursively constructed as 'lesbian' or 'gay', and that being (or doing) 'lesbian' or 'gay' isn't just about same sex sex.

In this chapter I will examine the consequences of these shifting constructions of 'homosexuality', and outline the case for the need for a material–discursive analysis. Through looking at the regulation of gay male and lesbian sexuality in the law and in sexual science, and drawing on the findings of a recent interview study conducted with a group of young lesbian women (Mooney-Somers and Ussher, forthcoming), I will argue that material and discursive elements are always intertwined in the negotiation of being 'lesbian' or 'gay'. To examine one level of analysis without the other will always give us an incomplete picture; to incorporate both emphasises the point that there are no easy or simple answers in this sphere.

REGULATING THE ACT OF SAME SEX SEX

Focusing on the flesh: a materialist approach

Prior to the late nineteenth century, medico-legal discourse on the subject of homosexuality focused almost entirely on the bodily act of same sex sex, the main target of legislation being sex between men. Thus the act of sodomy was historically described as a 'crime against nature' more heinous than murder (Dynes, 1989). In England, sodomy between men was first criminalised and made punishable by death, under an Act of 1533, promoted by King Henry VIII – thus instigating centuries of material regulation of male homosexuality. The death penalty remained on the statute books until 1861, when the Offences Against the Person Act imposed sentences instead of between ten years and life. This Act was extended in 1885 as part of an Act which was aimed at controlling prostitution, so that any acts of 'gross indecency' carried out between two men, either in public or private, were made illegal. It remained on the statute books in England until 1967, when consenting sex between two men over the age of 21, in private, was decriminalised (Weeks, 1981). Sex between two men in private continues to be illegal to this day in many countries: in the mid-1980s it was still illegal in Cyprus,

Eire, Mexico, New Zealand, the Soviet Union, and all Moslem countries (Howard League Working Party Report, 1984: 11). In 1993, it was illegal in twenty-four North American states, with the most severe state penalties being twenty years in jail (Rivera, 1991). In England, sex between men in public is still a crime. So men who engage in 'cottaging' (sex in public toilets), or who have sex with a third person present, can still be convicted of 'gross indecency' – even if both parties are consenting adults.

In contrast to the harsh legal treatment of sex between men, sex between women has been remarkably neglected by the statutes of the law. Yet it would be wrong to assume that women have had the freedom to engage in sex with each other, while men have been tortured and hanged for the same, for the warnings outlined in the New Testament concerning the dangers of women turning from the 'natural into the unnatural' (Paul 1.26) *have* appeared in secular law (see Robson, 1992). For example, in 1260, the 'Code of Orleans' was introduced in France, which prohibited sex between women, stating that, while for the first two offences a woman would 'lose her member', for the third she would be burned to death. In Italy in 1574, women who were found engaging in sex with other women, if they were over the age of 12, were sentenced to the following: 'she shall be fastened naked to a stake in the street of Locusts and shall remain there all day and night under a reliable guard and the following day be burned outside the city' (quoted in Crompton, 1985: 16).

Burning at the stake was also the punishment for women being caught having sex with women in medieval Spain, enshrined in the law code of 1256. Particular forms of sexual activity between women were deemed more worthy of such punishment. One Spanish jurist argued that 'burning should be mandatory only in cases where a woman has relations with another woman by means of a material instrument' (Faderman, 1985: 36). This edict was repeated in Italy, where it was decreed that if a woman merely made overtures to another woman she should be denounced; if she 'behaves corruptly with another woman only by rubbing' she should be 'punished'; yet if she 'introduces some wooden or glass instrument into the belly of another she should be condemned to death' (Brown, 1986: 14).

What is the focus of attention and is criminalised in all of these examples is the physical act of sex between women or between men, with that which is closest to the heterosexual norm – penetration – being most strongly condemned. It is an interesting irony. As Gayle Rubin has commented, 'the only adult sexual behaviour that is legal in every state is the placement of the penis in the vagina in wedlock' (Rubin, 1984: 291). It is also the one act which is likely to be deemed *illegal* if conducted between women or between men. Similarly, sodomy is used as incontrovertible evidence for, and indeed deemed to be the defining feature of, 'homosexual' sex between men.

Yet this realist definition of 'homosexual sex' isn't as simple as the law might suggest. First, what the law might view as a 'homosexual sexual act' is not always deemed to be the case by the participants involved. Penetrative sex between two men is common in closed communities, such as prisons, but in the majority of cases is not viewed as 'homosexual sex', particularly by the active penetrative partner. There is also evidence from anthropological research that same sex sexual practices are common in many societies, but are not interpreted as a sign of 'homosexuality'. The men of ancient Greece who simultaneously engaged in sexual relationships with young boys, prostitutes and their wives are the most oft-quoted example. In a different vein, anthropologists have recorded that in the Sambian tribe of the New Guinea Highlands, part of the initiation of boys into adulthood involves fellatio between young boys and men, with the young boys ingesting the adult male semen as an adolescent rite of passage (Herdt, 1984). All boys take part in this ritualised activity, so they can become strong and courageous warriors. Yet these young men do not subsequently take up a 'homosexual' identity, for after the rite of passage to become a courageous warrior is complete they marry women and, in the majority, cease engagement in same sex activity (Herdt, 1987). More contemporaneously, many men and women engage in consensual same sex sexual activities on an occasional or regular basis, while refusing to categorise themselves or indeed the acts they engage in as 'homosexual' (or 'gay' or 'lesbian') (Garber, 1995). So bodily acts can have many different meanings depending on the context in which they occur. We cannot make assumptions about what a sexual act means without examining its discursive construction and the cultural context in which it occurs.

Sex between women: an unspeakable offence

Within the law, the discursive representation of sex between women has arguably been more tightly regulated than the material practice. For example, one fifteenth-century cleric who deemed sex between women a sin against God and a crime against nature, proclaimed that 'women have each other by detestable and horrible means which *should not be named or written*' (Brown, 1986: 19). In the sixteenth century, in Switzerland, the authorities were advised that in the case of those women convicted of same sex sex, the death sentence should be passed, yet the crime itself should not be described, for 'a crime so horrible and against nature is so detestable and because of the horror of it, it cannot be named' (Monter, 1981: 41). When a woman was drowned for the crime of sex with another woman in Geneva in 1568, one jurist, Colladon, recommended that 'it is not necessary to describe minutely the circumstances of such a case, but only to say that it's for the detestable crime of unnatural fornication' (Monter, 1981: 43). Thus the material act was regulated, and the physical body punished (or destroyed), while at the same time there was an attempt to avoid discursively acknowledging its very existence.

In England, this legal silence has largely continued to this day (in contrast, sex between women *is* named (as illegal) in nearly 50 per cent of US states – Rivera, 1991: 82). It is widely reported that the current absence of *any* law regulating consenting sex between adult women in England is due to the fact that Queen Victoria refused to allow any mention of this concept in the sexual offences acts of the late nineteenth century, supposedly because she could not conceive of such perverse acts being actually carried out by women. Thus, to this day, there is no legal age of consent for sex between women in England.[1] A 1904 medical treatise entitled *Woman* claimed that sex between women had never been made a criminal offence because of 'the ignorance of the law-making power of the existence of this anomaly' (Faderman, 1991: 50). Yet it wasn't Queen Victoria's ignorance, but the ruling parliamentarian's fears, which led to the silence on this subject. They seemed to prefer absence of legislation to open acknowledgement of the threat of the lesbian.

For example, an uproar was provoked in 1920, by the attempt of the MP Mr Macquisten to introduce a change to the 1885 Criminal Amendment Act, which would recognise in law the crime of 'indecency between women'. If enacted, the change would have placed female and male homosexual sex in an equal position in the eyes of the law, as the working of the clause to be introduced was: 'Any act of gross indecency between female persons shall be a misdemeanour and punishable in the same manner as any such act committed by male persons under section eleven of the Criminal Law Amendment Act, 1885'.

The notion of 'sex' between women was clearly recognised as a possibility here. But what this 'sex' could possibly involve was still a conundrum. For, as one MP was driven to comment, 'How on earth are people to get convictions in a case of such a kind?' (Edwards, 1981: 44). Indeed, the contemplation of this sexual activity between women was so unthinkable to the learned men, that two of them, Colonel Webb and Sir Ernest Wild, declared that it 'was a beastly subject and they did not want to pollute the house with knowledge of it' (Edwards, 1981). This was despite the fact that Wild proclaimed that sex between women 'saps the fundamental institutions of society', 'stops childbirth', 'produces neurasthenia and insanity' and 'causes our race to decline'. The reason for maintaining this silence was thus: 'To adopt a clause of this kind would introduce into the minds of perfectly innocent people the most revolting thoughts' (Parliamentary Debates, Commons, 1921, vol. 145, 1977, quoted by Jeffreys, 1985: 114).

Women were deemed to be in need of the greatest protection from this supposed lesbian threat. Lord Desart, a former Director of Public Prosecutions, opposed the bill with the comment, 'You are going to tell the world that there is such an offence, to bring it to the notice of women who have never heard of it, never thought of it, never dreamt of it. I think it is a very great mischief.' The Lord Chancellor, Lord Birkenhead, reiterated these sentiments:

> I would be bold enough to say that of every thousand women, taken as a whole, 999 have never even heard a whisper of these practices. Among all

these, in the homes of this country . . . the taint of this noxious and horrible suspicion is to be imparted.

(Hyde, 1972: 200)

It seems that it was feared that if women knew of these practices they would then forsake men. In the words of one parliamentarian, 'any woman who indulges this vice will have nothing whatever to do with the other sex' (Parliamentary Debates, Commons, 1921, vol. 145, 1977, quoted by Jeffreys, 1985: 114).

Sexual activity between women *was* implicity recognised in English law in a number of divorce cases in the late 1940s, where a woman's 'unnatural sexual relations' with another woman were deemed grounds for her husband to divorce her (i.e. *Gardner* v. *Gardner*, 1947; and *Spicer* v. *Spicer*, 1945 – both cited by Edwards, 1981: 45). The 1956 Criminal Offences Act, sections 14 and 15, also acknowledged that a woman was capable of carrying out an indecent assault on another woman. But few cases have been brought before the courts. In cases when the law on female indecency *is* invoked, there is often an implicit assumption that sex between women is somehow of a different nature than sex between men. This was made clear within a 1957 Royal Commission on Homosexual Offences and Prostitution (section 103), which reported that it had 'found no case in which a female has been convicted of an act with another female which exhibits the libidinous features that characterise sexual acts between males' (Edwards, 1981: 45). This arguably reflects the common representation of lesbian sexuality as somehow more benign and innocuous than heterosexual, or gay male sexuality (what *do* they do in bed . . . ?). It is an assumption which sits strangely with the converse representation of 'the lesbian' as the epitome of the rapacious rampant female, with sex between women being positioned as orgiastic – part of a general absence of libidinous control. For example, the charge of *femina cum feminus* (woman with woman) was oft repeated during the witch trials of the Middle Ages, during which thousands of women were castigated and condemned for their supposedly voracious sexuality (Ussher, 1991). One account produced in Farnace in 1460 declared:

sometimes indeed indescribable outrages are perpetrated in exchanging women, by order of the presiding devil, by passing on a woman to another woman and a man to other men, an abuse against the nature of women by both parties and similarly against the nature of men.

(Evans, 1978: 76)

In the American army witch hunts of the 1950s, when lesbians were being sought out and unceremoniously discharged, stereotypes about the voracious sexuality of lesbians abounded. For example, as Lillian Faderman notes, 'lesbians were presented in the cliché of sexual vampires who seduced innocent young women into sexual experimentation that would lead them, like a drug, into the usual litany of horrors: addiction, degeneracy, loneliness, murder and suicide' (Faderman, 1991: 151). Today, the most common representation of rapacious 'lesbian' sexuality is in heterosexual pornography aimed at men. Here we see women engaging in sex with each other, invariably observed by a male voyeur, which then leads to an orgy of three-way sex between the women and the man (Ussher, 1997). The message might seem to be that lesbians are open to anything (or that any woman would really prefer to have sex with a man).

Lawmakers may have attempted to suppress knowledge of the existence of sex between women, but when it *is* acknowledged the penalties can be as severe as they were in the Middle Ages. In the parliamentary debates of the 1920s, one MP, Lieutenant Moor-Brabazon, suggested three ways of dealing with these female 'perverts': stamping them out with the death penalty, locking them up as lunatics or, best of all, ignoring them – not because they were innocuous, but because they would eventually extinguish themselves. These are sentiments reminiscent of the eugenics movement that advocated sterilisation for 'deviant' men and women. Thus it was declared:

> [we should] leave them entirely alone, not notice them, not advertise them. This is the method that has been adopted in England for many hundred years, and I believe it is the best method now . . . they have the merit of exterminating themselves, and consequently they do not spread or do very much harm to society at large.
>
> (quoted by Jeffreys, 1985: 114)

This latter sentiment clearly comes from an era where lesbian motherhood was unthinkable (or at least not publicly recognised). Today, it is arguably in the arena of lesbian motherhood that we see the most clear-cut regulation of lesbian sexuality within the law, as women in lesbian relationships continue to be deprived of custody – or even access – to their children, on the grounds of being unfit mothers. For example, in the 1981 case of *Dailey* v. *Dailey* the woman's ex-husband argued, 'Your honour, this is the bible belt. This [a lesbian raising her children] might be okay in New York or California, but this is the bible belt.' The woman lost custody of her children, with her access severely restricted, as her husband's attorney argued that in Tennessee the woman was technically a criminal for engaging in lesbian sex (Rivera, 1991: 95). In a similar case in Virginia, in 1993, a 22-year-old woman, Sharon Bottoms, was denied custody of her 2-year-old son, because the judge believed he would grow up not knowing the difference between men and women if he stayed with his lesbian mother. As the child's grandmother was granted custody, she commented, 'I don't care how my daughter lives, but Tyler [the child] will be mentally damaged by this. We can take care of ourselves, he can't' (*Guardian,* 9 September 1993, p. 11). Two conservative MPs, who commented on a recent British case where joint custody of a child was awarded to two lesbian women, reflected a similar view:

EMMA NICHOLSON   I am immensely unhappy when adult sexual behaviour inflicts a distorted lifestyle on children. I believe strenuously that every child deserves a mother and father.

SIR NICHOLAS FAIRBAIRN   We don't put children in the hands of the insane. Why should we put them in the hands of the perverted?

(reported in the *Guardian*, 30 June 1994)

Non-consensual sex between two women, if proven, is dealt with equally harshly by the law. One of the only women to be convicted of an indecent assault on another woman under the 1956 Criminal Offences Act, sections 14 and 15, was jailed for six years in 1991 for 'sexually assaulting' her two girlfriends and for impersonating a man – the case being brought after the mother of one of the girls discovered her daughter had a female lover (see Smyth, 1992: 23–24). The accused, Jennifer Saunders, argued in her own defence that both of her girlfriends had known she was a woman, and had wanted her to dress as a man in order to conceal the fact of their lesbian relationship. Whether the court was punishing 'assault' (which she argued had been consensual sex at the time it happened), or the audacity of a woman having sex with another woman while taking on a masculine masquerade, is open to speculation.

So in summary, while the law might position 'homosexuality' as a physical act, regulating the material body of the person who is caught engaging in this offence, it also serves to regulate the discursive representation of lesbian sexuality. Equally, it was only because certain acts were deemed 'homosexual' that they were condemned. So both material and discursive factors are interlinked in the construction and containment of homosexuality within the law.

Regulating homosexuality through sexology

Since the mid-nineteenth century, the professions of medicine, psychology and psychiatry have joined lawmakers in both the material and discursive regulation of homosexual sex. As positivism was the dominant epistemology in each of these professions, the focus continued to be on the material domain. However, it was the early sexologists who moved the focus from the physical act of same sex sex on to the analysis (and regulation) of sexual identity or orientation, through their 'discovery' of the homosexual and lesbian person in the 1850s, culminating in the first case histories of inversion appearing in the scientific literature in the 1870s. So 'homosexuality' became a categorisation for a type of person, rather than simply a physical act – a change which was reflected in the law. For example, in the years following the 1861 Act which abolished the death penalty for sodomy, the Home Office made attempts to distinguish between the occasional sodomite and the 'homosexual' man. Mr Justice Hawkins commented that 'for the most part that crime [bestiality] is committed by young persons, agricultural labourers etc. out of pure ignorance. The crime of sodomy with mankind stands on a *different* footing' (quoted by Weeks, 1981: 119, emphasis added). It was *different* in that it was almost unequivocally condemned.

The sexologist's early theories put forward to explain this phenomenon adopted an almost solely reductionist analysis, viewing homosexuality as an internal psychological or physical disorder. For example, Krafft-Ebing, writing in Germany in the late nineteenth century, had initially considered homosexuality as a manifestation of a neuropathic or psychopathic state – later changing his views to position it as more of an anomaly than as a disease (Krafft-Ebing, 1886). Havelock Ellis was more liberal, commenting that 'inverts *may* be healthy and normal in all respects outside their special aberration . . . I regard inversion as frequently in close relation to the minor neurotic conditions' (Ellis, 1893: 194, emphasis added). He reassured his readers that lots of distinguished people were inverts, but commented that 'usually only those of the lowest, most degenerate, and sometimes merce- nary class . . . are willing to betray their peculiarity' (Ellis, 1893: 205). One of the case vignettes he presented was of a physician whose moral traditions did not allow him to seek the satisfaction of his impulses – an early example of the status–conduct distinction which is central to debates concerning homosexuals in the army and the priesthood today.

For in US Federal law, a distinction is made between status (*being* gay or lesbian) and conduct (*acting* on it). Under the 14th Amendment, punishment or 'discrimination' cannot be based on status – being gay or lesbian is not proof of conduct. Direct evidence of 'deviant sexuality' is needed before discrimination is allowed. The 'don't ask, don't tell' policy introduced in the US army in the early 1990s was an attempt to enforce this 'status–conduct' distinction by not outlawing the homosexual person, but the act of homosexual sex. Equally, in the recent furore about 'gay vicars' in the Church of England, the official line is that if vicars do not act on their homosexual desires they cannot be punished or condemned. In contrast, there is no status–conduct distinction to complicate legislation in the British army. 'Homosexuality' is defined as sexual attraction to a person of the same sex – it is *desire* which is policed, not sexual conduct. For as is clearly stated in a 1994 army report outlining 'policy and guide- lines on homosexuality', 'homosexuality is defined as 'behaviour characterised by being sexually attracted to members of the same sex.' These thoughts and feelings, if admitted, will end a career, as homosexu- ality in the British army is still banned.

The sexological arguments could clearly be seen as confirming earlier theological or legal dictates on male homosexuality: that it was perverse and needed to be controlled and contained. The material consequences of the shift to a medical discourse to explain this deviance may have been that 'treatment' rather than punishment was offered as the main solution to the problem, but the end result was the same: officially sanctioned regulatory practices were extended towards gay men. However, the establishment of the term 'lesbian' or 'female invert' arguably had a much more significant material effect on the lives of many women. For, while sex between women had never been condoned, it had also rarely been spoken of openly, as we have seen. The sexologists changed this. Their writings on the horrors and dangers of lesbianism were widely disseminated in both medical and popular literature, casting suspicion on the motives and morality of thousands of women who had previously been able to engage openly in romantic friendships with other women. Prior to the 'discovery' of lesbianism, both physical and emotional intimacy between women was widely socially accepted and not construed as sexual. Many women, particularly in North American women's colleges, engaged in passionate romantic relationships with each other which were openly accepted, indeed encouraged (Faderman, 1991). These romantic friendships were not deemed to be antithetical or a threat to heterosexuality, but were seen as appropriate preparation for marriage, motherhood and domesticity in a rigidly gender-differentiated society where most of women's lives were spent in the company of other women (Smith-Rosenberg, 1985). The publicising of the writings of the sexologists irrevocably changed this. It resulted in accusations of 'perversion' being levied at women who engaged in intimate relationships with each other. Those who did not want their relationships with other women to be construed as sexual (and even contemporary records make it difficult to gauge whether they actually were), or who feared being categorised as 'lesbians', could no longer sustain what had undoubtedly been a positive supportive life with another woman. This is an interesting example of a shift in discourse influencing material practice, for, as long as it was construed as 'friendship', the physical reality of loving and living with another woman could exist unchallenged. As soon as it was categorised as 'lesbian' it was deemed unacceptable and condemned. At one level it is no different from being 'in the closet' today. But what is different with this example is that whilst the 'discovery' of lesbianism changed the societal view of these women, it also changed their view of themselves.

EXPLAINING HOMOSEXUALITY: A MATERIAL OR DISCURSIVE PHENOMENON?

Biological reductionism: seeing the body as to blame

In the writings of the early sexologists, lesbianism was seen to be irrevocably linked with masculinity, manifested through a physical deformity. Havelock Ellis commented that:

> among female inverts, there is usually some approximation to the masculine attitude and temperament . . . the sex organs . . . are sometimes

overdeveloped, or perhaps more usually underdeveloped . . . there may be a somewhat masculine development of the larynx.

(Ellis, 1893: 199–200)

Krafft-Ebing (1886) contributed a similar view, describing the female invert as having coarse male features, and a rough and rather deep voice. These clinical aberrations were put to the test in the 1930s in a series of studies carried out under the auspices of the Committee for the Study of Sex Variants in New York City, which set out to determine the characteristics of 'the lesbian' (Terry, 1990). Women volunteers were interviewed, observed and their bodies inspected. It was concluded that 'the lesbian' could be distinguished from the heterosexual woman on the basis of clear masculine or feminist tendencies, as well as enlarged genitalia. Here are two extracts from the psychiatrist George Henry's reports, on two different women:

Rose S: The labia majora are 10 cm long and the minora pigmented in a very pronounced fashion, notwithstanding the general coloration, and they protrude in pronounced, thick preputial curtains. The clitoris is 9 by 4 mm, and very erectile, the hymen worn and gone, admitting one or two fingers.

Frieda: She is a thorough feminist with intense sex bitterness. She will take nothing from any man. She will give herself to a man but only with feelings of contempt for him.

(Henry, 1948: 1023, 700)

Arguably, what is implicit within these early models of lesbianism is the notion that only physically masculine women could be actively sexual, as 'sex' was inconceivable without the presence of a man (or a penis). Thus a lesbian was expected to have a clitoris which was similar to a penis, or at the very least take up the position of 'man' (similar stereotyped beliefs are clearly still present today, with lesbian – and gay male – couples being questioned, 'Which of you is the man?'). So, while the focus is ostensibly on the material body, this is very much an example of scientific theory and practice being influenced by a particular discursive representation of 'the lesbian' and of 'sex'.

Interestingly, at the beginning of the century many women who identified as lesbian appear to have accepted these essentialist theories, finding much that was positive in the notion of being a congenital invert. One early lesbian, Frances Wilder, wrote in 1915 of her strong desire to caress and fondle other women, something which she explained as being as a result of her masculine mind. If she couldn't help herself, her sexuality could not be castigated (Faderman, 1991). This is perhaps an early example of biological theories being used to support the interests of those otherwise condemned – which we see in the attempts to identify a gay gene today.

In the late twentieth century there is still evidence of a strong biological discourse in sexology, which positions homosexuality as a biological phenomenon. This is not surprising, given the continued dominance of a positivist/realist epistemology in this field. As one sex researcher, Simon Le Vay has commented, 'It is not unrealistic to expect a gene or genes influencing sexual orientation to be identified within the next few years, since there are at least three laboratories in the United States alone that are working on the topic' (Le Vay, 1993: 127). There is a vast amount of funding being pumped into research attempting to isolate the biological causes of homosexuality (see Pattatucci and Hamer, 1995, for a review). Legions of twins and siblings have been studied to attempt to prove a genetic link. Early research, carried out in the 1950s, reported a 100 per cent concordance rate between thirty-seven male monozygotic (identical) twins – if one was gay, so was the other. The rate was 15 per cent for dizygotic (non-identical) twins (Kallman, 1952); compelling evidence for a genetic cause, or so one might think. More recent work carried out on twins and siblings by North American sex researchers Richard Pillard, Michael Bailey and colleagues has reported heritability rates of 50 per cent for both male and female homosexuality. For example, one study of gay men found concordance rates of 52 per cent for monozygotic twins, and 22 per cent for dizygotic twins (Bailey and Pillard, 1991). In lesbians, the concordance rate was 48 per cent for monozygotic twins and 16 per cent in dizygotic twins (Bailey *et al.*, 1993). These findings, and others like them, have led researchers to suggest that biological factors may play a stronger role in male homosexuality than they do in female homosexuality. For example, in a recent study of nearly 5000 Australian twins, researchers concluded that hereditary factors were important for men, whereas environmental influences were more important for women (Bailey, 1995). This begs the question of whether it is meaningful to talk about a 'homosexual' gene at all.

One of the criticisms of brain anatomy studies of homosexuality is that they are even more specific, focusing mainly on gay men who have died of AIDS complications. The widely cited research of Simon Le Vay, published in *Science*, which purported to show that the hypothalamus was smaller in gay men than in heterosexual men, has also been criticised for being based on very small numbers of men, and for there not being incontrovertible evidence of the sexual orientation of those studied – if 'sexual orientation' is something that can ever be established or fixed (see Garber, 1995) – the men were all dead when they were recruited for the study and therefore could not give any report. Yet, in both the popular and academic press, the results are generalised to the whole homosexual population. Another problem with this realist analysis is that one basic theory of brain difference can not even be agreed upon amongst the experts. Suggestions of a biological link have included the 'absence of linkage to micor satellite markers on the X chromosome' (Hamer, 1995); actions of the hypothalamic–pituitary–gonadal axis (Fedoroff *et al.*, 1995); and steroid 5-alpha-reductase deficiency (Alias, 1995). Comparative animal research has been conducted, examining the role of steroid hormones in sexual behaviour of a range of species – including rats, mice, fruit flies, as well as reptiles and primates. It is argued that changing hormone levels at certain stages of development changes sexual behaviour. Whether this research can be generalised to human populations where sexual behaviour is not simply mediated by hormonal factors, and whether *behaviour*, sexual identity or orientation are one and the same thing, is questionable. This type of research clearly marginalises or ignores the social and discursive construction of sexuality, and the complexity of human sexual experience. But perhaps the most important question is: Why are researchers so desperately searching for this elusive biological marker, and what are the implications of their (as yet) fruitless search?

If we can find a simple biological 'cause' for 'homosexuality', so the argument goes, we will have to stop enacting discriminatory practices at a social and legal level. We will have to see it as 'natural', and we can't condemn someone for their inescapable biological make-up. As the *Wall Street Journal* declared in 1993:

> the discovery of a definitive biological cause of homosexuality could go a long way toward advancing the gay-rights cause. If homosexuality were found to be an immutable trait, like skin color, then laws criminalising homosexual sex might be overturned.
>
> (quoted by Garber, 1995: 271)

It is a familiar argument – taken on in an emancipatory way by early twentieth-century lesbians who celebrated the notion of congenital inversion, as we have already seen above. The downside of this, in the era of DNA tests for genetic 'defects' in the womb, is that parents would potentially have the ability to test for a homosexual child and then terminate the pregnancy if so desired. Homosexuality could be screened out before birth.

Yet, as with all research which advocates a simple biological cause of behaviour – such as that on mental illness, criminality or aggression – there is both naivety and politics at play here. Fruit flies or rats may be primarily motivated by biological or evolutionary forces (although environmental factors are also influential even in these cases), but humans are a far more complicated case. Our behaviour – sexual as well as any other kind – results from a complex interaction of biological and social factors; a continuously shifting interplay between material and discursive factors. Genes or hormones may be one part of the jigsaw, but they are not the only one, or even necessarily the most important. To attest that a simple biological cause for *any* behaviour is proven is more a reflection of the ideological motives of the researcher than it is of the truth. To be fair, many of the scientific experts who work in this field assert that biology must be examined in its social context, stressing that genetic or hormonal factors may provide a potential or propensity for homosexuality. For example, while advocating the exploration of genetic factors, Pattatucci and Hamer (1995: 155) argue that 'it is our view that no single factor, be it genetic, physiological, or environmental, determines a given person's sexual orientation. Rather, we believe that certain factors may contribute to the development of an individuals sexual orientation.' However, this 'bio-psycho-social' explanation for sexuality still tends to focus on the individual, it still accepts the homo-sexual–heterosexual distinction as given, and invariably positions the body, or biology, as primary, with social or cultural factors merely being added on to explain why a biological propensity is acted out.

The social construction of homosexuality

Social constructionist theories of sexuality stand in stark opposition to the realist reductionist accounts which underpin both mainstream science and the law. Here, the body (or bodily acts) are not the starting point of any analysis of the phenomenon we know or do as 'sex'. Broadly, social constructionist accounts posit that our understanding and experience of sexuality is both shaped and regulated by social and cultural factors; that the meaning of bodily acts, or indeed what we define as 'sex', is always culturally and historically specific (see Weeks, 1985; Tiefer, 1987). Thus acts which are viewed as 'sex' in one context may not be in another; what is sexual deviance or crime at one point in history may be common practice at another (Ussher, 1997). Within this view, 'homosexuality' is neither a biological drive or an incontrovertible fact. The very concept only has meaning in a social and cultural context where heterosexuality is hegemonic, where normal and legal 'sex' is narrowly defined as heterosexual vaginal intercourse, and where the very machinery of state power is underpinned by the maintenance of this heterosexual norm (see Foucault, 1976; Butler, 1993).

In a theoretical vein, these approaches have shifted the focus from analyses of the mechanics of the flesh (what acts define homosexuality; what under-lying hormone is to blame . . .) to analyses of social discourse and power. Influenced by the work of Michel Foucault, sexuality has been 'decon-structed'. For example, Mary McIntosh, in an early and influential paper, argued that 'homosexuality' was not a 'condition' but a social role, with historical, social and individual variability shaping how this role was defined (McIntosh, 1968). The more recent work of Lillian Faderman, documenting a century of lesbian life in North America, has mapped the historical shifts in this role. In a similar vein, Kenneth Plummer has examined the way in which modern terminology for describing gay or lesbian sexuality evolved, and the impact of these linguistic changes on the men and women positioned as lesbian or gay (Plummer, 1981). Celia Kitzinger (1987) examined the different explanations for their lesbianism taken up by one group of women, demon-strating that their understanding of their sexuality was positioned within the dominant discourses which were circulating at this time.

Taking a slightly different stance, but still staying within the broad tenets of a social constructionist approach, Marjorie Garber has argued that the very notion of a 'homosexual' (or indeed heterosexual) identity or orientation is questionable. In talking of the shifting from male to female lovers and back again in the lives of the two women painters Frida Kahlo and Georgia O'Keefe, she comments that 'no one relationship, no one orientation, is for them the "real" one . What is real is what they are doing at the time' (Garber, 1995: 115). She also quotes Jonathon Dollimore (who, after many years of living with a male partner, is now living with a woman) as saying:

> We don't want a new hierarchy . . . that claims you're either one thing or the other . . . What I would not tolerate . . . is people who embrace that sort of thing in the exclusionary identity politics mode, saying 'I am now gay' as if their whole lives before that were a lie or don't count . . . I just don't think desire works like that.
>
> (Garber, 1995: 85)

In support of the view that 'homosexuality' is what you currently do, we could look to the fact that there are very few people within the gay or lesbian continuum who have had a uniquely 'homosexual' sexual life. The majority of people have had sexual relationships (or have engaged in sexual acts) with people of the opposite sex at some time in their lives. Arguably, this doesn't mean a great deal in a social milieu where heterosexuality is almost 'compulsory', as the American writer Adrienne Rich has suggested (Rich, 1980). This behaviour could be explained away by peer pressure, or attempts to assume a 'normal' sexual role. Or it could be explained within a model of 'choice', where 'homosexuality' is one of many possible sexual roles a person can perform; one of many possible identity positions that can be taken up.

This latter argument may seem to be borne out by the lesbian-feminist movement of the late 1970s, where lesbianism was advocated and adopted by many feminists as a revolutionary means of overthrowing patriarchal power. As one feminist who left her husband to become a lesbian commented in 1974, lesbianism was 'the only noble choice a committed feminist could make' (quoted by Faderman, 1991: 207). In this context the *role* of lesbian was taken up consciously, and primarily for political reasons – with some 'political lesbians' remaining celibate. The majority did enter into sexual relationships with other women – but this was not the defining feature of their newfound sexual identity; it was identification with other women. As a New York-based group Radical Lesbians argued in 1970:

> a lesbian is the rage of all women condensed to the point of explosion. She is a woman who . . . acts in accordance with her inner compulsion to be a more complete and free human being than her society . . . cares to allow her . . . She has not been able to accept the limitations and oppressions laid on her by the most basic role of her society – the female role.
>
> (Faderman, 1991: 206)

So 'lesbianism' was defined as rebellion against men, meaning that *any* woman could be classified as a lesbian – at least any woman who was angry enough. Politics, rather than sex and desire, was the basis for being lesbian. This view seems to have continued through to today in the minds of a small minority of active feminists. For example, Celia Kitzinger has argued that 'Lesbianism is a political identity', a 'blow against the patriarchy', not simply a 'sexual/emotional preference' (Kitzinger, 1987). As Lynne Segal has commented, this appears to position 'lesbianism as a voluntaristic choice, dictated by one's politics' (1994: 174).

The implications of both the Foucauldian and radical lesbian-feminist positions would seem to be the same, even though different routes are taken to reach this point: the material body is almost an irrelevance; it is discourse and power which are at issue here. Foucault's rejection of theorising at the physiological or psychological level, as well as at the level of specific social relations and cultural practices, has been criticised by many who are otherwise sympathetic to his arguments (Segal, 1994: 184). For, while cultural practices and discourses are central to the construction of 'sex' and of 'homosexuality', and knowing how to be (or do) 'lesbian' or 'gay' undoubtedly involves attention to the nuances of a social role, there is also a physical body involved (even for celibate political lesbians, whose *in*activity in the material sexual sphere underlined their political commitment to their goal). We cannot deny the importance of the material body, of bodily acts, or of the meaning of the physical intimacy that sex between two people evokes. Arguably, we cannot ignore or deny internal psychic forces, such as unconscious fears or desire: psychoanalysis, with its important insights about sexuality, is mostly absent from the social constructionist sphere. There is a danger in deconstructing sexuality so much that we are left with nothing left at all. As Carol Vance has argued, 'to the extent that social construction theory grants that sexual acts, identities and even desire are mediated by cultural and historical factors, the object of study – sexuality – becomes evanescent and threatens to disappear' (Vance, 1989: 21). Yet at the same time the reductionist material analysis which underpins the legal and scientific regulation of lesbian and gay sexuality is equally limited and problematic, as we have seen above.

What we need is a material–discursive analysis, so that we can acknowledge both the material body and social or discursive factors, without privileging one above the other, but seeing both levels of analysis as irrevocably interlinked.

Towards a material–discursive analysis of lesbian sexuality

Within a material–discursive approach it is implicitly acknowledged that we cannot separate out material and discursive factors in any analysis of sexuality. Our analysis of what it means to be lesbian or gay, or to engage in a sexual act which might be deemed 'homosexual', is irrevocably tied to the material body – to corporeal connections, to desire, to the performance of sexual acts which are deemed transgressive or normal at any point in time, and to physical appearance (the ways in which women and men signify their lesbian or gay status through dress or style). Yet it is also tied to discourse – to the shifting interpretations made about acts or attitudes, to the changing definitions and social meaning of being lesbian or gay. These two levels are irrevocably interlinked: the body cannot be conceptualised outside of discourse and, in the sphere of sex, discourse is always associated with the material body.

Lawmakers, scientists and critical theorists may be divided in their allegiance to material or discursive levels of analysis but, in contrast, many people who identify themselves as lesbian or gay draw on both material and discursive explanations when describing their own sexuality. This is a perspective which has historically been ignored, particularly in academic debates where the view of the supposedly objective expert is pre-eminent. The emerging discipline of gay and lesbian studies (or queer theory) has redressed this balance to a degree, as has the growing body of literary explo- ration of gay and lesbian life. In order to emphasise the importance of giving voice to those positioned as 'other' in a heterosexual sphere, and to illustrate the interrelationship between material and discursive factors in being (or doing) 'lesbian' or 'gay', I will end this chapter by turning to a recent interview study conducted with a group of young lesbian women, where the research focus was 'What does it mean to be a lesbian?' (see Ussher and Mooney-Somers, forthcoming, for more details of this research). Eight in-depth semi-structured interviews were analysed using thematic discourse analysis. After transcription, the data was coded in detail, and a number of different themes were identified. In this context I will draw on a small selection of the different interpretive repertoires on which the women drew in explaining what it meant to them to be lesbian, in order to demonstrate that these women positioned it as both a material and discursive experience.

Methodologically, this series of interviews may have appeared to have focused on the discursive construction of lesbianism, for our interest was in what these young women said about their sexuality and how they viewed themselves. Yet this is not just a case of talk, of a description of a sexual life. Taking up an identity as 'lesbian', in this group of young women, was arguably central to their lives – influencing both the material reality of how they spent their time, the way they experienced and described themselves, and the way in which they were positioned in the outside world. Being or doing 'lesbian' was a complicated multilayered experience. As one woman commented:

> what does it mean to me to be a, it means (*sigh*) god, it means (.) a complete hassle, (*laughing*) it's ahh, if anything, it's like ahmm, it means taking on a lot of pain, it means taking on society it means (.) it means standing out, it means it's about (.) about love, (.) it's about how society perceives you, it's everything, do you know what I mean, to be a lesbian is

to me, is, it's completely totally part of my life, it's everything, do you know what I mean, it's everything, but it's extremely dominant in who I am, and in what I am.

Here, we see the difficulty in openly taking up the position of sexual 'other', described both psychologically ('taking on a lot of pain') and socially ('it means standing out'). Being lesbian is both about 'love' and about taking up a political stance ('taking on society'). This interplay between psychological and performative aspects of sexuality is described by Judith Butler thus:

> gender is neither a purely psychic truth, conceived as 'internal' and 'hidden', nor is it reducible to a surface appearance; on the contrary, its undecidability is to be traced as the play *between* psyche and appearance (where the latter domain includes what appears in *words*). Further, this will be a 'play' regulated by heterosexist constraints though not, for that reason, fully reducible to them.
>
> (Butler, 1993: 234)

In this study, the interviewees clearly described both layers of experience (how they feel and who they are), as well as what they do and how they appear, as being central to the continuous negotiation of being or doing 'lesbian' in the material world. Thus, while it is their talk which was the focus of analysis, we were not negating the importance of the materiality of their lives, and of the function of their discursive explanations on both their experience of themselves and on the material practices in which they engaged.

EXPLAINING THE ROOTS OF LESBIANISM

As a pre-given desire – and as a social label

In explaining what it was to be a lesbian, this group of women drew on both a biological and a social discourse This is not surprising, as these are the dominant discursive explanations of gay and lesbian sexuality which currently circulate, as we have seen. However, in this study, these two apparently contradictory explanations were not positioned as opposite, but as complimentary.

A number of the women talked about their experience of being a lesbian as something which was inside them; it had always been there. It is a set of explanations that in many ways hints at essentialism:

> I started fancying women when I was in like the first year of infant school . . . we had a gorgeous piano teacher, but I only, ahmm, like knew I was like it was different from what everyone else was feeling when I was in, ahmm, when I was about 10 or 11 and only when I got to secondary school did I actually put a name to it. Up until that point I knew there was something going on in my head, but I didn't know what it was. I

chased sixth-formers, it was an all-girls' school . . . they just said 'are you a lesbian' although they had (.) said that as a joke . . . that's when I got the bells ringing. Awh, well, yeah this is a lesbian and hey this is what I feel.

In these extracts, the women position their lesbianism as both internal ('something going on in my head') and something which was there before they were old (or knowledgeable) enough to realise what their desires or feelings meant ('I didn't know what it was', 'in . . . the first year of infant school'). Here, desire or behaviour is positioned as coming before the categorisation of 'lesbian' – it is the label that is discovered later, not the feelings. This type of explanation might appear to reinforce reductionist biological accounts – that homosexuality is a pre-given state, waiting to be discovered or expressed, something over which a person has no control. It is one of the most common themes to emerge from the many 'coming out' stories which have now been published – the notion of always feeling 'different' from others, yet only later finding out what that meant. It may seem to provide support for the notion of lesbianism as a 'true' or pre-given sexual identity.

Yet many of the experiences related by these young women are also common to girls who never question their status as 'heterosexual'. The host of girls' boarding school stories attest to the normality of the schoolgirl 'crush', as is evidenced by the example below:

> Occasionally a 'pash' between a pretty junior and a receptive senior might lead to a secret meeting in the long grass at the end of the games field. They would usually just talk, unfamiliar with the vocabulary of desire, hardly knowing why they wanted to be alone, until by accident they brushed against each other's little breasts and discovered how nice it felt. But the prelude was so long and the subterfuge so elaborate that most 'pashes' were over before reaching even this innocent stage.
>
> (Lambert, 1991: 49)

Equally, girls' comics and teenage magazines are filled with stories about girls who both have strong feelings for other girls, and also 'feel different' (Ussher, 1997). Arguably, the interpretation of these feelings as 'lesbian' depends on whether the label is used by the girl herself, or by others:

> I was sitting next to her, yeah . . . and my knee was just like getting closer . . . you know, and I nearly exploded and this woman didn't touch my knee, you know . . . cause, you know, she hadn't a clue, I mean I was young and everything, but then I came home, like, cause my aunt said to me, you know, 'So do you think you're a dyke, then?'

I remember . . . *Dyke TV* . . . I was secretly watching it and I remember thinking, ahh, yeah, you know this is good, this is, this is what it is for me.

What is described by the interviewees above is an existing desire that was discovered to be 'lesbian' as a result of the comments of others, or because of seeing representations of lesbianism on television. The realisation described above was positive. However, making this particular interpretation was not always so:

> It's a complete hassle, being, coming out and being gay, I mean I didn't, I didn't like it . . . sometimes I still think God, you know, it would be so much easier to be straight . . . but you're sitting there and you have all these feelings and stuff.

J   I was growing up in a strict Muslim household and we talked about homosexuality generally (.) and it was bad, it, that's why I felt that I was sick and that it was a phase that I was going through and that I would be cured.

I   But you weren't.

J   No, no now I'd say I was born one.

Within all of these extracts above we see 'lesbianism' positioned as both material and discursive: a set of feelings over which the interviewee says she has no choice or control, yet at the same time a discursive position which is taken up after it is identified and named. Neither level is pre-eminent. Material and discursive factors act together to define what it is to be 'lesbian'.

'DOING' LESBIAN: 'WHAT YOU DO AND WHO YOU ARE'

Acquiring or taking up a lesbian identity, marked by the process of 'coming out' (see Mooney-Somers and Ussher, forthcoming), is only the first step. After this, lesbianism is arguably something women *do*, rather than something they *are*. This argument can be made about all gendered or sexual behaviour. For, as I have outlined elsewhere (Ussher, 1997), becoming 'woman', the process of acquiring expertise in the rules of femininity in order to 'do girl', involves a negotiation of the various representations of 'woman' and the myriad scripts of gendered roles which circulate in the symbolic sphere. As Judith Butler has argued, sexuality is always a set of repeated performances 'that congeal over time to produce the appearance of substance, of a natural sort of being' (Butler, 1990: 33). Heterosexual women may shift between the various subject positions of *being, doing, resisting* or *subverting* 'girl' (see Ussher, 1997, for a discussion of this), yet lesbians are arguably always resisting or rejecting the archetypal feminine script in 'doing lesbian', as the rules of femininity are framed within a heterosexual matrix. Thus there is an awareness of performance and of the negotiation of roles and rules which is not present to the same degree in the talk of young heterosexual women, for whom femininity (and heterosexuality) is so familiar and ingrained that it is taken for granted.

For the majority of these interviewees, *doing* or *being* lesbian was a multi-layered performance, which shifted and changed both across time and across situations. Many of the women spontaneously talked about how they used to be, as a comparison point for how they were now. Others talked about the many roles or performances that they currently adopt:

> I see myself as a lesbian avenger. I see myself as a lesbian film maker, within a group of lesbian film makers, and I see myself as a sometime disco bunny, sometime scene queen, you know, sometime bimbo.

So, while I will examine a number of the themes which emerged in the description of what it meant to 'do lesbian' below, it is important to note that this is a multiple shifting performance, not a static or rigid script (see Ussher, 1997).

Fashion and style

One of the dominant themes which emerged in the interviews was of expressing lesbian identity through dress or style:

> [What] is being a lesbian to me . . . well I suppose I would have to talk about the lesbian scene and the community and sort of lifestyle and culture and, you know, fashion. The lesbian fashion . . . and stuff like that . . . it gives me a really nice feeling to feel part of this, umm, this subculture . . . you know when you see people who are like yourself, you go 'God she's fab', and I sort of always think, ahh, dykes are really fab in the way they dress.

> To me it's the way I dress, the way I talk, the way I feel, my lifestyle, you know . . . If I was single I'd still go to gay places . . . it's a whole lifestyle for me.

The fact that 'doing lesbian' is both a material and discursive act is made clear in the extracts above. At one level it is the material reality of clothes, hairstyles, and ways of talking or behaving that is described. But the symbolic significance of these specific modes of dress or appearance is also implicitly revealed. Fashion and style are not arbitrary; they are central to the expression and interpretation of what it means to be (or subvert) 'woman' at any point in time (see Craik, 1993). Equally, what type of dress signifies 'lesbian' will change across cultural groups and across time, as Lillian Faderman (1991) has demonstrated in her exposure of the shifting physical expression of lesbian identity from stone butches and lesbian feminists, to SM advocates and lesbian chic. Women who don't conform to what is an accepted vision of 'lesbian' dress risk being assumed to be straight, as this interviewee comments:

> I hate people assuming that I'm straight. You get blokes coming up to you all the time and it's like [they] seem pretty disgusting and, ahmm, I hate it and if, like, women would come up to me I'd like that. But I don't like . . . like [it] being assumed I'm straight just cause of the way I look.

> I'd prefer [it] to be assumed I'm a dyke but . . . I'm not going to change my image just so I can fit in with their stereotype.

One of the functions of dress codes is arguably to be recognised as 'lesbian', both by other lesbians and by men. The interviewee above reported wearing a women's symbol because 'the only time I ever get people thinking that I'm a dyke is when I'm with someone else who looks like one'. The women's symbol may signify 'lesbian' to those who are cognisant with more subtle forms of communication. As is evidenced by the extract above, it does not work in a broader context, in warding off unwanted attention from men. So the different readings or interpretations of the symbolic representation of 'lesbian' can have marked material effects.

All about sex

The material body was also evoked in the theme 'lesbianism is all about sex', where the physical act of having sex with another women was positioned as both the defining feature and the demonstration of lesbian identity:

> The technical side of it, in that being a lesbian you're sort of, you're a woman who sleeps with women.

> It's pretty obviously about like sex . . . isn't it . . . you can talk about women's energy for as long as you like, but I think, ultimately, I think most women . . . adopt a lesbian identity because they want to shag women don't they, or they want to be shagged by women, or both.

> It's obviously a sexual thing first . . .

Again, this operates at both a material and discursive level. The women *are* having sex with other women, so material practice is involved. Yet it is the *meaning* of these physical acts which is important. So the first sexual contact can mark the woman taking up a legitimate status as 'lesbian'; it can be the event which draws attention to 'perv' desire:

> I was only probably really aware of kind of perv feelings (*laughing*) or sexual feelings . . . when we kissed which was completely . . . a big surprise, completely out of the blue and I didn't kind of try to kill her or take off my shoe and stab her in the eye . . . I kissed her back which was . . . quite cool . . . I just thought 'I've been kissed, I can join the human race.'

Here the interviewee draws attention to the strategy she could have adopted ('try to kill her or take off my shoe and stab her in the eye'), if she had wanted to continue to identify as 'straight'. But the fact she describes herself as having 'kissed her back' signified acceptance both of the act as sexual, and of herself as an active player in 'lesbian sex'.

This isn't inevitably the case. As was outlined above, both women and men engage in same sex sex without it being defined as signifying lesbian or gay status. One of the interviewees described her experience with a 'straight' women thus:

> It was very sexual, it was very romantic, it was total love, do ya know, it was, God, you know this . . . never happened to me before, you know, I was just completely, we were talking about the future, do you know what I mean, an' where're we gonna live, an' stuff, but she, I mean she looks really dykey . . . she did love me and it was very strong, and it was very real, but she is straight . . . I found it very difficult that she was, you know, going out with men and stuff, and like really flaunting it to everyone, because I think in a way she was like, you know, trying to put the whole thing behind her, but yet still needing me.

This again illustrates that 'lesbian sex' is both a material and discursive act; the physical act of sex can have many different meanings or many interpretations. To this 'straight' woman it was not positioned as 'lesbian sex', or at least as a sign of her own lesbian status, at all. We may want to evoke psychoanalytic or even sociological concepts in understanding why she repressed her desire – parental pressure and ambivalence about being openly positioned as 'lesbian' were the reasons given by the interviewee for her behaviour – but regardless of the explanation we adopt, it is clear that we cannot look to just the body or to the cultural construction placed upon 'sex', if we are to understand what it really means. The interviewee above describes a sexual relationship which was interpreted very differently by the two parties involved – something which is a common feature of couples therapy in any context (and is drawn out for comic effect in the television programme *Blind Date*). In this context it illustrates the fact that we cannot assume that a woman *is* lesbian, or defines herself as 'lesbian' just because she engages in sex with another woman.

The converse is also true, as is evidenced by the explanations and interpretations given by the interviewees who previously, or currently, desired or had sex with men. This did not negate the legitimacy of their being identified as 'lesbian', as that which could be seen as a sign of heterosexuality was either positioned as a past aberration or as lesser than sex with or desire for women:

> I had little things with men before, not men sort of people my age, I suppose, young, younger men, that I sort of I thought I was, like, had crushes on them, well, not crushes on them but (.) ahmm, and I, I actually used those things and maybe I sort of worked on those things to sort of deny the fact that at the time the most important person in my life was like that woman [the teacher].

J   Have you ever had sex with a man?
L   Yeah, so?
J   And it was (.)

L   Boring, I was just like waiting for something to happen, *EastEnders*
      was on in the background, ohh, oh so and so is going out with so and
      so, sorry, yeah it was boring it was just, thoroughly boring, and, I
      don't know, just, I just, I don't find the male body at all sexually attrac-
      tive so I think that's a real barrier to me even if I wanted to have sex
      with a man that would be a real barrier cause I wouldn't be able to get
      at all excited about it.

In these two extracts above, both desire for and sex with men are admitted,
but at the same time dismissed, thus in no way undermining the status of
these women as 'lesbian'. Indeed, the discursive interpretation placed on
both feelings and acts serves to reinforce their very lesbian identity, as feelings for and sex with women are implicitly positioned as so much more
important, or more powerful.

Women identified women

Another dominant theme to emerge from the interviews was of lesbianism
being defined by identification with other women. Reminiscent of the
lesbian–feminist rhetoric of the 1970s, this appears to position lesbianism as
a state of mind, or as a set of priorities:

   I think it means being pro-women, sort of very women-orientated, and
   that's where your interests are ... you know, women-conscious and
   women-centred ...

   Having strong feelings about women's rights and being aware, just having
   a higher awareness about our issues.

Given the provocative arguments of recent lesbian critics such as Monique
Wittig (1980) that 'lesbians are not women', because 'woman' is
constructed within heterosexual discourse, the continued identification with
both feminism and with women in this group is interesting. This identification with women was closely linked to a description of lesbianism as a
political stance; it is thus not necessarily an identification with *all* women.
Here, both material political action and the discursive meanings of this
action are clearly described:

   It does have political meaning ... my struggle against the straight
   community ... to me is political.

   My brand of lesbianism [is] really in your face, really out, really
   politically active in various things.

   It is political ... I don't think you can get away from that you know ...
   it's gonna be questioning their ... structure and their life and all this
   stuff.

The women interviewed here were all politically active as members of the direct action group 'Lesbian Avengers'. This means that they regularly engaged in material action to further their political ends, but at the same time being members of the group and engaging in these acts signified both group identity and personal power. It was both about what they did and what these actions discursively signified.

SUMMARY AND CONCLUSION

In this chapter I have examined the way in which both material and discursive factors have been used to define, express and regulate gay and lesbian sexuality. Traditionally defined through the material act of same sex sex, 'homosexuality' has been regulated and controlled for centuries at both the level of the material body and the level of discourse. In recent years, social constructionist, feminist and Foucauldian theorists have challenged the reductionist analyses which have dominated science and the law, demonstrating that 'sex' and the 'lesbian' or 'gay man' are products of discourse, not simply material acts or states, and that the meaning of lesbian and gay identities is dependent on and constructed within the social and discursive context in which a person is situated. In line with the other contributions to this book, it has been argued that we need to move away from the dichotomy of material or discursive, to acknowledge that both are interlinked. We need to shift our epistemological gaze from the narrowly focused to the broadly inclusive, and to acknowledge that these different approaches reflect the ideological and epistemological stance of the different experts and critics, rather than the 'truth' about 'homosexual sex', or about what it is to be lesbian or gay.

Through looking at a series of interviews conducted with a group of young lesbians, we have seen that material and discursive factors are irrevocably interconnected in the meaning of being lesbian. There are also many material and discursive consequences of taking up the position of lesbian – ranging from verbal and physical violence, parental rejection, social isolation, depression and anxiety, to feelings of empowerment, pleasure, group identification and sex. These issues are explored in detail elsewhere (see Ussher and Mooney-Somers, forthcoming).

Thus, in conclusion, it is argued that to examine only one level of experience – be it the material body or the discursive construction of 'homosexuality' – is to give only a partial and incomplete understanding of what it means to be 'lesbian' or 'gay'. Equally, to adopt either an essentialist or a strict social constructionist framework in describing and explaining lesbian or gay sexuality is to negate important aspects of experience. In contrast, to acknowledge and explore the relationship between the material and discursive is to move forwards towards a more comprehensive level of analysis, and one which appears to be a more meaningful reflection of the experiences of those who take up the position of 'lesbian' or 'gay'.

ACKNOWLEDGEMENTS

These arguments are explored in more detail in Ussher (1997), where parts of this chapter have previously appeared in a different form. Thanks are extended to Julie Mooney-Somers who conducted the interviews referred to above.

NOTE

1   Sex with a girl under the age of 16 could fall under the general laws protecting against child sexual abuse.

REFERENCES

Alias, A.G. (1995) 46 XY, 5-Alpha-Reductase Deficiency: A (Contrasting) Model to Understanding the Predisposition to Male Homosexuality?, poster presented at the 21st Annual Meeting of the International Academy of Sex Research, Provincetown, MA, 20–24 July.

Bailey, J.M. (1995) A Twin Registry Study of Sexual Orientation, paper presented at the 21st Annual Meeting of the International Academy of Sex Research, Provincetown, MA, 20–24 July.

Bailey, J.M. and Pillard, R.C. (1991) A Genetic Study of Male Sexual Orientation, *Archives of General Psychiatry*, 48, 1089–1096.

Bailey, J.M., Pillard, R.C., Neale, M.C. and Agyei, Y. (1993) Heritable Factors Influence Sexual Orientation in Women, *Archives of General Psychiatry* 50, 217–223.

Brown, J. (1986) *Immodest Acts*, Oxford: Oxford University Press.

Butler, J. (1990) *Gender Trouble: Feminism and the Subversion of Identity*, London: Routledge.

——(1993) *Bodies That Matter: On the Discursive Limits of 'Sex'*, London: Routledge.

Craik, J. (1993) *The Face of Fashion. Cultural Studies in Fashion*, London: Routledge.

Crompton, L. (1985) The Myth of Lesbian Impunity. In J. Licasta and R. Peterson (eds), *The Gay Past: A Collection of Historical Essays*, New York: Howorth Press.

Dynes, W.R. (1989) *Encyclopaedia of Homosexuality*, London: St James Press.

Edwards, S. (1981) *Female Sexuality and the Law*, Oxford: Martin Robertson.

Ellis, H. (1893) *Men and Women*, London: Contemporary Science Series.

Evans, A. (1978) *Witchcraft and the Gay Counterculture*, Boston: Fag Rag Books.

Faderman, L. (1985) *Surpassing the Love of Men,* London: The Women's Press.

——(1991) *Odd Girls and Twilight Lovers. A History of Lesbian Life in Twentieth Century America*, London: Penguin.

Fedoroff, J.P. *et al.* (1995) A GnRH Test of Androphiles, Gynephiles, Heterosexual Paedophiles, and Homosexual Paedophiles, paper presented at the 21st Annual Meeting of the International Academy of Sex Research, Provincetown, MA, 20–24 July.

Foucault, M. (1976) *The History of Sexuality*, vol. 1, London: Penguin.

Garber, M. (1995) *Vice Versa: Bisexuality and the Eroticism of Everyday Life*, London: Penguin.

Hamer, D. (1995) Sexual Orientation, Personality Traits, and Genes, paper presented at the 21st Annual Meeting of the International Academy of Sex Research, Provincetown, MA, 20–24 July.

Henry, G.W. (1948) *Sex Variants: A Study of Homosexual Patterns*, New York: Paul B. Hoeber Inc.

Herdt, G. (1984). *Ritualised Homosexuality in Melanesia,* Berkeley: University of California Press.

——(1987) *The Sambia: Ritual and Gender in New Guinea,* New York: Holt, Rinehart & Winston.

Howard League Working Party Report (1984) *Unlawful Sex: Offences, Victims and Offenders in the Criminal Justice System of England and Wales,* London: Waterlow.

Hyde, M.H. (1972) *The Other Love: An Historical and Contemporary Survey of Homosexuality in Britain,* Mayflower Books: London.

Jeffreys, S. (1985) *The Spinster and Her Enemies: Feminism and Sexuality 1880–1930,* London: Pandora.

Kallman, F.J. (1952) Comparative Twin Study on the Genetic Aspects of Male Homosexuality, *Journal of Nervous Mental Disorder,* 115: 282–298.

Kitzinger, C. (1987) *The Social Construction of Lesbianism,* London: Sage.

Krafft-Ebing, R. von (1886) *Psychopathia Sexualis,* trans. F.S. Klaf, New York: Bell.

Lambert, A. (1991) *No Talking After Lights,* London: Penguin.

Le Vay, S. (1993) *The Sexual Brain,* Cambridge, MA: MIT Press.

McIntosh, M. (1968) The Homosexual Role. In K. Plummer (1981) *The Making of the Modern Homosexual,* London: Hutchinson.

Monter, W. (1981) Sodomy and Heresy in Modern Switzerland, *Journal of Homosexuality,* 6, 41.

Mooney-Somers, J. and Ussher, J.M. (forthcoming) *Young Lesbian Women and Mental Health: A Discourse Analytic Study.*

Pattatucci, A.M.L. and Hamer, D.H. (1995) The Genetics of Sexual Orientation: From Fruit Flies to Humans. In P.R Abramson and S.D. Pinkerton (eds), *Sexual Nature, Sexual Culture,* Chicago: University of Chicago Press, pp. 154–174.

Plummer, K. (1981) *The Making of the Modern Homosexual,* London: Hutchinson.

Rich, A. (1980) Compulsory Heterosexuality and Lesbian Existence, *Signs,* 5(4), 651–666.

Rivera, R.R. (1991) Sexual Orientation and the Law. In J.C. Gonsiorek and J.D. Weinrich (eds), *Homosexuality: Research Implications for Public Policy,* London: Sage, pp. 81–100.

Robson, R. (1992) Legal Lesbicide. In J. Radford and D. Russell (eds), *Femicide: The Politics of Woman Killing,* Buckingham: Open University Press, pp. 40–45.

Rubin, G. (1984). Thinking Sex. In Vance, C. (ed), *Pleasure and Danger: Exploring Female Sexuality,* London: Routledge & Kegan Paul, p. 291.

Segal, L. (1994) *Straight Sex: The Politics of Pleasure,* London: Virago.

Smith-Rosenberg, C. (1985) The Female World of Love and Ritual: Relations Between Women in Nineteenth Century America, *Disorderly Conduct: Visions of Gender in Victorian America,* New York: Knopf.

Smyth, C. (1992) *Lesbians Talk: Queer Notions,* London: Scarlet Press, pp. 23–24.

Terry, J. (1990) Lesbians Under the Medical Gaze: Scientists Search for Remarkable Differences, *Journal of Sex Research,* 27(3), 317–399.

Tiefer, L. (1987) Social Constructionism and the Study of Human Sexuality. In P. Shaver and C. Hendrick (eds), *Sex and Gender,* Beverly Hills, CA: Sage.

——(1991) Commentary on the Status of Sex Research: Feminism, Sexuality and Sexology, *Journal of Psychology and Human Sexuality,* 43(3), 5–42.

Ussher, J.M. (1991) *Women's Madness: Misogyny or Mental Illness,* Hemel Hempstead: Harvester Wheatsheaf.

——(1997) *Fantasies of Femininity: Reframing the Boundaries of Sex,* London: Penguin.

Ussher, J.M. and Mooney-Somers, J. (forthcoming) Doing Lesbian: The Material-Discursive Construction of Lesbian Identities.

Vance, C. (1989) Social Construction Theory: Problems in the History of Sexuality. In H. Crowley and S. Himmelweit (eds), *Knowing Women: Feminism and Knowledge*, London: Polity Press.

Weeks, J. (1981) *Sex, Politics and Society. The Regulation of Sexuality Since 1800*, London: Longman.

——(1985) *Sexuality and its Discontents: Meanings, Myths and Modern Sexualities*, London: Routledge & Kegan Paul.

Wittig, M. (1980) The Straight Mind, *Feminist Issues*, 1(1) (Summer).

9 Intimacy and love in late modern conditions

Implications for unsafe sexual practices

Hélène Joffe

STUDYING REPRESENTATIONS OF INTIMACY

In this chapter I explore the valorisation of love and intimacy in contemporary society. Both love and intimacy are marked by their reference to states of closeness and attachment.[1] The idealisation of connection with others in late modernity manifests in aspects of sexual practice. I will focus on a striking finding which has emerged from the AIDS literature: the greater likelihood of failing to use condoms in sexual encounters which are considered more intimate, rather than more distant from the self. This phenomenon is explored within the rubric of social representations theory, a framework which is particularly useful in that in encompasses both the material and the discursive aspects of phenomena such as love and intimacy.

The growing body of empirical work on heterosexual, gay, bisexual and sex work[2] encounters indicates that people tend to practise unsafe sex in relationships which are viewed as intimate, and safer sex in relationships which are envisaged as more distant from the self. Few studies discern the complex interplay of factors which contribute to this polarisation. In this chapter I argue that the primary dynamic which is at work in this polarisation is the idealisation of love and intimacy. Current meanings of love and intimacy must be examined against a backdrop in which increasing numbers of people live alone, rather than in intimate contact with others. In keeping with Western trends, a third of the British population will form one person households by the year 2000 (Mintel survey, 20 March 1996). In commensurate proportion to the drift towards isolation, there is an idealisation of connection. The meanings and practices linked with love and intimacy are an idealised defence against a threat to the late modern individual's identity.

The chapter is conceived within a social representational framework, utilising the concepts of social identity and unconscious defensiveness, to examine the identity protective nature of representations. A social representation is a conceptualisation or explanation of a social object, such as 'love'. When one looks at social representations of a phenomenon one taps the contents of people's world-view, which are steeped in the assumptions of the culture. Social representations are forged in the interplay between the thoughts which form in the minds of individuals and the representations which exist in their social environment. This environment includes mass-mediated and other institutional messages and, at a more microsocial level, ideas heard in conversations with others. They are to be found both within individual minds and outside of them.

Social representations theory aims to capture constellations of thoughts concerning a social object. They can be accessed by tuning in to how people talk about phenomena, by gaining knowledge of how people act. The intentions of a social representational study are anthropological, though the concern is with contemporary, Western men and women. People's practices and their thoughts are regarded as manifestations of underlying representations (see Joffe 1996a, 1997). Consequently, the notion of a 'social representation' encompasses both thought and practice. In this chapter the central material practice under investigation is the use of condoms during penetrative sex as a preventive measure against HIV infection; it is presumed that talk about such practices reveals some of the thoughts which accompany condom use. When viewed in conjunction with one another, material practice and thought provide an inroad into the social representations which underpin love and intimate contact with others.

It is assumed that the individual's social identity, the individual's internalised affinity with certain groups, is integral to the social representations which the individual espouses. Gay men, for example, are likely to represent sex in a different way from heterosexual men in line with the status of their differing identities in the dominant culture. People establish and buy into codes of understanding common to the groups with which they identify. These codes of understanding form the basis of their social representations; they are the sedimentation of the 'we' in the composition of the 'I'. They are the outcome of efforts to become aligned with certain groups in fashioning a desirable sense of self. In addition to the salience of identity positioning, unconscious emotive dynamics are intrinsic to the process of representation. Representations protect the individual thinker from negative emotional states such as anxiety, in the same way that unconscious defences do (see Joffe, 1996b). So the gay man's representation of his sexuality, though influenced by dominant norms associated with his identity, will also defend him against adherence to ideas which are unwelcome.

In this chapter empirical work on gay men and sex workers is described in order to develop a conceptualisation of why there is a polarisation between loving thought/unsafe sexual practice and distant thought/safer sexual practice. The continuities and discontinuities with the meanings of love in the broader community are also explored. A developing corpus of research in the AIDS field has indicated that feelings of love and intimacy can increase the risk of exposure to HIV, and that gay men are more likely to have unprotected anal sex with regular partners than with casual partners (Weatherburn, *et al.*, 1992; Bochow, 1994). In a review of the studies on gay and bisexual men, Flowers *et al.* (1997) found that 'relationship status' was associated with unsafe sex more often and more consistently than any other psychosocial factor. The more intimate the relationship, the greater the likelihood that unsafe sex will be practised. Research on sex work also highlights the salience of emotional ties in the nature of the sexual act: high rates of condom use are found for anal intercourse among male sex workers, but condom use is not uniformly distributed across partners. Male sex workers are safest with male clients, less safe with male non-clients, and least safe with female non-clients (Pleak and Meyer-Bahlburg, 1990). This is echoed by Dorfman *et al.*'s (1992) finding that female sex workers use condoms more frequently with clients than with steady boyfriends or husbands. Day (1990) also finds strong evidence of a division between work and non-work practices among female sex workers. The condom is used in work-related sex and, by corollary, condom-free sex signals relationships outside of the realm of 'work'. Safer sex is a more accepted part of the sex workers' public world than of their more intimate, private life.

Two points of departure are utilised to advance the exploration of the division between intimacy/unsafe sex and distance/safer sex. First, I refer to studies concerning the behaviour of various out-groups and to the deep-seated meanings of intimacy for members of both in-groups and out-groups. Second, I link findings emerging from these studies with sociological work concerning how contemporary social life affects all members of society, how it constructs in-group and out-group alike as alienated, and how this impacts upon the status held by love and intimacy in late modernity.

THE REPRESENTATION OF INTIMACY AMONG MALE SEX WORKERS

I draw on an empirical study (Joffe and Dockrell, 1995)[3] which is concerned with male sex workers' (self-reported) bodily practices and their thoughts surrounding these practices. As part of a broader study, an in-depth analysis of the working and intimate lives of twenty male sex workers was conducted. A questionnaire was used to gauge their self-reported sexual practices, and was accompanied by a verbal account of their lives, in the context of a semi-structured interview. According to the derived measure of 'unsafe' sex – unprotected anal intercourse in at least one of the last five sexual encounters[4] – one-third of the respondents had practised unsafe sex. The meanings of both safe and unsafe sex which these men articulate provide access to their representations.

The data suggest that the male sex workers evaluate their partners on a continuum which ranges from a 'private' to a 'public' pole. This corresponds with a distinction between encounters which are conducted in order to satisfy desire as opposed to those carried out for monetary gain. The men were not generally asked about differences between their working and personal lifestyles. Rather the interviews suggested that the men spontaneously differentiated their private from their public sexual encounters. When the men entered this mode of differentiation, public life was associated with exploitation and with a lack of care, while private life was associated with the very antithesis:

> I'm going to tell you something, no, it's very strange, because, lots of times, when I was with a, in a relationship, and I would feel like I was, um, like I wanted control as well. But I'd forget 'I'm in a relationship now', 'what am I doing', 'switch off'. I couldn't switch off. I just felt like I was in bed with a punter, you know. My partner, my relationship, he would say to me 'Come on now, Norman, switch off, you're not on the streets, you're not with a client, you're with me. I care about you, I'm not looking for anything more from you except who you are, what you are. I love you very much.' I couldn't believe that this person loved me, you know. I've never ever believed anyone wanted me. When someone says to me they love me, I just don't believe them . . . I feel I've been abused, well, not abused, used, just like a piece of meat, you know, for someone to get their rocks off.
>
> (street worker, age 25, HIV negative)

Objectification, usury and manipulation – as well as the need to be vigilant – characterised thoughts about public life. While the sex worker quoted above aimed to maintain control with punters, he aimed to 'switch off' in the loving relationship. The search for quiescence and love, in private life, lay at the heart of many unsafe sexual acts in this sample. The condom was represented as a physical barrier to the romance and intimacy sought in the private realm. The incompatibility of the condom and love was clearly explained by the respondents:

> Well, just, I really resented the fact that I'd never actually been inside him without this plastic thing between us, and I wanted it to happen just once. Just to prove how much I loved him.
>
> (masseur, age 34, HIV negative)

In addition to viewing the condom as a plastic barrier to love, the absorption of semen is demarcated as important since it connotes having a lover 'inside of one' beyond the time frame of the act. This desire for a deep and long-lasting bond is illustrated in the following extract:

RESPONDENT   And when you don't use a condom you can say, 'I have got the person into me.' And it lasts three or four hours, I don't know. So you carry the idea of the person in you. So it is not only sex.

INTERVIEWER   So it is in your mind as well.

RESPONDENT   Because I remember when I left Japan we had sex just before I left Japan and I was on the plane and I said, 'OK he is home now but I am carrying him with me.' If it is somebody I don't like or I don't love, I really don't care. If

> it is just one night, I really don't care. But if the partner, the
> person I have sex with is someone I love . . .
>
> (masseur, age 25, HIV negative)

The search for intimacy can manifest in a willingness to absorb everything
that partners have to offer, even if it is the HIV:

> With my lover I thought, 'Well, I love the guy, if he has got it [AIDS] I
> am going to get it in some way, I want to give him everything, so it
> doesn't matter because we're in love.' It doesn't worry me that much.
>
> (street worker, age 21, HIV negative)

A pattern is evident in the content of the thoughts and actions of the sex
workers who refer to love. First and foremost, all of the men who practise
unsafe sex in the sample refer to love in talking about the thoughts which
surround this practice. Love presents as a major element of unsafe sexual
practice. The men create a division between their public and private
encounters, referring to the vigilance which needs to be maintained in the
more public sphere, and the desire to lower one's guard in the private sphere.
The condom symbolises this guard, a guard which would only serve as an
intruder in the sphere of physical and emotional connectedness. Absorbing
and keeping semen inside of oneself symbolises an ability to hold on to
someone else's essence, their insides, even when they are no longer present.
Penetration symbolises an inmost, deep-seated union. The desire to reach
this state of togetherness is far more salient in their talk than references to
the physical danger of contracting the HIV.

From the perspective of the health professional, one-third of the men in
the sample take considerable risks. Yet the sex workers are not centrally
concerned with risk. Rather, a yearning for the satisfaction of a desire for
intimacy lies at the heart of their representations of their sexual encounters.
I have stated that this yearning is an idealised one. Evidence for this lies in
the extreme language used in a number of the extracts:

> I loved him so much, and he wanted me so much, and we had the best sex
> in the world that I've ever had, and I never will have sex like that
> again . . . I suppose, it was just that climax of your relationship,
> everything that was just all right, and all the stop lights – well, we
> couldn't look.
>
> (masseur, age 36, HIV positive)

The word 'love', rather than a weaker version such as 'liking' or 'fondness',
is used in many ways: 'we're in love', 'someone I love', 'just to prove how
much I loved him'. In addition, the use of extreme language concerning sex
is striking in these extracts: 'best sex in the world', 'I never will have sex like
that again'. The 'love' extracts indicate that the material practice of penetration signifies different emotional states, depending on whether it is
accompanied by a condom or not. In these men penetration without a

condom – and the exchange of semen which is related to this – signifies emotional states of desire, intimacy and perfect union or wholeness. These states are valued so highly that material considerations regarding the potential infectivity of the body with the HIV pale into insignificance. I now turn to an exploration of reasons for the valorisation of intimacy and its manifestation in sexual practices, both within this group and beyond it.

THE REPRESENTATION OF INTIMACY IN OUT-GROUPS: TOWARDS AN EXPLANATION

A central aspect of the representations of 'prostitution' held in society at large relates to non-intimate sexuality and it is against the backdrop of such representations that the male sex workers formulate their thoughts and actions. Historically, sex work has been associated with immorality, with mercenary activity (Day *et al.*, 1987; Day, 1988) and with mass, incurable illnesses such as syphilis (e.g. Brandt, 1987; Gilman, 1988). Since these associations are highly negatively charged, it is an intrinsically stigmatised profession and, in out-groups, this stigma is related to the valorisation of intimacy. According to Goffman's (1963) now classic analysis, stigmatised people undergo 'identity ambivalence', since they are embedded in the wider norms of the society, norms which undermine their group. Identification with fellow stigmatised group members binds stigmatised people to these norms, which results in the creation of a 'spoiled identity'. This negative sense of one's identity stands in contrast to that of most people in the society who, according to the social identity tradition (Tajfel, 1981, 1982), are afforded a positive individual and in-group identity.

While stigma may damage the identities of the stigmatised, it is crucial to recognise that groups associated with stigmatised conditions are not purely victims of the stigmatising social representations. Individuals seek to reverse the effects of stigma by a number of mechanisms, one of which is to find the 'silver lining' of the stigmatised condition (Jones *et al.*, 1984). Since they are judged negatively in the social representations that surround them, sex workers are likely to experience a sense of 'spoiled identity'; however, like other out-group members, they may strive to resist the tarnishing of their identity by recasting their activities in a positive light. I will argue that the valorisation of intimacy is a sign of the recasting of sexuality in a positive light.

The 'search for the silver lining' can manifest as a conscious strategy, such as the strategies which underpin the 'gay pride' or 'black is beautiful' movements. Yet there is also an unconscious element in the search for a silver lining. A trace of an early psychodynamic defence against anxiety remains in the psyche throughout life. The trace of the 'splitting' defence manifests in people's proclivity to polarise the world into opposites and, more particularly, into bad and good: one side of what one looks at is devalued and the other idealised. Hate and love are emotions rooted in this polarisation. Polarising or splitting serves to keep the bad feelings from contaminating the good ones. In the thought patterns of the male sex workers, sexuality within the private realm is judged in idealised terms as a way of distancing it from the negative social judgements associated with sex work. The private identification with love is the sex worker's protection of himself from the 'bad', from an identity associated with usury.

There is a continuity between sex workers and the members of other out-groups in terms of the social stigma which they face, and of the heightened sense of anxiety which it produces. A theme which reappears in qualitative studies of various other out-groups is that of usury. In a study which examines gay men's discourse concerning their partners, the theme resurfaces:

> He just wants to be with me and that's nice. So you dun't feel like a cash machine, cos that's what I once said to Neil, I says, 'Thy makes me feel like a cash machine, press the right button and you get what you want.' With Jake you dun't, we just like being together and we enjoy together. That's it.
>
> (quoted in Smith *et al.*, 1997: 83)

A dislike of usury – 'Thy makes me feel like a cash machine', 'used, just like a piece of meat' – is evident in both the gay male and sex work data, and is juxtaposed with representations of a mutually enjoyable, authentic and intimate experience. Even though gay men have no need to distance themselves from the connotations carried by sex work, they need to gain distance from other negative social judgements.

The Smith *et al.* (1997) study bears similarity to that of the male sex workers, not only in terms of the exploitation versus authentic connection theme but in terms of how exploitation and intimacy are symbolised. Smith *et al.* talk of the way in which the exchange of semen is particularly important in forging intimacy since it represents a coming together of two disparate selves, which lasts beyond the moment of the sexual act. The condom symbolises an anathema to this ideal of togetherness:

> you're having to put a barrier between you and someone you love. And even if it's only a few inches of barrier, if you like, it's still something artificial that's there, which is otherwise a very sort of spiritual, animal type, primeval type of experience.
>
> (quoted in Smith *et al.*, 1997: 85)

The search for an ultimate experience of non-artificial togetherness emerges as a more important element than an attempt to avoid risk, in male sex worker and gay man alike. The similarity of the themes expressed in the two studies relates, at least in part, to the fact that both explore the representations of out-groups. The sexuality of both sex workers and gay men has been viewed as 'unnatural' in terms of heterosexual, monogamous, family-centred representations. Dominant norms are violated both by the bodily practices of these two groups and by their talk about them. Non-monogamous sexuality is endorsed by the activities of both groups, be it via anonymous, bathhouse sex (which is associated with a gay lifestyle) or via the multiplicity of nameless sexual contacts intrinsic to sex work. Being regarded as deviant may increase the need to dissociate oneself from deviance and to associate oneself with a societal ideal of exclusivity, which is represented by coupledom.[5]

Day's (1990) study of a further out-group, female sex workers, reveals a continuity across out-groups in terms of the symbolisation of intimacy and distance in sexual practices. These women's talk about their bodily practices can be framed in terms an almost identical representational structure to that of the male sex workers mentioned above: the women cast their activities as 'work' and draw a sharp contrast between work and intimate practices. Day's work is distinctive in its emphasis on protection of the 'self' from usury; the women in her sample delimit sex work as work so that a perceived 'true self' is protected from the stigma of that work. A central symbol of work, of the non-private, is the condom. It places a physical barrier between the sex worker and her client, which obstructs physical contact. The minimisation of contact with the client allows the 'self' to be preserved for the chosen private partners. While a number of different distancing strategies are used, all sex workers in Day's cohort are preoccupied with ways of keeping their distance: 'I don't want strangers' semen inside. I only drop the barrier with someone I really love' (quoted in Day, 1990: 101). This sex worker makes explicit a representation common in many studies of people's talk about AIDS. In parallel to private as opposed to public bodily contacts, so private as opposed to public emotional and social meanings are created. According to Day, the public is associated with a market morality (that of money), while the private is associated with a kinship morality (that of love). The private sphere not only excludes the emphasis on money, but is based upon ties of affection and procreation. In fact an emphasis on fertility and children among the female sex workers is the fundamental way of retaining a private self. The symbolic load attached to motherhood is very great. It not only counters the historically powerful representation of the 'barren prostitute' but also that of usury. The basic representation of the prostitute is of immorality and so sex workers legitimise their work as external, establishing a private self-identity infused with symbols of love and fertility.

These findings augment the claim that thoughts, actions and the representations which underpin them can be defensive, a way of distancing the self from stigma. They also show, in precise terms, that risk is not a dominant aspect of the sex workers' thoughts about their partners. The claims of social scientists concerning the centrality of 'under-estimation of risk' or 'sense of subjective immunity' regarding unsafe sex are out of kilter with the representations which reside within 'risk groups'. In fact, in Day's (1990) study half of the female sex workers with boyfriends know – rather than suspect – that these men are not monogamous. In addition, the female sex workers make the assumption that their boyfriends do not use condoms in their other relationships. So risk is not estimated in accordance with probability-type reasoning. Rather, the meanings with which the sexual acts are infused relate to preservation of a self uncontaminated by usury. These meanings originate in unconscious attempts to forge an idealised 'silver lining'. The sex workers' defences blind them to the very ways in which their private practices endanger their physical beings. A psychological search for intimacy and the sense of purity associated with loving relationships overrides considerations of material sources of infection.

Prior to examining whether this pattern of findings resonates with work on heterosexual men and women, it is useful to delve deeper into the association made between the loving relationship and purity. Evidence of this abounds in the symbolic representations of the sex workers. In Day's study, the semen of lovers is viewed as potentially fertile, while that of clients is seen as dirty. Joffe and Dockrell (1995) show that there is a desire to keep the semen of a lover inside of oneself, whereas that of clients is often regarded as disgusting. In line with Douglas's (1966) anthropological notions of purity and pollution, people draw a boundary around a pure self as protection against potential contamination by the outside world. In more psychodynamic terms, they split the 'good' feelings and objects from the 'bad' ones, in order to maintain the goodness.

Day points to the constant tension which she imagines the workers must feel, since the world of usury/work can scarcely be kept apart from the intimate/private realm: regular clients sometimes fall in love with the sex worker; boyfriends are often supported by the money procured through sex work. According to Day, the distinction between the two worlds is constantly under the threat of dissolution. However, I would argue that her account fails to consider that defences prevent the worker from perceiving that the two worlds may collapse into one another. Unconscious forces come to bear on the situation: an idealisation of the fertile, private realm and a denigration of clients (with their 'dirty semen') allows sex workers to split the one sphere off from the other, thereby protecting themselves from the anxiety created by the potential merging of the one into the other. In order to maintain a positive self and in-group identity, people strive to represent this identity as pure, as untainted by stigma. The challenge is more pronounced for out-group members, since they are faced with a plethora of negative representations concerning their identities. However, 'heterosexuals' may also face stigma. Since the categories 'gay', 'bisexual' and 'heterosexual' are not discrete or fixed, the experiences and desires of apparently dominant groups may be diverse and this may invoke similar anxieties to those of outgroups. I have suggested that a defensive structure grounded in a polarisation between idealisation and denegation operates in out-groups who face the anxiety created by stigmatising social constructions. However, the idealisation of love is far too pervasive in Western culture for it to be linked to stigma alone. Nevertheless, the idealisation of love may well be linked to anxiety, in a broader sense.

Having alluded to empirical work which suggests that intimacy is also venerated in heterosexual relationships, a theoretical conceptualisation of the phenomenon will be presented. Heterosexuals are more likely to practise safer sex within casual than within regular relationships (Health Education Authority, 1994). Condom use is associated with casual sex in heterosexual teenagers and adults alike (Willig, 1995). In heterosexual relationships, women, in particular, have exaggerated confidence in a stable partner's trust-worthiness (Fullilove *et al.*, 1990; Holland *et al.*, 1991; Maticka-Tyndale, 1992), making them willing to practise unsafe sex. Young women see sex in terms of love, relationships and romance, and this informs their reluctance to use condoms (Holland *et al.*, 1991). In fact, the act of discontinuing condom use signifies the establishment of trust in the transformation from a casual to a stable alliance. Similarly, the request that one's partner use a condom undermines the premise of trust in the exclusivity of the relation-ship (Willig, 1995). The data indicates that intimate relationships carry different meanings from casual encounters, and that actions – in terms of condom use – differ accordingly. The condom is experienced as more suited to distant encounters, in much the same vein as data on out-group practices have suggested. I turn to sociological theory to provide insight into the meanings of intimacy.

EXPLAINING THE LINK BETWEEN UNSAFE SEX AND LOVE: INTIMACY AND LATE MODERNITY

In recent years a number of prominent sociologists have shifted their attention from an exclusive focus on the public sphere to the private sphere of intimacy. They concur that intimacy is highly valued in contemporary, Western societies but differ in their judgement of the source of this phenomenon. Giddens (1992) links the valuing of intimacy with the growth in equality between men and women in recent decades, with a growing democratisation of the private sphere. For Giddens, the valuing of intimacy is a way of reappropriating emotional ties from which members of modern societies have become detached. Approaching the phenomenon from a different angle, Beck and Beck-Gernsheim (1995) also note that intimacy has prominence in late modern society, but for these theorists the *valorisa-tion of intimacy* is a reaction to an increasingly impersonal social universe.

The challenge is to discern whether the current status of intimacy is associated with a reappropriation of emotional ties, in accordance with Gidden's argument, or with the valorisation of connection, in the face of a dearth of attachments, in accordance with the argument of Beck and Beck-Gernsheim. Commentaries on modernity provide insight into social conditions which may impact upon the current meanings of intimacy. In his phenomenology of modern city life, Simmel (1903) pointed to the intensity of stimulation, the anonymity, the matter-of-fact soullessness, and the number and variety of human contacts. An intensification occurs in emotional life since there is a continuous flux in both external and internal stimuli. Yet the individual defends against this emotional intensity by shifting to the sphere of mental activity which is least sensitive, and which is removed from the depths of the personality. One of the defences that is erected is that of antipathy – the very opposite of the ability to relate emotionally to others. Relationships become both 'intellectualised' and more calculating, since monetary value is applied to everything. When these forces are combined, people's individual, particular value is undermined – people are dealt with in an indifferent and an interchangeable fashion.

During the twentieth century social theorists have refined Simmel's theory, increasingly emphasising how the individual distinguishes between a private and a more public identity as a form of self-protection. Modern people hide their interior, intimate self from the public realm (e.g. see Berger *et al.*, 1973). They distinguish between (what is experienced as) an authentic, private identity and a more anonymous, 'less real' public identity. These developments in the theory of the modern subject are pertinent, since the studies above indicate that people defend against a sense of anonymity with an image of the more 'authentic' and exclusive private space. The defence against images of usury can also be linked to distancing the 'self' from the sense of a calculating environment characterised by indifference and interchangeability. The condom may be experienced as a fitting protective barrier against a world of anonymity and usury, but as inappropriate for situations in which openness and emotional engagement are being pursued. Simmel's notion of 'antipathy', which characterises modern life, is symbolised by the condom, which keeps the self away from the sensation of the other.

Beck and Beck-Gernsheim's recent analysis (1995), which builds upon theories of modernity, appears to fit with the AIDS-related data. These data suggest that the exclusive, monogamous relationship is represented as that place in which all is potentially good and perfect. While Giddens's account corresponds with that of members of the Frankfurt School (e.g. Fromm, 1956), who proposed that uniting with others via authentic relationships is a way of maintaining sanity in the face of modernity, Beck and Beck-Gernsheim view the search for the authentic relationship as one of the delusions of late modernity.

According to Beck and Beck-Gernsheim, late modern life generates unprecedented levels of anxiety, even when compared with modern conditions of alienation. The media, in its dissemination of a wide array of medical and other technologies, makes members of society aware of an ever-increasing number of risks. Choices must be made in relation to such risks. One only has to think about the recent advances in the field of genetics to appreciate the proliferation of choices which face the individual. Each choice forces one to face one's likelihood of being affected by a threat. One of the ways in which we counteract the anxiety generated by modern life is by seeking out trusting relationships. Love is our alternative to doubt. It expresses the hope of finding security. The sense of security in late modernity is not shaken only by the increased sense of threat, but by the decreased support networks. In the past, reactions to anxiety have included the seeking out of religion and of family support. Yet traditional kinship ties have been severed: whereas in pre-industrial societies marriage was a union of two families or clans, in contemporary Western society partners are chosen in terms of personal wishes and intuitions, according to a notion of 'falling in love'. This frees people from tradition, to pursue a multitude of lifestyle choices, while simultaneously undermining the sense of 'home' offered by a close-knit society. Not only is there a loss of family-derived stability, but a loss of the spiritual support once offered by religion. With the decline in the belief in God, only people can offer existential meaning. In fact Beck and Beck-Gernsheim propose that in an analogous fashion to a longing for salvation via religion, there is currently a yearning for rescue via affection.[6] Intimate relationships absorb the role of religion in giving people a place of sanctuary. Love grants meaning to life in a post-Christian, late modern society. Since the social environment has become 'chilly' and filled with increasing uncertainty and risk, the desire for salvation via intimacy has become prominent:

> The direction in which modern developments are taking us is reflected in the way we idealize love. Glorifying it in the way we do acts as a counter-balance to the losses we feel in the way we live. If not God, or priests, or class, or neighbours, then at least there is still You. And the size of 'You' is inversely proportional to the emotional void which otherwise seems to prevail.
>
> (Beck and Gernsheim, 1995: 33)

CONCLUSION AND IMPLICATIONS

The social representations of both out-group and dominant group members express a need to distance the self from emotionally unauthentic relationships. This representation manifests in behaviour: condoms are used in casual (but not in regular) relationships. The conditions of late modernity – in which technology, alienation and a lack of kinship and spiritual support combine to give people a sense of anxiety – foster unsafe sexual practices in relationships which are deemed intimate. Out-group members face additional anxiety. This results from having to face stigmatising social representations of their groups. In order to maintain a sense of value and integrity, the private, 'true self' must be defended from social representations of a mercenary, diseased and immoral public persona. The response to anxiety, in all groups, is the idealisation of love and intimacy. By affiliating themselves to images of closeness and attachment to others, the anxiety generated by alienation can be held at bay.

While the empirical data presented in this chapter appears to support Beck and Beck-Gernsheim's (1995) notion of the 'valorisation' of love in late modern conditions, it is necessary to develop a conceptualisation of the processes which are at work in 'valorisation'. Beck and Beck-Gernsheim use the terms 'valorisation' and 'idealisation' in an interchangeable sense, without exploring the processes inherent in idealisation. Since this process reveals itself in fantasies of wholeness, perfection and goodness, it seems to map on to the psychodynamic notion of idealisation. The unconscious mechanism of splitting forms a particularly useful model of the dynamics which underpin the polarisation of objects into idealised and denigrated extremes. Loving, intimate sexuality fits with the former, while (one may argue) casual or sex work encounters fit the latter. This split is displayed in sexual behaviours which are either 'unsafe' or 'safe' in accordance with the representation of the level of intimacy experienced with the particular partner. Taken together, the chosen behaviours and the symbolic loads attached to them are manifestations of social representations.

Since this is a new way of conceptualising the trend which exists in the AIDS literature, the framework is preliminary and contains a number of unresolved issues. In a similar vein to the notion of 'false consciousness', the analysis abides by a notion that people's idealisation of intimacy is in some way delusional. Yet, at the level of experience, intimacy and 'making love' provide powerful sources of satisfaction. It does seem somewhat cynical to view love as a fabrication of minds anxious to procure a positive sense of existence in the face of an unpleasant social world. However, the image of intimacy as a late modern fantasy resonates. At the material level, people have multiple bodily contacts – either simultaneously or in serial monogamy – yet have fantasies of exclusive intimacy with an other. From a different angle, the data on growing divorce rates and increasing numbers of single occupant homes provide insight into the lack of material states of intimacy, despite the proliferation of messages in the society which demonstrate a yearning for it. It would be useful to study the phenomenon more directly, to find a gauge of whether intimacy is used as a *fantasised* place of sanctuary, a place in which happiness resides, or whether it is *experienced* as a place of sanctuary amidst alienated social conditions.

The analysis which I have presented has implications for research and prevention strategies regarding safer sex. Models of sexual behaviour currently view knowledge, attitude and belief states as predictors of intention to behave in a 'safer' or an 'unsafe' manner (see Joffe, 1996a), and the focus is generally on rational, conscious, cognitive precursors to behaviour. A more appropriate focus for such models would be the interlinked issues of emotion, identity and identity enhancement. Identity enhancement and emotional satisfaction appear to be far more closely related to sexual practice than appropriate knowledge or conscious evaluations of the danger posed by a potential partner. For out-group members, unsafe sex with lovers serves the function of positive identity enhancement. In the face of multiple social representations that stigmatise one's identity, the fantasy of a trusting, loving relationship bestows conventional respectability since it is valued in society. It also provides the potential for a subjective sense of satisfaction and for filling up the emotional void which is created by a 'chilly' social environment. Unsafe sex is not generally 'chosen' in line with rational intention. Rather, a series of forces which lie outside of awareness impact upon behaviour. Defence of a threatened identity, rather than an absence of volition, is one such force. Any attempt to modify unsafe sexual thoughts and actions must take into account the very inaccessibility of the cultural assumptions and defensive structures which underpin individuals' social representations.

If one follows the ideas of the all-pervasive health belief models, perceived risk of HIV leads to appropriate action. Beyond the critique that this is not borne out by a plethora of empirical studies (see Joffe, 1996a), this perspective neglects the internal rationality of the actor, favouring the social scientists' perspective on how people 'should' or 'are likely to' think. This shortcoming is well demonstrated by the more anthropological focus which has been presented. Sex workers, for example, face the risk of loneliness, the risk of being seen as a pariah, the risk of being seen as a contaminator, the risk of being seen as a sexual object. The very term 'to prostitute oneself' speaks of a representation that implies lowliness. Action expresses such representations. Sex workers act to protect a positive identity – to protect psychological rather than physical health. Unsafe sexual behaviour in sex workers' intimate sphere only appears to be perplexing if one operates from the assumption that people are risk-averse and, consequently, that knowledge of risks is followed by body-protective action. The sex workers' unsafe sex ,together with their talk of love, indicates the use of an altogether different lens – one structured by issues of identity enhancement and satisfaction. People practise unsafe sex, often with intention, because they are privileging certain representations in relation to their actions. This endorsement of certain ideas through action appears to be a more ecologically valid way of viewing current sexual practices than the available models.

The aforementioned health belief models have emphasised the salience of a sense of control and its link to practising healthy behaviours. There can be no doubt that when individuals experience themselves as having little control over a sexual encounter, they are not in a position to demand that a condom be used. There is an abundance of evidence for this in the AIDS field (e.g. see Bloor *et al.*, 1992; Crawford *et al.*, 1994; Amaro, 1995). Yet unsafe sex often occurs in relation to the joy of being out of control with someone, because this feeling is associated with a space in which one lowers the barriers which one erects around oneself in the public sphere. For a sexual encounter to be experienced as fulfilling, control must (by definition) be relinquished. Again, it is to the sex workers that I turn for elucidation. For the sex worker, work is associated with a desire for control of one's boundaries, of the substances that enter one, while being in a non-work relationship is (by definition) about 'switching off' these very concerns. A sense of openness is suggested by allusions to romance, feeling wanted, feeling lust, lowering one's guard, intimacy unfettered by a plastic object, the satisfaction of carrying one's partner's semen within oneself, and sharing everything even if this results in disease. By way of direct contrast, interactions with more casual, distant partners are often portrayed in terms of a need for self-protective strategies. These include endeavouring to remain in control, distant and indifferent. Even those sufficiently empowered to negotiate condom use may opt for the behaviours which express a fantasy of attachment and connection to others.

NOTES

1 Love is defined as 'That state of feeling with regard to a person which arises from recognition of attractive qualities, from sympathy, or from natural ties, and manifests itself in warm affection and attachment.' Intimacy is defined as 'close familiarity; intimate [inmost, most inward, deep-seated] connection or union' (Shorter Oxford English Dictionary, 1983).
2 The term 'sex work' is chosen in preference to the term 'prostitution'.
3 I would like to thank Julie Dockrell for allowing me to use this data, collected in a study funded by the Health Education Authority.
4 This is a more stringent criterion for 'unsafe' sex than is generally used in the literature.
5 It is important to note that representations rooted in resistance to dominant norms coexist with those which comply with dominant norms. Foucault (1976/1990) talks of the pleasure that those who are stigmatised for their sexuality gain from making a travesty of the dominant discourses. The more institutional laws oppress a group, the greater the pleasure group members find in the power of making a travesty of the laws. Power rests not only with mainstream institutional discourses but with those who have the ability to scandalise, to resist such discourses. However, it should not be assumed that, since sex workers transgress certain sexual conventions, they do not simultaneously hold a conventional outlook, an outlook coloured by contemporary morality. In this chapter the more conventionalised aspect of out-group members' social representations is emphasised.
6 Perhaps this argument overlooks the meaning of courtly love in past eras, thereby placing too much emphasis on the novelty of the search for intimacy. However, one might argue that courtly love did not contain the notion of an egalitarian type of connection with the other, which exists in the current ideal concerning intimacy: 'Intimacy is above all a matter of emotional communication, with others and with the self, in a context of interpersonal equality' (Giddens, 1992: 130).

REFERENCES

Amaro, H. (1995) Love, Sex and Power: Considering Women's Realities in HIV Prevention, *Journal of the American Psychological Association*, 50, 437–447.
Beck, U. and Beck-Gernsheim, E. (1995) *The Normal Chaos of Love*, Cambridge: Polity Press.
Berger, P.L., Berger, B. and Kellner, H. (1973) *The Homeless Mind: Modernisation and Consciousness*, New York: Random House.
Bloor, M.J., McKeganey, N.P., Finlay, A. and Barnard, M.A. (1992) The

Inappropriateness of Psycho-Social Models of Risk Behaviour for Understanding HIV-Related Practices Among Glasgow Male Prostitutes, *Aids Care*, 4, 131–137.

Bochow, M. (1994) A Wealth of Data, but a Dearth of Good Interpretation: Notes on the Deficiencies in Prevention-Orientated Research, Taking Gay Men as an Example, AIDS in Europe: European Conference on Methods and Results of Psycho-Social Research, Berlin.

Brandt, A.M. (1987) *No Magic Bullet*, Oxford: Oxford University Press.

Crawford, J., Kippax, S. and Waldby, C. (1994) Women's Sex Talk and Men's Sex Talk: Different Worlds, *Feminism and Psychology*, 4(4), 571–587.

Day, S. (1988) Prostitute Women and AIDS: Anthropology, *AIDS*, 1, 421–428.

——(1990) Prostitute Women and the Ideology of Work in London. In D.A. Feldman (ed.), *AIDS and Culture: The Global Pandemic*, New York: Praeger.

Day, S., Ward, H. and Wandsworth, J. (1987) Attitudes to Barrier Protection Among Female Prostitutes in London, Third International Meeting on AIDS, Paris.

Dorfman, L.E., Derish, P.A. and Cohen, J.B. (1992) Hey Girlfriend: An Evaluation of AIDS Prevention Among Women in the Sex Industry, *Health Education Quarterly*, 19(1), 25–40.

Douglas, M. (1966) *Purity and Danger*, London: Routledge & Kegan Paul.

Flowers, P., Sheeran, P., Beail, N. and Smith, J.A. (1997) The Role of Psychosocial Factors in HIV Risk-Reduction Among Gay and Bisexual Men: a Quantitative Review, *Psychology and Health*, 12, 197–230.

Foucault, M. (1976/1990) *The History of Sexuality*, vol. 1, London: Penguin.

Fromm, E. (1956) *The Sane Society*, London: Routledge & Kegan Paul.

Fullilove, M.T., Fullilove, R.E., Haynes, K. and Gross, S. (1990) Black Women and AIDS Prevention: A View Toward Understanding the Gender Rules, *Journal of Sex Research*, 7(1), 47–54.

Giddens, A. (1992) *The Transformation of Intimacy*, Cambridge: Polity Press.

Gilman, S. (1988) *Disease and representation: Images of illness from madness to AIDS*, Ithaca, NY: Cornell University Press.

Goffman, E. (1963) *Stigma: Notes on the Management of Spoiled Identity*, Harmondsworth: Penguin.

Health Education Authority (1994) *Health Update 4. Sexual Health*, London: Health Education Authority.

Holland, J., Ramazanoglu, C., Scott, S., Sharpe, S. and Thompson, R. (1991) Between Embarrassment and Trust: Young Women and the Diversity of Condom Use. In P. Aggleton, G. Hart and P. Davies (eds), *AIDS: Responses, Interventions and Care*, London: Falmer Press.

Joffe, H. (1996a) AIDS Research and Prevention: A Social Representational Approach, *British Journal of Medical Psychology*, 69(3),169–190.

——(1996b) The Shock of the New: A Psycho-Dynamic Extension of Social Representations Theory, *Journal for the Theory of Social Behaviour* 26(2), 169–190.

——(1997) The Relationship Between Representational and Materialist Perspectives: AIDS and 'the Other'. In L. Yardley (ed.), *Material Discourses of Health and Illness*, London: Routledge.

Joffe, H. and Dockrell, J. (1995) Safer Sex: Lessons from the Male Sex Industry, *Journal of Community and Applied Social Psychology*, 5, 333–346.

Jones, E.E., Farina, A., Hastorf, A.H., Markus, H., Miller, D.T. and Scott, R.A. (1984) *Social Stigma: The Psychology of the Marked Relationship*, New York: W.H. Freeman and Co.

Maticka-Tyndale, E. (1992) Social Construction of HIV Transmission and Prevention Among Heterosexual Young Adults, *Social Problems*, 39(3), 238–252.

Moscovici, S. (1982) The Coming Era of Representations. In J.P. Codol and J.P. Leyens (eds), *Cognitive Approaches to Social Behaviour*, La Haye: Nijhoff.

Pleak, R. and Meyer-Bahlburg, H. (1990) Sexual Behaviour and AIDS Knowledge of Young Male Prostitutes in Manhattan, *Journal of Sex Research*, 27, 557–587.

Simmel, G. (1903) The Metropolis and Mental Life. Reproduced in K. Wolff (ed.), *The Sociology of Georg Simmel*, Glencoe: The Free Press (1950).

Smith, J.A., Osborn, M. and Flowers, P. (1997) Interpretative Phenomenological Analysis and the Psychology of Health and Illness. In L. Yardley (ed.), *Material Discourses of Health and Illness*, London: Routledge.

Tajfel, H. (1981) *Human Groups and Social Categories*, Cambridge: Cambridge University Press.

——(1982) The Social Psychology of Minorities. In C. Husband (ed.), *Race in Britain: Continuity and Change*, London: Hutchinson.

Weatherburn, P., Hunt, A.J., Hickson, F. and Davies, P.M. (1992) *The Sexual Lifestyles of Gay and Bisexual Men in England and Wales*, Project Sigma.

Willig, C. (1995) 'I Wouldn't Have Married the Guy if I'd Have to do That': Heterosexual Adults' Constructions of Condom Use and Their Implications for Sexual Practice, *Journal of Community and Applied Social Psychology*, 5, 75–87.

10 Reading the bleeding body
Discourses of premenstrual syndrome

Catherine Swann

This chapter begins with a brief review of the historical context of premenstrual syndrome (PMS), the recent theoretical 'crisis' in menstrual cycle research and the reconstructed theoretical approaches to menstrual cycle and PMS research which have emerged from this. Setting out a theoretical framework which draws upon standpoint epistemology and strands of poststructuralist argument, I use discourse analysis to explore the construction and meanings of PMS through a thematic decomposition of interviews with women attending their first appointment at a PMS clinic The aim of this chapter is threefold: to review the relationship between epistemology and research strategy in the context of the experience of PMS; to present qualitative and feminist research; and to conclude by considering the ways in which a constructionist analysis of PMS may serve to refocus and redirect research into the experience of women (see Swann, 1995a, 1995b, 1996).

PMS – A BRIEF HISTORY?[1]

The material processes associated with the menstrual cycle are a universal physical experience for the vast majority of women of a reproductive age. Menarche (the first menstrual bleed) normally occurs between the ages of 9 and 16 (Golub, 1992), beginning a cycle of hormonal and physiological changes that will continue for the greater portion of women's lives. Many different cultures have linked menstruation, menstrual blood and the menstrual cycle with a variety of diseases and disorders (Sayers, 1982; Ussher, 1989), and Western attitudes to the menstrual cycle have been shaped and formed alongside developing medical knowledge and technologies.

The term 'premenstrual tension' made its first appearance almost simultaneously in medical and psychoanalytic literature, in 1931 (Frank, 1931; Horney, 1931). Gynaecologist R.T. Frank noted 'indescribable tension' (1931: 1054) in some of his female patients before menstruation. Little more was written on the subject for some twenty years, until Greene and Dalton (1953) reported more general disturbances and symptoms occurring premenstrually, and coined the term 'premenstrual syndrome' (PMS). The

1970s saw the beginning of an explosion of research into PMS, and into paramenstrual detriment to performance and behaviour (See Ussher, 1992a). Since then, a vast amount of research has been carried out in the area. Over 150 different symptoms have been recorded (Moos, 1969; Warner and Bancroft, 1990), ranging from sore breasts and water retention to depression, loss of libido and aggression. Recent estimates suggest that 10–40 per cent of women of a reproductive age experience serious disruption to their lives as a result of PMS (Mortola, 1992).

The prevailing medical and social construction is that the symptoms experienced premenstrually by women are related in some way to fluctuating levels of reproductive hormones (Golub, 1992). So, although as a medical 'problem' PMS has a relatively brief history (Richardson, 1993), it has rapidly gained medical status and respectability. 1994 saw the inclusion of 'Late Luteal Phase Dysphoric Disorder' in the Diagnostic and Statistical Manual of the American Psychiatric Association (APA, 1994), a category referring largely to negative psychological symptoms which may occur in the late luteal (post-ovulatory) phase of the menstrual cycle. Several clinical instruments exist to measure and diagnose PMS (see Moos, 1968; Chesney and Tato, 1975; Halbreich and Endicott, 1982), although each has been contested and arguably none is without serious conceptual and methodological problems (Richardson, 1990; Bancroft, 1993).

In spite of this apparent general medical acceptance, a number of recent reviews in the area point to the same conclusion: There is no simple biological substrate that marks PMS, nor any simple or measurable relationship between hormone levels and symptom experience (Bancroft, 1993; O'Brien, 1993). While many medical treatments prove (transiently) effective in reducing PMS symptoms, no one treatment has been proven to be consistently more effective than placebo. This would seem to indicate that, although there is a lack of any evidence (other than circumstantial) for PMS as a disorder or disease of the body, a vast number of women report that they are regularly disabled by symptoms that occur in the premenstrual phase of their menstrual cycles.

From the 1980s, the positioning of the female body as the 'cause' of premenstrual symptoms and experience was vociferously challenged both from within the scientific mainstream, and by critical and feminist theoreticians. From the mode of social science, research investigated the role of cultural factors such as beliefs and expectations in the experience of premenstrual symptoms (e.g. Koeske, 1980). Feminist critics questioned the disease category of PMS, suggesting for example that it marks the extreme end of a spectrum of femininity; that its existence as a 'disorder' serves to negate what is in fact quite legitimate anger or depression – a social construct that regulates and controls the behaviour of women (see Parlee, 1991). Importantly, too, feminist theoreticians such as Ussher (1989, 1991) have drawn disturbing parallels between the twentieth-century phenomenon of premenstrual syndrome and earlier female 'disorders' such as hysteria and neurasthenia. PMS may have a brief history, but it is arguable that the scientific and historical discourses that contribute to this phenomenon predate modern medical technology by many centuries.

Obviously, the view of PMS as being determined by sociocultural factors, or as an epiphenomenon of cultural practices, is difficult (if not impossible) to reconcile with the strict 'biomedical' model within which PMS is most commonly placed (Ussher, 1992a). Both theoretical positions are exclusive and univariate in their accounts – the biomedical model cannot account for the complexity of premenstrual experience, yet social and feminist critiques which locate PMS in the social realm alone provide no explanation or solution to that percentage of women who report severe disruption to their lives premenstrually.

The arguments around causes and constructions of PMS have been rehearsed at length elsewhere (see, for example, Ussher, 1992a; Bancroft, 1993; Swann, 1995a). It is useful at this point to step back from the debate around the influence of hormones, social and psychological factors upon experience, and to evaluate critically the evolution of different theoretical strands within the construction of PMS as either medical or social phenomenon. It was from here, influenced by the arguments of Foucault (1984), Parker (1992) and Harding (1987), that I began the final piece of research for my doctoral thesis.

A CRISIS IN MENSTRUAL CYCLE RESEARCH?

I began my research into women's experience of PMS at a time when some academics and clinicians were moving away from the theoretical stand-off between univariate biomedical and social accounts. Variations on bio-psycho-social models of PMS have been proposed over the last few years (Rubinow and Schmidt, 1989; Ussher, 1992a; Bancroft, 1993; O'Brien, 1993) which reflect a growing acceptance (by some) of the contribution of different internal and external factors to the outcome response of self-diagnosis and medical-help seeking. In such models, menstrual cycle experience is placed in the context of many other factors – such as cyclical variations in stress and arousal, beliefs and expectations, and social support – all of which may contribute to a woman's status as a PMS sufferer. Supposedly, no one facet of experience is privileged over another (Ussher, 1992b), and in this way it is suggested that multi-factor approaches may partly reconcile the tensions between divergent research positions.

But there is a broader problem within traditional multi-factor approaches (e.g. Rubinow and Schmidt, 1989), in that they may still operate within a narrow positivist epistemology, concentrating on quantitative methodologies and simple causational relationships between bio-psycho-social variables and PMS. In other words, the traditional bio-psycho-social approach to health and illness experience operates from a 'realist' position, where health and illness (or, in this example, premenstrual symptomatology) are framed as biological events, which finite and measurable psychosocial variables may intersect and influence. The underlying set of assumptions, or epistemology, maintains a biomedical orientation (Swann, 1995a). The theoretical accounts of experience produced by such models are thus constrained by the absence of sociohistorical context, or attention to the dynamics of subjective experience.

To move towards less partial accounts of the experience of PMS and the menstrual cycle, I have argued that an 'epistemological shift' (Swann, 1995a: 127; 1996), or challenge to traditional assumptions underlying menstrual cycle research (Walker, 1995; Ussher, 1997) is necessary. The menstrual cycle need not be conceptualised as a biological, independent variable (a model of experience with limited explanatory power), or as a socially constructed phenomenon (an approach which cannot legitimate lived physical experience). These two divergent perspectives indicate clearly that menstrual cycle experience is rather more complex. Instead, it can be argued that (like cognition) the menstrual cycle is positioned upon an experiential interface (Richardson, 1992), between the realms of the social (external) and the biological (internal). Bio-psycho-social accounts cannot encompass the full implications of this within their conceptual frameworks, as this experiential interface represents the 'subjective' state, the dynamic interplay of all modes of experience. In the same way that a 'turn to language' followed the crisis in social psychology (Parker, 1989), so menstrual cycle and PMS research needs to move away from the limitations of positivism and towards an account that allows us to question these modes of culture, gender and power, and their relationship to lived experience.

From this position, 'bio', 'psycho' and 'social' are all considered from a critical distance: rather than taking reported experience at face value, we use our epistemological framework, assumptions about the world and knowledge (Harding, 1991) to question our research process, practice and production. Experience (or subjectivity) is positioned not as having a taken-for-granted biological or social origin, rather, this approach emphasises the 'relational character of their mutual effects' (Henriques *et al.*, 1984: 22). This opens the way for use of different qualitative methodologies in researching PMS, and should afford an analysis that is (unlike previous research) considered within its sociohistorical context.

STANDPOINT THEORY AND STRATEGIES OF RESEARCH

The relationship between material and social modes of experience is taken up and explored within different contexts throughout this book, with a shared concern to find space in which critical readings of texts of the body may be reconciled with undeniable material aspects of bodily experience. I had become interested in the social construction of the female body as the site of a myriad of women's problems – the enduring medical construction of PMS, at best tenuous, has become firmly entrenched in Western culture.

Nearly all women of a reproductive age menstruate, many of these women (whether or not they conform to any clinical parameters) will report varying degrees of premenstrual symptomatology. Yet the voices of women themselves, and the sociohistorical context in which PMS is experienced, have been absent from the literature. Despite many years of claim and counter-claim from within the naturalist tradition, there has been little analysis of PMS that has either focused upon women's own accounts, or that has critically evaluated the relationship between experience and prevailing constructions of gender and the body.

Feminist critiques, founded in observations such as this, were central to my shift in epistemological concern. Two strands of argument are relevant here: the gendered nature of PMS as a disease category, and the use of science in defining and measuring PMS.

In the first place, the construction of the category 'PMS' within the social arena configures and marks out a 'gendered illness' (Parlee, 1991). This, in turn, can be said to reinforce and reproduce power relationships of gender. For example, a parallel may be drawn between the modern 'illness' of PMS and historic references to neurasthenia and hysteria, in the way in which the female body is positioned at the site of dysfunction (Ussher, 1991; Rodin, 1992). In turn, only women may be labelled 'hysteric' or 'premenstrual', as only women have the unavoidable physical characteristics necessary for these conditions. Thus different disease categories reinforce gender differences, and inequalities. There are also socio-economic roots to PMS: it may be used as an explanatory framework for interpreting the behaviour of women. Its appearance, first in 1931 and later in the 1970s, marks points in history when women were challenging the social and economic order (Rittenhouse, 1991).[2] Furthermore, the menstrual cycle has effectively regulated (by exclusion) the presence of women in some sectors of work (Martin, 1987; see Ussher, 1989) .

Second, a number of feminists have rejected the methods and mores of traditional 'science'. Positivism, they argue, has excluded women's voices and experience from the 'pictures' created by scientific methods, situating women only as the 'objects' of the scientific gaze. Feminist standpoint theory (Smith, 1987; Harding, 1987, 1991; Henwood and Pidgeon, 1994) critically evaluates the use of positivistic research frameworks, and notes the absence of women's experiences in the workings of science and psychology. Standpoint theorists argue that science is not isolated from the social order (and is not an objective, transparent means of acquiring knowledge), and should therefore be placed on the same 'causal plane' (Henwood and Pidgeon, 1995) as the phenomena that it tries to explain. Scientific accounts, because of the gendered nature of their gaze (science is largely practised by men, and interpreted through frameworks that are subject to the same power relations as the broader social context) are therefore only partial, since they only account for the activities of the powerful. It is easy to see how this argument is relevant to PMS, a syndrome with varying timing and symptoms, backed up by little or no consistent evidence, and yet one that endures as a medical category. Perhaps this is reflective not so much of an epidemic of faulty hormones, but more of the regulatory nature of the science which identifies and evaluates it?

This is an important point, and relates back to the shift from realist to critical orientation in understanding women's experiences of PMS and the menstrual cycle. I have argued that an advantage of this shift is the ability to use research strategies and modes of thought which question the relationship between facets of gender, sociocultural and historic influences upon experience. The critique of science provided by standpoint theory highlights actions of scientific discourse in defining and regulating women's bodies and experience.

At the centre of feminist standpoint epistemology is the notion of doing research in order to 'see through the eyes of our participants' (Henwood and Pidgeon, 1994). In this way, the accounts produced by research are grounded firmly in the experience of the participants – experiences which are all too often invisible in traditional epistemologies. They are also less partial than those accounts produced by traditional 'science', as research questions and practice centre around the 'subjects' of the research. As Sue Wilkinson has argued, 'If you want to know why a person did what they did, ask them, they might just tell you' (Wilkinson, 1986). While this comment oversimplifies the process of women-centred research, disregarding the concept of 'critical distance' (Parker, 1992), it illustrates well a fundamental premise of the feminist standpoint. From here, all methods and research are open to scrutiny. This does not mean that standpoint research *has* to be qualitative, however: discourse analysis with the tools of reflexivity and deconstruction, allows just such a critical consideration of the relationship between 'subject' and 'method'.

This standpoint neither founds any theory of subjective experience within some biologically given component, nor denies biology (or material experience) any role in our interpretations. Rather, subjectivity and subjective experience of PMS are positioned upon an interface between the social and material realms. By placing women's accounts at the centre of research into PMS, we may ask what PMS means to women and how discourses are employed to constitute this experience. As Rose Braidotti argues, 'The "body" is to be thought of as the point of intersection, between the biological and the social . . . between the sociopolitical field of the microphysics of power, and the subjective dimension' (Braidotti, 1989: 97). Within a discursive research framework, the 'size' of critical distance (the degree to which you take accounts at 'face value', if you like) will vary, depending upon the underlying assumptions of the researcher. Although it draws upon strands of poststructuralist and constructionist argument, standpoint theory is a 'critical realist' orientation (Bhaskar, 1989; Doherty, 1994), a theoretical approach that both acknowledges some material realities of lived experience, while recognising the constructing and representative mediation of culture, language and political interests (see Ussher, 1997; see also Chapter 3). In other words, feminist standpoint research that uses a discourse analytic strategy will read data at the level of the text (a critical distance), but will also consider the function of particular discourses in the accounts of women, and their relationship to lived experience. Standpoint approaches privilege particular sets of accounts (those that are commonly excluded from the mainstream), with the aim of emancipation.

WOMEN'S ACCOUNTS OF PMS

From this standpoint, I set out to investigate why women self-report PMS, and the different meanings that PMS had to them. I wanted to explore the discursive construction of PMS by women, and functions of different discourses within women's accounts. What particularly interested me was the configuration and positions of the 'body' within these discourses. However, I attempted to be data-driven (or 'grounded') rather than theory-driven in my analysis (Henwood and Pidgeon, 1994). Proponents of grounded theory (see Henwood and Pidgeon, 1994) argue that obtaining theoretical accounts of phenomena through the systematic collection and analysis of data (rather than relying upon a priori theories and assumptions) may generate important new theoretical accounts (Swann and Ussher, 1995). In an area where little systematic or qualitative analysis has been applied, this seemed particularly important.

I interviewed fourteen women in total, all of whom were attending their first appointment at a PMS clinic in a London hospital. The women were aged from 26 to 44, and had been referred to the clinic by their GPs. They also came from a variety of ethnic and socio-economic backgrounds. These women probably represented the moderate to severe end of any spectrum of perceived symptom experience, and it had in many cases taken a great deal of time and pressure to obtain specialist treatment.

I used a semi-structured interview technique, with questions focused around women's beliefs about PMS, their histories and experiences. The interviews were recorded, and later transcribed using a system based on that of Potter and Wetherell (1987). Analysis entailed reading and rereading, breaking down the texts of the interviews and gradually piecing together themed open-ended categories (Stenner, 1993). My reading of the texts was influenced by the historical context of discourses of the body (e.g. Foucault, 1984; McNay, 1992), and by Parker's (1992) approach to discourse analysis.

Discourse analytic techniques read data at the level of the text, rather than taking language to be a transparent medium between the social actor and the world (Wetherell and White, 1992). A critical distance is placed between the researcher and the text, in which the action of the research and researcher are bought into the analysis and questioned, through the practice of reflexivity. Because the underlying epistemology is influenced by constructionist and poststructuralist arguments, my research is not positioned as a fact- or truth-finding exercise, but examines instead different constructions of experience or different 'realities'. This focus on textual analysis does not have to preclude consideration of material or physical existence; rather, my assumption is that material experience may be framed, interpreted and represented through discourse. It is here that modes of the social and of the body may be reconciled, through the conceptualisation of subjectivity as being on a dynamic interface between the two realms.

Through this process of analysis and decomposition, I identified four major discourses. There are many apparent contradictions and differences both within and between different women's accounts: the process of discourse analysis allows us to identify and include them in the analytic process. These discourses (all containing constitutive elements or themes) relate to the female body, femininity, a discourse of dualism between body/mind and premenstrual/normal, and the privileging of the body as a cause of experience. The following sections describe these different discourses and themes. I conclude with a consideration of the implications of this research, and use of a material–discursive perspective, both for theory and research practice in the arena of PMS research.

THE DETERMINING BODY

Since the prevailing construction of PMS is biological, most usually as a hormonal imbalance (Vines, 1993), it is not surprising that the discourse to emerge most frequently centres on the dysfunctional body. The clinical setting of the interviews, conducted in a material situation most commonly associated with physical ailments and disease, will probably have influenced the texts produced in the interviews. Given the biological construction of PMS in the public arena, however, one would probably expect similar reports elsewhere. In this sense, it is a discourse of embodiment, for the problems associated with PMS (whether physiological or not) are mapped on to the body.

All of the women I interviewed use this biological discourse at some point in their narrative, in describing the nature and cause of their problems. It is drawn upon at certain common points in the women's accounts – for example as they come to describe the events leading up to their self diagnosis. This discourse permeates the texts, and is made up of sometimes tacit themes as different reproductive life events are used to map out and 'tell the story' of their symptoms.

PAULA   I think it [PMS] was worse since coming off the pill (C: Right) and I was 27 then I got sterilised . . . you know, sort of I was on the pill at 18 so I suppose I didn't really notice until coming off the pill, you know, my husband would sometimes say, 'Oh, I can tell YOU'RE [her emphasis] going to come on' (*laughs*). I don't know, you just get on with it really (C: Right) but recently I thought, 'Why keep putting up with it?'

ANDREA   It's got worse definitely since I got sterilised. I mean, I was saying to my Mum (.) before I fell for my last daughter I was on the pill (.) and (.) I never knew when I was gettin' a period (.) never (.) never had feelings like this but I'd say definitely since I've been sterilised (..) I've noticed . . .

Dalton (1991) suggests that reproductive life events (e.g. childbirth, coming off the pill) often trigger PMS, but it is interesting that the artificial control of one's hormonal cycle is positioned as containing and controlling the woman's own unruly hormones. Paula's comment, 'you just get on with it really', implies that disorder and discomfort are normal – to be expected. This inevitability, or biological determinism, clearly focuses on negative aspects of menstruation. Further, detailed descriptions of reproductive life histories were common, used as textual warranting devices to construct the 'reality' of PMS. For example:

JANE   By then I'd realised that it was something that was happening to me regular, I thought maybe it's me, I'm a bit depressed and things (.) you know it took a good few years for me to suss it out that the (.) there was something wrong and then I started reading things about PMS (.) and it's sort of like all coming home I've got all these sort of things wrong with me . . . I thought it was a bit of postnatal depression (.) it might have been [. . .] it was just (.) being depressed and feeling (..) feeling depressed.

Jane's reference to postnatal depression established at quite a late point in her narrative that hormones and the menstrual cycle are at the root of her depression – she presented it as a sort of 'road to Damascus' insight. However, this is framed by a long, reflective preamble in which she consults other sources of knowledge, before realisation dawns. Woolgar (1988) has noted similar discursive strategies in the speech of scientists, as discoveries are converted into 'facts' through the use of logic and positivist reasoning. Within this excerpt, reflection and discovery are employed to uncover the 'real' (biological) cause of Jane's symptoms. These narratives about women's reproductive life histories, used as warranting devices within the texts in the context of help-seeking for PMS, illustrate the action of a biological discourse in constructing and representing experience.

Of course, 'hormones' occupy a central place within this discourse. Although they are often referred to in an oblique manner, through refer-ence to the changes brought about by childbirth or the contraceptive pill, the effects of hormones are frequently positioned as causal. For example,

ALICE   My assumption IS [her emphasis] *that it's (.) some sort of (.) probably quite normal hormonal changes (.) which are occurring . . . it HAS [her emphasis] been suggested that it could be (.) a possibility something to do with hormones . . . and IF that's*

> *hormonal (.) if that is to do with sort of (.) imbalance or whatever (.) chemistry that can be just kind of levelled out (.) why not, you know.*

SANDY   Previous to going on the hormones last March, oh, for (.) near on a year when they [her symptoms] started getting worse again . . . so I started the hormone replacement therapy.

Alice draws upon a theme of hormonal change to frame her experience of her menstrual cycle. The categories of biology and female reproductive hormones are used to contain her description of her symptoms, positioning her 'hormones' as a causal factor. The cultural construction of female hormones, as a cause of perceived female lability, has taken a central place in the last fifty years in the understanding of gender and behaviour (Vines, 1993). This perhaps does not reflect an increasing public understanding about hormones (which is often vague or confused). It can be argued instead (see Keller, 1985; Swann, 1995a) that there is a direct relationship between the accounts of gendered bodies produced by science, the increasing acceptance of science as a primary ideology in the West, and the reproduction of power relationships of gender.

In a Foucauldian analysis, the increasing technology around sex and sexual function represent the tools of social and political power, which act or inscribe upon the body and the individual (see Foucault, 1984). This argument reveals the real and tangible action of discourse upon the body. Furthermore, this discourse is historically located: writers have drawn disturbing parallels between 'hormones' and the power accorded to them within culture/scientific discourse, and themes of spiritual possession around witchcraft in the Middle Ages (Ussher, 1989, 1991). Of course, the regulated body is also gendered, and Foucault has argued that the 'hysterisation' of women's bodies is an axis of knowledge and power, used as just such as tool: 'the female body was analysed – qualified and disqualified – as being thoroughly saturated with sexuality; whereby it was integrated into the sphere of medical practices, by means of a pathology intrinsic to it' (Foucault, 1979: 104).

There are positions of resistance and anger within this biological discourse, where women reflect on their experiences of PMS, and search for other means of expressing them. However, taking up these positions serves only to confirm the overlying discourse of female pathology grounded in female biology. For example:

ALICE   Well as a woman (.) and as a probation officer (.) I mean (.) you know I can well understand it but I also know that some women can be a bit clever and uh (.) they know that they can use that as an excuse but people use all sorts of excuses for bad behaviour don't they (.) because they want to blame anybody but themselves for bad behaviour . . . I mean obviously it's [PMS] always been there (.) erm, but (.) you know I don't know what the things are that impact on it (.) that make it more (.) maybe it's, er (.) partly a sort of attitude of mind that you have that (.) you put up with it for years and years (.) and why should you (.) you know if there's something that can be done.

NADINE   I think it can really disrupt women's lives a hell of a lot (.) and – and there should be some kind of alternative or it should be recognised in a way that the solution isn't just to go back on the pill (.) I don't see why I should spend (.) all my time on the pill.

Alice distances herself from her body here, and engages in a process of intellectualisation: by considering other explanations (or even the concept of PMS as an excuse), or by becoming angry, women resist cultural prescriptions for their experience. But this form of agency is very limited, especially in the context of an explanatory tool as seductive (and powerful) as biology.

Similarly, Jenny describes a process of self-reflection, in which she questions her own status as a PMS sufferer, and its possible causes:

JENNY   I HAVE [her emphasis] *wondered this* (C: Yeah) and I've wondered if I went out looking for it (C: Mmm) you know to – you know, looking for the symptoms sort of bu, er, I do question myself, you know, in all sorts of areas anyway erm [. . .] BECAUSE erm th-that doubt is still there . . . I think to myself, you know, how much is real, how much is imagined, you know, how much are other factors responsible . . . but I stopped taking the evening primrose tablets on two occasions and noticed the difference.

'Hormones' (as a discursive category) are constituted as having a mysterious and somewhat sinister quality. The female body is constituted as bad, or dysfunctional, with a myriad series of aches and pains, and symptoms, which for Alice is 'out of control', and which makes Jane feel clumsy and overweight, so that she is unrecognisable to others.

ALICE   There'll be (.) physically would be [. . .] getting extremely . . . probably the worst thing that happens to me . . . that I get terribly tired (.) during the day (.) more tired than usual and I get knackered anyway 'cos I'm getting old, go to bed really early (.) and sleep too early (.) wake up at three (..) feeling energised (.) only to start the whole thing the following day (.) when I say feeling energised feeling (..) erm (.) almost manic . . . in the early hours of the morning (.) and erm everything you know out of kilter . . . the other thing . . . for me that premenstrual period as well it's a COMPULSION [her emphasis], an urge to eat or drink . . . yes I've noticed what it is now and that's why I'm wondering if there's . . . it's sugar, it's a kind of chocolate craze.

JANE   I'm aching all over (.) erm I feel like I put five stone on (.) and I've only been laying in bed for an hour (.) and erm I don't go to the toilet as much (..) feel like I want to go but I don't go (.) erm (..) headaches (.) joints (.) eating [...] er, depressed (.) it just goes on everything ... everything I've ever looked at (.) it's hard to think now it's sort of 'cos I feel like (.) I do everything's round the wrong way (.) back to front (.) can't talk properly sometimes try to talk and I'm (.) you know (C: Mmm) I walk into things and I get bruises all over me.

JANE   You know, it's not my body it don't feel like my body (.) clomping about with these great big legs like I've put two stone on ... I put a stone on (.) (C: Really) mmm, people say they don't recognise me.

The body is also constituted as a burden, something heavy or unpleasant that the woman must carry around with her and cope with, along with everything else in her life:

ANNE   Well it certainly would ... to be able to be free of all those, um (.) handicapping symptoms (.) which to me take up too much time (.) if it was two days I wouldn't mind at all (.) but it's often ten.

In contrast, this embodied discourse of biology is also used to reframe, or refocus experience, making distressing events more manageable:

SAMIRA   It's not every month, when I really will be as depressed as I was depressed when I was depressed (C: Mmm) only it's for a shorter time. But because it's that intense I can almost [...] it becomes quite hard to think that it's just PMT, this is all right, it's gonna go away.

JOANNE   It's the greyness, you know (C: Yeah) erm, the feeling, I mean, i-i-it just suddenly seems to present itself, it j-just seems to be there and (.) it's like to step back from it, you know, at the time and say (.) it's OK, you know (.) this is just part of a monthly problem you know it will go away ... at the time I feel gripped by it, you know, and, er, I think, (.) 'God, this is never going to go away, why am I feeling like this and why do things look so bad, and why do they make me feel so bad.' (.) It's not until the depression lessens with hindsight that you know.

The excerpt from Samira's interview illustrates how this discourse of female biology is employed in the representation of experience. When Samira terms her depression 'PMS', it becomes less distressing, as the problem will disappear when her period starts. Thus self-diagnosis of PMS could be seen as a coping strategy for other problems in itself. Certainly, other research (Koeske, 1983; Bains and Slade, 1989) suggests that the menstrual cycle acts as a salient source of attribution for aversive events and experience. It is interesting to note that the reproductive body is blamed for the *worst* of Samira's depression. In this way, social power relations of gender are reproduced and conflated (Ussher, 1989). By framing experience through the lens of PMS, the body is positioned as bad, or faulty, and most certainly as gendered.

The presence of a biological discourse within these texts might have been expected, as biological or biomedical (Ussher, 1992b) models of PMS are predominant in both medical and popular literature (Martin, 1987; Rittenhouse, 1991). Perhaps here it reflects a debate in the public arena as much as any private 'reality', or subjective experience. However, the way in which the biological discourse is utilised in the context of the reflective processes of self-diagnosis illustrates the way in which public discourse has permeated into the subjective.

What is more, the conflation of gender and pathology in the material body serves to reproduce power relations. This process is apparent in other 'gendered' conditions such as anorexia, where the female body is constructed as excessive, in need of control and containment to conform to exaggerated feminine 'ideals' (Malson, 1995). Here, this relationship between the material and social realms is apparent in a second discourse – a discourse of femininity.

EMBODYING THE SOCIAL: FEMININE CONFLICTS

The discourse of female biology overlaps and contrasts with a discourse of femininity. I use the term 'embodied' to denote the way in which the discursively constituted body frames women's subjective experiences. The category of 'PMS' is used to signify 'bad' or unfeminine behaviour – intersecting with biology. Again, there are different themes within this discourse, of anger, violence, bad mothering and bad behaviour. Taken together, they constitute a major discourse of bad (versus ideal) femininity.

HANNAH   I hit my fiancé [*laughs*] he woke up with, erm, a black eye and a thick lip (.) I must have gived him a hell of a whack, I dunno why . . . he was just sleeping there, poor bugger (.) and (.) I just got up and whacked him.

JANE   He [her partner] just sort of like grabbed my hand and things and tried to stop me from hitting him (..) and he says, 'You're like a mad possessed person.' (.) He hit me once and (.) I ended up on the floor and then I was straight back up again (.) it was like there's something inside you (.) he said, 'You're ANGRY, you're really angry.'

ANDREA   The first sign is normally the crying . . . or (.) the only other way I can put it is that someone's talking to you – you wanna say shut up, you don't wanna hear it, you don't wanna speak to anybody (.) you just want to be left alone . . . I can't be bothered (.) with anything or anybody (..) . . . I just wanna go away and sit in a room somewhere (.) you know an-and it's hard with the children 'cos they'll want something and you – my fists will go, I clench my fists a lot 'cos it's horrible, it's horrendous . . . I'd say the worst month was when I actually attacked my daughter.

These accounts of premenstrual behaviour and experience constitute a discourse of (bad) femininity within the texts in which difficult emotions, inappropriate responses, and aspects of behaviour and experience incongruent with archetypal notions of femininity are attributed to the menstrual cycle. In other words, because of the emphasis on forms of 'bad' femininity, within this discourse there is a textual reference to 'good' or ideal femininity.

Hannah, who was on remand in a local prison at the time, speaks of being violent towards her fiancé. She positions this act as premenstrual behaviour, but relates hitting her partner while he is asleep, avoiding the problem of retaliation. Violence towards one's partner is both bad and 'unfeminine': Female violence, towards men or children, even when influenced by 'hormones', represents a cultural taboo (Vines, 1993).

Within this discourse, the 'bad mother' is constituted as uncaring, neglectful, violent and related to the overlying construct of PMS. Andrea's life, at the time of the interview, was chaotic and difficult. She told me that effective treatment for PMS was her last chance for keeping custody of her children – if she did not begin to manage her anger and aggression, they would be taken into local authority care. Another example of the 'bad mother' can be seen in the text of my interview with Jenny.

JENNY   My daughter does, my son's two (.) he doesn't really understand, my (.) my daughter, she does (.) she says when I'm better, she says, 'Oh you're better now, you've been to the doctor's, and she thinks I'm at the doctor's and I'm getting tablets and I'm not well (..) and it's sad to (.) look at your little girl (.) and one minute you're a nice (.) calm and placid mum (.) got all the time in the world and the next minute you're just (.) got no time, I don't want to read a book, I don't want to sit there, I don't want to be touched, or (.) I just want to go upstairs and I sit in the bathroom on my own (..) just to have that peace and quiet, and I get annoyed if they (.) knock on the door or they want to come in (.) and it's normal for them to come in because they want to be with their mum and I just want to be away.

Jenny's narrative contains both a discourse of embodied femininity and a reference to a discourse of ideal (and unattainable) motherhood – a mother 'with all the time in the world', one who never needs to take time out for herself.

Loss of control is also a central theme to this discourse.

ALICE   It just [. . .] (C: And is that how you feel?) yeah (.) yeah, this is probably quite a good way of putting it (C: Right) that there is a sense of, um (.) not being in control (.) I don't mean (.) it's not,

erm (.) DANGEROUS [her emphasis] out of control (.) but it's, uh
(.) um, somehow feeling that (.) being swept along, you know (.) (C:
Mmm) you want to kind of check at each point what's happening.

ANDREA   You know some women will get these feelings but can look into
them (.) I couldn't, I just blew (.) (C: Right) no questions
asked . . . at that point it was – got to the point where I was self-
inflicting injuries as well as (..) hurting children (C: What sort of
self-inflicted injuries?) I gave myself black eyes.

Andrea speaks of loss of temper premenstrually, to the point where she 'just
blew' and has harmed her children and sometimes herself. Alice feels 'swept
along', a side-reference perhaps to the tide of her hormones and of feeling
dangerous.

These aspects of subjective experience that do not fit in with Western
ideals of femininity are often positioned as premenstrual, unfeminine
behaviour, and therefore undesirable or unwanted. These references to
socially unacceptable behaviour represent powerful regulatory mechanisms
in the construction of female identity. The cultural pressure on women to be
placid, calm, 'feminine' is tremendous, and in these interviews the cracks
start to show. Women who step outside of their gendered roles and behave
'inappropriately' are positioned in one of two ways – as either 'bad' or 'mad'
(Ussher, 1991).

So, the premenstrual woman describes herself as angry, violent, a bad
mother, dangerous and out of control; personal experiences that also relate
closely to public stereotypes. Taken together, these different positions form a
discourse of 'bad' femininity realised in the texts, which positions itself in
opposition to any notion of 'ideal' (but desirable) femininity. I would argue
that the way this discourse of femininity is employed within the social
context of PMS illustrates traditional constructs of femininity – for
example, the good mother/good wife. It also relates back to, and is tied to,
the discourse of biology and the female body.

THE BODY/SELF DIVIDE

A body/mind dualism, where the action of the 'rational' mind is valued over
and above that of the 'irrational' body, is deeply entrenched in Western
culture and medical science (Kirmayer, 1992). This Cartesian dualism is
particularly pronounced in cultural constructions of gender, where the categories of 'female' and 'male' take up positions of 'irrational/body' versus
'rational/mind'. The discourses of biology and femininity in women's
accounts of PMS illustrate both this mind/body divide and the action of
gender on subjective experience. For these women, an unruly body is the
prime site of their distress. But another dualist discourse is apparent within
these texts – one in which the premenstrual woman is separated from her

'normal' self. This discursive 'splitting' of the premenstrual woman/experience from the 'normal' woman/experience links closely with the theme of loss of control, and acts as a regulatory mechanism. Thus:

JENNY   She [a doctor] just said, um (.) um, 'Oh you're suffering from (.) you're depressed, um' (.) and I said, 'It's up to my periods', because I did write out a chart of how I was for a good few months before that and, um (.) (C: So you had an idea) had an idea there was something going on but I, I thought it was ME [her emphasis] I'm going mad (.) this thing takes over me every month.

JANE   This is uncontrollable what I've got (.) it just takes over (.) it's like my mouth goes off and I'm screaming and shouting and swearing and [. . .] there's nothing I can do to stop it.

ANDREA   Th-they all said, 'How are you?', and I said, 'Fine', and then ten minutes later they heard this almighty din and again I don't remember anything happening . . . with my daughter, she (.) I was drying her hair one minute and the next minute she had a black eye and was on the floor.

Andrea describes the uncontrollable harming of herself or her child, and this 'splitting' process is so powerful that she actually blacks out, remembers nothing of what she has done. She is literally 'overtaken' by her body, forcing her to do things that are beyond her control because 'she' wasn't there at the time. If Andrea's body does these dreadful things, and not Andrea, then this relates back to the theme of the female body as 'bad'.

Both Jenny and Jane speak of being 'taken over' every month. This discourse has its roots in notions of spiritual possession that were used to control women in the Middle Ages (Ussher, 1989, 1991). Within the postmodern social arena, it acts as a regulator, marking boundaries for women of acceptable and unacceptable behaviour, and highlights their unpredictable and uncontrollable tendencies ('at the mercy of their hormones'). It regulates by policing the presence of women and the interpretation of their behaviour in different arenas. But in taking up this discourse, and positioning themselves therein, these women are actively negotiating something for themselves rather than simply being, as Foucault (1984) might suggest, passive bodies upon which discourses of power inscribe their mark:

JANE   He's [her partner] not really [supportive] because he doesn't know how to deal with them, he thinks it's ME [her emphasis] actually having a go at him all the time (.) and not this thing that takes over me.

SARAH   . . . Erm, the mood swings (.) it's like being two different people (.) (C: Right) as I said earlier on it's the one that's shouting is enjoying it (.) and yet the normal side of me is standing next to me

> thinking WHY [her emphasis] are you doing this, you're (.) you
> can't help it.

It is possible to argue that these women's expressions of anger are a secret (and by definition unacceptable) pleasure. Women, I would suggest, use this 'Jekyll and Hyde' position as a metaphor for their experience, as a way of negotiating the expression of 'unacceptable' emotions and behaviours from within a pre-existing (and oppressive) social framework. It may also be a source of shame and guilt, both of which themes come across very clearly from the interview texts.

It is perhaps the social emphasis on the primacy of women's reproductive role, and their public biological functions, that actually produces this splitting process, rather than the other way around. Kirmayer (1992) argues that our bodies seek discursive expression, using a language that is itself grounded in and driven by bodily experience. Given the interfacial position of the menstrual cycle (between material and social modes), the female body not only 'insists' on discursive meaning, but the discourses of the female body themselves use the body as a site of expression. Here, this is achieved through the adoption of particular metaphoric strategies. In taking up this dualism and its metaphoric structure, it can be argued that women, rather than being controlled by discursive prescriptions and limits, actually use this strategy to negotiate a way of expressing the inexpressible. In this sense, the women are not passive subjects but active agents in the construction of their experience.

THE SPEAKING BODY: REGULATING LIVED EXPERIENCE

Discourses of femininity and biology frame women's experience. Parlee (1991) has argued that PMS effectively trivialises anger and resistance, rendering it meaningless. Further, PMS supports and represents the interests of certain (male) institutions. If the discursive 'splitting' of the premenstrual and 'normal' self illustrates the way in which discursive meaning is imposed upon bodily experience, then this final discourse illustrates the way in which all experience is reframed and reinterpreted through the lens of the body.

Within the texts, the discursive body was often used to explain or interpret other aspects of experience. This I found particularly distressing, as women disclosed the most intimate and disturbing details of their lives, framed only by the discursive category of PMS. For example:

HANNAH Because the reason for that [a criminal offence] is that I suffer from migraines (C: Right) I – I was on, I had PMT, I got very ratty and, er, as well as get very bad migraines on top as well as the alcohol (C: Mmm) and, er, the sexual abuse (C: Mmm) It's all just crammed in my head ... my head feels like it's gonna explode 'cos I've got everything to cram in.

ANDREA   Well I didn't have any control over (.) my life (.) (C: Right), erm, and I was taken into a family centre because things became so bad (.) er, ultimately the reason I came off the (.) antidepressants was 'cos I took an overdose (.) er, last January.

[I was in prison for] fraud (..) erm, and I had Charlotte [daughter] erm, we split up when I was pregnant and (.) I've had injunctions and that, he's quite violent . . . I don't know, at the moment it's the [PMS] symptoms, everything else in my life is fine.

In both of these excerpts, experience is very clearly framed by the body, and by PMS. Andrea also draws upon a romantic discourse at the end of this piece of text, positioning herself as having just the one problem: if only the PMS could be cured, then everything else in her life would be fine. This is contradicted by the other information that she gives throughout the interview, a strategy that firmly locates the blame for her problems within and upon her body.

SAMIRA   I mean, I just had quite a sort of (.) emotionally abusive rather than sexually abusive relationship with my parents (C: Mmm), I mean a BIT [her emphasis] physically (.) I mean I got hit quite a lot probably more than most (.) teenagers get hit, I mean, I was sort of HIT [her emphasis] quite a lot at sort of 15, 16 and sort of hit with objects and sort of belted and sort of whipped and things.

NADINE   Work's [teaching] very stressful (..) also, erm, not having a place of my own (.) . . . my own space to work when I come home 'cos I only have a small room . . . and I don't have the space to do it (.) and that stresses me out an awful lot, erm (.) and that again stresses me out at work because I haven't got the stuff that I need for the next day (.) Neil [boyfriend] that's a big area of stress 'cos I was constantly up and down (.) one minute everything's fine and the next minute it's not (.) that's really difficult . . . I actually go and see a therapist as well now.

It seems to me that there are graphic and illustrative themes of stress, pain and hardship in these texts, which are all but negated by positioning them within the category of 'PMS'. Why, for example, were these women not seeking legal aid, or being given help to find better housing? Why were they locating blame upon their bodies and not upon the violent or distant partner, the abusive father, or on poverty? These other material problems do not appear salient as causes of distress, when compared to the gendered body.

PMS is a socially acceptable category, positioned within a particular medical and social ideology, within which there is a (limited) framework for understanding and treatment. By positioning themselves within a particular medical diagnosis, perhaps women win some 'space' away from everyone and everything else. By adopting a sick role, they no longer have to cope with other material problems. The framework that exists for dealing with violent partners, abuse, depression or rape, or other material aspects of being a woman in Western culture is, perhaps, even less available than treatment for PMS.

By privileging the body as an attribution for distress, experiences that might in other circumstances be usefully alleviated are negated. And although the taking up of a particular position within a dualist discourse may be, in some senses, emancipatory (as it affords particular and otherwise prohibited behaviours), it also highlights the distinctly oppressive nature of the social context within which these women exist. Nicolson (1986) observes that the women she interviewed, who traditionally would be seen as chronically depressed, could equally, from a feminist position, be seen as chronically oppressed. I was left to consider the reasons why many of these women were seeking help for PMS, and not for the other myriad (and, to me, equally compelling) problems in their lives. It struck me that there were perhaps two explanations for this. In the first place, it may be that seeking help for a gynaecological problem is the most readily available avenue for help for many women, that it is easier to visit a GP than, say, to seek legal aid or deal with a violent partner.

A second explanation may be that the body is a more legitimate site for blame than the mind: perhaps it is more palatable to be labelled as physically, rather than mentally, ill. This does not, however, fully explain why these women specifically report premenstrual problems, and not one of the many other predominantly female disorders such as anorexia or depression. In many respects, as a middle-class, educated, childless white woman, my reaction could be explained by my privileged position within many of these discourses. I have available to me many different alternatives, explanatory frameworks and material resources that these women do not. However, the most striking implication of this discourse of bodily primacy is the way in which it illustrates the shortcomings, contradictions and oppressive practices embodied in Western constructions of femininity.

CONCLUSIONS

PMS is constituted through closely intertwined discourses of the body and of femininity. By taking up positions within body/mind and premenstrual/'normal' dualisms, women may negotiate and maintain their feminine status in spite of behaviour and experience that does not always conform to archetypal feminine ideals. However, these dualisms also reproduce and reinforce gendered relations of power in the social arena. A discourse of primary embodiment which positions the female body as causal in all of the experiences associated with PMS highlights the action of this power, and the fragmentations and oppressions of Western constructions of femininity and the female body. Importantly, a material-discursive approach places the body within its sociohistorical context, and the realm of the social in the context of bodily experience. As such, this approach provides a potential solution to the impasse or crisis in menstrual cycle research (see Ussher, 1997), and an avenue for greater insight in many other areas of the study of health and illness experience.

My analysis of these texts has a number of implications for women who self-report PMS. The other material circumstances which, in the context of these interviews, are framed by the female body (poor housing, violence against women, sexual abuse and poverty) are constantly debated in the feminist arena. Any analysis which places PMS in the broader social context should add weight to the feminist argument. Second, by deconstructing the disease category of PMS, we may create new and less oppressive discursive resources for interpreting and representing subjective experience.

Use of this particular qualitative approach places the experience of PMS firmly within its sociohistorical context, and links this interpretation to broader discussions of the construction of gender. These issues have largely been neglected in PMS research, despite the centrality of notions of gender and the body within recent theoretical developments. This failure of traditional approaches to take women's experiences into account renders their explanatory powers quite weak, whereas a theoretical account that is firmly grounded in subjective experience potentially has the power for social and political change.

There are a number of limitations to this particular piece of research. Different people will read texts in different ways, depending upon the experiences they bring to their research. My analysis is just one of many possible interpretations. Furthermore, these women represent a small sample, interviewed in a clinical context. It would be useful to explore the constructions of the reproductive body and PMS from within different contexts – for example, there are many public texts around menstruation (e.g. advertisements for sanitary products, women's magazines) that configure the body in powerful and meaningful ways, and that have yet to be analysed and related to the subjective realm. However, in recognising PMS as a complex interplay of the internal and the external, of the orders of the body and the text, an important step towards breaching the impasse in PMS research (Ussher, 1992a, 1997) is reached.

NOTES

1 Apologies to John Richardson, whose paper of the same name provides an excellent review of the historical context of PMS. See Richardson (1993).
2 See Rittenhouse (1991), Martin (1987) and Parlee (1991) for thorough reviews of socio-economic factors in the emergence of PMS.

REFERENCES

American Psychiatric Association (1994) *Diagnostic and Statistical Manual of*

Mental Disorders, 4th edition, Washington DC: American Psychiatric Association.

Bains, G.K. and Slade, P. (1989) Attributional Patterns, Mood and the Menstrual Cycle, *Psychosomatic Medicine*, 50, 469–476.

Bancroft, J. (1993) The Premenstrual Syndrome: A Reappraisal of the Concept and the Evidence, *Psychological Medicine Monograph Supplement 24*, Cambridge: Cambridge University Press.

Bhaskar, R. (1989) *Reclaiming Reality: A Critical Introduction to Contemporary philosophy*, London: Verso.

Braidotti, R. (1989) The Politics of Ontological Difference. In T. Brennan (ed.), *Between Feminism and Psychoanalysis*, London: Routledge.

Chesney, M.A. and Tasto, D.L. (1975) The Development of the Menstrual Symptom Questionnaire, *Behaviour Research and Therapy*,13, 237–244.

Dalton, K. (1991) *Once a Month*, London: Fontana.

Doherty, K. (1994) Subjectivity, Reflexivity and the Analysis of Discourse, paper presented to the Annual Conference of the British Psychological Society, December.

Foucault, M. (1979) *The History of Sexuality*, vol. 1, London: Penguin.

—— (1984) *The History of Sexuality*, vol. 3, *The Care of the Self*, trans. Robert Hurley, London: Penguin (1989).

Frank, R.T. (1931) The Normal Causes of Premenstrual Tension, *Archives of Neurology and Psychiatry*, 26, 1053–1057.

Golub, S. (1992) *Periods: From Menarche to Menopause*, London: Sage.

Greene, R. and Dalton, K. (1953) The Premenstrual Syndrome, *British Medical Journal*, 1, 1007–1014.

Halbreich, U. and Endicott, J. (1982) Classification of Premenstrual Syndromes. In R.C. Friedman (ed.), *Behaviour and the Menstrual Cycle*, New York: Marcel Dekker Inc.

Harding, S. (ed.) (1987) *Feminism and Methodology*, Indianapolis: Indiana University Press.

——(1991) *Whose Science? Whose Knowledge? Thinking from Women's Lives*, Milton Keynes: Open University Press.

——(1993) Rethinking Standpoint Epistemology: 'What is Strong Objectivity'? In L. Alcoff and E. Potter (eds), *Feminist Epistemologies*, London: Routledge.

Henriques, J., Hollway, W., Urwin, C., Venn, C. and Walkerdine, V. (1984) *Changing the Subject: Psychology, Social Regulation and subjectivity*, London: Methuen.

Henwood, K. and Pidgeon, N. (1994) Beyond the Qualitative Paradigm: A Framework for Introducing Diversity Within Qualitative Psychology, *Journal of Community and Applied Social Psychology*, 4, 225–238.

——(1995) Remaking the Link: Qualitative Research and Feminist Standpoint Theory, *Feminism & Psychology*, 5(1), 7–30.

Horney, K. (1931) Premenstrual Tension. In K. Horney, *Feminine Psychology*, ed. and trans. H. Kelman, London: Routledge (1967).

Keller, E.F. (1985) *Reflections on Gender and Science*, London: Yale University Press.

Kirmayer, L.J. (1992) The Body's Insistence on Meaning: Metaphor as Presentation and Representation in Illness Experience, *Medical Anthropology Quarterly*, 6(4), 323–346.

Koeske, R.D. (1980) Theoretical Perspectives on Menstrual Cycle Research: The Relevance of Attributional Approaches for the Perception and Explanation of Premenstrual Emotionality. In A.J. Dan, E. Graham and C. Beecher (eds), *The Menstrual Cycle*, vol. 1, New York: Springer Verlag.

——(1983) Sociocultural Factors in the Premenstrual Syndrome: Review, Critique and Directions, paper presented to the Premenstrual Syndrome Workshop, Intramural Research Program, NIMH, Rockville, MA, 14–15 April.

McNay, L. (1992) *Foucault and Feminism: Power, Gender and the Self*, Oxford: Polity Press.

Malson, H. (1995) Anorexia Nervosa: Discourses of Gender, Subjectivity and the Body, unpublished Ph.D. thesis, University of London.

Martin, E. (1987) *The Woman in the Body: A Cultural Analysis of Reproduction*, Milton Keynes: Open University Press.

Moos, R.H. (1968) The Development of a Menstrual Distress Questionnaire, *Psychosomatic Medicine*, 30, 853–867.

——(1969) Typology of Menstrual Cycle Symptoms, *American Journal of Obstetrics and Gynaecology*, 103, 390–402.

Mortola, J. (1992) Assessment and Management of Premenstrual Syndrome, *Current Opinion in Obstetrics and Gynaecology*, 4, 877–885.

Nicolson, P. (1986) Developing a Feminist Approach to Depression Following Childbirth. In S. Wilkinson (ed.), *Feminist Social Psychology: Developing Theory and Practice*, Milton Keynes: Open University Press.

O'Brien, P.M.S. (1993) Helping Women with Premenstrual Syndrome, *British Medical Journal*, 307, 1474–1478.

Parker, I. (1989) *The Crisis in Modern Social Psychology, and How to End it*, London: Routledge.

——(1992) *Discourse Dynamics: Critical Analysis for Social and Individual Psychology*, London: Routledge.

Parlee, M.B. (1991) The Social Construction of PMS: A Case Study of Scientific Discourse as Cultural Contestation, paper presented to the conference on The Good Body: Asceticism in Contemporary Culture, Institute for the Medical Humanities, Texas University, Galveston, 12–13 April.

Potter, J. and Wetherell, M. (1987) *Discourse and Social Psychology: Beyond Attitudes and Behaviour*, London: Sage.

Richardson, J.T.E. (1990) Questionnaire Studies of Paramenstrual Symptoms, *Psychology of Women Quarterly*, 14, 15–42.

——(ed.) (1992) *Cognition and the Menstrual Cycle*, New York: Springer Verlag.

——(1993) The Premenstrual Syndrome: A Brief History, paper presented to the Annual Conference of the British Psychological Society, Blackpool, 4 April.

Rittenhouse, C.A. (1991) The Emergence of PMS as a Social Problem, *Social Problems*, 38(3), 412–425.

Rodin, M. (1992) The Social Construction of Premenstrual Syndrome, *Social Science and Medicine*, 35(1), 49–56.

Rubinow, D.R. and Schmidt, P.J. (1989) Models for the Development and Expression of Symptoms in PMS, *Women's Disorders, Psychiatric Clinics of North America*, 12(1), 53–69.

Sayers (1982) *Biological Politics: Feminist and Anti-Feminist Perspectives*, London: Tavistock.

Smith, D. (1987) *The Everyday World as Problematic: A Feminist Sociology*, Toronto: University of Toronto Press.

Stenner, P. (1993) Discoursing Jealousy. In E. Burman and I. Parker, (eds), *Discourse Analytic Research: Repertoires and Readings of Texts in Action*, London: Routledge.

Swann, C.J. (1995a) Psychology and Self-Reported PMS: An Evaluation of Different Research Strategies, unpublished Ph.D. thesis, University of London.

——(1995b) Reconstructing the Reproductive Woman, paper presented to the Annual Conference of the British Psychological Society, Warwick University, April.

——(1996) Premenstrual Tensions: Feminism, Psychology and Epistemology, paper presented to the Annual Conference of the British Psychological Society, Brighton, April.

Swann, C.J. and Ussher, J.M. (1995) A Discourse Analytic Approach to Women's Experience of Premenstrual Syndrome, *Journal of Mental Health*, 4(3), 359–367.

Ussher, J.M. (1989) *The Psychology of the Female Body*, London: Routledge.

——(1991) *Women's Madness: Misogyny or Mental Illness?*, London: Harvester Wheatsheaf.

——(1992a) The Demise of Dissent and the Rise of Cognition in Menstrual Cycle Research. In I.T.E. Richardson (ed.), *Cognition and the Menstrual Cycle*, New York: Springer Verlag.

——(1992b) Research and Theory Related to Female Reproduction: Implications for Clinical Psychology, *British Journal of Clinical Psychology*, 31, 129–151.

——(1997) Premenstrual Syndrome: Reconciling Disciplinary Divides Through the Adoption of a Material Discursive Standpoint, *Annual Review of Sex Research*.

Vines, G. (1993) *Raging Hormones: Do They Rule Our Lives?*, Berkeley: University of California Press.

Walker, A. (1995) Theory and Methodology in Premenstrual Syndrome Research, *Social Science and Medicine*, 41(6), 793–800.

Warner, P. and Bancroft, J. (1990) Factors Related to Self-Reporting of the Premenstrual Syndrome, *British Journal of Psychiatry*, 157, 249–260.

Wetherell, M. and White, S. (1992) Fear of Fat: Young Women Talking About Eating, Dieting and Body Image, unpublished MA thesis, Open University.

Wilkinson, S. (ed.) (1986) *Feminist Social Psychology: Developing Theory and Practice*, Milton Keynes: Open University Press.

Woolgar, S. (1988) *Science: The Very Idea*, London: Routledge.

11 Menopause

Bodily changes and multiple meanings

Myra S. Hunter and Irene O'Dea

INTRODUCTION

The menopause, defined as a woman's last menstrual period, takes place in a gradual process of physiological change, occurring concurrently with age and developmental changes, within a psychosocial and cultural context. Bodily changes during the menopause transition occur at different levels and include hormonal changes (lowering of oestrogen levels and raised follicle stimulating hormone), menstrual irregularity and cessation of periods, and for many women hot flushes and night sweats. However, women's experience of these changes varies considerably; some, for example, have no experience of hormone changes or hot flushes. In addition, the menopause can be seen as a marker of reproductive state, a stage of the life cycle and of age. The meaning of bodily changes is likely to be intimately related to sociolinguistic influences, such as discourses of gender, ageing and reproduction. A woman's subjectivity is therefore positioned between her perception of biological changes and the discursive constructions of the menopause, which are influenced by social, political and cultural practices and traditions. In this chapter we are interested in how women experience and negotiate the varied (largely negative and often conflicting) multiple meanings of the menopause.

We begin with a brief overview of the historical theories and treatments of menopausal women. Current theoretical perspectives are described, including biomedical, psychological and sociocultural. However, it is biomedical discourse that currently dominates research literature and media accounts of menopause. We argue that for the most part these approaches are polarised and fragmented and fail to account for the varied experiences of women. A material-discursive framework is proposed and used in a qualitative study of women's accounts of the menopause. Thirty-seven 50-year-old women who were currently or had recently experienced menopause were interviewed. The research is approached from a feminist perspective in that the focus is on the women's own accounts, and a critical stance is taken towards the prevailing gendered constructions of the menopause. Discourse analysis was used to explore women's accounts of the impact of menopause and the extent to which bodily changes are imbued with discursive meanings.

HISTORICAL INFLUENCES

The scientific discourses of the Western world relating to menopause and mid-age have contributed to the evolution of a stereotypic picture of the menopausal woman as irritable, depressed, asexual and besieged by hot flushes (Dickson, 1990). Analysis of historical accounts provides rich examples of how social constructions of the menopause have served to legitimise sexist and ageist attitudes towards mid-aged and older women (Martin, 1987; Hunter, 1990; Ussher, 1991). Negative views of menopause date back at least as far as Roman times, when menstrual blood was seen as poisonous. It was argued that after the cessation of menstruation, toxins previously excreted via menstruation were 'retained', destroying the body from within and causing physical, sexual and emotional decline. Blood-letting, by cutting veins or applying leeches, was a common treatment used to attempt to preserve well-being, physical and sexual attractiveness (Wilbush, 1979).

The link between a woman's reproductive capacity and emotional well-being, and even her sanity, was perpetuated by psychoanalytic, psychiatric and gynaecological thinking in the nineteenth century. Expressions of distress or dissatisfaction could be seen as sexual or 'hysterical' in origin and gynaecological surgery was used as a treatment (Showalter, 1987). Until 1980, when it was removed from the DSM-III (Diagnostic and Statistical Manual of the American Psychiatric Association) classification of psychiatric disorders, it was believed that the menopause was a cause of psychosis (involutional melancholia) (Krafft-Ebing, 1877). Psychoanalytic theories promoted the menopause as a neurosis, in which women mourned their loss of femininity and sexuality. A pessimistic picture was painted when this phase of life comes to an end, 'for reality has actually become poor in prospects, and resignation without compensation is often the only solution' (Deutsch, 1945). Thus the end of reproductive life is expected to signal a morass of misery and an end to any sense of usefulness (Ussher, 1989).

Historical examples clearly show how the female body can be variously constituted. It is usually defined as a problem or an illness, thus serving to maintain and reproduce inequalities in gendered power relationships. For example, if a woman's menopause is assumed to signify inevitable loss and the body is imbued with negative meanings, then this construction of the menopause may well lead to depression and misery for women, thus rein-forcing the link between loss and the menopause. Similarly, the assumption, in some psychoanalytic writings, that a woman's sexuality is embedded within her reproductive status, can be seen as a discursive strategy to define and regulate women's sexuality. By defining sexuality in this way approxi-mately one-third of all women, particularly infertile, postmenopausal and older women, are positioned as asexual.

THE BIOMEDICAL DISCOURSE

It is the biomedical discourse that currently dominates research literature and media accounts of the menopause. The menopause is seen as a oestrogen-deficiency disease, a cluster of physical and emotional symptoms that should be treated by hormone replacement therapy (HRT).

For example, in his book *Feminine Forever*, Robert Wilson (1966), a major proponent of HRT, claimed that his 'youth pill' (oestrogen) could avert twenty-six psychological and physical complaints; 'Total femininity' could be preserved. The menopausal woman was depicted as 'an unstable oestrogen starved' woman who is responsible for 'untold misery of alcoholism, drug addiction, divorce and broken homes'. Although this position is now considered extreme, it has been assimilated into mainstream gynaecological texts:

> The declining oestrogen levels of the climacteric are also thought to give rise to a variety of symptoms, collectively referred to as the climacteric syndrome, namely insomnia, depression, generalised headaches and pains, dyspareunia, loss of libido, poor concentration, irritability, poor memory, anxiety and urinary frequency.
>
> (Studd and Smith, 1993: 210)

Within medical discourse the focus has tended to be upon women in relation to men, with an emphasis on staying young and attractive and sexually responsive for their heterosexual partners (Seibold *et al.*, 1994). For example, 'loss of libido' is often regarded as a symptom of the menopause. As a result the relational context is overlooked, as are the woman's sexual needs. Moreover, little is known about the views and experiences of menopause of lesbian women. In the promotion of HRT youthful images of attractive women are commonly used, often embracing a male partner. Until recently the medical profession or 'masters of menopause' (Greer, 1991) have been the major voices speaking about what is essentially a female experience.

The boundaries of the 'disease' have shifted markedly over the past twenty years from a transitional state to a more permanent postmenopausal condition, rendering women prone to chronic health problems such as osteoporosis and cardiovascular vulnerability. While increasing research interest into the health problems of older women, this perspective implies that the menopause is to be avoided (by HRT), since a host of problems might ensue if HRT is not sought. The broadening of the definition also implies that HRT should be used by the majority of women, even if they are not experiencing problems. This is an unusual situation, in that a large cohort of women would be rendered as in need of medication. The promotion of HRT frames the menopause within a very medical discourse and plays on fears of ill health and particularly on women's fears of cancer and ageing. This process discourages women from exploring their experiences of the menopause and developing alternative perspectives.

Such images of mid-aged and older women have not gone unchallenged. Feminist writers have critically examined assumptions about the menopause, which serve to oppress and limit the lives of women. The biomedical perspective positions women as deficient in relation to men and sets norms for what beliefs and actions are 'appropriate' for mid-aged women. Thus the production of medical knowledge maintains and reinforces both sexist and ageist attitudes, and enables the pharmaceutical industry to profit. There is, however, a diversity in both medical and feminist opinions about HRT and the menopause (see Hunt, 1994).

PSYCHOLOGICAL MODELS

There has been little psychological research in this area. However, what has been carried out has been based broadly within a bio-psycho-social framework. Typically, quantitative measures of psychosocial variables, such as attitudes and beliefs (Leiblum and Swartzman, 1986; Hunter, 1992; Avis *et al.*, 1993) and psychosocial stresses (Ballinger *et al.*, 1979; Greene and Cooke, 1980) have been correlated with symptoms (such as hot flushes) and mood during the menopause. Bio-psycho-social models draw attention to the interrelationships between social, psychological and biological variables – for example, Greene (1983) proposed a 'vulnerability model', in which the hormone changes preceding the menopause were seen as rendering women more susceptible to the impact of life stresses during mid-life.

It is not that this research has not had positive impact, in that assumptions about mid-aged and older women have been challenged from within medical institutions (see Whitehead, 1994; Hunter, 1996). For example, prospective epidemiological studies surveying large general population samples of women have provided evidence that the menopause is not experienced as such a negative event as might be expected from medical texts, and that depression and emotional problems do not necessarily increase at this time (Matthews *et al.*, 1990; Holte, 1992; Hunter, 1992; Kaufert *et al.*, 1992; McKinlay *et al.*, 1992). One major finding was that women's experience of all aspects of the menopause varied considerably.

However, the tendency has been for psychosocial variables to be regarded by the medical profession as peripheral to biological variables, which are seen as the main elements of research and clinical practice; psychosocial factors are seen as problematic in terms of measurement and are often 'added on' rather than being afforded equal weight. Within these models biological, psychological and social variables are generally regarded as fairly separate entities.

Similarly, the methodology of psychological studies limits our understanding of the variability of women's accounts in different contexts. Questionnaire studies are problematic in that they have tended to tap medical discourses, with talk about hot flushes, vaginal dryness and irregular periods. Bio-psycho-social models position the menopause primarily as a problem for the individual. This can lead to individualised explanations and the tendency to pathologise any problems that menopausal women might experience, thus averting accountability from social and political structures. For example, a woman's depression may be attributed to stress, coping style or her expectations of menopause. Critics of bio-psycho-social models point out that insufficient attention has been paid to the sociocultural context of health and illness (Marks, 1996).

The above problems can be seen as stemming largely from the positivist epistemology which underpins both bio-psycho-social and biomedical models. A material-discursive framework enables exploration of the fluid relationships between social construction and material changes; the body is afforded discursive meaning and material circumstances influence the production and function of discourse.

SOCIOCULTURAL APPROACHES

The sociocultural perspective on the menopause developed in the 1970s, by feminists, sociologists, anthropologists and others, partly in reaction to the growing predominance of medical model. From this perspective, menopause is viewed as a natural developmental process having little or no direct effect upon women (see Kaufert, 1982). Here menopausal problems are seen as socially determined, being the result of negative stereotypes towards menopause and ageing, as well as women's limited social roles (Parlee, 1976; Neugarten, 1979). Sociological studies of attitudes to the menopause and experience of symptoms within and between cultures demonstrate the variability of 'menopausal symptoms' (Avis *et al.*, 1993). However, although the menopause is conceptualised in terms of social construction, traditional quantitative methods of inquiry have generally been used in sociological research.

Anthropological studies provide examples of how menopause can be a positive event, particularly when it signifies a change in social status (Flint, 1975; Davis, 1986; Rice, 1995). In general, women living in non-Western societies appear to report fewer symptoms during the menopause compared with those living in Western societies (Payer, 1991). However, once again the integration of these findings into existing models of the menopause has been problematic. For example, how do cultural factors influence women's experience? Interestingly, a study carried out in Mexico and in India has drawn attention to the material differences between cultures – such as diet, reproductive practices and exercise – which might, in addition to attitudes and values, explain the marked differences in reports of menopausal experiences (Beyenne, 1986). A material–discursive framework could take account of these findings by acknowledging material differences, and by examining the ways in which sociocultural discourses influence the significance of material differences.

A MATERIAL–DISCURSIVE APPROACH

The biomedical and the sociocultural/feminist theories represent very polarised positions (Kaufert *et al.*, 1992). The biomedical view neglects social influences and we would argue that the sociocultural view has traditionally ignored the body. The biomedical, psychological/bio-psycho-social and sociocultural models all tend to adopt a positivistic framework to understand the menopause in terms of hormonal changes or attitudes and values which reside within the individual woman; the truth about the menopause can be unravelled which is apolitical and value-free. The development of discursive theory and social constructionist methods in social psychology had led to criticisms of the objective status given to biomedical and psychosocial variables and of the assumption that the subject is consistent and the researcher 'objective' (see Henriques *et al.*, 1984; Potter and Wetherell, 1987; Hollway, 1989). In this framework, subjectivity and the meaning of the menopause would be seen as constituted within language and is the result of historically specific discursive relations and social practices (Foucault, 1972; Walkerdine, 1986). Consistent with feminist research, social constructionist approaches focus upon women's experiences and analyse the social meanings and power relationships within language.

There have been few qualitative studies of how women discursively construct the menopause. Those that have been published include descriptions of the pervasiveness of biomedical discourse (whether women's language reflected or resisted it – see Dickson, 1990), or how the medical discourse can function to enable some women to acknowledge distress and seek help (Daly, 1995). In a study comparing women of different ages, Martin (1987) found that the vast majority of older women she interviewed saw the menopause in a positive light, while younger women tended to share the medical view of the menopause. She concluded that 'women choose – at least to some extent – whether or not to treat . . . menopause as a medical event.' In addition, it would seem that the experience of the menopause could well have modified its meaning for the older women.

The material–discursive approach, which constitutes the common theme in this book, draws upon a social constructionist perspective but does not ignore the material body. By 'material' we refer to biological changes such as the timing of the menopause (whether it happens in a woman's early forties or fifties), health problems, hot flushes and menstrual periods, but also social and economic factors, such as experience of employment and social support. The 'discursive' element refers to the symbolic representations of menopause and the older woman. This approach enables us to think about the menopause as a complex process involving varied bodily changes, the meaning of which are very much influenced by the material context and discursive constructions of gender, ageing and reproduction. The question addressed in the following study is: How do women negotiate these two levels – the material and the discursive – as they make sense of their own experience of the menopause?

A STUDY OF WOMEN'S ACCOUNTS OF MENOPAUSE

The study described below aims to explore women's accounts of menopause using a feminist, material–discursive approach. We used a qualitative methodology (thematic discourse analysis – Potter and Wetherell, 1987), based on interviews with mid-aged women, to examine the ways in which discourses around the menopause, gender and ageing are reproduced in women's accounts. We were interested in the extent to which the menopause influenced a woman's sense of herself, what discourses are available to mid-aged women, and how women subjectively position themselves in relation to these discourses. In particular, we were keen to explore how women talked about bodily changes in the context of often negative, and potentially conflicting, discourses surrounding the menopause.

The term 'discourse analysis' subsumes a variety of qualitative, language-oriented approaches to research (Potter and Wetherell, 1987; Burman and Parker, 1993). In general, discourse analysis focuses upon content and form in talk and texts and is concerned with the analysis of action, construction and variability. Our aim was to map out broad themes within women's accounts which relate to social and historical discourses, rather than attempt a detailed linguistic analysis.

As female psychologists in our late thirties/early forties, we inevitably approached the interviews and analysis from particular perspectives. However, like the women who were interviewed, we both inhabit a multiplicity of subject positions. Within the interviews, the role of the interviewer as research psychologist, the content of the questions, and the setting are likely to have the effect of positioning the participants as 'menopausal women', when other aspects of their identities may well be more salient in different contexts. Nevertheless, our aim was to explore the discourses used by women when they are offered the opportunity to talk openly about their thoughts and experiences.

Forty-five women, aged 49 to 51, were recruited from the age/sex register of a general practice in North London, that served a large socially mixed catchment area. Ninety-two women were initially contacted by letter and forty-five responded to an invitation to talk to a researcher about their health, well-being and their lives, at a convenient time at the practice. Appointments, lasting up to an hour were arranged by telephone.

Their mean age was 50.04 (SD = 0.74) years. Eighty-two per cent were married or cohabiting, 9 per cent single and 9 per cent divorced. Seventy-five per cent classified themselves as white British, 9 per cent as non-white British and 16 per cent as white, non-British. Sixty-two per cent worked outside the home. Socio-economic status was assessed by years of education. Fifty-six per cent left school at the age of 16, while 44 per cent continued education for a further one or more years. Fifty-one per cent felt that they were currently going through the menopause, 16 per cent were taking HRT, 20 per cent were unsure as to their stage of menopause, and 13 per cent felt that they had not started it yet. The following analysis was based on the responses of the thirty-seven women who saw themselves as menopausal, post-menopausal or who were taking HRT.

We used semi-structured interviews, which included open questions about their lives, their general health and the menopause. The interviews took place in a comfortable office, at a time when no clinics were occurring, and lasted between twenty-five and fifty-five minutes. The interviews were tape-recorded with the permission of participants. This analysis focuses upon the accounts women gave in response to the following broad questions.

First, they were asked generally about the menopause and where they felt they were in relation to the menopause. Second, they were asked about any consequences of the menopause for them personally. (Prompts included: 'What is its main impact upon you; and has it affected the way you see your-self generally?').

The taped interviews were transcribed verbatim. The texts and the tapes were repeatedly read and listened to by both authors, and discussed. Potter's (Potter and Wetherell, 1987) ten stages of analysis were used as a basis for detecting interpretive repertoires or broad themes. These were taken to a peer-group discussion and elaborated further. The focus on women's accounts enabled us to consider bodily experiences framed within discourse. In other words a material–discursive analysis to some extent can help to reconcile the sociolinguistic–material/body split by conceptualising a constant interplay between the two. We identified six broad themes in response to the women's accounts. These themes included: accounts of menopause as bodily experiences; menopause as a non-event; changes in menstruation; as relating to reproduction; menopause as a sign of ageing and finally menopause as an unspoken taboo. More than one theme was mentioned by a number of women.

The menopause defined by bodily changes

The first question – how women positioned themselves in relation to the menopause, i.e. how did they define being menopausal – tended to elicit physical symptoms and signs, in particular hot flushes, night sweats and menstrual changes and minor physical and emotional symptoms. However, it was hot flushes that were most prevalent in women's accounts and were most commonly described as 'symptoms', rather than hormone or menstrual changes. These bodily changes were described broadly within a biomedical discourse, but the meaning of the changes varied with social and material circumstances:

> The first time I got it I felt that everyone was looking at me; I used to go bright red and feel embarrassed. It only lasted a few minutes but does happen sometimes when I'm talking to people now: I feel uncomfortable. All the blood rushes to my face. Some people say I get a little bit red but

as I say there's nothing you can do about it. It's nature and that's it really. I did mention it to the doctor once but I don't think they want to know anyway. My periods stopped for three months and then started again. This went on for two years and it's completely finished now. I was kind of uncomfortable but I knew what was happening to me. I just took it in my stride.

Anna's account above shows how her experience of flushes is very much in the social arena. She feels embarrassed and uncomfortable about her bodily reactions, particularly in social contexts. The experience of being hot and red signifies flushing and the menopause, but also triggers reactions of shame and embarrassment. She minimises this discomfort by positioning hot flushes as 'natural', which for her implies there is nothing she can do about them. However, later she says with a degree of pride that she took it in her stride. She mentions hot flushes to the doctor, but did not feel that this was a legitimate place to talk about them. We can see here a negotiation between biomedical discourse, which might potentially provide a place to talk about her experience, and a sociocultural discourse which positions menopause as natural.

Accounts of the nature and severity of hot flushes varied within and between women:

Maybe, about two years ago I was feeling hot at times, hot flushes but no more . . . It wasn't for long and then I thought well that's it.

I get hot at times but it doesn't bother me. If it's hot I just open the window but otherwise I don't have any ill effects at all.

For these two women hot flushes and the menopause were not seen as problematic. In the second quote the experience is presented in relation to a medical discourse – no ill effects. However, Joanne described a different experience:

You think hot flushes – poof nothing, easy peasy, but you can actually feel the sweat trickling down your head when you wake up during the night and then you're tired the next day, desperately because you can't sleep . . . and then you go to work and you're sat on the Underground and because there's no movement of air, so it's drip, you want to take all your clothes off. Another thing is you worry that you're going to smell. I don't think people realise what an awful nuisance it is, because they think it's just an inconvenience.

Here Joanne is clear that for her hot flushes are troublesome, particularly when they affect her sleep and she has to go to work and in situations where there is little air, or she is not free to remove clothing. As well as these material constraints, she is also concerned about other people's reactions to her. She feels different to others and misunderstood; others do not understand that hot flushes can be such a nuisance. She appears to be relating here to a discourse of menopause as natural or unproblematic and which dismisses hot flushes as 'easy peasy . . . just an inconvenience'.

The potential split between inner bodily experience and the outer social experience was common in women's accounts. Hot flushes were difficult to acknowledge and often experienced in a very private way:

> My first sign was when I had those, what they call hot flushes. They don't start off at the feet and come very hot. Mine is more of a funny feeling, like when you've been sunburnt. I get very, very hot. If I'm sitting here and I'm talking to you and I get hot and uncomfortable I don't suddenly go 'Phew, it's terrible'. I'd just continue talking to you and if I got really hot I'd just take my cardigan off. I don't even think I'd mention it.

Again, this quote suggests some external social norm of common experience ('what *they* call hot flushes' – emphasis added) that the individual women is not party to, and feels different from. However, a common theme is that these bodily signs of menopause are best dealt with privately.

Jill's account of her menopause nicely illustrates the dual influences of both her perceptions of her bodily changes – she did not like her body changing – *and* the social impact of the menopause which is defined and constructed within social relationships:

> I think I'm in the menopause . . . just. Physically I have just a slight change in temperature, warm, not uncomfortable. I don't like it, changing, just in my face, but I feel it. It's very difficult to sort out. (*Pause*) I don't know. There's so many strands, ageing, sexuality, being attracted to men, then there's your mother, your husband and there's your children, everyone reacting to you. It's not just one thing.

Hot flushes have a bodily reality that is variable in intensity but which clearly has a social significance. Meanings of menopause in relation to gendered discourses of ageing and reproduction are considered in sections that follow.

Menopause as non-event: continuation of the self

The most commonly voiced theme was that the menopause had no or few consequences for the women at all. This was by far the most common response to the second main question about the impact of the menopause. They described a continuance of the self that was not dramatically changed by the menopause. This is consistent with the results of epidemiological studies (Kaufert *et al.*, 1992; McKinlay *et al.*, 1992), and it challenges a biomedical, deficiency-disease, model of the menopause. The quotes below appear to be more consistent with a view of menopause as a natural developmental stage, having little impact upon women:

Nothing particular. I'm more concerned with getting on with the next week.

Nothing really, it's part of life.

It hasn't made me anything better or anything worse. I feel no different in myself.

It didn't have any consequences for me.

Discussions of bodily changes were to some extent separated from changes 'in themselves', which was perhaps partly due to the framing of the questions and partly a reflection of the mind–body dualism which is pervasive in Western cultures. Thus there may be a splitting between the 'normal' self and the less controllable body. To ignore or separate bodily changes from evaluations of themselves could also be a discursive strategy actively to avoid the potential impact of negative social constructions of the menopause – the menopause happens to the body, not to the self:

I didn't like my periods being irregular or my body feeling different but in myself, well, I still felt that inside I hadn't changed.

I had a few physical changes but nothing else; I'm still the same person.

In the following quote Nicky discriminated between different aspects of her menopause:

Physically it was nice not to have periods but that was counterbalanced by the sweats. Emotionally I was quite happy about it.

By constructing the menopause as a low impact event, these women had a sense of the continuity of themselves across the menopause transition.

No more periods!

The cessation of menstruation is the main sign of the menopause in medical and scientific discourse. However, when women talked about this change they generally talked about it as a *positive* change in their lives. Again this theme brings together material bodily change and their discursive meanings. In their accounts menstruation is positioned as unpleasant and troublesome; the cessation of menstruation is then experienced as a relief, since something unpleasant is taken away:

It's nice to get it over with and not have periods any more.

I'll be quite happy when it's all over and done with.

I've never enjoyed having periods.

Relief was expressed particularly by women who had experienced heavy periods. For example, Joan recounted:

I was a person who suffered an awful lot with my periods and it stopped me doing a lot of things when I was younger because I had such heavy periods and now I can do anything I want. At one time if we planned to go away for the weekend and I had a period I was in such a state that I didn't want to go away. But now I've lost all that now which is beautiful!

It might make life a lot easier maybe having gone through it. I won't have to bother about periods. On such heavy days it's quite difficult to go out anywhere. I don't use Tampax now. I've read it can cause toxic shock. I've read it in the paper and heard about it on television so I try not to use it now. It would make life easier and be a relief.

It is noteworthy that none of the women talked about the cessation of menstruation in negative terms – the ending of periods was not seen as a loss but a gain. Within this theme traditional stereotypes of the grieving menopausal woman are challenged and replaced by an image of the menopause as having positive consequences.

The cessation of periods was constituted as a positive change in women's lives, and this was particularly the case for those for whom periods had been problematic, i.e. either heavy or painful. Menstruation was constructed as a nuisance, as limiting activities, and even a health hazard (toxic shock). It is interesting that the experience of menstruation was separated in women's accounts from the issue of reproduction and fertility. The ending of periods was experienced as a relief by practically all of the women who mentioned it. On the one hand this theme challenges traditional stereotypes of the depressed menopausal woman, but on the other hand it is consistent with wider cultural discourses and practices that associate menstruation with incapacity, shame and dirt (Laws, 1990; Ussher, 1991).

Menopause as end of reproductive life

An awareness of the menopause as the end of a woman's reproductive phase of life was apparent in several women's accounts. However, the majority challenged the view of the menopausal woman experiencing loss and grief at this time. In the contexts of most women's lives, reproductive decisions tended to be made earlier. For example:

I never really wanted to have children so it never really worried me in that way. I'll be quite pleased in some ways.

It won't make any difference for me because I was sterilised at 38 and I won't feel that I can't have children any more because I've been quite happy not having children for the last twelve years.

It gives you the feeling it's the end of something, your reproductive time. But I mean I think that ended a little time ago. I wouldn't have dreamt of having a baby after 45 I mean, so I'm not looking for that.

Nevertheless, there was an awareness that some – *other* – women might feel unhappy about not having reproductive potential:

> Whether there comes a point when you think that I can't have any more children or whatever, I don't know.

Several, however, made tentative comments referring rather obliquely to the possibility of feeling 'incomplete' after the menopause. Susan had had a hysterectomy, after having three children:

> I've never felt an incomplete person. I've got three healthy children and it's never bothered me.

Fiona clearly expressed concerns about 'completeness' even though she had had children:

> Emotionally, I can't give birth. I can't have children any more. I think that might be a huge block. Not that you might want to have any more but psychologically you know that you can't have any kids any more . . . I would never have another child anyway, but I have thought about it. God, I can never have children any more, so I think there's part of you maybe feels that you're not a complete woman any more.

Here, a 'complete' woman is one who is fertile and has reproductive potential. Female sexuality has also been linked to reproductive potential which is then seen to end at the menopause (Gannon, 1994). The women's comments appeared to reflect a broad gendered discourse which positions only fertile or reproductive women as 'complete' and valued. For one woman, Toni, this process was obvious in that within her culture she was deemed unfit for marriage because she had fertility problems:

> It affected me in the sense that I couldn't have children. Being of Greek parents they used to try and organise your life and marry you off and I used to find that there was no way I could ever marry because I couldn't have children. It was just one of those things. That was the only thing that really upset me, not being able to get married and having children. The doctors might be able to do something about it now. It's a bit late now.

To conform to social and cultural norms Toni needed to be fertile in order to be considered as a potential marriage partner.

Material events also influenced the meaning of the menopause as a reproductive event for Maria, who described how eight years ago her 4-year-old son was killed in a car accident:

> . . . that's had a devastating effect on my life and also on my relationship with my husband. It's just not a happy situation and it's not something I've got over.

When asked about the consequences of the menopause, she said:

> In terms of periods and all that kind of thing life is much easier. It means
> that I'm not concerned about being pregnant if that's a concern, but for
> me I would have been happy if I had been, given my personal circum-
> stances.

While she acknowledges relief from concerns about periods and pregnancy,
in the context of her grief, she reflects on the possibility that she possibly
could have been.

Most women actively challenged the stereotypical view of the
menopausal woman as grieving lost fertility, although there was an awareness of a view of the older woman as being 'incomplete'. Particular material
events and cultural influences also shaped the meaning of the menopause as
a reproductive event.

The menopause as a sign of ageing

Here the menopause was seen to signify ageing. However, ageing, like
menopause, had multiple meanings in women's accounts and could signify
mortality, physical changes and a change in social status as an older woman.
The menopause is inextricably linked to age, and this was evident in several
of the women's accounts. Being 50 and the menopause were talked about
interchangeably. However, the majority challenged the assumption that the
menopause marks the beginning of old age.

Several women included comments about ageing in their accounts of the
consequences of the menopause, but many also resisted this discourse by not
applying it to their own experience:

> It doesn't make me feel older if that's what you mean.

> Getting old (*laughs*) but it doesn't bother me that much. I don't get hang-
> ups about it.

These two women linked menopause and ageing but distanced themselves
from seeing themselves as 'older', which was negatively connoted with the
expectation that 'hang-ups' would result.

Several women did voice concerns about ageing. For Jill, age had always
been a concern and had negative meanings including mortality, time running
out and fears of being old:

> I think once the menopause is over you feel as though you're fast
> approaching retirement and it doesn't seen so very long now to being old.
> It's a bit frightening that it's only a few years away and there's still lots of
> things to do. I think in ten years' time I'll be old. But then I'm somebody
> who worried about my age. I don't like to think or talk about my age so I
> think that's the consequence of the menopause probably for me.

Anne worked with older people and felt that this influenced the meaning of
the menopause:

I'm more concerned with getting on with my life . . . As far as the future is concerned I've stopped looking too far ahead, each day is too precious. When you see the problems of advanced age you just learn to live for one day or one week at a time. As far as myself is concerned, so long as I'm independent that's all that matters.

For Anne, awareness of ageing led her to appreciate current life, in contrast to Jill, who saw ageing as a frightening process. In both these accounts the menopause draws women's attention to the ageing process and ultimately to their own mortality.

Other women located the meaning of ageing and the menopause more clearly within their social context. Toni talked about feeling older at work:

I've never looked at myself as being in my fifties but I find that I do feel it more now . . . because I'm working with people that are 17, 18, and I feel older now because of the way they are, unless it's me that's changed because they're whispering, oh, what did you get up to last night, blah, blah, blah, blah. It suddenly makes you think, 'God I'm 50, where has my life gone', but before I never had these feelings at all. I don't know whether it's to do with the menopause or not or just your working environment.

In this context being 50 meant being different from her peers. She was grappling with the reasons for feeling suddenly older: Was it the menopause or her work (feeling excluded or separate from the younger people at work) which exacerbated her other feelings about being 50? This is a clear example of the complex interplay between age, which materially involves physical change, and its discursive meaning, and also how the salience of age and the menopause can be modified by social context.

In the next example, Ruth talks about ageing and physical appearance and draws upon discourses of both gender and ageing when discussing her menopause:

I think it's awful. I don't think it's fair that women should have this at all but there you are. But I feel that over 50, women, generally, it's difficult. They may not look older, because modern things, dyeing hair or exercise or what have you. I still think that after 50, it's very hard for a woman . . . she can look quite good but she loses that girlishness in most cases, there are few exceptions. Men have the advantage. Generally speaking much harder over 50 for a woman to be young in her mind as well as how she looks.

Here ageing is distressing because, in contrast to men, the 'ideal woman' has to both look *and* feel young to be valued. There is a conflict between how mid-aged women are and how they 'should' be. To look and feel good means to look and feel young. In this account, women are seen to have a difficulty or problem, although this view is resisted to some extent – 'I don't think it's fair'.

The older woman is variously represented in these accounts as being different – for example from younger people at work and in physical appearance – and faces an additional task of negotiating the gap between inevitable physical ageing and perceived demands, as a woman, to look young. Here, discourses about ageing and gender combined to devalue older women. While the majority challenged and resisted these assumptions some women clearly felt diminished by them. Itzin (1986) describes the pervasiveness and oppressive nature of ageism and sexism, and the split created in women's experience:

> Because of the extent to which we have internalised age-sex stereotypes we lead double lives. We live both our 'reality' and the 'reality' of the oppression. That is to say, we live the lie about us. We submit to the stereotypes and resist them simultaneously.
>
> (Itzin, 1986:129)

Veronica recounted a direct experience of discrimination at home:

> Emotionally, I don't see it as an emotional problem. I just think it's part of living. My son and husband tease me, I'm old, I'm stupid, I'm this, that and the other.

There is a direct contrast here between her own construction of the menopause, which normalises her experience, and her family's perspective that diminishes her.

An alternative, more emancipatory discourse relating to age, voiced by several women, was of the menopause as a marker or point in time to reflect about the past and to move on to a future that could be planned:

> It brings home to you that perhaps you're in the last half of life. You know 50 is the mid-century, but there's more you can do, fit in, take up. I think as a consequence of that I've sat and taken stock a little bit about life. You sit and think, where are we going from here, what do I want to do now? It's a time for a bit of reflection about where you're going over the next few years.

Women's constructions of the menopause in terms of ageing were variable: it could be a neutral process, a distressing concern or a positive marker in life. Discourses around ageing and gender which position the older woman as unattractive or invisible clearly influence the subjectivity of the 50-year-old woman. However, these stereotypes were also challenged in the women's accounts. Some women voiced concern about mortality, which could lead to fear or a greater appreciation of life.

Staving off the unknown: menopause as unspoken taboo

This theme very much reflects women's use of language and their negotiation of available discourses when asked about the menopause. Although the interviewer used the word 'menopause', the women tended not to. Nor did they use other terms, such as 'change' in their accounts. 'It' and 'this' were frequently used, and the menopause was referred to obliquely, suggesting that the menopause is not commonly discussed directly. It is also possible that, given the negative connotations of menopause reflected in many of the themes above, women choose not to position themselves as menopausal. The absence of a positive language was noticeable. For example:

. . . that side of it is out of the way.

. . . not fair that women should have this.

I've accepted it, wishing it was all over.

Within this theme women referred to some process or event which they appeared not to be currently experiencing, but were attempting to stave off or avoid. However, implicit in their accounts is the idea that if they did stop to find out what 'it' was, there would be negative consequences. For example, Denise said:

You have to put yourself in order as well because when you go through something like that you become like you are not interested in yourself . . . like you want to let yourself go. If I was indoors, if I didn't have to go out to the business I would have been worse. You have to occupy your mind. So I think for some women who have nothing to do it must be really terrible for them. They must sit down and think about it and become depressed.

When talking about other women, who were not working or occupied, she reveals concerns about becoming depressed or out of control ('let[ting] yourself go'). Denise implies that if she did not keep in control she too might experience negative consequences of the menopause. Ironically, this strategy might itself prevent her from finding out what would happen if she did experience her menopause without keeping control or keeping busy. Keeping busy was mentioned by several women. For example:

I'm busy, I really don't think about it a lot.

ANNA I don't think it will affect my life at all because I don't think I would let it anyway because if there were problems then I'm the sort of person who would get it sorted. I'm too busy anyway to worry about it.

As well as keeping busy, Anna positions herself as someone who would not let 'it' affect her, thereby avoiding negative expectations of her own menopause. For others, there was talk of acceptance of something that was vague and unspecified, but again had negative connotations:

Not to let it get to you basically. I mean it's something that you can't particularly stop. It's something that you're going to have to deal with and accept presumably and accept it gracefully.

> There's a lot to go through from 45 onwards. I've accepted it and I'm wishing it was all over and done with and finished with. I take it in my stride, it's nature and that's it.

Here there is a sense of inevitability of having to go through a vague but difficult process, but it is not clear where the difficulty lies in these accounts. There is a feeling of something happening that these women did not like but which was not named or expressed. Rather, there was a need to accept, and even to do so with grace.

Two women described how by taking HRT they avoided imagined consequences of the menopause. Sue said that she had been feeling depressed and irritable, particularly with her husband, before she took HRT. She commented:

> Now it's wiped out. It's a non-event.

Her irritability and depression were, it seems, reframed within a biomedical discourse, in the context of her relationship, as menopausal symptoms and 'treated' by HRT.

Marie is married with a young daughter. She described how she felt that her image of a menopausal woman did not fit within the context of her current life. Taking HRT was seen to be a way of resolving this conflict:

> I don't know because I'm staving them off. Well, I feel OK about myself, it's what other people desire and need from me that's the difficulty. It's how I have to be as a wife and a mother to a young child. I've got to be there and I've got to be in action but personally I wouldn't mind going around with a granny cardigan, taking up knitting . . . but it's not right for the family. So I've staved off the menopause for a while until my husband catches up with me [her husband is younger than she is]. Until he catches up with me I've got to keep the pace going.

For Marie, being a mother and a wife meant being very actively looking after other people's needs. She was very much aware of prescribed roles in the family, and how as a mother of a young child she 'should' be and act differently than she felt she was able to do. In this context the menopause was seen as positive in that the 'granny' could slow down and do as she wished, without having to conform to family demands.

Discussion

The final theme, 'staving off the unknown: menopause as unspoken taboo', seems to relate in complex ways to the other themes described above. By referring obliquely to the menopause ('it', 'this', etc.) and by keeping busy, avoiding and staving off the menopause with HRT, women were going through the menopause but attempting to control or avoid its experience. Concerns about 'let[ting] yourself go', 'becoming depressed', it being 'terrible' and 'suffering' were indirectly mentioned. Instead of voicing fears or concerns openly, the women talked about keeping busy, putting oneself in order, getting it sorted, not letting it get to you and taking HRT.

There appeared to be a fear of the unspoken and the unknown. Images of chaos and loss of control and inability to deal with life came to mind when reading the transcripts, as if some women were negotiating the varied and often contradictory constructions of the menopause, which were difficult to locate in language and directly challenge. The other themes, which may underpin these fears, drew upon discourses around gender and ageing, about reproduction and the position of mid-aged and older women as 'other' than ideal (young, reproductive, fertile and attractive [looking young]). These negative constructions of the menopause and ageing were challenged by some women, but 'staved off' by others. Perhaps, in order to retain self-esteem in this context, some women took HRT and others avoided the issue by keeping busy.

These accounts may also reflect polarised social discourses of menopause, as disease and decline on the one hand and as an unproblematic natural phase of life on the other. These dichotomous constructions frame women's experiences in unnecessary extremes. For example, in order to avoid the unknown horrors of one pole (problematic), many of the women we interviewed faced a complex discursive task in interpreting their menopause in terms of the other pole (no problem).

There was also a sense, in some of the women's accounts, of fears of being out of control which might relate to long-standing stereotypes of the menopausal woman as mad, masculine or witch-like (Greer, 1991). It is interesting that within these gendered discourses the older woman becomes either invisible, or attempts to conform to the 'ideal', or becomes a threat (difficult to control). During the reproductive years, the causes of women's distress have been located in their reproductive bodies (Ussher, 1989). After the menopause we might expect to become free from such biological attributions in view of the change in reproductive status. It is ironic that at the menopause 'lack of hormones' becomes the problem and another explanation for female problems.

It is interesting that, in contrast to those applied to women, cultural stereotypes of sexuality in the ageing male reflect expectations of continuity, virility and potency. Sexual difficulties in men have often been attributed to the female partner in studies of heterosexual couples, i.e. women cause men's sexual problems (Gannon, 1994). Within medical discourses there is an expectation that older women should retain their sexuality, by using hormonal treatments (Sheehy, 1992). Here the woman's sexuality is positioned very much as being within her body. Thus the menopausal women can be seen as losing her sexuality, but at the same time having it redeemed by medical treatment. Such discursive practices are likely to increase anxiety about sexuality and perpetuate images of the older woman that limit her freedom to make her own choices. In fact, studies suggest that the menopause is not necessarily associated with changes in sexuality: some women report a decrease, others an increase, but the majority no change in sexual activity and enjoyment (Gannon, 1994).

The promotion of HRT can be seen as one way of attempting to maintain women within traditional gender roles – her essential womanhood can be restored. Portrayals of the post-menopausal woman without HRT emphasise what 'proper' or 'desirable' femininity is by showing what women are like when they no longer have it (Hunt, 1994). Nonetheless, there is, particularly in the UK, a concern by some doctors and pharmaceutical companies about the 'low' uptake and adherence rates for HRT (Spector, 1989). It is estimated that 10 per cent of menopausal women currently take HRT in the UK, and that a sizeable proportion stop taking it within the first six months. So a large proportion of menopausal women are in practice resisting this 'solution' to the menopause. In a recent interview study (Hunter *et al.*, 1996), we found that there was a general preference not to take medication (including HRT) amongst mid-aged women, unless severe symptoms were experienced. Whether or not symptoms were described as severe or not was influenced by both material and discursive factors, such as the frequency of night sweats and the reactions of others. Once again we see the split between constructions of the menopause (disease/natural event) and the way in which the menopause can shift from being a natural process to a medical problem. In order to legitimately receive (medical) help the menopause is to be constructed as a problem, and can then be 'normalised' by HRT (Daly, 1995).

CONCLUSIONS

Despite the pervasiveness of the medical model in scientific and media accounts, biomedical language and practice does not adequately reflect women's complex subjectivity about the menopause which is varied, multidimensional and contextually determined. The biomedical discourse was used when women initially defined themselves in relation to the menopause (in terms of bodily changes), but less so when they talked about the impact of the menopause upon themselves. In general, the women described the menopause as having little overall impact, they talked of continuation of the self and relief from menstruation; reproductive decisions, on the whole, were faced earlier in their lives. Women's accounts of the impact of the menopause were complex, varying with material circumstances – for example, working environment, hot flushes, past pregnancies and heavy periods. Six main themes were described, drawing upon social and cultural discourses about gender, reproduction and ageing, which the participants in the study challenged to varying degrees. The accounts illustrate how bodily changes are socially constructed and how social constructions influence experience of the body in an interactive process.

Women can face a considerable discursive task at the menopause – to maintain a positive sense of self amidst menopause and age changes (both bodily and discursive) which are unduly negatively connoted. The majority of the women we spoke to did this by describing menopause as having little impact on themselves, being pleased to be free from periods and unaffected by not being able to have children. While women challenged assumptions based on biomedical and psychoanalytical theories, they did so by positioning themselves in relation to these discourses – for example, by saying the end of the reproductive life-stage is not a problem or the menopause did not produce symptoms. Other ways of negotiating negative images of menopause was to see other women as being more prone to problems, and by avoiding or staving off the menopause by keeping busy or taking HRT.

We would argue that fears engendered by sexist and ageist discourses were difficult to talk about directly, and tended to be avoided in a variety of ways. By 'staving off' the menopause some women did not have the opportunity to find out whether their experience would in fact conform to their image; in this way taboos about menopause are easily maintained. In general, we would expect that experience of the menopause would be more positive than expectations (Neugarten, 1979; Martin, 1987). A similar process has been described by Rich (1990) in relation to the maintenance of ageist attitudes:

> Given the hazards of passing and the fact that so many old people themselves have lived a lifetime of fear, contempt and patronizing of the old, it is easy to see why most old people share with other members of society the stereotyped view of old people and also refuse to define themselves as old.

> (Rich, 1990: 56)

Such avoidance divides woman and depoliticises the menopause and ageing.

In negotiating discursive meanings of bodily changes, the women grappled with several dichotomies when making sense of their own experience: for example, the menopause as disease or natural process; menopause as private or public experience. The split between body and self was also evident. The lack of an emancipatory language with which to talk about menopause, which did not polarise the experience, was noticeable. Theoretical models, such as the biomedical and the bio-psycho-social model, reflect and maintain these dichotomies. A material–discursive framework would seem to be a more helpful way of understanding the complex interplay between bodily, social and cultural meanings.

'Menopause' is a vague, blanket term which has multiple meanings. In order to demystify the menopause it might be beneficial to promote a language which is more specific and which discriminates between different aspects of the process. For example, the women we interviewed talked about and evaluated hot flushes, menstrual and reproductive changes quite differently. Several women commented that the menopause is still a taboo and that few opportunities exist at this stage of life to discuss feelings and experiences in depth. One of us has been working with groups of mid-aged women in order to provide a place for discussion about social and cultural meanings of the menopause and to examine their impact upon experience of this stage of life (Liao and Hunter, 1994; Hunter and Liao, 1995). Such groups might help to develop common understandings, to acknowledge differences between women and to reinforce the sense of agency and resistance to stereotyped images that the mid-aged women in this study clearly voiced in their personal accounts.

Further understanding is needed of the differences between women, in terms of sexuality, culture, economic and life experiences, as well as the cohort of differences as each generation approaches the menopause.

REFERENCES

Avis, N.E., Kaufert, P.A., Lock, M., McKinlay, S.M. and Vass, K. (1993) The Evolution of Menopausal Symptoms. In H.G. Burger (ed.), *The Menopause*, London: Baillière Tindall.

Ballinger, S., Cobbin, D., Krivanek, J. and Saunders, D. (1979) Life Stresses and Depression in the Menopause, *Maturitas*, 1, 191–199.

Beyenne, Y. (1986) Cultural Significance and Physiological Manifestations of Menopause: A Biocultural Analysis, *Culture, Medicine and Psychiatry*, 10, 47–71.

Burman, E. and Parker, I. (eds) (1993) *Discourse Analytic Research: Repertoires and Readings of Texts in Action*, London: Routledge.

Daly, J. (1995) Caught in the Web: The Social Construction of Menopause as Disease, *Journal of Reproductive and Infant Psychology*, 13, 115–126.

Davis, D.L. (1986) The Meaning of Menopause in a Newfoundland Fishing Village, *Culture, Medicine and Society*, 10, 73–94.

Deutsch, H. (1945) *The Psychology of Women*, vol. 2, New York: Grune and Stratton.

Dickson, G.L. (1990) A Feminist Poststructural Analysis of the Knowledge of Menopause, *Advances in Nursing Science*, 12, 15–31.

Flint, M. (1975) The Menopause: Reward or Punishment, *Psychosomatics*, 16, 161–163.

Foucault, M. (1972) *The Archaeology of Knowledge and the Discourse on Language*, New York: Pantheon.

Gannon, L. (1994) Sexuality and the Menopause. In P.Y.L. Choi and P. Nicholson (eds), *Female Sexuality*, London: Harvester Wheatsheaf.

Greene, J.G. (1983) Bereavement and Social Support at the Climacteric, *Maturitas*, 5, 115–125.

Greene, J.G. and Cooke, D.J. (1980) Life Stress and Symptoms at the Climacterium, *British Journal of Psychiatry*, 136, 486–491.

Greer, G. (1991) *The Change*, London: Hamish Hamilton.

Henriques, J., Hollway, W., Urwin, C., Venn, C. and Walkerdine, V. (1984) *Changing the Subject: Psychology, Social Regulation and Subjectivity*, London: Methuen.

Hollway, W. (1989) *Subjectivity and Method in Psychology: Gender, Meaning and Science*, London: Sage.

Holte, A. (1992) Influences of Natural Menopause on Health Complaints: A Prospective Study of Healthy Norwegian Women, *Maturitas*, 14(2), 127–141.

Hunt, K. (1994) A Cure for All Ills? Constructions of the Menopause and the Chequered Fortunes of Hormone Replacement Therapy. In S. Wilkinson and C. Kitzinger (eds), *Women and Health: Feminist Perspectives*, London: Taylor Francis.

Hunter, M.S. (1990) *Your Menopause*, London: Pandora Press.
——(1992) The SE England Longitudinal Study of the Climacteric and Postmenopause, *Maturitas*, 14(2), 117–126.
——(1996) Editorial: Depression and the Menopause, *British Medical Journal*, 313, 1217–1218.
Hunter, M.S. and Liao, K.L.M. (1995) Problem Solving Groups for Mid-Aged Women in General Practice: A Pilot Study, *Journal of Reproductive and Infant Psychology*, 13(2), 147–151.
Hunter, M.S., O'Dea, I. and Britten, N. (1996) Decision Making and Hormone Replacement Therapy: A Qualitative Analysis, *Social Science and Medicine*, (in press).
Itzin, C. (1986) Media Images of Women: The Social Construction of Ageism and Sexism. In S. Wilkinson (ed.), *Feminist Social Psychology*, Milton Keynes, Open University Press.
Kaufert, P.A. (1982) Myth and Menopause, *Society, Health and Illness*, 11, 141–166.
Kaufert, P.A., Gilbert, P. and Tate, R. (1992) The Manitoba Project: A Re-Examination of the Relationship Between Menopause and Depression, *Maturitas*, 14(2), 143–156.
Krafft-Ebing, R. von (1877) Uber Imesin in Klimakterium, *Psychiatry*, 34, 407.
Laws, S. (1990) *Issues of Blood*, London: Macmillan.
Leiblum, S. R. and Swartzman, L.S. (1986) Women's Attitudes About the Menopause: An Update, *Maturitas*, 81, 47–56.
Liao, K.L.M. and Hunter, M.S. (1994) The Women's Midlife Project: An Evaluation of Psychological Services for Mid-Aged Women in General Practice, *Clinical Psychology Forum*, 65, 19–22.
McKinlay, S.M., Brambilla, D.J. and Posner, J. (1992) The Normal Menopause Transition, *Maturitas*, 14(2), 103–116.
Marks, D.F. (1996) Health Psychology in Context, *Journal of Health Psychology*, 1, 7–21.
Martin, E. (1987) *The Woman in the Body*, Milton Keynes: Open University Press.
Matthews, K.A., Wing, R.R. and Kuller, L.H. (1990) Influences of Natural Menopause on Psychological Characteristics and Symptoms of Middle-Aged Healthy Women, *Journal of Consulting and Clinical Psychology*, 58, 345–363.
Neugarten, B. (1979) Time, Age and the Life Cycle, *American Journal of Psychiatry*, 136, 887–894.
Parlee, M. (1976) Social Factors in the Psychology of Menstruation, Birth and Menopause, *Primary Care*, 3, 477–490.
Payer, L. (1991) The Menopause in Various Cultures. In H. Burger and M. Boulet (eds), *A Portrait of the Menopause*, London: Parthenon.
Potter, J. and Wetherell, M. (1987) *Discourse and Social Psychology: Beyond Attitudes and Beliefs*, London: Sage.
Rice, P.L. (1995) Pog laus tsis khaub hcaws lawm: The Meaning of Menopause in Hmong Women, *Journal of Reproductive and Infant Psychology*, 3, 79–92.
Rich C. (1990) Ageing, Ageism and Feminist Avoidance. In H. Crowley and S. Himmelweit (eds), *Knowing Women*, Milton Keynes: Open University Press.
Seibold, C., Richards, L.R. and Simon, D. (1994) Feminist Method and Qualitative Research About Midlife, *Journal of Advanced Nursing*, 19, 394–402.
Sheehy, G. (1992) *Menopause: The Silent Passage*, New York: Random House.
Showalter, E. (1987) *The Female Malady*, London: Virago.
Spector, T.D. (1989) Use of Oestrogen Replacement Therapy in High Risk Groups in the United Kingdom, *British Medical Journal*, 299, 1434–1435.
Studd, J.W.W. and Smith, R.N.J. (1993) Oestradiol and Testosterone Implants in Menopause. In H. Burger (ed), *The Menopause*, London: Baillière Tindall.

Ussher, J.M. (1989) *The Psychology of the Female Body*, London: Routledge.

——(1991) *Women's Madness: Misogyny or Mental Illness?*, London: Harvester Wheatsheaf.

Walkerdine, V. (1986) Post-Structural Theory and Everyday Social Practices: The Family and the School. In S. Wilkinson (ed.), *Feminist Social Psychology*, Milton Keynes: Open University Press.

Whitehead, M.I. (1994) The Pieter van Keep Memorial Lecture. In G. Berg and M. Hammar (eds), *The Modern Management of the Menopause*, London: Parthenon.

Wilbush, J. (1979) La Menespausie – The Birth of a Syndrome, 1, 145–157.

Wilson, R.A. (1966) *Feminine Forever*, New York: Evans.

Worcester, N. and Whatley, M.H. (1992) The Selling of HRT: Playing the Fear Factor, *Feminist Review*, 41, 1–26.

12 Anorexic bodies and the discursive production of feminine excess*

Helen M. Malson

INTRODUCTION

Over the last three decades the subject of 'anorexia nervosa' has received considerable attention in psychology and elsewhere, and there is now a vast literature seeking to characterise and explain 'anorexia' from a variety of perspectives (see e.g. Hsu, 1989; Malson, 1997a). Underlying this apparent diversity in knowledges of 'anorexia' there are also, however, a number of theoretical and philosophical assumptions that many 'mainstream' perspectives share in common. Many psychological perspectives remain firmly allied to positivist research agendas and retain, at least implicitly, a medical or quasi-medical conception of 'anorexia' as a distinct clinical entity. Hence, theory and research in this field has been largely concerned with producing objective 'facts' about 'anorexia nervosa' as an *individual* pathology; with identifying *individual* characteristics thought to be typical of those diagnosed as anorexic and with seeking to provide individualistic (and often universalistic) causal explanations (Yager, 1982). These shared assumptions lead to a repeated re-production of otherwise varied accounts which, first, reify the concept of 'anorexia nervosa' as a 'natural' clinical entity and which, second, tend to produce decontextualised and individualistic understandings of 'anorexia' by representing 'anorexia' in terms of *individual* characteristics and *individual* personal histories and by emphasising differences rather than similarities between those diagnosed as 'anorexic' and those not. Within this context the production of 'anorexic' bodies and of (psychological) meanings associated with those bodies has often been conceptualised as an individual rather than a sociocultural matter, while attention to the physical aspects of 'anorexia' – whether in terms of proposed organic aetiology or secondary effects of starvation – has retained an almost exclusive biomedical orientation.

It is, however, increasingly acknowledged that social factors must play some part in explanations of 'anorexia' (Shaw, 1995). The cultural idealisation of female thinness (Garner and Garfinkel, 1980) and the concomitant prevalence of body dissatisfaction, dieting, bingeing and purging among women (Grunewald, 1985; Gilbert, 1986) and girls (Wardle and Marshland,

1990; Hill and Robinson, 1991) has been well documented. Indeed, dieting and an attendant 'diet mentality' might now be described as both descriptively and prescriptively normative (Polivy and Herman, 1987). And it is clearly important that eating disorders be understood within this contemporary cultural context (Hsu, 1989). Hence researchers have, for example, examined the effects that fashion magazines may have on 'eating psychopathogy' in young women (e.g. Shaw, 1995). Such research very usefully moves the focus away from the (pathologised) individual girl or woman towards her social context. However, much of this socioculturally oriented work on 'anorexia' is also limited in two important respects.

First, there is a tendency to focus only on social pressures to 'diet' and attain a 'fashionably thin' physique to the exclusion of other sociocultural factors that may be pertinent (thus suggesting, perhaps inadvertently, that societal factors play a role in eating disorders *only* up to a point). It is of course essential that the pernicious cultural dictates about the female body promulgated by the fashion and diet industries come under severe critical scrutiny. But it is also essential that sociocultural analyses of 'anorexia' go further by analysing the *multiple* meanings of women's 'dieting' and 'thinness' and by exploring how other aspects of the sociocultural context may also be imbricated in the problem of 'anorexia'. For, 'anorexics' are not simply 'super-dieters' (e.g. Polivy and Herman, 1985), striving (overly) hard to achieve feminine beauty; 'anorexia' is a much more complex problem. As several feminist authors (e.g. Brumberg, 1988; Orbach, 1993) have argued, 'anorexia' is expressive of complex gender-political issues and dilemmas. Women's concerns with controlling their bodies have, for example, been interpreted in terms of our lack of power in other areas of life (Lawrence, 1984), while the diminutive 'anorexic' figure has been interpreted as an expression of women's lack of status in our patriarchal society (Chernin, 1981). The ways in which contemporary Western culture is imbricated in the problem of 'anorexia' are multiple and the 'anorexic' body may sustain a variety of complex and even contradictory meanings.

Second, there is often a lack of adequate theorising of the relationship between individual and society; of *how* society is imbricated in the seemingly individual problem of 'anorexia'. There is a tendency to rely on undertheorised notions such as (over-) 'internalisation' (of cultural messages about dieting and female beauty) which fail to question or transgress the 'traditional' individual–society dichotomy and which ultimately leave unchallenged the (socially constructed) notion of 'anorexia' as '*individual* pathology'. Yet, the high profile of 'anorexia' in both the popular and academic press suggests a cultural fascination with eating disorders. It indicates that 'anorexia' is not simply an *individual* pathology but is also of wider cultural significance (see also Malson and Ussher, 1996b). Like some other conditions (see Sontag 1978, 1989), 'anorexia', can be understood as a metaphor for, and a manifestation of, particular sociocultural concerns and dilemmas. It is 'expressive' of cultural conflicts between mass consumption and normative thinness (Turner, 1992); between the indulgent consumer and the controlled and abstinent worker of capitalist society (Bordo, 1990); and between feminist politics and normative ideologies of femininity. In short, 'anorexia' may be expressive of a multiplicity of societal as well as individual concerns and conflicts about femininity, gender power relations, consumption, control and individualistic competitiveness (Brumberg, 1988; Malson and Ussher, 1996b).

'Anorexia' can thus be understood to be profoundly embedded in a variety of contemporary gender-specific cultural practices and ideologies so that 'anorexic' bodies are always-already located within multiple systems of significations and power relations (Malson, 1997). And from this perspective it is essential that 'anorexia' be theorised and researched in ways which attend to the multiple culturally constituted meanings of the 'anorexic body'; which place gender at the centre of analysis; and which seek to transgress the individual–society dichotomy that underlies the individualistic 'mainstream' knowledges of 'anorexia' as individual pathology.

The discourse-oriented approaches (see below), promoted in psychology by Walkerdine (1988), Potter and Wetherell (1987), Burman and Parker (1993) and others, seem particularly suited to such a task; first, because meaning is seen as constituted in discourses and discursive practices. Hence, 'anorexia' can be be more thoroughly located within its socioculturally specific contexts. And, second, such an approach thereby facilitates an analysis of the *multiple* and often contradictory meanings of 'anorexia' and 'anorexic' bodies as they are constituted in different discourses. However, in focusing on discourse, discursive approaches in psychology have often failed to attend to the physicality of the body or to other aspects of extra-discursive, material reality (see Chapter 1). Discourse analytic work, it has been argued, seems to attend to the (discursively constructed) *meanings* and not the corpo-*reality* of the body.

Discourse analysis of 'anorexic' bodies – and similarly of female reproductive bodies (see Chapters 10 and 11), of sexual bodies (see Chapters 5–9) or pathologised 'unruly' bodies (see Chapters 2–4) – brings this issue to the fore. For the 'anorexic' body is clearly embedded in a variety of discourses and discursive practices but it is equally clear that there are very serious physical dimensions to the problem of 'anorexia'.

Analyses of 'anorexia' must then seek to engage both with the discursive and the extra-discursive of 'anorexic' bodies. In this chapter I shall, therefore, explore how a discursive approach, informed by feminist poststructuralist and psychoanalytic theory, might also engage with the material physicality of the corpo-real (anorexic) body. Hence, after outlining the theoretical and method-ological approach adopted here, my discussion will draw on a discursive analysis of a series of interviews with twenty-three women, twenty-one of whom had been diagnosed as 'anorexic' and two who were self-diagnosed.[1] In particular, my analysis will explore the discursive production(s) of 'anorexic' bodies and female (reproductive) bodies, focusing on the discursive–material production (and destruction) of 'feminine excess'. In so doing I shall seek to illustrate how a discursive approach can attend to the physical extra-discursive as well as the discursive aspects of 'anorexic' and female reproductive embodiment.

A FEMINIST POSTSTRUCTURALIST APPROACH TO DISCOURSE

Like other discursive approaches in psychology, feminist poststructuralist approaches are premised on a reconceptualisation of language and discourse. Language is viewed not as a transparent medium through which the world can be objectively accessed. It does not simply describe or reflect some underlying reality (Potter and Wetherell, 1987). Rather, following de Saussure (1960), the relationship between the signifier and the signified, between language and reality, is problematised. It is an arbitrary relationship, maintained (and changed) through social convention. In poststructuralist approaches language is understood to be constitutive rather than reflective of reality (Parker, 1990). Discourses are viewed as social 'practices that systematically form the objects of which they speak' (Foucault, 1972: 49).

As Hall argues, this view of language is very different from the notion of language as reflective, for 'It implies the active work of selecting and presenting, of structuring and shaping; not merely the transmitting of an already-existing meaning, but the more active labour of *making things mean*' (Hall, 1982: 64).

Objects do not exist 'anterior' to discourse 'waiting' to be discovered and more or less accurately, objectively described (Foucault, 1977a). Rather, a discourse 'finds a way of limiting its domain, of defining what it is talking about, of giving it the status of an object – and therefore of making it manifest, nameable, and describable' (Foucault, 1972: 41). 'Anorexic' bodies and female reproductive bodies, like other bodies, are always-already caught up in discourse, in systems of meaning, of symbolic representations and power relations. And it is these discourses and discursive constructions that a poststructuralist discourse analysis seeks to explicate.

In viewing objects, events and experiences as constituted in discourse, a discourse-oriented approach also thereby transgresses the individual–society dichotomy inherent in conceptions of 'anorexia' as individual pathology and in psychology generally where identity is conceptualised as something residing within the sovereign unitary individual. From a poststructuralist perspective 'identity' is retheorised in terms of multiple subject positions constituted in discourse. Discourses do not simply reflect individual identities; rather, they produce a variety of subject positions from which a person speaks or is addressed (Foucault, 1972; Henriques et al., 1984). Subjectivity is constituted and reconstituted in talk and text (Wetherell and White, 1992), in social practice. In poststructuralist theory, then, subjectivity is both decentred and multiple. Foucault did not consider that discourses emerged

from 'the unity of the subject': 'discourse is not the majestic unfolding manifestation of a thinking, knowing, speaking subject, but, on the contrary, a
totality in which dispersion of the subject and his [*sic*] discontinuity with
himself may be determined' (1972: 54–55). That is, the subject is constituted
outside of herself in discourse: 'discoursing subjects are part of the discursive field . . . The discourse is not the place where pure subjectivity irrupts; it
is a space of positions and of differentiated functions for subjects'
(Foucault, 1978: 13). And because the subject is interpellated by many
discourses she is also multiply produced; dispersed across a number of
discourses. 'Femininity', for example, cannot therefore be considered to be a
consistent or unitary identity, originating from the female body or from the
individual woman. Rather, from a poststructuralist perspective, 'femininity'
is an 'unreliable' category that takes on a variety of sociohistorically contin-
gent shapes (Jardine, 1985; Poovey, 1988; Riley, 1988). It is multiply
produced in the various discourses that simultaneously constitute and regulate the female body in a variety of often conflicting ways.

In short, a discourse-oriented approach (particularly one informed by
feminist poststructuralist theory) enables attention to the multiple discursively constructed meanings of the female body and the 'anorexic' body. It
also provides a more thorough theorisation of the ways in which society is
imbricated in the problem of 'anorexia nervosa'. It transgresses the individual–society, internal–external dichotomy, locating (anorexic) subjectivities
within their sociocultural and gender-specific discursive contexts.

DISCOURSING THE PHYSICAL BODY

A poststructuralist discursive approach is, therefore, particularly useful in
understanding anorexia and many other social psychological phenomena
because it locates the (anorexic) body in its multiple sociocultural and
gender-specific discursive contexts; because it attends to meanings, to the
ways in which objects, bodies and 'identities' are multiply constituted in
discourse; and because it thereby provides a theoretical framework which
goes beyond any individual–society dichotomy (see Henriques *et al.*, 1984;
Parker, 1990).

However, as noted above (see also the other authors in this volume), one
of the potential problems with some discursive approaches within
psychology is their tendency to focus on the (discursively constructed)
meanings (of the body or whatever) while excluding the extra-discursive, the
material, from consideration. By reductively equating 'discourse' with
'language' or text (see Foucault, 1972), some forms of discourse analysis fail
to (or choose not to) address that which is (in the narrow sense) outside of
the (conceptually dis-embodied) text. Discourse analysis can, and often
does, stop short of an engagement with the complex relationships between
the discursive and the extra-discursive. It can thereby re-produce a too-rigid
division between texts (of the body) and material realities (of the body) that

parallels rather than challenges the meaning–reality, mind–body, individual–society dichotomies of mainstream psychology and that again leaves
consideration of the physical body to the biomedical disciplines.

Excluding the material corpo-*reality* of the body from analysis clearly
becomes particularly problematic (and irresponsible) when considering
'anorexic' bodies. 'Anorexic' bodies, I have argued, cannot be adequately
theorised and researched apart from their sociocultural discursive contexts.
But neither should the material reality of women's self-starvation and
emaciation be disregarded. What I would like to argue here, however, is that
to engage with the discursive field, to explore the discursive constructions
(and regulations) of the female 'anorexic' body need not entail a disregard
for the extra-discursive, for the physicality of that body. For, as Foucault
(1978) argues, a *poststructuralist* discourse analysis is concerned not only
with an exploration of intra- and inter-discursive relations. In exploring the
discursive productions of objects, subject positions and truths, it also
precisely seeks to engage with the complex dependencies between the
discursive and the extra-discursive; between, for example, the transforma-
tions in 'medical discourse and a whole play of economic, political and
social changes' that clearly have extra-discursive, material dimensions to
them (Foucault, 1978: 13).

Poststructuralist discourse analysis engages, then, with the extra-discursive of social reality (social practices, institutions, etc.) and of corpo-real
bodies (their physical being) in a number of ways; first, because discourses
do not simply describe the body in one way or another, but are themselves
social practices with very real effects (Walkerdine, 1986, 1988). A discourse
is not simply a text that constructs one version of the world (or the body)
rather than another. By constituting bodies (or other objects) in particular
ways, discourses thereby constitute 'regimes of truth' that position subjects
in different ways, in different power relations; that engender particular social
practices and regulate (embodied) ways of being. Discourses of femininity,
as Dorothy Smith (1990) points out, involve whole sets of body management
practices, purchasing skills and the like which are simultaneously material
and discursive; they are worked out upon the corpo-real body and are integral to late capitalist modes of production and consumption.

A discourse is, then, a social practice 'composed of a whole assemblage
of activities, events, objects, selfings and epistemological precepts' (Prior,
1989: 3, quoted in Sutton, 1994). And discursive relations are neither simply
'internal to discourse' nor

> exterior to discourse . . . they are in a sense, at the limit of discourse . . .
> Of course, discourses are composed of signs; but what they do is more
> than use these signs to designate things. It is this *more* that renders them
> irreducible to the language (*langue*) and to speech.
>
> (Foucault, 1972: 46, 49)

That is, discourses as social practice have powerful, 'real' material effects (Walkerdine, 1986) on embodied subjects. They regulate subjects, defining what is normal and abnormal in various social settings and for various groups of people (Foucault, 1977a, 1979; Walkerdine, 1986). For instance, medical discourses that have constituted women's bodies as essentially pathological have had very serious consequences for women as embodied subjects. As many feminist and poststructuralist authors have demonstrated, the female reproductive body has been surrounded by numerous discourses and cultural practices (see Foucault, 1979; Ussher, 1991); both popular and medical discourses that have constituted that body in various conflicting, and often misogynistic, ways. The *female* reproductive body has been made a particular target of discourses and discursive practices surrounding sexuality, reproduction and the body (Foucault, 1979). It has, with very real material consequences, frequently been constituted as Other, as dangerous, uncontrolled or pathological; as a site and source of feminine excess (see e.g. Sayers, 1982; Showalter, 1985; Ussher, 1991).

A poststructuralist discursive approach is, therefore, particularly useful in analysing female bodies and 'anorexic' bodies from a feminist perspective, because discourses are understood to be about power (Foucault, 1977a, 1980; Couzens Hoy, 1986; Walkerdine, 1986). As Foucault (1979: 100) argued, 'it is in discourse that power and knowledge are joined together'. In constituting a field of knowledge, a discourse rules out other truths. 'The manifest discourse . . . is really no more than the repressive presence of what it does not say' (Foucault, 1972: 25), and:

> we should admit . . . that power produces knowledge (and not simply by encouraging it because it serves power or by applying it because it is useful); that power and knowledge directly imply one another; that there is no power relation without the correlative constitution of a field of knowledge, nor any knowledge that does not presuppose at the same time power relations.
>
> (Foucault, 1977a: 27)

Discourses regulate and discipline populations, individuals, bodies by constituting fields of knowledge, instituting truths, constituting subjectivities in particular ways. The embodied subject is positioned in discourse and subjected to normalising judgements (Foucault, 1977a, 1979; Walkerdine, 1988). Yet 'this micro-physics of power' that functions in discourse is not simply a repression. Rather, power/knowledge produces its reality:

> We must cease once and for all to describe the effects of power in negative terms: it 'excludes', it 'represses', it 'censors', it 'abstracts', it 'masks', it 'conceals'. In fact power produces; it produces reality, it produces domains of objects and rituals of truth.
>
> (Foucault, 1977a: 194)

And a discursive approach that can elucidate the multiple discursively constituted meanings of the body and the power relations embedded therein is, I would argue, a particularly fruitful way of theorising and researching the female (and 'anorexic') body. Discourses that produce the fat (female) body as ugly, uncontrolled and gluttonous and the thin female body as beautiful, heterosexually attractive and successful form a part of discursive practices such as dieting, self-starvation, bingeing and purging that result in psychological distress, physical damage and even death for increasing numbers of girls and women. As Foucault (1977a: 138) argues, discourses 'discipline' the body through 'a multiplicity of minor processes of domination'. Discourses constitute the (female) body by 'exercising upon it a subtle co-ercion, . . . obtaining holds upon it at the level of the mechanism itself – movements, gestures, attitudes, [habits] . . . an infinitesimal power over the active body' (1977a: 137). In short, from a poststructuralist perspective, we can suggest that discourses have 'powerful and 'real' effects' because by constituting 'truth' they thereby regulate embodied (female, anorexic) subjects. Yet at the same time we must acknowledge that their 'truth' is historically mutable; it is never absolute (Walkerdine, 1986: 64).

In refuting the notion of objective, absolute truth, poststructuralist theory, like some feminist theories (Fee, 1981; Harding, 1987; Jordanova, 1989), thus disputes the objective status of any field of knowledge including biomedical discourse. This should not be interpreted, however, as a denial of the physicality of the body. Bio-medical discourses enjoy a naturalised status in which they appear to transparently describe physical processes. Yet, as we have seen, biomedical fields of knowledge are also fields of power relations (Foucault, 1972, 1979; see Sayers, 1982; Jordanova, 1989) which have often functioned to maintain the sexual status quo; hystericising the female body and constituting it as essentially pathological (see e.g. Showalter, 1985). Bio-medical discourses are discourses about the body but, like other discourses, they nevertheless must be *made* to refer to the body (Woodiwiss, 1990; Sutton, 1994). They consist of the same signifying relations that Saussure (1960) and then Foucault (1972) have elucidated in discourses generally. Hence, to refute the claims of objective truth made for scientific biomedical discourse is not to dispute the physicality of the body but, rather, to problematise the relationship between biomedical discourse and the physical body it purports to know.

To question the legitimacy of pathologising medical accounts of the female reproductive body (see Sayers, 1982; Ussher, 1991) is not, then, to deny women's reproductive capacity. To question reductive biomedical explanations of 'anorexia' (see e.g. Kaplan and Woodside, 1987) is not to deny that self-starvation has serious physical consequences. Indeed, as McNay (1992) argues, the physical body is central to Foucault's work. Poststructuralist theory seeks to transgress the classical dichotomies between ideology and truth, individual and society, mind and body. And, having 'deconstructed' the notion of the unitary self-knowing individual (at the centre of history), Foucault's work places the body at the centre of analysis (McNay, 1992); the corpo-real, material body that is discursively constituted and regulated in its specificities; that is worked upon by power/knowledges; that is 'the inscribed surface of events . . . totally imprinted by history' (Foucault, 1977b: 148). Poststructuralist theory is therefore particularly useful for feminist theory and research in that it provides a radically anti-essentialist account of material corpo-*real* (female) bodies, of physical bodies which are 'always-already' multiply produced and regulated by sociohistorically specific (patriarchal) discourses and discursive practices (McNay, 1992).[2]

Finally, a poststructuralist discursive approach can attend to the physicality of the body by exploring the ways in which discursively produced meaning leans on corpo-reality. The physical body can be thought of as a condition of possibility, what Foucault calls 'a surface of emergence' of discourses about the body (Sutton, 1994). Its weight and fat or emaciation, its pains, processes, sensations and capacities, are not only constituted in discourse; they also make possible or plausible particular discursive constructions of a body. As Foucault (1972) argues, discourses do not emerge in a vacuum. Rather, their emergence and development is made possible by a variety of sociocultural conditions, both discursive and extra-discursive. And among these conditions of possibility is the physical body (Sutton, 1994). The discursive production(s) of bodies lean on the extra-discursive, material physicality of bodies. Just as discourses constitute and regulate the body, so they also lean(s) on the physical body to support their 'truths' (see also McNay, 1992). Through the discursive/physical practice of self-starvation, the 'anorexic' body becomes progressively thinner, and eventually emaciated. Within any particular discourse, its physical emaciation sustains meanings that a fatter body would not. For instance, it eventually loses its physical reproductive capacity and thereby physically/discursively constitutes a means of contesting and rejecting those feminine subjectivities signified by the fatter female body with its physical reproductive capacities.

In short, poststructuralist discursive approaches can attend to the physical as well as the discursive dimensions of bodies: first, by explicating the ways in which discourses constitute regimes of truth, fields of knowledge about the world and about bodies; second, by analysing how discourses thereby regulate embodied subjects and engender particular discursive–material practices that work upon bodies and embodied subjects; and, third, by exploring the corpo-real body as one of the conditions of possibility of discourses about the body – that is, by theorising and researching the body as a complex and dynamic interface of the discursive and the extra-discursive, as a product *and* a precondition of the micro-physics of power that function in discourse.

LIBIDINAL BODIES OF GENDERED DISCOURSE

This conception of the body at the interface of the physical and the symbolic or discursive is also found (in a different form) in psychoanalytic theory. For Freud 'the ego is first and foremost a body-ego', but 'it is not merely a surface entity, but is itself the projection of a surface' (1923: 703). In psychoanalytic theory, identity is conceptualised as profoundly gendered. Yet femininity and masculinity are not mechanistically determined by the body (Sayers, 1982; Grosz, 1990); rather, they are the precarious consequences of a complex process of psychosexual development, the effects of society's *ideas* about the body (Mitchell, 1974). Psychoanalysis conceptualises gender, not as a natural given, but as the possible and probable consequence of unconscious *interpretations* of genital sex differences (Sayers, 1982).

Lacan's rereading of Freud further emphasises the importance for psychosexual development of this projection or interpretation of the body. For Lacan, the unconscious is 'the site of interaction between the body, history and psychic representation' (Coward *et al.*, 1976: 8). As Mitchell argues:

> In each man's [*sic*] unconscious lies all mankind's 'ideas' of his history; a history that can not start afresh with each individual but must be acquired and contributed to over time. Understanding the laws of the unconscious thus amounts to a start in understanding how ideology functions, how we acquire and live the ideas and laws within which we must exist. A primary aspect of the law is that we live according to our sexed identity, our ever imperfect 'masculinity' and 'femininity'.
>
> (Mitchell, 1974: 403)

Hence, Lacan's description of the unconscious simultaneously refers to what is 'within' the subject and also to what is beyond her. More specifically, Lacan argues that the unconscious is 'precisely constructed in the acquisition of language' (Coward *et al.*, 1976: 17) which always precedes the individual and comes to her (or him) from outside of herself (Mitchell and Rose, 1982). Hence, there 'is no subject independent of language' (Sarup, 1988: 12); gendered subjectivity is constituted as an effect of Symbolic representation of the (libidinal) body (Rose, 1982).

Like Foucault, Lacan thus 'deconstructs' the subject, showing it to be social (Sarup, 1988), decentred (MacCannell, 1986), and fictional (Lacan, 1992) or literary (MacCannell, 1986): ' "identity" and "wholeness" remain precisely at the level of fantasy' (Rose, 1982: 32) because subjectivity does not arise from within the individual, from the Real, but from without, created by and within the Symbolic order. But Lacan, following Freud, also elucidates the specifically gendered patriarchal nature of this process of signifying the body, of constituting gendered libidinal subjectivity in language. For Freud (1984), both masculine and feminine identities are constructed in relation only to the penis. For Lacan (see Mitchell and Rose, 1982) sexual difference is signified by the phallus.[3] The phallus has 'the privileged function of ... representing human identity' (Benvenuto and Kennedy, 1986: 187). It signifies the effect of the signifier, of language or the

Symbolic order in creating (gendered) subjectivity (Lacan, 1992). And, because the phallus is a 'masculine' signifier, masculinity is positively signified as 'I', while femininity is negatively signified as the 'not-I', as the Other of identity (Benvenuto and Kennedy, 1986).

Like Foucault, Lacan, provides a theorisation of the body as always-already caught up in systems of meaning, symbolic representations and power relations. Gendered subjectivity is shown to be the effect of (unconscious) interpretation of the libidinal body within the Symbolic, within language. The physical body is not the origin of its gendered meaning nor of its desires. Rather, the body and its physical genital difference is a condition of possibility of symbolic representations of the body but it is the Symbolic order (or discourse) that constitutes the body as masculine or feminine and it is in discourse, not the body, that desire is produced.

In short, Lacanian psychoanalytic theory elucidates the profoundly patriarchal nature of the Symbolic order that inscribes the body as either masculine or feminine, that produces the body as a gendered and libidinal body. Hence, a feminist poststructuralist approach, informed by psychoanalytic theory, provides a fruitful theoretical framework within which to theorise and research the (female) 'anorexic' body in ways which, I have argued, can attend to the multiple discursively constituted meanings of the body and to the physicality of that body as it is constituted within patriarchal orders of discourse. In the remainder of this chapter I shall, therefore, use this approach to explore the discursive production of 'anorexic' bodies and female reproductive bodies, focusing on how these bodies are constituted within a discourse of Cartesian dualism. In so doing I hope to illustrate further how a feminist poststructuralist discourse analysis can attend to the materiality of the discursively produced body.

ANALYSING 'ANOREXIC' BODIES

A discourse of Cartesian dualism

As noted above, this analysis of 'anorexic' bodies draws on a series of semi-structured interviews conducted with twenty-three women diagnosed or self-diagnosed as anorexic (see Malson, 1995b). These interviews covered a wide range of issues and drew on a variety of different discourses and discursive resources. However, I am concerned here with only one such discourse – that of Cartesian dualism (see also Malson and Ussher, 1996a, 1996b). In this discourse human existence is constructed so that the spiritual or mental is seen as entirely separate from the physical realm (Bordo, 1990, 1992). 'Mind' is identified as 'self' and the body is construed as alien to that self and as something that threatens self-integrity. Dualist discourse thus constitutes the body in a specific way, as Other of the self and as potentially eruptive, dangerous and excessive (Bordo, 1990, 1992). This dualist construction of the body is, moreover, frequently figured as a female body.

'Woman' is often made to signify bodily-ness, in opposition to masculine intellect (Fee, 1981; Jordanova, 1989) and the female body has frequently been portrayed as the Other (see Ussher, 1991) as alien, eruptive, dangerous and excessive.

In the interviews, this discourse of Cartesian dualism was evident in, for example, constructions of eating as a bodily urge, entirely dissociated from the conscious mind. Without constant vigilance by the mind/self over the body, the alien body might take over and eat, erupting in a frantic, uncontrollable mess. (Malson and Ussher, 1996b).[4]

EMMA   You know everything that you're forbidden to have and you have to eat it *all* at once [. . .] it's just the franticness that I hate [. . .] In a way it feels like it's not me. It feels *it* takes over. (H: Mm). It's not me saying: oh, you know, do it. (H: Right) It's something completely (.) something completely dissociated from me (H: right) that just kicks in and says: yeah, do it, you know. But I'm not thinking about it at all. (H: Right) I have to clear up the mess once I've done it and sort out, you know, what's been going on (H: Mm) because I haven't been there all the time that that's all been happening. [. . .] I try and stop it from happening but then without even thinking about it I find myself in the kitchen and it's going (H: Mm) you know. And once it's started you can't stop.

Eating is construed not as something desired or initiated by 'the self' but as a bodily process and as an antithesis to any mindful intention. It is an instance of the alien body 'taking over' and defeating the mind/self. This discourse of Cartesian dualism thus constitutes the body and (embodied) subjectivity in a very particular way. It locates desire in the alienated body and therefore produces the need to control that body, to resist its desires (to eat). It thereby simultaneously produces the desire not to eat, engendering (and forming a part of) specific material, embodied practices of body management such as 'dieting' and self-starvation.

This discourse further consolidates this regulation of embodied subjects by construing, categorising and valuing the specificities of bodies in particular ways. Like many other discourses (Malson, 1997), this discourse construes the thin body positively, in this case as proof of the mind/self's control of the body.

H   Was there something that, say, being thin meant to you?
WENDY   Yes, it made me feel successful, as if I was kind of (.) I don't know, in control.
NICKI   There are a lot of characteristics that I admire like being slim [. . .] It's the kind of idea of being in control of your life and doing all your work and sticking to deadlines and (H: Mm) you know (H: Being competent) sort of perfection, yeah the perfection ideal.

JACKIE I achieve also control (H: Mm) definitely 'cos (H: Right) you
know no none of my, however much people try and make you eat
no one can (.) (H: Right) you know, control *that*. I mean it's sh'
it's *me* doing what I want.

Thinness is valued here because it signifies the mind's triumph over the body
and its desires (to eat). The thin body is discursively produced as a
controlled body, signifying the perfection and integrity of the mind/self. It is
a discursive construction that clearly also leans on the extra-discursive of
bodies. That not eating makes bodies thinner is one of the (material) conditions of possibility of this discursive construction of thin bodies. In
contrast, then, fatness signifies indulgence and an inability to control the
alien, eruptive body of dualist discourse (Malson and Ussher, 1996b).

TERESA Passivity is linked in my mind to being fat and to being indulgent, (H: Right) to being out of control.
ZOE I felt like such a loser because *I* felt like *I couldn't control my
weight because I was overweight*. (H: Right) *So there must* be
something wrong with me because you know: oh well, I didn't
have enough self-control.
EMMA I want to lose the fat. [. . .] I hate it being in me and it feels
completely alien (H: Right) and I just want it away. You know. I
want it *off*. [. . .] It just doesn't feel like it should be part of me
(H: Mm) you know. It feels all wrong. [. . .] I just do feel like this
big, monstrous size.
JANE I just wanted to get rid of all this weight an' (H: Right) (.) it
made me feel I was better 'cos there was less fat (H: Mm) as if
there was less (H: Mm) bad.

Just as in previous extracts, the body is construed as alien to the self, so in these
extracts, it is body fat that is produced as 'completely alien' and as 'all wrong'.
Indeed, it is produced as the *source* of estrangement of the self from the body.

It epitomises all that is negative about the alien and excessive body of
dualist discourse and metonymically signifies the body of dualist discourse
(Malson and Ussher, 1996b); by which I mean that it signifies something,
the body, of which it is only a part. Like the body, body fat is constituted as
alien, as eruptive, threatening and excessive.

Regulating embodied 'woman'

As numerous feminist authors (e.g. Fee, 1981; Jordanova, 1989) have argued,
the mind–body dichotomy of Cartesian dualism is a gendered, patriarchal
dichotomy in which 'man' is associated with the mind, rationality and
science and 'woman' with the body, nature and emotion. Hence, as noted
above, the body of dualist discourse is frequently figured as a female body.
This discursive relationship between woman and body can be seen to pivot

around particular discursive constructions of body fat. For, as we have seen, body fat comes to stand for all that is negative about the body of dualist discourse. But body fat is also culturally and physiologically related to the reproductive female body (see Caskey, 1989). This discursive production of body fat as 'feminine' is one that again leans on the corpo-real specificities of the female body – on the flesh of breasts and hips, on the body fat necessary for female reproductive functioning.[5] Body fat thus signifies a feminine bodily excess as well as a dualistic bodily excess.

As Lacan (among others) has illustrated, woman generically has been made to signify excess. Using the concept of *jouissance* (literally 'orgasm' but, more particularly, a bodily ecstasy/excess that is in excess of the Symbolic), Lacan theorises 'woman's' (Symbolic) relation to the phallus in terms of feminine bodily excess: 'There is a jouissance . . . a jouissance of the body which is, if the expression be allowed, beyond the phallus . . . There is a jouissance proper to her, to this "her" which does not exist and which signifies nothing . . . ' (Lacan, in Mitchell and Rose, 1982: 144–145). This figure of 'woman as excess' is evident in a variety of cultural myths of 'woman'. 'She' is sometimes, as Simone de Beauvoir notes, celebrated as the eternal infinity of Nature: ' . . . endowed with mind and spirit, but she belongs to Nature, the infinite current of life flows through her; she appears, therefore, as a mediatrix between the individual and the cosmos' (1953: 204). 'She' has also been celebrated by feminists, for example by Luce Irigaray (1988) and by Mary Daly (1984). Women's lust, Daly writes, 'is in essence astral. It is pure Passion: unadulterated absolute, simple sheer striving for abundance of be-ing. It is unlimited, unlimiting desire/fire' (1984: 3).

More frequently, however, the figure of 'woman as excess' is not so much celebrated as reviled. As Lacan argues, 'she' is the obverse of woman as Other, as not-all: ' . . . if she is excluded by the nature of things, it is precisely that in being not-all, she has, in relation to what the phallic function designates of *jouissance*, a supplementary *jouissance*' (Lacan, in Mitchell and Rose, 1982: 144). It is precisely in being negatively signified as lacking, in being not-all in relation to the phallus that the feminine position is also *in excess* of the Symbolic (or discursive). And, as psychoanalytic theory has illustrated, the construction of 'woman' as Other, as not-all (and therefore as excess) is predicated on the physical absence of a penis (Freud, 1984), on the cultural representation of 'woman' as lacking, as 'castrated' (Mitchell, 1974; Mitchell and Rose, 1982). This definition of the feminine as a lack/excess is, then, a construction that leans upon the corpo-real specificities of female and male bodies. But it is nevertheless a construction that can only ever be symbolic rather than 'real' since, as Rose (1982: 42) argues, 'something can only be seen to be missing according to a pre-existing hierarchy of values' ('there is nothing missing in the real', p.113).

Lacanian psychoanalytic theory thus elucidates the patriarchal nature of the Symbolic (or discursive) production of 'woman' as lack and obversely of 'woman' as excess. The female body is always-already discursively produced within a patriarchal order that constitutes woman as Other. But this process of discursive/Symbolic production leans on the corpo-real specificities of male and female bodies. The female body is a condition of possibility, a surface of emergence of its discursive production(s). 'Feminine excess' is a discursive construction that leans on the (always-already discursively consti-tuted) specificities of physical genital difference (Freud, 1984: Lacan, 1992) and on the discursive–material relationship between femininity and body fat. This figure of 'woman as excess' is evident, I would argue, in contemporary discursive constructions of women talking too much, having too much emotion, too much need, 'taking up too much space', being 'too much there' (Bordo, 1992: 103). In the interviews in this study and in the wider field of discourse, 'she' is epitomised in two figures of 'woman' – in the figures of the mother and the sexual woman.

The maternal body as a site of excess

TERESA   For me there is this sort of, there is this terrible (.) fear, anger of femininity in terms of passivity [. . .]. You know, kind of images of the kind of, the mother figure as this sort of cow-like unintel-ligent person that like, that just feeds (H: Mm). You know the, um, figure out of *The Bell Jar* [. . .] I mean Sylvia Plath's just very, um (.) I mean awful about her. She paints this awful picture of this very unintelligent working-class American mother who just feeds the kids on ice-creams, and ice-cream and marshmal-lows 'cos that, just has them like one after the other like this (H: Mm). She presents her as this cow without a, (H: Mm) without a brain, (H: Mm) who's just massively fat and unattractive. (H: Mm). Her, her whole, um, motive in life is just to have, mind-lessly have more children and breed more (H: Right), more and more and more. And not have any life of her own. All that is just like devoted to caring for other people (H: Mm). And that is I s'pose an image of horror for me.

In this extract 'the mother' is discursively constructed as feminine and passive and simultaneously as 'an image of horror'. This 'image of horror' leans, I would argue, on a discourse of Cartesian dualism in its re-produc-tion of the mind–body dichotomy. 'The mother' is constructed here as entirely bodily rather than spiritual, wilful or intelligent: she is 'mindless'. The 'maternal body', like 'the body' of dualist discourse, is construed as the antithesis of the mind, will or spirit. It is animal-like – 'cow-like' – uncon-trolled, and excessive. And its lack of control, its excess, is emphasised by its being 'massively fat'. This maternal body has an excess of excess flesh.

This feminine bodily excess is similarly evident in the discursive construc-tion of the (necessarily embodied and body-oriented) maternal role.[6] 'The mother . . . just feeds the kids on ice-creams . . . and marshmallows', comfort foods that are also commonly constituted as 'bad' foods which will engulf her children in the same amorphous massive fatness that engulfs her. And just as she engulfs her children (in 'fattening foods') so 'she' too is engulfed by the maternal role. 'She' does 'not have any life of her own'. She is *selflessly* devoted to caring for others. There is nothing else to her but motherhood and as a mother 'she' is constructed as entirely bodily, as uncontrollable, excessive, engulfing, mindless and selfless, as lacking in subjectivity.[7] 'She' just 'breeds' and 'feeds the kids'. Indeed, 'she' 'breed[s] more [. . .], more and more and more.' 'Her' mindless fecundity again signifies an uncontrollable bodily feminine excess that is again signified by her body fat. For, as we have seen, within the discourse of Cartesian dualism body fat signifies uncontrolled bodily excess and a specifically feminine excess. Being 'in excess' of male reproductive capabilities, women's reproductive capabilities are inscribed within patriarchal discourse as excessive – a feminine (discursive–material) excess signified by women's body fat. It is 'the mother's' fat body that is here discursively constituted as a trope of this feminine, maternal excess. Body-fat is then a material, corpo-real condition of possibility of maternal bodies but (women's) body fat is also always-already discursively constructed within patriarchal systems of symbolic representations and power relations.

The excesses of the sexual woman

A second figure of feminine excess is that of 'the sexual woman'. In these next extracts 'the sexual woman', like 'the mother', is constructed as bodily, uncontrollable and excessive. And again this feminine excess is signified by body fat, by the fat female body.

TRICIA   I s'pose for me [being fat] was (.) I felt being clumsy and being ugly, (H: Right) (.) being out of control, (.) (H: Mm) but I think, uh, as far as a woman goes, being (.) sexually so desirable to men and not being able to say no [. . .] much more open to sexual to sexual advances from men (.) (H: Right) *but* (.) because of course being a woman one's not allowed to say no. [. . .] And also maybe it (.) more of a link with my mother which I (H: Mm) particularly wanted to dis', I mean not that my mother was fat (H: Right) but it's just the image of being a mother.

TERESA   I think there was a big issues for me around being sexual (.) 'cos my sister wasn't sexual; she was mad. She was sexual, well, she was sexual in a really awful way (H: Right) and (.) um, and quite overweight (H: Mm) and (.) so for me being anorexic and being quite promiscuous was almost, um, I think the sexuality was in rebellion [. . .] it was a sexuality that was completely in my control (H: Right) because I slept around with people but I never, emotionally, let it touch me.

While the heterosexually attractive woman is most frequently portrayed as slim, the fat female body may, nevertheless, be construed as sexual. Yet it is the obverse of any idealised feminine sexuality. It signifies an uncontrolled female sexual excess; a feminine sexuality that is mad, bad, awful; uncontrolled and unable to say 'no'; a feminine sexuality that is bodily, alien, threatening and excessive (see also Ussher, 1991). It is a discursive (patriarchal) production of feminine excess that both constitutes and regulates/oppresses embodied female subjects and that is predicated on the always-already discursively constituted corpo-real specificities of female bodies – on the flesh of breasts and hips, on the discursive–material relationship between body fat and femininity.

The 'anorexic' body as absence of feminine excess

The discourse of Cartesian dualism thus constitutes the female (reproductive) body as a site and source of feminine excess. And this feminine excess, epitomised in the two figures of 'the mother' and 'the sexual woman', is signified in particular by female body fat. Within this discursive context the 'anorexic' body can be understood as a material–discursive evasion of this feminine bodily excess. In her account of an 'anorexic' experience Jennifer Shute vividly described this desire to evade the (discursively constituted) alien and distasteful excesses of the female reproductive body:

> Who, given the choice, would really opt to menstruate, invite the monthly haemorrhage – a reminder that the body is nothing but a bag of blood, liable to seep or spatter at any moment . . . One day I will be thin enough. Just the bones, no disfiguring flesh, just the pure, clear shape of me. Bones. That is what we are, after all, what we're made of, and everything else is storage, deposit, waste. Strip it away.
>
> (Shute, 1992: 5, 9)

The female reproductive body is constituted here as 'a bag of blood . . . storage, deposit, waste'. It is alien, disfiguring and uncontrolled, 'liable to seep or spatter at any moment'.[8] In contrast, the 'anorexic' body, stripped of its flesh/fat, signifies an absence of this feminine bodily excess. It is, as I have already illustrated, constituted as controlled. It signifies the mind's triumph over the body, over its desires, its (feminine, bodily) excesses. It indicates an 'ideal' non-body: 'no disfiguring flesh, just the pure, clear shape of me', a dis-embodied subjectivity dissociated from the feminine excess signified by the fatter female body.

TERESA   It was something to do with not, not being in my body . . . transcending my position, my sexuality . . . There's something about being anorexic can be powerful.

ELAINE   What, what they would be trying to do through their anorexia?

H   Yeah (.)

ELAINE   A lot of things. (H: Mm) They'd be trying to isolate themselves. They'd be (.) stopping having their periods and not being a woman any more. They'd be (.) avoiding emotions (.) (H: Mm) All kinds of things like that (H: Mm) in that range.

NICKI   If I didn't have it [anorexia], if I wasn't thin (H: Mm) then I wouldn't have an identity. I'd just be this big bad blob.

H   Righ' mm. What sort of identity did you feel it was or it is or whatever?

NICKI   It was, um, it was very powerful. (H: Mm) It made me feel good and in control.

In these extracts 'anorexia' is about 'not being in my body' and therefore 'not being a woman any more'. It is about 'transcending . . . my sexuality' by destroying all traces of body fat, by destroying the female body (fat) that signifies feminine excess (see also Malson and Ussher, 1996b). In this discourse of Cartesian dualism, having a thin body, being 'anorexic' is about being dissociated from a figure of femininity that is bodily, alien, threatening and excessive; a 'femininity' that is signified by the fatter female reproductive body. 'Anorexia' can thus be understood within a wider field of (patriarchal) discourses about gender, subjectivity and embodiment; discourses that lean on, constitute and regulate the (always-already discursively constituted) specificities of corpo-real bodies; discourses that constitute and regulate embodied subjects. The eradication of body fat that produces 'anorexic' bodies (through self-starvation) is clearly a discursive practice that functions at the interface of the discursive and the extra-discursive of the female body with very drastic physical consequences.

NICKI   It's just a way of like trying to disappear (H: Mm) and trying to be in control and feel pure. (H: Right) It's just the perfection (H: Mm) thing. [. . .] You just want to get smaller and smaller.

CONCLUSIONS

In this chapter I have used a feminist poststructuralist perspective to explore how a discourse of Cartesian dualism constitutes the body, and particularly the female body, as alien and threatening, as Other and as a site and source of excess while, (conversely), the female 'anorexic' body is constituted as an absence of this excess. Drawing on interviews with women diagnosed and self-diagnosed as 'anorexic', I have sought to elucidate how the female reproductive body may be discursively constituted as excessive; how female fatness is constituted as a metaphor of this feminine, bodily excess; and how two figures of 'the mother' and 'the sexual woman' can be seen as epitomising this 'feminine excess'. By focusing on this one discourse of Cartesian dualism, I have sought to show the necessity of locating the 'anorexic' body in its discursive contexts; of locating it within that field of discourses that also constitute the female reproductive body and the fatter female body negatively as Other, as threatening and as a site and source of excess.

Clearly, there are also more positive images of the female body, of the maternal body and of female sexuality, than the images I have discussed here. What I would like to argue here is, however, that these figures of reproductive femininity as excess are figures that are prevalent throughout our society. They are not peculiar to women who have been diagnosed or self-diagnosed as anorexic. Rather, they pervade a variety of academic, clinical and popular discourses in images of women as bodily, as threatening, uncontrolled and voraciously sexual, or as pathogenic, overbearing and engulfing mothers. That there are other more positive constructions of the female reproductive body, articulated in these interviews and in the wider cultural context, illustrates that *this* female body is the product of discourse. Its Otherness and excess do not reside in the extra-discursive reality of the body but are constituted in discourse. Similarly, there are a variety of often conflicting constructions of the 'anorexic' body. In contrast with the construction discussed above, the 'anorexic' body may also itself be construed as the product of excess.

PENNY   I didn't want to lose, I thought I was fat. I needed to lose weight more. Nothing was ever good enough. Every half a stone I lost I wanted to lose another one. (H: Mm) And I keep saying: no I'll stop when I get to six stone, you know. It carried on so you know, it just took a snowball and I couldn't let go 'cos I wanted (H: Mm) that control that I thought I didn't have over my life.

NICKI   I just went on this rampage of like being hungry (H: Mm) which felt wonderful, and finding ways to lose weight and everything. (H: Right) And it was just, it's hard to put into words. It was just the only important thing. And it was like a matter of life and death. (H: Mm) And it was the only way of being able to feel on top of things.

'Anorexia' may paradoxically be construed as uncontrolled, as an excessive control as well as a renunciation of feminine bodily excess. This excess or absence of excess resides, then, not in the extra-discursive of the body but in the discourses that converge upon it. Yet, at the same time, these meanings also lean on the corpo-reality of that body, on its extra-discursive physicality. The material-discursive practice of self-starvation results in a literal dematerialisation of the body. It produces a body devoid of flesh and which no longer has a reproductive capacity.

Within any particular discourse, the physically thin or emaciated body will sustain meanings that the fatter female body, with its reproductive capacity, will not. In this chapter I have explored how a discourse of Cartesian dualism produces the body, and particularly the female (reproductive) body, as Other and as a site and source of excess. This gendered, patriarchal/misogynistic discourse thus produces a desire to be dissociated from this denigrated body. It forms part of a dispersed system of discourses and discursive practices that produce 'anorexic' bodies. In analysing the discursive production of the 'anorexic' in relation to the female reproductive body I have sought to illustrate the necessity of locating 'anorexic' bodies in their multiple discursive contexts. I have also sought to transgress the discourse–material dichotomy that parallels the mind–body dichotomy of Cartesian dualism. That is, I have explored how the physicality of the body is imbricated in its discursive production. First, because these discourses and discursive practices are themselves material processes that have very real, physical effects on the body – the physical process of, for example, women's self-starvation is not something exterior to the field of discourse but is itself constituted in a variety of discourses and discursive practices; and second, because these discourses simultaneously *lean on* the physicality of the body, on its fat or emaciation, its pains, sensations, its (reproductive) capacities and incapacities in this process of discursive–material production.

NOTES

* Thanks to Paul Sulton and to Jane Ussher for their invaluable discussion of ideas and helpful comments on earlier drafts of this chapter.
1 See Malson and Ussher (1996a and b) for a discussion of the methodology of this study.
2 This is not to argue that bodies are passive targets of power/knowledge, since discourses also produce their own resistances to their 'infinitesimal controls' (see Foucault, 1979).
3 The phallus, in Lacanian theory, is not the penis but the masculine sign in relation to which gender identity is constituted either positively or negatively as 'masculine' or 'feminine'. The phallus functions, therefore, as 'a signifier whose reference is the cultural order' (Coward and Ellis, 1977: 57).
4 In the extracts from the transcripts used in this chapter, italics indicate where words are stressed; = indicates an absence of any gap between two utterances; a pause is indicated by (.); and [. . .] indicates that that part of the transcript has been omitted. Editorial comments/explanations are given in square brackets [ ] and interjections are transcribed as (H: Mm).
5 The accumulation of a certain amount of body fat is a physical precondition for menarche and women's subsequent reproductive capacity (Caskey, 1989). Similarly, the eradication of body fat in 'anorexia' results in amenorrhoea and the loss of reproductive capabilities (see Malson and Ussher, 1996a).
6 See also Chernin (1981) and Malson and Ussher (1997b) for a discussion of 'the mother' in relation to eating disorders.
7 See also Irigaray (1988) and Whitford (1989) for a discussion of the cultural production of the mother as lacking in agentic subjectivity.
8 See also Malson and Ussher (1996a) for an analysis of the menstruating body in relation to amenorrhoea as a symptom of 'anorexia'.

REFERENCES

de Beauvoir, S. (1953) *The Second Sex,* trans. J. Cape, London: Penguin (1984).

Benvenuto, B. and Kennedy, R. (1986) *The Works of Jacques Lacan: An Introduction,* London: Free Association Books.

Bordo, S. (1990) Reading the Slender Body. In M. Jacobus, E. Fox-Keller and S. Shuttleworth (eds), *Body/Politics: Women and the Discourses of Science,* London: Routledge, pp. 83–112.

——(1992) Anorexia Nervosa: Psychopathology as the Crystallization of Culture. In H. Crowley and S. Himmelweit (eds), *Knowing Women: Feminism and Knowledge,* Cambridge/Oxford: Polity Press/Open University Press.

Bruch, H. (1974) *Eating Disorders: Obesity and Anorexia Nervosa and the Person Within,* London: Routledge.

Brumberg, J. (1988) *Fasting Girls: The Emergence of Anorexia Nervosa as a Modern Disease,* Cambridge, MA: Harvard University Press.

Burman, E. and Parker, I. (eds) (1993) *Discourse Analytic Research: Repertoires and Readings of Texts in Action,* London: Routledge.

Caskey, N. (1989) Interpreting Anorexia Nervosa. In S.R. Sueleiman (ed.), *The Female Body in Western Culture,* Cambridge, MA: Harvard University Press, pp. 175–189.

Chernin, K. (1981) *The Obsession: Reflections on the Tyranny of Slenderness,* New York: Harper and Row.

Couzens Hoy, D. (1986) Power, Repression, Progress: Foucault, Lukes and the Frankfurt School, in Couzens Holy, D. (ed.) *Foucault: A Critical Reader,* Oxford: Basil Blackwell, pp. 123–147.

Coward, R. and Ellis, J. (1977) *Language and Materialism: Developments in the Semiology and the Theory of the Subject,* London, Routledge.

Coward, R., Lipshitz, S. and Cowie, E. (1976) Psychoanalysis and Patriarchal Structure. In *Papers on Patriarchy* (Patriarchy Conference, London), Brighton: Women's Publishing Collective.

Daly, M. (1984) *Pure Lust: Elemental Feminist Philosophy,* London: The Women's Press.

Fee, E. (1981) Is Feminism a Threat to Scientific Objectivity, *International Journal of Women's Studies,* 4, 378–392.

Foucault, M. (1972) *The Archaeology of Knowledge and the Discourse on Language,* trans. A. Sheridan, New York: Pantheon Books.

——(1977a) *Discipline and Punish: The Birth of the Prison,* London: Penguin (1987).

——(1977b) Nietzsche, Genealogy, History. In D.F. Bouchard (ed.), *Language, Counter-Memory, Practice: Selected Essays and Interviews,* Ithaca, NY: Cornell University Press, pp. 139–164.

——(1978) Politics and the Study of Discourse, *Ideology and Consciousness* 3, 7–26.

——(1979) *The History of Sexuality,* vol. 1, *An Introduction,* London: Penguin (1990).

——(1980) *Power/Knowledge: Selected Interviews and Other Writings 1972–1977,* (ed.) C. Gordon, London: Harvester Wheatsheaf.

Freud, S. (1923) *The Ego and the Id, Standard Edition,* vol. 19, London: Hogarth Press/Institute of Psychoanalysis.

——(1984) *On Sexuality,* London: Penguin.

Garner, D.M. and Garfinkel, P.E. (1980) Socio-Cultural Factors in the Development of Anorexia Nervosa, *Psychological Medicine,* 10, 647–656.

Gilbert, S. (1986) *Pathology of Eating: Psychology and Treatment,* London: Routledge.

Grosz, E. (1990) *Jacques Lacan: A Feminist Introduction,* London: Routledge.

Grunewald, K.K. (1985) Weight Control in Young College Women: Who Are the Dieters?, *Journal of the American Dietetic Association*, 85(11), 1445–1450.

Hall, S. (1982) The Rediscovery of 'Ideology': Returning to the Repressed in Media Studies. In M. Gurevitch, T. Bennett, J. Curran and J. Woollacott (eds), *Culture, Society and the Media*, London: Methuen.

Harding, S. (1987) Is There a Feminist Methodology. In S. Harding (ed.), *Feminism and Methodology: Social Science Issues*, Milton Keynes: Open University Press, pp. 1–14.

Henriques, J., Hollway, W., Urwin, C., Venn, C. and Walkerdine, V. (1984) *Changing the Subject: Psychology, Social Regulation and Subjectivity*, London: Methuen.

Hill, A.J. and Robinson, A. (1991) Dieting Concerns Have a Functional Effect on the Behaviour of Nine Year Old Girls, *British Journal of Clinical Psychology*, 30, 265–267.

Hsu, L.K.G. (1989) The Gender Gap in Eating Disorders: Why Are the Eating Disorders More Common Among Women?, *Clinical Psychology Review*, 9, 393–407.

Irigaray, L. (1988) Luce Irigaray. In H.E. Baruch and L.J. Sorrono (eds), *Women Analyse Women: In France, England and the United States*, New York: Harvester Wheatsheaf, pp. 149–164.

Jardine, A. (1985) *Gynesis: Configurations of Woman and Modernity*, Ithaca, NY: Cornell University Press.

Jordanova, L. (1989) *Sexual Visions: Images of Gender in Science and Medicine Between the Eighteenth and Twentieth Centuries*, London: Harvester Wheatsheaf.

Kaplan, A. and Woodside, B. (1987) Biological Aspects of Anorexia Nervosa and Bulimia Nervosa, *Journal of Consulting and Clinical Psychology*, 55(5), 645–652.

Lacan, J. (1992) *Écrits: A Selection*, trans. A. Sheridan, London: Routledge.

Lawrence. M. (1984) *The Anorexic Experience*, London: The Women's Press.

MacCannell, J.F. (1986) *Figuring Lacan: Criticism and the Cultural Unconscious*, Beckenham: Croom Helm.

McNay, L. (1992) *Foucault and Feminism: Power, Gender and the Self*, Oxford: Polity Press.

Malson, H. (1995a) Anorexia Nervosa: Discourses of Gender, Subjectivity and the Body, *Feminism and Psychology*, 5(1), 87–93.

——(1995b) Discursive Constructions of Anorexia Nervosa: Gender, Subjectivity and the Body, unpublished Ph.D. thesis, University College London.

——(1997) *The Thin Woman*, London: Routledge.

Malson, H. and Ussher, J.M. (1996a) Bloody Women: A Discourse Analysis of Amenorrhea as a Symptom of Anorexia Nervosa, *Feminism and Psychology*, 6(4), 505–521.

——(1996b) Body Poly-Texts: An Analysis of Discursive Constructions of 'The Anorexic Body', *Journal of Community and Applied Social Psychology*, 6, 267–280.

——(1997b) Beyond This Mortal Coil: Femininity, Death and Discursive Constructions of the Anorexic Body, *Mortality*, 2 (1) 43–61.

Mitchell, J. (1974) *Psychoanalysis and Feminism*, London: Penguin (1990).

Mitchell, J. and Rose, J. (eds) (1982) *Feminine Sexuality: Jacques Lacan and the École Freudienne*, Basingstoke: Macmillan.

Orbach, S. (1993) *Hunger Strike*, London: Penguin.

Parker, I. (1990) Discourse: Definitions and Contradictions, *Philosophical Psychology*, 3(2), 189–204.

Polivy, J. and Herman, C.P. (1985) Dieting and Bingeing, *American Psychologist*, 40(2), 193–201.

——(1987) Diagnosis and Treatment of Normal Eating, *Journal of Consulting and Clinical Psychology*, special issue on eating disorders, 55(5), 635–644.

Poovey, M. (1988) Feminism and Deconstruction, *Feminist Studies*, 14(1), 51–65.

Potter, J. and Wetherell, M. (1987) *Discourse and Social Psychology: Beyond Attitudes and Behaviour*, London: Sage.

Prior, L. (1989) *The Social Organization of Death, Medical Discourse and Social Practice in Belfast*, Basingstoke: Macmillan.

Riley, D. (1988) *Am I That Name? Feminism and the Category of 'Women' in History*, Basingstoke: Macmillan.

Rose, J. (1982) Introduction 2. In J. Mitchell and J. Rose (eds), *Feminine Sexuality: Jacques Lacan and the École Freudienne*, Basingstoke: Macmillan, pp. 27–57.

Sarup, M. (1988) *An Introductory Guide to Poststructuralism and Post-Modernism*, New York: Harvester Wheatsheaf.

de Saussure, F. (1960) *Course in General Linguistics*, London: Peter Owen.

Sayers, J. (1982) *Biological Politics: Feminist and Anti-Feminist Perspectives*, London: Tavistock.

Shaw, J. (1995) Effects of Fashion Magazines on Body Dissatisfaction and Eating Psychopathology in Adolescent and Adult Females, *European Eating Disorders Review*, 3(1), 15–23.

Showalter, E. (1985) *The Female Malady: Women, Madness and English Culture, 1830–1980*, London: Virago.

Shute, J. (1992) *Life Size*, London: Mandarin.

Smith, D. (1990) *Texts, Facts and Femininity: Exploring the Relations of Ruling*, London: Routledge.

Sontag, S. (1978) *Illness as Metaphor*, New York: Farrar, Straus and Giroux.

——(1989) *AIDS and its Metaphors*, New York: Farrar, Straus and Giroux.

Sutton, P. (1994) Metropolitan Artisans and the Discourse of the Trade c. 1750–1825, unpublished Ph.D. thesis, University of Essex.

Turner, B.S. (1992) *Regulating Bodies: Essays in Medical Sociology*, London: Routledge.

Ussher, J. (1991) *Women's Madness: Misogyny or Mental Illness*, London: Harvester Wheatsheaf.

Walkerdine, V. (1986) Poststructuralist Theory and Everyday Social Practices: The Family and the School. In S. Wilkinson (ed.), *Feminist Social Psychology*, Milton Keynes: Open University Press, pp. 57–76.

——(1988) *The Mastery of Reason: Cognitive Development and the Production of Rationality*, London: Routledge.

Wardle, J. and Marshland, L. (1990) Adolescent Concerns About Weight and Eating: A Social Developmental Perspective, *Journal of Psychosomatic Research*, 34, 377–391.

Wetherell, M. and White, S. (1992) *Fear of Fat: Young Women Talk About Eating, Dieting and Body Image*, unpublished manuscript, Open University.

Whitford, M. (1989) Re-Reading Irigaray. In T. Brennan (ed.), *Between Feminism and Psychoanalysis*, London: Routledge, pp. 106–126.

Woodiwiss, A. (1990) *Social Theory After Post-Modernism: Rethinking Production, Law and Class*, London: Press.

Yager, J. (1982) Family Issues in the Pathogenesis of Anorexia Nervosa, *Psychosomatic Medicine*, 44(1), 43–60.

Index